Listening to Charles Ives

Charles Ives in Battery Park around 1913.

Listening to Charles Ives

Variations on His America

J. Peter Burkholder

Foreword by Leonard Slatkin

AMADEUS PRESS
Lanham · Boulder · New York · London

Published by Amadeus Press
An imprint of The Rowman & Littlefield Publishing Group, Inc.
4501 Forbes Boulevard, Suite 200, Lanham, Maryland 20706
www.rowman.com

6 Tinworth Street, London SE11 5AL, United Kingdom

British Library Cataloguing in Publication Information Available

Library of Congress Cataloging-in-Publication Data

Names: Burkholder, J. Peter (James Peter) author.
Title: Listening to Charles Ives : variations on his America / J. Peter
   Burkholder.
Description: Lanham : Amadeus Press, 2020. | Includes bibliographical
   references and index. | Summary: "Award-winning music historian J. Peter
   Burkholder explores Charles Ives's diverse musical output and unusual
   career, discussing about forty of the best and most characteristic
   pieces framed with biographical sketches. Offering readers of any
   background a guide to listening, this book is an ideal introduction to
   the iconic American composer"— Provided by publisher.
Identifiers: LCCN 2020037537 (print) | LCCN 2020037538 (ebook) | ISBN
   9781442247949 (cloth) | ISBN 9781442247956 (epub)
Subjects: LCSH: Ives, Charles, 1874-1954—Criticism and interpretation.
Classification: LCC ML410.I94 B49 2020 (print) | LCC ML410.I94 (ebook) |
   DDC 780.92 [B]—dc23
LC record available at https://lccn.loc.gov/2020037537
LC ebook record available at https://lccn.loc.gov/2020037538

In memory of my father
Donald L. Burkholder
1927–2013
who first introduced me to Ives's music

Contents

List of Figures

Foreword

Leonard Slatkin

$\mathcal{D}$uring the first thirty or so years of my life, I hated Charles Ives. The music seemed naive on one hand and overly thick on the other. The only pieces I liked were a few songs. After a while things changed. Why? Because I started to think about how to actually listen to the works as well as understand the historical context in which they existed.

We really did not have American music for the concert hall at the turn of the twentieth century. Wagner, Beethoven, and other Austro-Germanic composers dominated. And they influenced, almost to the degree of plagiarism, composers in the years before 1900. Ives was among them. Several years ago, I performed all four of his symphonies in one concert at Carnegie Hall. What was amazing was to hear how his musical voice and language changed in a rather short period of time.

Understanding more about his use of spirituals, church hymns, and patriotic tunes made a big difference. In addition, one could see how he was leaving the dust of the past behind, looking forward to a path that would make him a trailblazer, although at the time he was only appreciated by a few.

By the time Leonard Bernstein got around to premiering Ives's Second Symphony, not until 1951, the American public seemed to wake up and not be frightened by the brashness and distortions of their favorite melodies. And when Leopold Stokowski gave the first performance of the Fourth Symphony in 1965—and I was at Carnegie Hall that day—excitement and a full house made this one of the most memorable events in my own musical life.

Understanding how to listen to the music of Ives is critical, to the point where I believe you cannot just dive in without this knowledge. In the following pages, you will learn about key passages, important motives, and sonorities that are both subtle and thrilling. Whether an experienced Ivesian or coming to the music for the first time, read, listen, and enjoy.

—Leonard Slatkin

Acknowledgments

&very book is a collaboration, and I have many people to thank for their help. First and foremost is Charles Ives himself, for writing all this wonderful and intriguing music. I have been studying Ives and his music for over forty-five years, have come to know the pieces I discuss in this book like intimate friends, and am still finding something new in them almost every time I hear them. His joy, his exuberance, his craft, his ability to convey deep feelings, and his sometimes wicked sense of humor have sustained me throughout this project.

Over the years my friends in the Ives community have sustained me as well. I am indebted to John Kirkpatrick, H. Wiley Hitchcock, Vivian Perlis, and Clayton Henderson, all now passed on, for their seminal contributions to Ives studies and for their continual support. Deep thanks to James Sinclair for his incomparable catalogue and his many editions and performances of Ives's music, and to Gayle Sherwood Magee for her splendid work on dating Ives's manuscripts, on his choral music, and on his place in American culture. Thanks to Geoffrey Block for our many collaborations, for his endless enthusiasm, for helpful advice, and for nudging me to do this guidebook on how to listen to Ives, the sort of book I have always wanted to write. Thanks also to Kyle Gann for his book on the *Concord Sonata* and for fun discussions about the piece; to Tom Brodhead for many long, productive conversations; and to Larry Starr, Jan Swafford, Neely Bruce, and Don Berman for their insights and ideas. I am honored to call all of them friends, and I deeply appreciate their support and assistance.

I especially appreciate the comments and suggestions of my friends Charley Roush, Chris Freitag, Andy Durkin, and Gary Ebbs, who are not Ives experts but were interested in the book, read drafts, and offered feedback that helped me make my writing accessible to the widest range of readers. Thanks to Danny Ashkenasi for accompanying me on my tour of Ives's Manhattan addresses, and to Danny and his husband Ed Elder for hosting me on my visits to New York.

I am grateful for support from Indiana University through a sabbatical leave and the Distinguished Faculty Research Fund. My colleagues and students in the Department of Musicology and the Jacobs School of Music were encouraging from the start through the finish, offering suggestions and asking useful questions. My students in classes and seminars on Ives contributed many new ideas and perspectives that have shaped my thinking. Matthew Leone helped with research errands and scanning.

Many thanks to Suzanne Eggleston Lovejoy, Music Librarian for Reference and Instruction at the Irving S. Gilmore Music Library of Yale University Library, for providing scans of photographs and concert programs from MSS 14, The Charles Ives Papers in the Music Library of Yale University; from MSS 32, The Horatio Parker Papers in the Music Library of Yale University; and from MSS 56, The John Kirkpatrick Papers in the Music Library of Yale University. Thanks also to Michael Frost, Public Services Librarian for Manuscripts and Archives at Yale's Sterling Memorial Library, for the photograph of William Lyon Phelps. The photograph of Augustus Saint-Gaudens's bronze relief sculpture on the *Memorial to Robert Gould Shaw and the Massachusetts Fifty-Fourth Regiment* is from Royal Cortissoz and Bruce Rogers, *Augustus Saint-Gaudens* (Boston: Houghton, Mifflin, 1907), 58.

I am indebted to everyone at Rowman & Littlefield who shepherded this project from initial idea to fruition. Bennett Graff first suggested the idea and commissioned this book. Gregg Akkerman and Natalie Mandziuk were supervising editors in the early stages, and John Cerullo in the final months. Thanks to them for keeping me on task, if not exactly on time. Michael Tan worked closely with me, providing almost instant feedback every time I sent him a chapter and making many helpful suggestions that improved the book. Thanks to Rae-Ann Goodwin for excellent copyediting; to Rhonda Baker for the beautiful design, typesetting, and layout; and to Paula Williamson and Naomi Minkoff for steering the book through production.

Thanks finally and most of all to my husband of almost three decades, Doug McKinney, for his unflagging support, cheerful patience, willingness to listen, and helpful advice, and for listening to me read passages out loud and telling me candidly what works and what does not.

In his self-deprecating and wickedly witty way, Ives dedicated his *Concord Sonata* and *Essays Before a Sonata* to those who could not stand either one. I offer this book to you, my reader, with the hope that you will like it, but even more that you will enjoy Ives's music and come to love it.

Timeline

1874   Born on October 20 in Danbury, Connecticut, to Mary Parmalee Ives and George Edward Ives.

1876   Ives's only sibling Joseph Moss Ives II, known as Moss, born on February 5.

1881   Begins school at the New Street School in Danbury.

1887   Plays a tarantella for piano by Stephen Heller on a joint student recital on May 11.

1888   First public performance of an Ives work, *Holiday Quickstep*, on January 16.

1889   First position as church organist begins on February 10 at Danbury's Second Congregational Church. Moves to Baptist Church in October on his fifteenth birthday. Organ lessons with J. R. Hall begin on May 21 and with Alexander Gibson begin on October 22.

1891   Begins school at the Danbury Academy in September.

1892   Plays premiere of *Variations on "America"* in Brewster, New York, on February 17.

1893   Enrolls at Hopkins Grammar School in New Haven in April. Becomes organist at St. Thomas Episcopal Church in New Haven on May 7. Travels with his uncle Lyman Brewster to the Chicago World's Fair in August and September.

1894   Begins college at Yale and becomes organist at Center Church in New Haven in September. Father dies on November 4 from a stroke.

1895   Elected to sophomore society Hé Boulé.

1896   Joins Delta Kappa Epsilon fraternity. First publications: Part song *For You and Me!*; *March "Intercollegiate"*; *William Will*, a campaign song for William McKinley; and *A Scotch Lullaby* in the *Yale Courant*. Meets Harmony Twichell, his future wife, through her brother David Twichell, a Yale friend.

1897   Tapped for Wolf's Head, third most prestigious secret society at Yale.

1898   Graduates from Yale, moves to New York, and begins work at Mutual Life Insurance Company and as organist at Bloomfield Presbyterian Church.

1899   Moves to Charles H. Raymond & Co. in New York and meets Julian Myrick.

1900   Becomes organist and choirmaster at Central Presbyterian Church in New York.

1902   Directs premiere of his cantata *The Celestial Country* on April 18. Resigns from his last position as church organist.

1905   Begins to grow closer to Harmony Twichell.

1906   Composes *The Cage* and *Central Park in the Dark*.

1907   On January 1 founds his own insurance agency, Ives & Co., in partnership with Julian Myrick. On October 22 proposes to Harmony Twichell, and she accepts.

1908   Marries Harmony on June 9 with her father Joseph Twichell officiating.

1909   Cofounds Ives & Myrick agency on January 1 with Julian Myrick. In April Harmony miscarries, followed by hysterectomy.

1910   Walter Damrosch conducts a private reading of Ives's First Symphony by the New York Symphony Orchestra on March 19.

1911   Completes Third Symphony and has it copied.

1912   Charles and Harmony Ives buy property in West Redding, Connecticut, and begin building a summer house.

1913   Iveses' first summer in their West Redding house.

1914   Composes *General William Booth Enters into Heaven* and Third Violin Sonata.

1915   Begins *From Hanover Square North*.

1916   Charles and Harmony Ives adopt their daughter Edith on October 18.

1917   United States enters the Great War on April 6. Private performances that month of *In Flanders Fields* at a luncheon for Mutual Life Insurance and of Third Violin Sonata at Carnegie Recital Hall.

1918   Diagnosed with diabetes in August. Medical crisis in October.

1919   Revises and copies Second Piano Sonata (*Concord Sonata*), writes *Essays Before a Sonata*.

1920   *Essays Before a Sonata* printed and mailed out.

1921   *Concord Sonata* mailed out and reviewed.

1922   *114 Songs* printed, mailed out, and reviewed.

1924   Second Violin Sonata premiered on March 18.

1926   Last new composition, *Sunrise*.

1927   First two movements of Fourth Symphony premiered at Town Hall in New York on January 29, played by members of the New York Philharmonic conducted by Eugene Goossens. First major article on Ives appears, by Henry Bellamann.

1928 Movements from the Second Piano Sonata (*Concord Sonata*) are first Ives pieces played in Europe: *Emerson* (first movement) by Katherine Heyman in March on Paris radio, and *The Alcotts* (third movement) by Oscar Ziegler in July at Salzburg. In November, *The Celestial Railroad* and First Violin Sonata premiered.

1929 Second movement of Fourth Symphony published in Henry Cowell's *New Music Quarterly*. Mother dies on January 25.

1930 Ives retires from Ives & Myrick on January 1.

1931 *Three Places in New England* premiered in New York on January 10 and played again in Boston, Havana, and Paris, conducted by Nicolas Slonimsky. Ives hears the work in New York and Boston in January, then consults diabetes specialist and is put on insulin. *Washington's Birthday* premiered in San Francisco on September 3 and *Decoration Day* in Havana on December 27.

1932 *The Fourth of July* premiered in Paris on February 21 by Orchestre Symphonique de Paris, conducted by Nicolas Slonimsky. Aaron Copland accompanies seven Ives songs (including five premieres) on May 1. That month Ives and his family travel to Europe for fifteen months.

1933 *General William Booth Enters into Heaven* premiered in San Francisco on September 26. *Thirty-Four Songs* published.

1935 *Nineteen Songs* published.

1937 *Psalm 67* premiered. *Washington's Birthday* published.

1938 John Kirkpatrick premieres complete *Concord Sonata* at Cos Cob, Connecticut, on November 28.

1939 John Kirkpatrick plays *Concord Sonata* in New York on January 20 and February 24 to glowing reviews. Brother Moss Ives dies on April 7 from a stroke. Daughter Edith marries George Tyler on July 29 at West Redding house.

1940 Fourth Violin Sonata premiered in New York on January 14.

1942 Public premiere of Third Violin Sonata in Los Angeles on March 16.

1945 Elected to National Institute of Arts and Letters.

1946 Third Symphony premiered by the New York Little Symphony under Lou Harrison at Carnegie Chamber Music Hall on April 5. Played again on May 11 in an all-Ives concert at Columbia University that also includes premieres of *Central Park in the Dark*, *The Unanswered Question*, and Second String Quartet. Iveses' only grandchild Charles Ives Tyler born June 29.

1947 Third Symphony published. Wins Pulitzer Prize in Music for the Third Symphony and gives the prize money away. Second edition of *Concord Sonata* published.

1948   Recording of *Concord Sonata* by John Kirkpatrick released.

1949   First Piano Sonata premiered on February 17.

1951   Second Symphony premiered at Carnegie Hall by New York Philharmonic on February 22, conducted by Leonard Bernstein, and published later in the year.

1953   Premiere of First Symphony in Washington, DC, on April 26, conducted by Richard Bales.

1954   First performance of *Thanksgiving* and of complete *Holidays Symphony* by Minneapolis Symphony, conducted by Antal Dorati, on April 9. Dies on May 19 in New York from a stroke after a hernia operation.

Introduction

Charles Ives has the most diverse output of any major composer, from marches to symphonies, from delicate simplicity to dense complexity, from humorous stunts to spiritual journeys, from Romantic styles to modernist sounds, from sweet melodies to crunching dissonances that still surprise listeners a century later. Listening to Ives is an adventure. Hearing how a piece begins may not prepare you for what comes next, or how it ends. Knowing one Ives piece may not prepare you for another.

This diversity can be unsettling. It can also be enormously appealing. Joseph Haydn sought to make each symphony and string quartet a unique individual; Ludwig van Beethoven made his symphonies, string quartets, and sonatas into instrumental dramas; Gustav Mahler spoke of the symphony as a world and said "it must contain everything." Ives's orchestral works, chamber music, sonatas, and art songs build on these ideas. Each work is different, but all represent a kind of lived experience, as if we have entered Ives's world—or as if he is painting a sound-picture of the world he shared with the people around him, spinning variations on the America he knew. Experiencing one of Ives's mature works for orchestra can be like life itself, as we encounter the familiar juxtaposed with the new, the strange, or the unexpected, in a multidimensional space with more going on around us than we can take in. Other Ives pieces are lyrical, like the extended meditations on hymn tunes in his Third Symphony and violin sonatas. Many of his pieces play with style, like those that evoke ragtime, band music, or popular songs. Some works are frankly experiments, trying out a new technique for its own sake, just to see what happens. He speaks many languages as a composer, often mixing them in a single piece, and he uses them to convey feelings and experiences that could not be expressed in any other way.

The variety in style, approach, sound, and meaning from one Ives piece to another also means that there is an Ives for everyone. Tell me what kinds of music you like, and I can find a piece by Ives that you will love—probably

1

many of them. Others you may like less, or not at all. Ives himself said he liked some of his pieces better than others, called at least a handful the best he had ever written, criticized some, and then changed his mind, encouraging performers to give them a try. When after thirty-five years of composing he published a collection of *114 Songs*, he put almost everything in it, representing all the types and styles of song he had ever written, from his most recent back to his very first, from sentimental to mocking, from conventional to entirely new in style, using texts that range from Shakespeare, Goethe, and Robert Browning to poems he read in the newspaper or were written by family members or by Ives himself. It is astonishing to listen to them all and consider how such contrasting, inventive, and distinctive songs could all spring from the same brain and hands.

The best way to approach Ives is with an open mind—anything may happen—and an understanding of the multifaceted background that made him and his music the way they are. Ives was a social chameleon, fitting into a variety of roles from football team captain to church musician and from businessman to composer. In a similar way, he was a musical chameleon, changing his colors in different contexts. As a composer of symphonies, string quartets, sonatas, and art songs, he inherited the mainstream of European classical music, the tradition based on the repertoire of great works from the eighteenth and nineteenth centuries that are performed in concert halls and listened to with rapt attention. His favorite composers were Johann Sebastian Bach, Beethoven, Johannes Brahms, and César Franck, and he knew the recent music of Richard Wagner, Pyotr Tchaikovsky, Antonín Dvořák, Claude Debussy, Richard Strauss, and Alexander Scriabin. The influence of all these composers and more can be heard in his music, suffusing his early works but echoing in later ones as well. At the same time, as a New England native who played drums in his father's band, sang hymns in church and at outdoor revivals, worked as a professional church organist throughout his teens and twenties, and heard popular music from Stephen Foster to Tin Pan Alley songs and from fiddle tunes to ragtime, he brought the sounds of American music into that European framework, synthesizing traditions and creating music that was unlike anything heard before. Through that synthesis he put American music on the world stage and brought American life into the tradition of classical music.

This book aims to be true to Ives's diversity while offering an introduction to about forty of his best and most characteristic pieces. After an opening chapter that explores some unusual aspects of Ives's career and music through an imagined experience at a concert of songs, the book proceeds roughly chronologically, tracing Ives's path from his early exposure to several musical traditions, through his training in European classical music and his incorporation of American music and experimental techniques, to the astonishing works of his maturity. Each chapter focuses on pieces that reflect Ives's changing vision and the range of his music at each stage.

By going in roughly chronological order, we can follow Ives's development. He started with the commonplace and became extraordinary. The pieces we will encounter represent steps along his path, as he learns his craft in four musical traditions; masters the methods and conventions of each tradition, including its characteristic genres (types of piece), forms (standard ways of structuring a piece), and styles; combines aspects of these traditions in new ways; invents new musical techniques; and creates an individual idiom and musical personality unlike anyone else. The music he knew inspired his own, and what he knew and how he used it changed over time, so a chronological presentation is the best way to explain the variety of his music and the traits of each piece. It also helps us understand Ives's music in the context of his artistic aims, which vary greatly from piece to piece, and his many ways of reshaping borrowed musical material to make new music, which developed from traditional methods to remarkably innovative approaches.

Our focus throughout will be on the pieces themselves, getting to know each one on its own terms. Each chapter features descriptions of works by Ives, including vignettes that attempt to capture the experience of listening to the music. Recommended recordings for each piece mentioned in this book are listed in the Selected Listening at the back. An ideal way to use this book is to pause before reading each description, listen to the piece about to be discussed, then read the section on the piece, and finally listen again, perhaps following the description as you listen; this allows you to hear and respond to each work on your own terms, learn about it with the music still resounding in your ears, and then hear it again, focusing on the characteristics, effects, and events described in the commentary. There is more than one way to listen to and interpret each piece. My ways of understanding and hearing Ives's music are not the only ones. I hope they will inspire you to delve into each of his works and explore your own approaches to hearing and making sense of this music.

In providing background for and describing each piece, I will avoid specialist terminology whenever possible, introducing and defining musical terms only when they can help to make a description clearer and simpler.

The central purpose of this book is to offer guidance to listeners, including what to listen for and where to focus your attention. As the title says, this is a book about *listening* to Ives's music. As often as possible I will describe pieces not as one might visualize them or encounter them on the page, but as you can hear them in real time. Often I will attempt to depict a piece in live performance: as a historical recreation of a performance in

Ives's lifetime, or of a concert, real or imagined, in the present or recent past. In these passages, marked with horizontal braces, I have allowed myself a novelist's license to bring the event to life, filling in the gaps in the historical record (which are many), and imagining how it might have been.

Although the focus is on listening to Ives's music, this book is also in a way a biography—a specifically musical biography. These pieces fit into a narrative, tracing Ives's changes throughout his career. We know the outlines of that career well: his youth in Danbury, Connecticut; his early training as a pianist and organist; his studies in music theory, harmony, counterpoint, and composition with his father, George Ives; the churches where he was employed as an organist; his schooling, from grammar school through college at Yale, where he studied with the composer Horatio Parker; his work in New York as a businessman, culminating in his cofounding of one of the most successful insurance agencies of his time; his family life, friendships, and marriage to the always supportive and wonderfully named Harmony Twichell; and his pieces that were performed, reviewed, and published. The Timeline highlights the major events of his life and career.

But placing his music in the context of that career is far from simple, because of uncertainty about when he wrote each piece. For most of his adult life he earned his living in the insurance business, while composing evenings, weekends, and vacations. He worked on most of his larger works intermittently over many years, usually alternating his efforts between several pieces at once, and most of his compositions were first performed or published long after they were conceived. Ives was inconsistent and sometimes inaccurate in dating his manuscripts, and the dates for each piece that he recorded in his memoranda or his lists of works seem more often to apply to his initial idea than to the final completion. Thus most pieces had long gestations, and we cannot always tell when Ives began or finished work on them, much less when he dreamed up or finalized a particular feature. In the 1990s, Gayle Sherwood Magee established dates for when most types of music paper (sheets printed with staff lines for music notation) that Ives used were published, and she has been able to use that information along with handwriting analysis to date many of his handwritten manuscripts, from sketches where he jotted down a first idea or worked out a passage, to drafts of longer sections, to copies of whole pieces in pencil or ink. Her dates remain approximate and are not universally accepted, but they have been incorporated into the standard catalogue of Ives's musical works, *A Descriptive Catalogue of the Music of Charles Ives* by James B. Sinclair, and into the article on Ives in *The New Grove Dictionary of Music and Musicians*, available online through Grove Music Online. I use the dates given in Sinclair's *Catalogue* or in *Grove*, recognizing that though uncertain, they are the best we have.[1]

I have relied throughout on the biographies of Ives by Frank R. Rossiter (1975), Stuart Feder (1992), Jan Swafford (1996), Gayle Sherwood Magee (2008), and Stephen Budiansky (2014), as well as my own earlier books and articles. Descriptions of Ives's works draw on my published analyses.[2] Ives is eminently quotable, and I often include passages from his writings, from those around him, or from reviews. Especially valuable are his self-published book *Essays Before a Sonata*; his informal memoirs published posthumously as *Memos*, which provide the background to dozens of pieces and are laced with wicked and self-deprecating anecdotes; and the interviews with many of Ives's family members, friends, and colleagues in Vivian Perlis's *Charles Ives Remembered: An Oral History*. These and other sources on Ives's life, music, and career can be found in the Selected Reading.

A particularly useful resource is the website of the Charles Ives Society (charlesives.org), which provides audio recordings of most tunes Ives borrowed (see the box below). Those tunes are printed (with their words when they have a text) in *The Charles Ives Tunebook*, edited by Clayton W. Henderson.

This book is designed to accompany you on a journey through Ives's music. Its ultimate aim is to make some of that music a lifelong companion for you, music you return to, music you cannot forget, music that shapes your experience of other music and perhaps of life itself. I write this book for you—if you have read this far, you are my audience—and I dedicate it to the memory of my father, an avid reader who was also an avid listener to classical music. He was an adventurous sort who loved finding new music and finding out more about music that was already familiar. It was on recordings he brought home when I was a teenager that I first heard Ives's music. He found Ives endlessly fascinating, always worth another listen. So do I.

AUDIO RECORDINGS OF BORROWED TUNES

To hear the hymn tunes, popular songs, patriotic songs, and fiddle tunes Ives borrowed and reworked in his music, listen to the audio recordings on the Charles Ives Society website, at charlesives.org/borrowed-tunes. Since many hymn tunes are sung to more than one set of words, the hymn tunes are listed on the website by the name of the tune rather than by the first line of the text (e.g., *Bethany* rather than "Nearer, my God, to Thee").

A Most Unusual Career—
and a Recital of Songs

$\mathcal{Y}$ou walk into the recital hall and take a seat, eager to hear the well-known singer in a live concert. He strides onto the stage to applause, followed by the pianist who will accompany him. Both bow, the pianist takes her seat, and they begin to perform *Dichterliebe*, a cycle of songs by Robert Schumann.[1] The songs offer a range of emotions, now yearning and delicate, now hopeful and happy, now urgent and dramatic, now sad and contemplative, always reflecting the feelings of the German poetry as you follow the translations in your program booklet. This is the kind of music you came to hear, the height of the nineteenth-century art song tradition, in the richly expressive musical language of that era, known as the Romantic style. But it is only the beginning of a varied program you look forward to with anticipation.

Next up is a set of songs by Charles Ives, an American composer whose music you have never heard. The singer nods to the pianist, signaling that he is ready to begin. Then the pianist attacks the keyboard, pounding both hands down on a horribly dissonant group of notes that sounds more like a child beating their palms on the keys than like any music you know. But it is not just random pounding, or a regrettable mistake; again and again she hits the same notes, the left hand always striking the low notes just after the right hand hits the high ones, like a rebounding echo. BANG! BANG! BANG, bang (pause) bang-BANG! The rhythm reminds you of the drum corps of your school's marching band. While the pianist keeps pounding away, sometimes changing the notes or varying the rhythm, the singer starts to sing a melody that sounds like a familiar tune. It rises and falls, at first loud and punchy, then soft and hymnlike, then forceful again, but all seemingly in a different musical universe from the piano.

> Booth led boldly with his big bass drum—
> (Are you washed in the blood of the Lamb?)[2]

The drumming, the dissonance, the sound of hymns, the language of a religious revival—this is all quite unexpected, very different from the lovely Schumann songs you were just hearing. You look back at your program. This song is called *General William Booth Enters into Heaven*. What sort of raucous, noisy, drum-filled, bloody heaven is this? What kind of composer writes such a song, and why?

IVES AND HIS MUSIC

Welcome to the world of Charles Ives. He composed his songs for exactly this sort of occasion: a voice recital, a concert by a featured artist with an accompanist, on which you might hear music from various composers, written over several generations and in individual, highly contrasting styles. He did not intend to disrupt the proceedings or knock his listeners back on their heels—well, maybe a little, since he later wrote that he wanted to create music that exercised his listeners' ear muscles rather than soothing them with well-worn sounds:

> Beauty in music is too often confused with something that lets the ears lie back in an easy chair. Many sounds that we are used to do not bother us, and for that reason we are inclined to call them beautiful.[3]

But like Schumann, who was one of his models for song writing when he was young, Ives was trying to convey an experience through music, reflecting the feelings and images in the text. His music is so different from Schumann's because the experiences he sought to convey are different, and the music he knew was different. The march-like drumming, the new chords, the hymnlike melodies, and the stark and sudden contrasts of style were all as much a part of him as was the musical tradition he learned from Schumann and other European composers. He sought to bring the music and the life he knew as an American into the realm of the international concert stage and the classical masterworks, and he wanted to have his music heard in the concert hall side by side with Bach, Beethoven, Schumann, Brahms, Dvořák, and Debussy.

This is easier to hear and understand if the first piece you encounter by Ives is not quite so different from the music you know as *General William Booth* is from Schumann's songs. Yet that sudden shock of the new is exactly how the world of music came to know Charles Ives. Like other composers, Ives studied performance and composition when he was young, learned styles and genres of music that were current in his time, wrote music that fit into those traditions, and gradually developed an individual idiom. But unlike most composers, the crucial parts of Ives's development happened out of public view. He did not make his career as a performer or teacher of music, as composers have done since the Middle Ages, or from composing alone, as a fortunate few have been able to do since the nineteenth century. His only paid positions in music were as a church organist, and he quit the last of those at age twenty-seven. He made his living instead in the insurance business, where he was one of the great innovators. He composed evenings, weekends, and vacations, producing hundreds of works, few of which were performed. Then a health crisis in 1918, in his mid-forties, gave him a sense of the limited time he had left on earth, spurring him to use his financial resources to promote his music and get it out to performers and the public. And—of course—it was his most recent music that he started with and promoted the hardest, for that was the music that was dearest to his heart and most expressive of who he was then.

As a result of this unusual career, musicians and the public learned Ives's music in reverse chronological order, encountering late, complex pieces such as the Second Piano Sonata (known as the *Concord Sonata*) and the Fourth Symphony in the 1920s; the American-flavored orchestral works *Three Places in New England* and *A Symphony: New England Holidays* in the 1930s; the more approachable Third Symphony in the 1940s; and the Romantic-style Second and First Symphonies only in the early 1950s, shortly before his death and over four decades after their completion. The first pieces to become known were among his most radical, and many listeners found them hard to digest. He was attacked as an amateur, praised or reviled as an avant-gardist, regarded as a hundred percent American without influence from Europe, considered a philosopher in music because of the Transcendentalist associations of his *Concord Sonata,* and believed to not care about musical style or craft because of passages widely quoted from his writings. All of these views of Ives are wrong, misunderstandings created by the way we came to know his music.

The solution is to consider his music in more or less chronological order and understand each piece against the background of Ives's own past. For all I know, you will take to *General William Booth Enters into Heaven* like a duck takes to water, and love it immediately, even when it bumps up against Schumann in a song recital and provides a shocking contrast. But no matter whether you love it or hate it or are simply nonplussed on first hearing, your understanding of the song can be enriched by knowing how it draws on the musical traditions Ives knew, and even what it has in common with songs like Schumann's.

"ALMOST EVERY KIND OF SONG IMAGINABLE"

Our chronological journey through Ives's life and music will begin in the next chapter. For now, let us start in the middle of the story, return to the imaginary song recital with which this chapter began, and listen to some songs that will give us a sense of his craft and of the diversity of his music.

Ives's songs are a good place to start because they are central to his work as a composer. About half of his roughly four hundred compositions are songs. When he set out to promote his music in the early 1920s, his second project (after his *Concord Sonata*) was self-publishing a book of *114 Songs*, a sort of omnium-gatherum of music covering his entire career from his first song in 1887 to his most recent ones from 1921. Characteristically, he arranged the book in roughly reverse chronological order, so his newest songs came first and those in more conventional idioms were buried deep inside. He had 1,500 copies printed and sent them out to libraries, periodicals, musicians, and critics, hoping to interest someone in his music.[4]

Ives made the collection as varied as possible, apparently hoping that everyone would find in it something to like. As the composer Aaron Copland put it in his review,

> Almost every kind of song imaginable can be found—delicate lyrics, dramatic poems, sentimental ballads, German, French, and Italian songs, war songs, songs of religious sentiment, street songs, humorous songs, hymn tunes, folk tunes, encore songs; songs adapted from orchestral scores, piano works, and violin sonatas; intimate songs, cowboy songs and mass songs. Songs of every character and description, songs bristling with dissonances, tone clusters and "elbow chords" next to songs of the most elementary harmonic simplicity.[5]

Unfortunately, most people's tastes are not as all-encompassing as Ives's. There may have been something for everyone to like in the collection, but that meant there was also something for almost everyone to dislike. Copland approved of the songs in modern styles, but he criticized the songs in more traditional Romantic styles and in the idioms of popular music and wondered why Ives bothered to include them. Others hated the songs that were the most radical in style, including the first one in the book, *Majority*, which used tone clusters—all the notes one can play on the piano with the flat of one's hand or one's forearm—to suggest masses of people. Ives himself suggested that some people would not even look at the rest of the songbook after seeing that on the first page.[6]

Because Ives's songs are so diverse, sampling a few of them can illustrate the variety of his music. They can also help us understand how Ives used references to musical styles and types to convey meaning. We all have a sense that music can mean something; music can elate us, move us to tears, bring back memories, make us dance, inspire us to action, calm us down, and affect us in many other ways. But how music does this is a very complicated question. The songs are a good laboratory for exploring how Ives's music conveys meaning, because the range of possible meanings is suggested by the text. So instead of asking how music can be meaningful in the abstract, we can consider how Ives's music in his songs changes or deepens how we understand the words. As we will see, Ives often creates meaning by evoking familiar music that carries particular associations.

MEMORIES

You notice on your program that *General William Booth* is the first of a half dozen songs by Ives. After that initial shock, you do not know what to expect. The next one is *Memories*, which Ives composed in 1897, when he was in his early twenties. You see in the program booklet that it has a subtitle—"A, Very Pleasant; B, Rather Sad"—and that Ives wrote the words for it himself. You brace yourself for drums and dissonance, but that is not what you get.

The pianist begins, quickly alternating low notes with her left hand and chords with her right—boom-chick boom-chick boom-chick and so on. It sounds very familiar, a kind of musical background you have heard hundreds of times before. After all the novel sounds of the previous song, you recognize this as *tonal* music, music that follows the same rules of harmony that Bach, Beethoven, and Brahms observed, using the progressions from chord to chord and the relations between notes to define a *key*—a sense of home base, where the music starts and to which it returns at the end. Usually this would not be a surprise—you hardly noticed that Schumann's music was tonal since you expected it would be—but given your recent experience with *General William Booth* you cannot help but observe how different this song sounds.

As the pianist continues, the singer comes in, breathlessly singing in a lilting rhythm, starting each phrase with a leap up to a peak, bouncing down, and then undulating up and down, spitting the words out as quickly as he can. The melody conveys a sense of fun and excitement, a perfect fit for the text. Although the title of the song is *Memories*, the words are all in the present tense, those of a child talking about sitting in the "opera house" waiting for the curtain to go up, hearing the orchestra, and whistling and humming along with the music. And then the singer, embodying that child's experience in the moment, starts to whistle—an extraordinary and unexpected effect in the middle of a song recital.

It is as if the passage of time has fallen away and we are back in our childhood—or Ives's childhood in the 1880s. The "opera house" is not the Metropolitan Opera House in New York or Covent Garden in London but the theater or auditorium in small cities and towns all over the United States (like the one in his home town of Danbury, Connecticut, shown in the next chapter), where touring companies came to present operas and operettas as well as plays, minstrel shows, variety shows, vaudeville, magic, and all sorts of public entertainments, and where local performers also took the stage. This song, with its rapid declamation of a light-hearted text in a lilting melody over light accompaniment with very few places to stop for breath, is in a style that was heard often in such theaters in the second half of the nineteenth century, like a patter song in a Gilbert and Sullivan operetta.

You are in a recital hall in the twenty-first century listening to a program of art songs, songs that are part of the classical tradition and are intended to be listened to with rapt attention, while you keep quiet. But the words and the music are telling you that it is the late nineteenth century and you are a child in a theater in your home town, getting excited and making noise along with the orchestra as it starts to play before the show begins. This magical effect has been called "fictional music": a piece of music that enacts a performance by a different set of musicians in a different setting for a different audience, and invites you to imagine yourself as a member of that audience in that time and place.[7] Ives did not invent this effect—there are many famous examples, like the moment in Berlioz's *Symphonie fantastique* when we hear an English horn and an oboe imitate cowherds playing their pipes and imagine ourselves out in the country—but he uses it often. In this song, the combination of a familiar musical style with the words' present tense description of what we are doing places us in the middle of a particularly vivid memory. This is music about the experience of listening to music.

The music reaches a climax of excitement, and the singer shouts "Curtain!" Shouting in a song is again extraordinary. The music has lured you into a music hall from a century and a half ago and has wound you up with anticipation, and then the curtain goes up before your eyes. What happens next? After a pause, what sounds like an entirely new song begins, in a new key, as if this is the show you have been waiting to hear. The singer, who has been acting the part of a child excited to be at the opera house, is now playing the part of a performer onstage, and you are part of the audience in that theater. The music is now much slower and softer, in a completely different mood and style. Instead of alternating low notes and chords, the piano slowly plays each chord as an *arpeggio*, sounding each note in the harmony from lowest to highest, dropping part of the way back down, and repeating the gesture in a series of waves, creating a gently arching accompaniment that reminds you of a nocturne by Fryderyk Chopin. The singer joins in with a melody that sounds like a sentimental parlor song of the mid-nineteenth century, a song for amateurs to sing at home, in the style of Stephen Foster's *Gentle Annie* or *Jeanie with the Light Brown Hair*. The words are also nostalgic: overhearing an old song that seems tattered and worn with use, the singer remembers it as the tune his uncle hummed, sweet but a little sad. The music is gorgeous, and the effect is dreamy. Like the first part of *Memories*, this portion uses an old and familiar musical style to create fictional music, a song about the experience of hearing an old and familiar song, which we assume had the same slow and sentimental character as the melody we are hearing now. Although this part of Ives's song, like the first, begins in the present tense, the words lead explicitly into the world of the past, as the overheard tune brings to the singer's mind memories of hearing his uncle hum and seeing him shuffle to the barn.

Juxtaposing Musical Styles

Memories is a wonderfully clever song, using familiar musical styles to take us to a particular time and place and evoke specific moods. The juxtaposition of different musical styles is characteristic of Ives's music, and we will hear it in most (though not all) of the pieces we encounter.[8] Using these juxtapositions to create fictional music, music about the experience of listening to music, also became characteristic, especially in his later pieces.

Style is a word often used in discussions of music, and it is worth pausing a moment to consider what we mean when we use it. A style is a characteristic manner or mode of composing or performing, an overall effect, that is created from the combination of many individual aspects of music and is distinctive from other styles. We recognize different styles of clothing for different purposes, groups of people, and historical eras: one wears a tuxedo or gown to a formal party, but not to the beach or to plant tulip bulbs in the garden; people from different nations, ethnic groups, economic classes, professions, or cliques in high school can often be identified by what they wear; and a teacher today does not dress like teachers did in the 1700s or the 1400s. In the same way, styles of music are associated with different social functions, nations, groups, and historical periods. We can identify musical styles and distinguish them from each other easily, almost immediately, if we are familiar with them. The differences between country music and hip hop are obvious, and if we hear a musical style out of its usual place—square dance music at a church service, for instance, or a hymn at a square dance—we are struck by how it breaks our expectations, whether that is meaningful (say, to honor the memory of a favorite fiddler) or just inappropriate. We can talk about style at many levels: the style of an era, a nation, or a type of music, but also the style of an individual composer, of a particular piece, or even—as in *Memories*—of one part of a piece. The many differences of style are part of what makes music so endlessly fascinating.

Because Ives uses so many different styles in his music, and often features contrasts between them within his pieces, style will be a recurring theme throughout this book. Sometimes we will have to wade into the weeds of technical description to make clear how these styles sound or how to tell one from another, but often the styles will be familiar ones and their differences will be obvious.

<hr>

THE CIRCUS BAND

The next song in the recital is called *The Circus Band*, and band music is what you hear. The pianist plays a brief introduction, establishing the key and the character of a march. Then the singer joins in with a tune in band style, singing about the circus parade on Main Street, led by the band. The words are again written by Ives and in the present tense—the band is coming down the street right *now*—but from a boy's perspective, suggesting that this is another song about a memory of hearing music years ago during one's childhood. The parade is brought to life by the sights described in the text and by music in the style of a band march. The only thing you notice out of the ordinary is that sometimes the rhythm is syncopated, when the singer or pianist lands on a note a bit sooner or later than you expect, just before or after a beat rather than on it, creating an offbeat accent against the steady background beats that makes the music sound even more exciting. These offbeat accents add up, leading to a moment of syncopation that departs from how a real marching band would sound and reminds you that you are listening to an art song *about* a parade, not the parade itself.

Typical of a march, the first section—called a *strain* in the band world—repeats exactly, followed by another repeated strain in a closely related key. If this were a march by John Philip Sousa, you would expect these two strains to be followed by a *trio*, an extended section in a new key. What comes is a bit of a surprise: the music has been tonal throughout, but now the pianist plays a big dissonant chord, her right hand on the high notes followed immediately by the left playing low notes. The shock of this sudden change of style makes you sit up straighter in your seat. As she repeats the chord—BANG! BANG! BANG, bang (pause) bang-BANG!—you recognize the rhythm and effect you heard at the beginning of *General William Booth Enters into Heaven*, and you realize that this is Ives imitating drumming. These sounds might be startling when played on the piano, but to hear drummers play this familiar rhythmic pattern before or during a march is a perfectly ordinary event.

The use of strange sounds to evoke something very familiar reinforces the sense that this song is fictional music, like *Memories*: a song that asks its listeners to imagine that we are on Main Street long ago listening to the band in a circus parade rather than in a recital listening to a singer and pianist. *Memories* sounds like the music it evokes, and so does most of *The Circus Band*, but the piano-drumming is a stylization, musical sounds that pretend to be other music. Although it does not really sound like drums, we recognize through the bang-y chords and the familiar rhythm that it is referring to drumming, and we understand in context that these chords are acting out the part of the drums, just as the voice and piano are acting out the parts of the other instruments in the band.

As the song continues, you get exactly what you expect from the trio of a Sousa march: a brief introduction, a new strain of melody, a dramatic episode known to band aficionados as a "dogfight," and a repetition of the new melody, all in the style of a late-nineteenth-century march. The "dogfight" is so called because its dramatic back-and-forth between the high and low instruments sounds a bit like dogs snapping and barking at each other, with lots of colorful notes and chords from outside the key to heighten the tension. The last repetition of the trio strain is as loud and full as possible, thickening the texture of the music with a highly energetic rising and falling line that imitates the trombones in the band (Ives even marks this passage "Hear the trombones!"), and the song ends with a bang.

WALKING

Next up is *Walking*. As usual, the piano begins first, but this time the introduction is longer. It starts loud, alternating low notes—what musicians call the bass line, the lowest part—and high chords. The chords are what you notice most: more dissonant than in *Memories* but not as crunchy or harsh as the piano-drumming. As the right hand alternates two chords in irregular rhythm and the bass line in the left hand keeps a steady pulse, you notice that each note and chord continues to sound even after the next one is played, muddying the texture. This blurring effect is created on the piano when the player presses a pedal that lifts off all the dampers, the weighted pieces of felt that normally drop onto each string and stop the sound as soon as the player stops holding down the key she pressed to play the note. The pianist releases the pedal, the blurring ceases, and you hear rich, slightly dissonant chords harmonizing a jaunty tune, soon taken up by the singer as he describes the sights on a morning walk in October, from church steeples to glowing autumn leaves.

Unlike *Memories* and *The Circus Band,* this song does not immediately remind you of any music you have heard before. It is not exactly tonal—at any rate, it does not follow the same rules of harmony as music by Bach, Beethoven, or Brahms—but it is not far away from tonal music. Both melody and harmony sound as fresh and rugged as an October morning. As the title suggests, this is a song about taking a walk and all the things we see and hear along the way. The steady rhythms and up-and-down motions of the music neatly portray energetic walking. The blurred chords in the piano introduction are explained when the singer mentions "the village church-bells"; like the piano-drumming in *The Circus Band,* the passage with the dampers off is a musical stylization, a way to convey on the piano an impression of the resonant reverberations of tolling church bells. Twice the voice rises to a peak and falls back down, illustrating the sights of the ridge and the hills.

The piano introduces a new section with faster motion, and the singer pushes on with a steady gait. Suddenly the music slows and quiets, the church-bell chords return in the piano, and over them the singer speaks of seeing a church where a funeral is taking place. Then the pace picks up again as he points out a tavern where a dance is happening, and the piano plays a syncopated melody reminiscent of square dance tunes with a touch of ragtime, like the fragments of dance music we might hear from a distance as we pass by. The music that opened the song returns, and the first section repeats with new words as the walk continues: "today we do not choose to die or to dance, but to live and walk." On "walk," the singer keeps repeating the two notes he just sang for "to live," subtly drawing an equivalence between living and walking, that lively movement that is poised midway between the stillness of the grave and the jauntiness of dancing. The music quiets and fades without slowing down, as if the walkers continue moving at the same pace and gradually disappear into the distance.

Music about Experiences

Like the two previous songs, *Walking* is about an experience. Instead of a remembered experience from childhood, this is one in the present. Instead of a direct focus on hearing music—in a theater, on the street, in a parade—where the music itself is the center of attention, this is a walk through a landscape. But it is a landscape with people in it, represented by the music—church bells, dance music—that is associated with their activities. As we will see, many of Ives's pieces are about experiences, both of music directly and of events in which music plays a role and therefore can represent people and what they are doing.[9]

Thinking over the last three songs, you realize that all of them describe shared activities: *we* are waiting for the show to begin, watching the parade, or walking with a friend. Ives often focuses on such shared experiences. His landscape pieces are usually populated by crowds. But some works, like the next song, speak of an individual experience.

THE CAGE

As you have come to expect by now, *The Cage* is different from every other Ives song you have heard tonight. The pianist plays only chords, dissonant chords that mostly sound like the same chord moving up and down the piano keyboard, with an occasional bigger and even more dissonant chord as punctuation. The singer goes up and down in a directionless, all but tuneless melody. The sentiment in Ives's poem is as bleak as the music, describing a leopard who paces back and forth in his cage, stopping only when the keeper brings him some food; in reaction, a boy who has watched this for hours wonders, "Is life anything like that?"

The song is over in less than a minute. In its printed version, *The Cage* is all of one page long. It is a little gem, like a haiku that captures an image and poses a question. The aimlessness of the leopard, glumly pacing like a life-spirit imprisoned, is portrayed by the almost featureless melody that steps up and down in notes mostly of the same rhythm, stopping on a longer note only now and then to illustrate or emphasize a word, as when the leopard himself stops. The chords are the bars on the cage, easier to see as vertical lines on the page than to hear in performance—the Germans call such things *Augenmusik*, eye-music—but the chords' persistence throughout the piece and their motion up and down the piano keyboard neatly convey the leopard's perspective of vertical bars everywhere, no matter where he turns.

New Ways of Composing Music

To figure out how Ives achieves these effects, we need to look at how his music departs from our expectations for tonal music.

First, the aimless back and forth of the singer's melody. Tonal music draws on the notes available in a certain key, which can be arranged as a series of rising or falling steps called a scale. Melodies often move mostly by step—a motion from one note to the next one above or below it in the scale—but also typically include skips and leaps, skipping over a note to land on the next one or leaping over two or more. Mixing it up like this gives a melody more variety and expressivity, like the bouncy and vigorous melody from the first half of *Memories* or the haunting sad song in its second half. Relentlessly going up and down the scale by step, as the melody in *The Cage* does, makes for a dull, unvaried, and expressionless melody, perfect for the bored pacing leopard.

This melody is made even more dull because almost all the steps are the same size. Tonal music uses *diatonic scales*, in which some of the steps are smaller than others. If you sing *Happy Birthday to You*, the step between "birth-" and "-day" is larger than the step between "to" and "you." Musicians call the larger one a *whole step* or *whole tone*, and the smaller one a *half step* or *semitone*. The placement of whole tones and semitones in a diatonic scale gives a sense of where you are in the scale and helps you anticipate the direction of the melody. Tonal melodies, like those in *Memories* and *The Circus Band*, typically move up and down in arching phrases and home in at the end on the main note in the key, which always has a whole step above it and a half step below it.

But *The Cage* does not use this sort of scale. The voice mostly rises and falls in whole steps, outlining a *whole-tone scale*, a scale made up only of whole tones. Just a handful of times during the song do we hear a half step, shifting the melody from one whole-tone scale to another and then back again. There is no differentiation in a whole-tone scale. Every step is of equal size: everything is the same, no matter where you go, so there is no sense of location or direction, no indication that you have arrived at a resolution. It is a perfect musical device for representing aimless motion, when—from the perspective of the leopard—everywhere you go it is always the same. Going back and forth between two whole-tone scales is a musical metaphor for the leopard's changes of direction, going to the right and then to the left but never able to reach a satisfactory conclusion.

Second, those chords. In *Memories* and *The Circus Band*, the chords support the melody, and the succession from one chord to the next works with the melody to shape phrases and create the sense of progress, the feeling of beginnings, middles, and ends at every level from the phrase to the whole piece, that is the core of our experience with tonal music. But in *The Cage*, there is no sense of progress. To convey the futility described in the text, Ives has to avoid using chords that would suggest progression and resolution.

How does he do this? By using different intervals to build his chords. An interval is the distance between two notes, whether played successively in a melody or simultaneously in the harmony. Intervals are named by the number of notes they encompass in a diatonic scale. Starting anywhere in the scale and counting where you start as the first note, the interval from that note to the one just above or below it is a *second*, the interval from the first to the third note is a *third*, from the first to the fourth note is a *fourth*, from the first to the fifth note is a *fifth*, and so on. Chords in tonal music are built out of thirds; for instance, the first, third, and fifth notes of a diatonic scale form a chord with two successive thirds, one stacked on the other. This chord is *consonant*, rather than dissonant, because all the notes harmonize sweetly with each other, and the chord sounds stable. Tonal music works because chords built from thirds support notes in the melody and form logical progressions from one chord to the next, ultimately leading back to the main note and chord in the key.

In *The Cage*, Ives avoids chords like this in order to avoid any sense of progress. What he uses instead is chords built out of fourths. (If you sing the first two notes of *Here Comes the Bride*, that is a rising fourth.) Most of the chords in *The Cage* are made of five notes, with each note separated by a fourth from the notes above and below it. This type of chord is dissonant; the notes do not all harmonize sweetly, and several directly clash with each other. But a chord of stacked fourths *sounds* remarkably stable. It does not sound like it needs to resolve—which is the function of dissonance in tonal music—and so it does not create an impulse to move. When one such chord is followed by another, there is no sense of progression, no resolution of dissonance to consonance as in tonal music; all the notes just move in parallel from one chord to the next, as directionless as the melody in the voice. A series of chords like this is an apt symbol in sounds for the row of unyielding iron bars that keeps the leopard in his cage.

In this song, Ives creates a new way of composing music. For the scales used in tonal music, he substitutes whole-tone scales, and for chords made out of thirds, he substitutes chords made of fourths. It is not that he follows no rules but rather that he replaces the traditional rules of tonal music with new ones. As we will see in the next few chapters, this is a characteristic of his experimental music. But alongside these radical new rules, there are many traditional features of *The Cage*. It is, after all, an art song, setting a text in a meaningful way, with a melody in the voice and an accompaniment in the piano, just like *Memories* and *The Circus Band*. It even does something very typical of tonal music by returning at the end to where it began; the closing phrase is set to the same melody and chords as the opening phrase. We will discover that experimentation with new musical resources is a feature throughout Ives's career and that in every case there remains something traditional for us to hang on to.

DOWN EAST

The last Ives song on the program is *Down East,* again with a text by Ives. The pianist begins with soft dissonant chords under a melody in parallel thirds that slowly descends, one half step after another. This is a *chromatic* melody, all semitones, lacking the mix of whole steps and half steps typical of most melodies in tonal music. The mood is dreamy, mysterious, serious. When the voice comes in, the words suggest that this will be another song about memories, especially memories of songs sung or heard in childhood. But the music does not have the flavor of music from the past, as in *Memories* and *The Circus Band.* The piano plays the same soft, slow, and shadowy music several times, with chromatic figures repeating over a sustained note in the bass, and the voice moves very slowly, repeating a melody in a narrow range, rising and then sinking down. Despite the repeating figures, there is no sense of a key, just a vague sense of being located somewhere in musical space, floating, hardly moving.

Then everything changes. The music moves faster, the vocal melody is suddenly in a bright key with a lilting rhythm, and the piano accompanies with familiar tonal harmonies. The contrast with the preceding chromatic music could hardly be stronger. You realize in retrospect that the first section was like an incantation, like Homer calling to the muses to inspire him at the beginning of *The Iliad*—here, Ives summoning his memories, the songs of childhood. The tune you are hearing now, in the style of a nineteenth-century song, must be part of the memory.

The singer describes an old house in a seaside village and the memories that draw him nearer to it. Something about the melody sounds familiar, like hints of a tune that is vaguely remembered and just beyond recognition. He mentions the chores on Sunday morning and the playing of the old pump organ, then sings the opening phrase and words of "Nearer, my God, to Thee" (*Bethany*), a familiar hymn that must have sounded from the organ many a Sunday morning. Suddenly it comes into focus: this is the tune Ives has been hinting at from the beginning, in the piano's opening chromatic melody, in the vocal melody, in parts of the accompaniment. After the chromatic incantation, the whole vocal line is a paraphrase of the hymn tune, following a similar melodic contour but adding notes, dropping others, altering the rhythm, and changing the style from hymn tune to sentimental song. Just as the text is about a memory of hearing this hymn played on the family's pump organ, the music of Ives's song is all about that tune, giving us fragments and variants and finally presenting the most recognizable phrase of the melody with its text in unvaried form.

As we will see, this is a frequent procedure of Ives, hinting at a tune before giving it to us directly. It is a way of drawing in the listener, evoking something familiar to pique our interest without giving the whole game away at once. And the moral the song proclaims in its last line is also classic Ives: "With those strains a stronger hope comes nearer to me." The past—the childhood home, the chores, the memories, the hymn that encapsulates them all—is still useful in the present, bringing hope and sustaining the spirit. The flipping of perspective in the final phrase sums it up: the hymn is about drawing "nearer to Thee," to God, but Ives's song is about drawing memories and the strength they bring nearer to *me*, in my daily life—because I need them now. This is not nostalgia for a lost past but reaching back to the past for something that remains valuable today. At the words "a stronger hope comes" the music gradually grows more grand, with more expansive chords than ever before in the song, conveying this sense of strength. Then the last few notes return to the previous simplicity, with a last echo of the hymn tune in the piano forming a fleeting "Amen."

GENERAL WILLIAM BOOTH ENTERS INTO HEAVEN

The concert is over, and you and most of the audience are on your feet, giving the performers a standing ovation. As sometimes happens, after they come out a third time to take a bow, the pianist sits again at the piano, the singer signals for all of you to sit down, and then he announces that they are so grateful for the warm response that they will perform an encore. Usually this is something new, an extra treat that is not on the printed program. But then he says that the most difficult item they performed tonight, for them as performers and, he guesses, for you as an audience, was Ives's *General William Booth Enters into Heaven*. He and his accompanist would like a second chance at it, and he hopes you will indulge them. Remember, he says, William Booth was the founder of the Salvation Army. The poem Ives set in this song, by American poet Vachel Lindsay, is a fantasy about what happened when Booth died, imagining him going to Heaven at the head of the army of souls he had saved from poverty and homelessness. Ives's music is challenging, the singer says, but so is the message of the song. And with that, he signals to the pianist, and they begin again.[10]

This time through, having heard this piece once before and having experienced all those other Ives songs, you find yourself understanding much better what Ives is after in this extraordinary music. You know from *The Circus Band* that the loud chords at the beginning are Ives imitating drumming, and you guess from having heard *Down East* that the melody in the voice is based on a hymn tune. The juxtaposition of drumming with a hymn is startling, but it fits the poem, which juxtaposes Booth's drum with religious imagery:

> Booth led boldly with his big bass drum—
> (Are you washed in the blood of the Lamb?)
> . . . Saints smiled gravely and they said: "He's come."
> (Are you washed in the blood of the Lamb?)

You notice that the chords and bass notes representing the drumming change for each new phrase and sometimes in the middle of a phrase, as if Ives is using them to harmonize the melody in a strange not-quite-tonal way, which makes the drumming and the diatonic melody sound less disconnected. The melody at "Saints smiled gravely" is echoed in the piano, weaving voice and piano together still more. The drumming and the hymn, different as they are, are somehow both manifestations of Booth's faith.

The piano turns to dissonant repeating figures as the singer begins to describe the marchers in Booth's parade. Each group, from "walking lepers" to "vermin-eaten saints," is accompanied by its own figuration in voice and piano over a continuing drumbeat in the background. You remember that Ives shifted figuration and style from patter song to parlor song in *Memories*, and from misty chromaticism to familiar tonal music in *Down East*, and you begin to hear each of these phrases as its own "style"—each an invention of Ives, not much like any musical style you have heard before, but each different from the others and all quite different from the drumming and hymn styles you heard earlier in the song. Through these changes of "style," Ives is suggesting the variety in the crowd and also setting off each line of poetry from the next. "Are you washed in the blood of the Lamb?" repeats again as a refrain at the end of this section. You notice that each time you hear this phrase, it is set to a different variant of the same music, always sounding like a tonal melody surrounded by less familiar sounds.

The drumming quiets, then ceases. It seems the marchers have stopped and are milling around, represented by new dissonant repeating figures in the piano that move up and down in waves and by a vocal melody that mean-ders up and down a whole-tone scale. The words describe the milling crowd evoked in the music:

> Every slum had set its half-a-score
> The round world over. (Booth had groaned for more.)
> Every banner that the wide world flies
> Bloomed with glory and transcendent dyes.

Then all of a sudden you're in the middle of a revival. "Big-voiced lassies made their banjos bang," playing—on the piano, of course—an energetic popular song. (Although few listeners today would recognize the tune, it has a heavenly connection; it is a nineteenth-century minstrel song by African American composer James A. Bland, called *Golden Slippers*, about going to Heaven and walking on the golden streets.) The music builds in intensity, and the singer bursts into another chorus of "Are you washed in the blood of the Lamb?" and cries of "Hallelujah!" The words describe the unusual scene, which includes "bull-necked convicts" and others moving freely around Heaven while loons trumpet fanfares overhead, represented by different bugle-call figures in the voice and piano, like trumpets echoing from many directions in a huge space. "Are you washed in the blood of the Lamb?" returns over quick arpeggios in the piano, repeats many times, and gradually calms.

Booth and his legions are in the center of Heaven, which Vachel Lindsay imagines as like a court-house square in a county seat somewhere in the American Midwest. Now Jesus appears:

> Jesus came from out the court-house door,
> Stretched his hands above the passing poor.
> Booth saw not, but led his queer ones there
> Round and round . . .

After all the dissonance and activity, the music for this passage is serene, slow, dignified, and tonal. The singer goes "round and round" on three notes, while the piano plays chords and a broad tune in the baritone range (just above the bass). This is the hymn tune *Fountain*, an early-nineteenth-century melody arranged as a hymn by Lowell Mason and usually sung to these words:

> There is a fountain filled with blood
> Drawn from Immanuel's veins;
> And sinners, plunged beneath that flood,
> Lose all their guilty stains.

The bloody imagery fits with the similar imagery in the poem. Indeed, Ives has been using variations of the second phrase of this hymn tune—"Drawn from Immanuel's veins"—for each appearance of the refrain line, "Are you washed in the blood of the Lamb?" Now the tune appears almost whole, missing a couple of notes. Ives syncopates and repeats its last phrase, which circles up twice through the same three notes the singer is repeatedly descending, so that the piano and singer circle "round and round" each other in opposite directions, as both slow down and fade.

Suddenly, the drum chords from the beginning of the song return, and the marchers are transformed:

> . . . in an instant all the blear review
> Marched on spotless, clad in raiment new.
> The lame were straightened, withered limbs uncurled
> And blind eyes opened on a new, sweet world.

Over the drumming, the singer recites on a single pitch, gradually growing louder, then adds fanfare figures as he repeats "marched on" seven times. At the moment of transformation, "Marched on spotless, clad in raiment new," the pianist settles into the drum pattern and the singer sings the whole melody of *Fountain*. This is the climax of the song, where the hymn tune Ives has been hinting at since the beginning takes center stage, and the combination of hymn-singing over drumming represents the full fervor of Booth's faith and the culmination of his mission to save the poor, disabled, forgotten, and neglected. The fact that the hymn tune fits Lindsay's poetry rather awkwardly is not a defect in Ives's song, but a sign of the force of Booth's will and the miracle of the marchers' transformation.

After the climax, suddenly there is a pause, and all is still. What more is there to say? The singer repeats the question again twice: "Are you washed in the blood of the Lamb?" The first time, the pianist accompanies with soft arpeggios, tonal but spiced with sweet dissonance. The second time, the pianist plays traditional harmony that recalls the style of hymn settings for four voice parts in Protestant hymnals. The sudden appearance of such a familiar style in the midst of a song that has been full of extraordinary sounds brings the events we have just witnessed down to earth. It is as if the poet, the composer, the singer, and the pianist, having told the story of Booth's entry into Heaven, now turn to us and ask us directly to examine our own faith: could we do what Booth did? This is the challenging message the singer mentioned. Then, just as quickly, the moment is over; the drumbeats return in the piano, growing softer and breaking up as the march moves off into the distance.

VARIATIONS ON AMERICAN LIFE AND MUSIC

What have we heard in these six songs? Songs about experiences, some in the present (like *Walking* and *The Cage*), some remembered (as in *Memories*, *The Circus Band*, and *Down East*), some imagined (like *General William Booth*); songs that celebrate American popular music, from marches to par-

lor songs to ragtime; songs based on hymns, the central music of the Prot-
estant church; songs that experiment with new musical resources, like *The
Cage*, or use such new resources for expressive effect, as in *General William
Booth*. The five songs with words by Ives capture variations on American
life: attending a show at the town theater, watching a circus parade down
Main Street, taking a brisk walk in October, contemplating a leopard at
the zoo, and reminiscing about one's childhood home. Even the vision of
Heaven in *General William Booth* resounds with American drum patterns,
hymns, banjos, and trumpet calls. And all six of them are art songs, in the
classical tradition. A popular song or march may be for entertainment, and
a hymn for use in worship, but these are art songs *about* popular music or
about a hymn, and indeed about how popular music is used for entertainment and how hymns can draw us nearer to the divine.

These songs draw on four distinctive traditions: American popular music, Protestant church music, European art music, and experimental music.
Ives encountered all of them in his youth and learned how to write pieces in
each of these traditions, before mixing them together in his later music. How
did he come to know each one? We turn now to that story.

· 2 ·

An American Musical Childhood

$\mathcal{B}$orn in 1874, Charles Ives grew up in Danbury, a small city in western Connecticut, roughly fifty miles northeast of New York City and two hours away by train. It lies in the foothills of the Berkshires along the Still River, a small tributary that flows eastward through town and then turns north to meet the Housatonic River about a dozen miles on. Founded in the 1680s, Danbury had grown to a population of about six thousand in 1850, twelve thousand in 1880, and over nineteen thousand by 1890. Most residents were of Yankee stock and worshiped at the Congregationalist, Episcopal, Methodist, or Baptist churches, but there was a new Catholic Church on Main Street to serve a rising population of Irish and Italian families. Townsfolk were proud of their heritage as a farming community marked by the New England virtues of hard work, service, education, social equality, and participation in civic life. The cemetery north of town was named for Revolutionary War hero General David Wooster. Over a thousand local men had served in the Union Army during the Civil War—including some who lay in Wooster Cemetery, commemorated every May 30 on Decoration Day. Danbury was a thriving industrial city famed for hatmaking; by the 1880s its thirty factories were making five million hats each year, a fourth of the annual production in the entire United States. Jobs in the factories were well paid, and the great majority of people in town owned their own homes. During the late 1870s and 1880s, progress was visible everywhere: City Hall, a new library, new commercial buildings, a hospital, sewers, electric streetlights, telephones. But there were downsides: struggles for better working conditions led to strikes in the early 1880s; the mercury used in hat production slowly poisoned the hatmakers, producing tremors; and waste from the factories and sewers flowed right into the river.[1]

The Iveses were among the city's most prominent families. They had been in Connecticut since William Ives cofounded New Haven in 1638. His great-great-great-grandson Isaac Ives (1764–1845) grew up in Meriden, graduated from Yale in 1785, and moved to Danbury to practice law. After his first wife, a descendent of one of Danbury's founders, died in her early twenties, he married Sarah Amelia White (1773–1851), whose family had been in town for several generations and whose father Joseph Moss White and grandfather Ebeneezer White had also graduated from Yale. Isaac helped the hat business grow, and made his fortune, by establishing an outlet in New York City that sold Danbury's hats wholesale. In 1829 he retired to Danbury and bought the house at 210 Main Street shown in Figure 2.1, where four generations of Iveses would live and where Charles would be born forty-five years later. Isaac's son George White Ives (1798–1862), Charles Ives's grandfather, continued his father's business and became one of Danbury's leading citizens. He cofounded the Danbury Savings Bank—the town's first bank—in 1849, serving as its secretary-treasurer, and watched it grow from a wooden chest in his dining room to become a central engine for the town's prosperity. He also helped create the railroad that ran from Danbury to New York; the company that brought gas lighting into Danbury homes; and Wooster Cemetery, which he designed in the new style pioneered at Boston's Mount Auburn Cemetery, as an open, tree-filled space like a public park. George and his wife Sarah Hotchkiss Wilcox Ives (1808–1899) were deeply committed to social justice and liberal Christian causes, especially the abolition of slavery.[2]

Figure 2.1.   The Ives house at 210 Main Street in Danbury around 1895. In the carriage are Charles Ives's uncle Isaac Wilcox Ives and his wife.

MSS 14, The Charles Ives Papers in the Music Library of Yale University, Series VI, Item 4.

Ives's father George Edward Ives (1845–1894) was the youngest of George and Sarah's children and the only one to take an interest in music, studying flute, violin, piano, and cornet (a mellower cousin of the trumpet) and later making a career as a performer and music teacher in Danbury. As a professional musician, and not very successful businessman, he was something of an odd man out in the family. His oldest brother, Joseph Moss Ives (named after their great-grandfather Joseph Moss White), was the first in the family since Isaac Ives to go to Yale, but he was sent home in his sophomore year after he participated in a prank—putting plaster in the chapel bell to keep it from sounding the summons to compulsory morning chapel services. He never returned to college, and spent his life in business, first in Boston and then in Danbury. The second brother, Isaac Wilcox Ives (named for both of his grandfathers), was also a businessman, running a lumber yard in Danbury alongside several other ventures, some successful and others not. George's sister Sarah Amelia (named after her grandmother but known by her middle name) married Lyman Brewster, a lawyer who had moved to Danbury after graduating from Yale in 1855 and became a judge and state senator; he was from a distinguished New England family, a descendant of William Brewster, who came over on the Mayflower in 1620 and became leader of the Plymouth Colony.[3]

As the youngest, George Ives was the last to wed, marrying Mary Elizabeth Parmalee (1849–1929) on New Year's Day 1874. Known as Mollie, she was the daughter of a local farmer and an amateur choral singer from nearby Bethel. On October 20 that year, Charles Edward Ives was born in the Ives family homestead, followed sixteen months later by his brother Joseph Moss Ives II, named for his uncle but known to everyone as Moss. Moss grew up to be a lawyer and judge in Danbury, like his Uncle Lyman. When Charlie was around five years old Aunt Amelia wanted to move with Uncle Lyman back into the family house, so George and his family moved to 16 Stevens Street, a few blocks away; nine years later, they moved again, into a house behind the Ives house that had once been the family barn.[4]

The boys had a regular small-town childhood, playing games and sports with friends and going to school and church. Among their more elaborate games were playing shopkeepers, setting up a grocery store in the woodshed in imitation of their uncles, and running the Ives Bros. Railroad under the clothesline and through the back yard. They spent a month at the beach in Westbrook most summers with their mother, staying in Uncle Lyman's vacation house near other relatives, while George stayed home to work, sometimes coming down for weekends. Charlie was active in sports, especially baseball, which was later a source of inspiration for several of his compositions. He joined an amateur baseball team called the Alerts in the spring of 1889, when he was fourteen, playing in the outfield and then becoming the pitcher. In September 1891 he moved from the New Street School, where he had been for ten years, to the Danbury Academy, and joined their football team; the following year he was their captain.[5]

In between all these other activities, Ives had music lessons: drums with a local barber, piano and music theory with his father, and then piano, organ, violin, and cornet with other teachers. He listened to all the music going on around him and participated in much of it. His early experiences with music, through his father and his home town, helped to form his musical tastes, and they echo throughout his mature music.[6]

DANBURY AND THE FOUR MUSICAL TRADITIONS

The most important characteristic of Ives's music is not its dissonance nor its complexity nor its advanced style, for not all of his music is dissonant, complex, or unusual in sound. Rather, as we saw in the introduction and experienced in chapter 1, the most important trait of his music is how varied it is, how different one piece can be from another.

Ives grew up in Danbury in the last quarter of the nineteenth century surrounded by music that was in circulation in his day, some of it old and some quite new. By the time he was twenty-five he had heard, learned, performed, and composed music in four different musical traditions: American popular music, Protestant church music, European classical music, and experimental music. Over time he blended elements of those traditions to create his most personal and individual compositions. In a sense he was a native speaker of four different musical languages, while most composers master only one or two. Many of his pieces stick to one style and tradition, but he often integrates diverse styles and traditions within a single work. It is the diversity of his background, and his willingness to mix such separate types of music, that explains both the variety of his music overall and the unique sound of his mature works.[7]

AMERICAN POPULAR MUSIC

The first tradition Ives mastered was American popular music, music whose function was to entertain an audience, appeal to amateur performers, and make money for its composers and publishers. During his childhood and teen years, he encountered all kinds of popular music from his own time and earlier generations. His father, George Ives, had served as the youngest bandleader in the Union Army during the Civil War, which ended just nine years before Charles Ives was born.[8] Songs from the Civil War like *The Battle Cry of Freedom* by George F. Root, *Marching Through Georgia* by Henry Clay Work, and *Tenting on the Old Camp Ground* by Walter Kittredge were known to everyone in Danbury, often sung in commemorations of the war or around the parlor piano. The songs of Stephen Foster, from the decades just before the Civil War, were also widely sung and a particular favorite in the Ives household. Old favorites like *Home! Sweet Home!* by Henry R. Bishop were heard alongside new hits like Michael Nolan's *Little Annie Rooney* and James A. Bland's *Golden Slippers* (which we heard Ives quote in *General William Booth*). There were also the fiddle tunes used for quadrilles and square dances, from Scottish and Irish standards like *The Campbells Are Coming* and *Irish Washerwoman* to traditional American tunes like *Arkansas Traveller* and *Turkey in the Straw*. These and hundreds of other popular melodies were virtually inescapable in nineteenth-century America, part of the mental furniture of anyone growing up in Danbury.

Ives had a close family connection to public performance of popular music through his father. George Ives played cornet at a high level—he had studied the instrument in New York with a professional—and led Danbury's most prominent amateur band. Figure 2.2 shows him in his bandmaster's uniform around 1890. Charles Ives played drums in the band as a boy, and through participating in and listening to his father's group he got to know the sounds, customs, and music of small-town amateur bands. The repertoire ranged from marches, dances, medleys of popular songs, and virtuosic pieces for featured soloists, including his father on cornet, to excerpts from operas and orchestral works arranged for band, especially overtures that introduced an opera or were played as freestanding pieces. He also saw his father participate in other performances, sometimes directing a theater orchestra, the kind of ensemble that plays in the pit to accompany a show or takes the stage to play a mixed program. George also directed

Figure 2.2.   George Ives with his cornet in his bandmaster's uniform around 1890.

MSS 14, The Charles Ives Papers in the Music Library of Yale University, Series VI, Item 33.

amateur bands in nearby Bethel and performed in other towns or traveled with touring shows in the region, jobbing around as musicians must do to put food on the table.[9]

Holiday Quickstep

In his teens and early twenties, drawing on these experiences with popular music, Ives wrote a number of marches for band, piano, or theater orchestra. One of them became his first piece performed in public: *Holiday Quickstep,* dated "Xmas '87" on the manuscript and played at Taylor's Opera House on Main Street in Danbury, shown in Figure 2.3. The parts survive in George Ives's hand, and he no doubt guided his son in composing the piece. It was a conventional march for its time, reflecting the type of repertoire George had been performing with his bands since becoming a bandmaster in the Civil War a quarter century before, but the music shows Charles Ives's ear for the style and genre of the march, including the Sousa trademarks of ending after the trio and including a "dogfight."[10]

Figure 2.3. Taylor's Opera House in Danbury around 1892, with the Civil War memorial to the left.
Cinema Treasures (at cinematreasures.org/theaters/10277/photos/238764).

Let us go back 130 years and imagine that concert as witnessed by the person who documented it for us in the first published review of an Ives piece.[11]

As the arts reviewer for the *Danbury Evening News,* you try to attend every important artistic event in town. On Monday, January 16, 1888, you find yourself at Taylor's Opera House, where the German Dramatic Association is presenting an evening of diverse entertainment. The 1,250-seat house is packed; most of Danbury's elite is here, along with hundreds of other citizens.

The main feature is a comic play in four acts, *Raising the Rent,* which has you and the rest of the audience in stitches. The play ends around 10 p.m., and an amateur chorus from the nearby town of New Milford takes the stage, performing songs in German as well as in English. The evening ends with dancing in the foyer that continues well past midnight to music provided by the Standard Orchestra, a small theater orchestra. They also perform concert pieces throughout the evening, as overtures before each act of the play, as a warm-up before the dancing, and as interludes to give the dancers some rest. You notice that they are playing very well, up to their usual high artistic standards.

At one point in the festivities they settle in for the march *Holiday Quickstep* by Charles Ives, who just turned thirteen three months ago. The boy should know his marches, you think, since he is the son of George Ives, whose band you have heard on many occasions and who directs the Standard Orchestra. The march tonight will be performed not by the band but by members of the orchestra: two groups of violins, two cornets, a piccolo, and a piano. The composer's proud father will be leading the group and playing the first cornet part.

Like every march, this one has two main beats per measure, perfect for marching (left-right, left-right). But as the title says, this is a quickstep, a fast type of march common in the United States since the 1830s. In most quickstep marches, each of the main beats is subdivided into three shorter beats, so there are six quick beats in each measure. This gives the music a swinging lilt, as groups of three alternate with pairs of long and short notes.

You hear such lilting rhythms right away as the music begins. The cornets play a brief rising fanfare—da *DID*-dle-y DID-dle-y *DUMM*-da DUMM—answered by the other instruments playing in unison—*DID*-dle-y DID-dle-y *DUMM* drrrUMM! Then the first strain of the march begins, a spritely eight-measure-long tune in the violins and piccolo with the repeating rhythm da *DUM*-da DID-dle-y *DUM*-da DUM, while the piano and cornets accompany. After the first strain repeats, the piano breaks in with a dramatic descending bass line that swiftly darkens the harmony from a bright major key to a more somber minor key. Tonal music uses two kinds of keys, major and minor, and the differences between them are part of the expressive palette of every composer, like shades of paint to an artist. The piano is answered by a rising figure in the cornets, and the piano and cornets go back and forth in a dramatic "dogfight." Then the first strain returns in the home key, all light and lilt again. The conversation between instruments, the changes of key, and the contrasts of style and mood between fanfare, jollity, and drama are all typical of marches and seem well handled.

Another brief cornet fanfare and response from the other instruments introduce the trio, the second half of the march. A new strain presents a charming, lyrical melody in a new combination of instruments, cornets and violins, while the piano keeps time and marks the changes of harmony. When this strain repeats, the piccolo adds sparkling flourishes. After this soft interlude, the much louder final strain begins with rising arpeggios in the cornets over rising scales in the bass line of the piano. This final strain reminds you of the trio from the *Second Regiment Connecticut National Guard March* by David Wallis Reeves, which you have heard the Danbury Band play many times; you once were told that it is one of George Ives's favorite marches. The pattern of rising arpeggios in the cornets is similar, and the quick notes that embellish the cornet line in Reeves's march are echoed in Ives's march in the violins and piccolo. You smile: clearly the boy is using the well-known march as a model for his own, but he shifts the borrowed elements around and makes sure every phrase that echoes the Reeves ends up going in a different direction, demonstrating his mastery of the idiom of the march while tipping his hat to a distinguished predecessor. The final strain repeats, the march ends with three repeated chords, and you join the hearty applause. Young Ives set out to show that he could write a march in popular style, and he carried it off.

When your review is published the next day on page 3 of the *Danbury Evening News*, you praise each part of the program. At the end you single out Ives's piece for special notice:

> The feature of the evening, in the musical line, was the rendition of the "Holiday Quickstep," composed and arranged for orchestra by Charlie Ives, a thirteen-year-old son of George E. Ives. Master Ives is certainly a musical genius, being an accomplished performer on several instruments, as well as a composer and arranger. The "Holiday Quickstep" is worthy a place with productions of much older heads, and Master Charlie should be encouraged to further efforts in this line. We shall expect more from this talented youngster in the future.[12]

Your prediction will of course come true, although you could hardly anticipate at the time how much music he would write and how diverse and innovative it would be.

Holiday Quickstep itself went on to become a local favorite: played again on
Christmas Day in 1888 by the Sunday school youth orchestra at the Methodist Church where George Ives was the music director, then performed in a
band arrangement by George's Danbury Band on October 11, 1889, and by
Ives himself on the organ on May 25 and June 15, 1890, as a prelude during
Sunday services at the Baptist Church where he was the organist. The success of the piece was a lesson for Ives in how to compose for his audience
and how to adapt music to new groups of instruments. The latter would be
a habit that lasted until the end of Ives's life. Composing for one's audience
was something he pursued assiduously during his apprentice years and never
completely forgot, even during his later years of writing music for an imagined ideal listener.[13]

AMERICAN PROTESTANT CHURCH MUSIC

At the same time that he was surrounded by popular music, Ives was learning a second tradition: American Protestant church music. While his father
played cornet at the Methodist Church and directed the choir there beginning
in 1885, the rest of the family attended the First Congregational Church right
next door to their house. There, as a boy, Ives learned to sing dozens of hymns,
from *Abide with Me* to *When I Survey the Wondrous Cross*. His father often led
the singing at outdoor revival meetings, which included not only traditional
hymns but a newer body of gospel hymns like *Bringing in the Sheaves* and *In
the Sweet By-and-By*. Beyond hymn tunes, church services included organ
pieces as preludes before the service and postludes at the end; anthems (sacred
choral works) from the choir; and solos, duets, trios, or quartets by featured
singers. Ives may have sung in the choir as a boy, and family diaries record Ives
singing solos and duets in the children's services. In his later teens, a teacher
told him he had "a good high tenor voice." He did not take many voice lessons, but his experiences singing in church as well as in the family parlor come
through in his compositions, almost half of which are songs.[14]

    After initial training on piano from his father, from around the age of
ten Ives took piano and later organ lessons with Ella Hollister, organist and

Figure 2.4.   Charles Ives at age fourteen.
MSS 14, The Charles Ives Papers in the Music
Library of Yale University, Series VI, Item 46.

choirmaster at the Disciples
Church. She had confidence in his
abilities, as he filled in for her playing organ at services on two Sun-
days in August 1888, when he was
only thirteen. When she moved to
the Second Congregational Church
on West Street as their new choir
director, Ives followed her and became the regular organist there
in February 1889 at age fourteen,
beginning a career as a professional
church organist that would last for
the next thirteen years. Figure 2.4
shows Ives at that age. That summer, he took organ lessons twice a week
with J. R. Hall, organist at the First Congregational Church, practicing four
hours a day. He moved to the Second Baptist Church on October 20, his
fifteenth birthday; the *Danbury Evening News* took note and crowed that he
was "the youngest organist in the state." He continued to take organ lessons
for at least the next two years, now with Alexander Gibson, an organist from
Norwalk who taught him increasingly difficult concert pieces that Ives played
in recitals and also for church. He played at the Baptist Church until he left
Danbury in 1893, then worked at Episcopal and Congregational churches in
New Haven and at Presbyterian churches in New Jersey and New York until
1902. The habits of organists and traits of organ music became fundamental
to Ives's approach to composition and performance.[15]

In all of these positions, and at revivals, Ives accompanied the congregations as they sang hymns, building a repertoire of tunes that would remain in
his head and under his fingers for the rest of his life. Many of them appear
in his mature works, dozens of which are based on hymn tunes. He described
one such work, the Third Violin Sonata, as "an attempt to express the feeling
and fervor—a fervor that was often more vociferous than religious—with
which the hymns and revival tunes were sung at the Camp Meetings held
extensively in New England in the [18]70's and 80's"—outdoor revivals for
which Ives often played the organ as a teenager. He recalled "how the great
waves of sound used to come through the trees—when things like *Beulah
Land, Woodworth, Nearer My God To Thee, The Shining Shore, Nettleton, In the
Sweet Bye and Bye* and the like were sung by thousands of 'let out' souls. . . .

There was power and exaltation in these great conclaves of sound from humanity."[16] He tried to capture that spirit in his later music based on hymns.

In church services Ives also accompanied vocalists singing solos and the choir singing anthems, psalms, and canticles (psalm-like passages from parts of the Bible other than the Book of Psalms)—including pieces he composed. At the Baptist Church he often accompanied a quartet or double quartet of soloists, indicating that the choir was a quartet choir: one in which each of the four standard groups in a choir—sopranos, altos, tenors, and basses, groups of high and low women's and men's voices respectively—was led by one or two particularly strong singers who could keep the others in their group on pitch and could also serve as soloists. The singers were apparently all amateur volunteers, although at other churches the singers in the lead quartet were usually paid. Ives composed for them both choral works like *Easter Anthem* and *Psalm 42 (As Pants the Hart)* and solos like his setting of *Rock of Ages*, all in a style typical of functional church music of the time, with songlike melodies and rich harmonies touched with chromaticism.[17]

EUROPEAN CLASSICAL MUSIC

The third tradition Ives encountered in Danbury was classical music, based on the repertoire of musical classics from Bach and George Frideric Handel through Haydn, Mozart, Beethoven, Franz Schubert, Felix Mendelssohn, Schumann, and Brahms. His father had studied how to write music in this tradition as a young man, taking lessons with a German immigrant musician in New York and filling a notebook with exercises in harmony (the combination of simultaneous tones), counterpoint (the combination of simultaneous melodies), and orchestration (arranging music for particular instruments), following the common practice of composers from the eighteenth and nineteenth centuries. George Ives had no ambition to be a composer, but he had written short pieces in order to learn how the music he played was constructed, as music students had been doing for centuries. George then taught these techniques to his son, using the same notebook and similar exercises. Ives learned to compose by imitating the music he knew, as we have seen with *Holiday Quickstep* and will see again throughout his early works.[18]

Classical music was performed in Danbury with increasing frequency during Ives's childhood and teen years. Classical works from opera overtures to sonatas and symphonies were sometimes included in the concerts at Taylor's Opera House, played by touring groups or by local talent, often with George Ives participating and his son likely in attendance. Harry Rowe

Shelley, a composer and organist from New York, conducted the Danbury Choral Society in performances of oratorios from 1889 on. Musical clubs like the Mozart Musicale, the Rossini Musical Soirée, and the Mendelssohn Musicale, mostly run by women from the leading families of Danbury, sponsored private gatherings centered on musical performances, sometimes with Ives's participation.[19]

Meanwhile Ives was studying pieces from the classical tradition in his piano and organ lessons and playing some in concerts. Piano practice included preludes and fugues from Bach's famous collection *The Well-Tempered Clavier*, which Ives continued to play almost daily well into his final years. At age twelve, on a May 1887 recital with fellow students, he played a tarantella for piano by the nineteenth-century piano virtuoso Stephen Heller. In his organ lessons and at church services he often played classic organ works, including several of Bach's preludes and fugues, Mendelssohn's preludes and fugues and first two organ sonatas, and works by Beethoven, Schubert, Schumann, Chopin, Wagner, and other classical composers that had been arranged for organ.[20]

The summer he was fifteen, at a benefit concert for the new church building fund at the Baptist Church on June 11, 1890, he performed five major works on the organ: Gioachino Rossini's *William Tell Overture* as arranged for organ by American organist and composer Dudley Buck; Bach's *Dorian* Toccata and Fugue in D Minor; Dudley Buck's *Variations on "Home, Sweet Home"*; Mendelssohn's Organ Sonata No. 1 in F Minor; and the "Marche Pontificale" (third movement) from Jacques-Nicolas Lemmens's Organ Sonata No. 1 in D Minor. This is challenging repertoire, and it shows what an excellent musician he was already in his early teens. The review of the benefit concert in the *Danbury Evening News* said that he "is to be congratulated on his marked ability as a master of the keys for one so young. We predict for him a brilliant future as an organist." Two and a half weeks later, on a Saturday afternoon solo recital on June 28, he played another Bach prelude and fugue, Mendelssohn's Organ Sonata No. 2 in C Minor, and arrangements for organ of the overture to Friedrich von Flotow's opera *Stradella* and the march from Wagner's opera *Tannhaüser*, along with shorter organ works by French composers. The *Danbury Evening News* review praised him for playing with a "skill almost phenomenal." The following May, at another fundraiser for the Baptist new church building fund, Ives played arrangements of the overture and march from Carl Maria von Weber's opera *Oberon* and the Adagio from Beethoven's first piano sonata, followed by Mendelssohn's Prelude and Fugue No. 1 in C Minor and Jacques-Nicolas Lemmens's *Grand Fantasia in E Minor (The Storm)*, a virtuoso showpiece.[21]

All of these pieces had a double function. For Ives, they were organ recital material, guaranteed to impress and entertain the audience. But for those who considered themselves connoisseurs of the best in music, they were also pieces from the classical tradition, music one sits and listens to with rapt attention, music one goes back to again and again, always finding something new in it. It is not clear from Ives's own diaries and letters, from reviews in the *Danbury Evening News*, or from other accounts of the concerts in Danbury how much Ives himself or those around him regarded the music of Bach, Mendelssohn, or Wagner as classics. From his diary entries about how well he played (or what mistakes he made), it appears he may have been focused on getting the notes right as he climbed up the mountain of the organ repertoire, taking on more and more challenging pieces.

Variations on "America"

In the midst of these challenges he took up another: writing a virtuoso organ work of his own, his *Variations on "America."* This was his first major piece in a classical form, theme and variations, and it has become the earliest piece of his to be played regularly, whether on the organ, arranged for orchestra, or—especially—arranged for band, where it has become one of the hundred most frequently performed pieces in the concert band repertoire. He wrote it in 1891–1892 and premiered it on February 17, 1892, at a concert in nearby Brewster, New York.[22] What might it have sounded like that evening?

You won't be writing a review because the concert is out of town, but your curiosity gets the better of you. You have been following young Charlie Ives for four years, since you lauded his *Holiday Quickstep* in the *Danbury Evening News*. His recent organ recitals have shown an impressive command of the instrument, playing difficult repertoire by French and German composers, but he has not included any music of his own. When you heard that he would be playing a new organ piece on a recital across the state line, you decided you would go, to see what happens when he brings together his growing virtuosity as a performer with his abilities as a composer.

So on a winter Wednesday evening, you take your seat in Brewster's Methodist Episcopal Church for a mixed program that includes appearances by Alvin Kranich, a twenty-six-year-old virtuoso pianist and composer from New York City, and the revered hymn writer Fannie Crosby. Young Ives is clearly not the star of this show, but he plays very well, impressing the audience with Bach's Prelude and Fugue in D Minor (BWV 539) and Lemmens's *The Storm*. Then comes the piece you came for: his *Variations on "America"* ("My country, 'tis of thee," the same tune as *God Save the Queen*).

It starts with a surprise. Instead of playing the theme first, followed by a series of variations, Ives begins with an introduction, loud and fast. You recognize the opening notes of the tune ("My country, 'tis—"), but the rhythm is different, more bouncy. Instead of continuing with the familiar melody, each phrase seems to vary the last one. At first it gets further and further from the tune you know, but then you start hearing familiar fragments: "Of thee I sing. Land where my fathers died!—" And just as quickly it goes back to a kind of continuous variation, leading at last to a repetition of the opening few phrases. The atmosphere throughout is of excited anticipation. You wonder what could possibly come next.

Surprise! It's the tune you expected at the beginning, *America*, at a moderate tempo and harmonized like a hymn, with the merest flip of a flourish at the close. So Ives is presenting the theme, not at the outset, but after he hints at it and makes you *want* it. His is not the first set of variations to take this approach, but you find it clever and satisfying.

Then come the variations. In a traditional set of variations, after the theme is presented, each variation treats the theme in a new way: sometimes the tune is accompanied by new figuration, sometimes the tune itself is embellished, sometimes only a general outline can be heard amid new material. There are many strategies. Some variation sets gradually increase in intensity—for instance by using faster note values in each successive variation—and then may change course, perhaps by shifting the key from major to minor and back. Beginning in the middle nineteenth century, composers like Brahms wrote what have been called character variations, in which each variation has not just different figuration but a different character, sometimes marked by a change of tempo or key, often suggesting a different style or kind of music, so that the variations are quite diverse in flavor. You wonder what path Ives will choose.

The first variation presents the theme, again in hymnlike harmony, adding above it a much faster countermelody, a rapidly running line. In the second half, that added melody doubles in pace at times and includes some chromatic flourishes. Well, you think, he can't play much faster than that. Indeed, the second variation does not try to outdo the first in speed of figuration, but picks up on the chromaticism, using lots of chromatic motion in the harmony to accompany the melody. The tune is back on top, with either the bass line or lines in the middle of the texture constantly moving to keep up momentum. It seems that what Ives has in mind is a set of character variations, each one different in style and tempo.

Indeed! The third variation suddenly changes not only tempo and style but also key and meter—the pattern of accented and unaccented beats in each measure. This is in the fast tempo, six-beat meter, and rollicking style of a quickstep march. The tune is again on top, recast from hymnlike to a lilting song but immediately recognizable, like an old friend in a costume. There are chromatic touches, linking back to the previous two variations, and a pervasive figure of a note decorated by the note just a half step below it, with the lower note quick and on the beat. Somehow—maybe it's that figure, or the quickstep rhythm, or both—this variation sounds like music played on a circus calliope; it feels witty, jesting, almost sarcastic, worlds away from the sober mood of the theme or the excitement of the introduction. Ives repeats the tune and adds a running melodic line in a middle voice, recalling his procedures in both the first and second variations.

The fourth variation is back in the original triple meter (three beats per measure), and in the original key, but now minor instead of major. The accompaniment sets up the rhythm of a polonaise—DUM-didda dut-dut DUM-dut, DUM-didda dut-dut DUM-dut—giving this variation again a completely different character from what you have heard so far. When the melody comes in, it is played straight—in its original rhythm, though in a minor key—but because of the accompaniment it sounds to you not like a hymn but like a song in an opera, or a cornet solo the band might play. The second half of the tune repeats, now with little two-note flourishes in the organ's flute stop (the organ pipes that sound like a flute). This again reminds you of both opera and band music, which often have little decorative touches like this. It occurs to you that since bands so often play excerpts from popular operas, maybe Ives means to invoke both traditions.

Every set of variations for the organ needs to show off the pedals at some point, and the fifth variation does just that. Organists play on keyboards with their ten fingers, like pianists, but have an extra pedal keyboard for their feet, used to play bass notes, the lowest notes in the musical texture. In most music, the bass line moves more slowly than the other parts, and that has been true so far in Ives's piece. In this variation, however, the bass line, played in the pedals, marches along at twice the pace of the melody and chords above it, propelling the music forward. After the first phrase the pace in the pedals nearly doubles, reminding you of the rapidly running countermelody in the first variation.

After playing the tune all the way through, Ives repeats it in the same texture, only more so: the bass line continues its propulsive march in the pedals, the melody and chords jump into a higher range, the tempo is suddenly faster, and a middle voice adds a repeating half-step figure like the one in the third variation. It sounds like the music is driving toward a grand ending.

But then the tune gets stuck on the next-to-last phrase—"From every mountainside"—with the last note falling back instead of leading upward into the last phrase. The harmony leads off in a new direction, the next-to-last phrase repeats and is varied, and the music seems to struggle to find the right continuation. Suddenly the very opening of the piece's introduction, last heard about seven minutes ago, breaks in, now saturated with rapid running notes over a climbing bass line and sounding more ponderous than sprightly. Then that breaks off as well, and you watch as Ives's fingers leap from one keyboard to the other, playing rapid, brief figures that alternate between loud and softer, close and more distant, in a powerful, dissonant climax. Finally Ives literally pulls out all the stops—meaning all the pipes on the organ are sounding—as he marches up and down the pedal keyboard under grand chords that hint at the tune, and reaches at last the final phrase of the song: "Let freedom ring!" He makes you wait for it, and when it comes, that final phrase makes a fulfilling ending to an energetic and very satisfying piece.

Although it has become one of Ives's best-known pieces, *Variations on "America"* took years to see print. A few months after its premiere, his father copied it out neatly and sent it off to a publisher, who sat on it for a couple of years and then sent it back. More than fifty years later, the prominent American organist E. Power Biggs asked Ives for an organ piece, and Ives sent him these variations, the longest and most assured piece he had written for the instrument. Biggs played it in 1948 and oversaw its publication in 1949, but he sought to simplify the climactic passage near the end, cutting out the acrobatics of leaping between keyboards. Ives wrote to the publisher requesting that they be restored in the published version, and they were, though they were marked "ad lib" (*ad libitum*, at the discretion of the player) so that they could be omitted "if Mr. Biggs doesn't like to play them." It is a remarkable testament to Ives's prowess as a seventeen-year-old organist that he was playing music that challenged a professional half a century later.[23]

One feature that Biggs and other modern players include in *Variations on "America"* that did not appear in Ives's 1892 performance is a pair of brief interludes that he penciled into his ink manuscript around 1902.[24] They raise eyebrows, because both are in two keys at once, with an upper stream of music in one key and a lower stream in another, at two very different levels of audibility. An interlude after the second variation has the upper parts playing loudly in the key we just heard, while the lower parts play very softly in the key of the forthcoming third variation. The effect is of hearing music close by while vaguely sensing other music at a distance, as if you were standing in the door of one church listening to the organ while you can just barely hear the organ sounding from another church across the street. The second interlude, between the fourth and fifth variations, is similar, but now the loud music is at the bottom of the texture and the soft music at the top. This combination of separate streams of sound, set off from each other by key and by a sense of distance, one close and one farther away, is a frequent and distinctive feature of Ives's later music. The effect is ruined in most performances of *Variations on "America,"* when the organist (or orchestra or band) plays both layers equally loudly.[25] And the addition of these interludes makes the piece into something different from the virtuoso vehicle that Ives played at Brewster that February. With those interludes, it represents a combination of organ recital music in the classical tradition with another strain in Ives's career, the fourth and most idiosyncratic tradition he knew in his youth.

EXPERIMENTAL MUSIC

The fourth musical tradition Ives participated in during his Danbury years was experimental music, defined as music written for the purpose of exploring new musical techniques for their own sakes, to try them out, rather than in pursuit of a larger aesthetic or philosophical goal. Perhaps "tradition" is the wrong word: experimental music became a current in the twentieth century, encompassing younger composers such as Henry Cowell and John Cage, but Ives appears to be the first composer to experiment repeatedly and systematically with new musical resources. He was, in a sense, the founder of the American experimental tradition in music.[26]

During his youth, Ives treated his musical experiments as an almost entirely private affair, akin to his exercises in harmony and counterpoint, shared with no one but his father and perhaps a few family members and friends. His typical approach was to take the existing rules of music, rules he was learning in his music theory and composition lessons with his father, and change one or two of them just to see what happens. As he asks in his *Memos*, recalling his attitude as a teenager,

> if two major or minor 3rds can make up a chord, why not more? And also, if you can play a tune in one key, why can't a feller, if he feels like [it], play one in two keys?[27]

So alongside his exercises in traditional harmony, where chords can be made by stacking two or three thirds on top of each other, Ives tried piling on *more* thirds, both major thirds (the size of two whole steps) and minor thirds (a whole step plus a half step). The result was chords of five to eight notes separated by thirds, with each note in the chord grinding in dissonance against one or two of the others. Instead of creating tension and resolution in a phrase through traditional chord progressions, in some brief sketches he set up two streams of chords, one sinking by half step while the other rises by half step, so that they create unheard-of clashing combinations as they move, and then converge at the end to sound a single consonant chord that has the effect of resolving the previous dissonances. While he was learning to write canons, pieces in which a melody in one voice is imitated exactly in another voice starting a little later (as in *Row, Row, Row Your Boat*), he not only created canons that followed the traditional rules of counterpoint and harmony but also tried out ones where each voice was in a different key—an effect called *polytonality*, because more than one tonality or key is being heard simultaneously. Along the same lines, he wrote little pieces where *London Bridge Is Falling Down* is played in one key while the accompaniment is in another key, usually a whole step or half step away to create maximum dissonance. Such unusual resources—novel chords, streams of parallel chords moving in opposite directions, and polytonal counterpoint and harmony—were tried out for their own sakes in these little pieces that Ives wrote as a teenager, but many of these techniques proved useful in his later music for creating effects that could help to convey a meaning or depict an image or an event.[28]

One such experiment that later bore fruit was trying to imitate the sound of drums on the piano. This is the origin of that striking effect in the middle of *The Circus Band* and the beginning of *General William Booth* that we noticed in chapter 1. Half a century later, Ives told the story in his *Memos*:

> When I was a boy, I played in my father's brass band, usually one of the drums. . . . In practising the drum parts on the piano (not on the drum—neighbours' requests), I . . . got to trying out sets of notes to go with or take-off the drums—for the snare drum, right-hand notes usually closer together—and for the bass drum, wider chords. They had little to do with the harmony of the piece, and were used only as sound-combinations as such. . . .
>
> Father didn't object to all of this, if it was done with some musical sense—that is, if I would make some effort to find out what was going on, with some reason. . . . Sometimes, when practising with others or in the school orchestra, I would play drum parts on the piano, and I noticed that it didn't seem to bother the other players—*if* I would keep away from [chords] that suggested a key. . . .
>
> I just mention the above, not that in itself it is much, but to show how the human ear (not one but all) will learn to digest and handle sounds, the more they are heard and then understood. In this example, what started as boy's play and in fun, gradually worked into something that had a serious side to it that opened up possibilities—and in ways sometimes valuable, as the ears got used to and acquainted with these various and many dissonant sound combinations.[29]

Here Ives credits his father with keeping an open mind, letting him experiment if he did so "with some musical sense." Typically that meant, as in any good experiment, keeping some variables unchanged—here, the rhythmic patterns played on the drums—while changing others, in this case the sounds used to produce those rhythms. Ives also recalled his father experimenting with sound, trying to capture the sound of a church bell in a rainstorm by using intervals too small to be played on the piano, and encouraging his sons to sing a song in one key while he played the accompaniment on the piano in a different key, just to see how long they could stick it out. But George Ives was not a composer. All he gave to his son, including an openness to experimentation, a first exposure to Bach and other classics, his first lessons in piano and composition, and experiences with a wide variety of music from band marches and Stephen Foster songs to church music and concert music, found its realization in Ives's later music.[30]

LEAVING DANBURY

In the spring of 1893, at age eighteen, Ives left Danbury for good. In February, he enrolled in Hopkins Grammar School, a preparatory school in New Haven whose principal goal was to get its students into Yale and prepare them to pass the entrance exams. The family—George, of course, but also Uncle Lyman and Aunt Amelia—had decided that Ives must go to Yale, the family college, aiming for the success in business that had eluded his father, and Hopkins was the vehicle to get him admitted. Ives took a room in a boarding house and joined the school's baseball and football teams; his greatest triumph came the next spring when he pitched as the Hopkins team defeated Yale. Figure 2.5 shows him in uniform with his catcher, Franklin Hobart Miles. At first he came home weekends to see his family and continue his organ duties. In March 1893 he traveled down to Carnegie Hall in New York City, probably with his father, to hear the great Polish piano virtuoso Ignacy Paderewski perform a program including music of Bach, Beethoven, Chopin, and Franz Liszt. On April 16, Ives played at the dedication of the new church building in Danbury, then two weeks later came his last Sunday service as organist of the Baptist Church. The following week, May 7, he played his first Sunday in his new position as organist at St. Thomas Episcopal Church in New Haven. After that, he came home less and less often, although he kept up frequent correspondence with his family, especially his father.[31]

In May, George wrote to say that Uncle Lyman, who was chairman of the American Bar Association's Committee on Uniform State Laws, would

be attending the national conference in Milwaukee the first week
of September, had funding to
pay for a secretary to travel with
him, and wondered if Ives would
like to go. It was an exciting opportunity, farther than Ives had
ever traveled, and would allow
him and his uncle to attend
the World's Columbian Exposition in Chicago, the greatest as-
semblage of peoples, technology,
fine arts, music, and culture the
United States had ever seen. Ives
jumped at the chance.[32]

That August at the World's
Fair, Ives and his uncle took in
its spectacle, bustle, and electric-
ity (literally—it was all lit by
electric power, still a recent and
novel innovation), but especially
its music. The latest hits from
Tin Pan Alley sounded in the
Midway. John Philip Sousa, soon
to be dubbed "The March King,"

Figure 2.5. Charles Ives and Franklin Hobart Miles, pitcher and catcher for the Hopkins Grammar School baseball team that beat Yale in spring 1894.

MSS 14, The Charles Ives Papers in the Music Library of Yale University, Series VI, Item 54.

led daily free concerts by his band, a professional outfit far superior to the
amateur bands George Ives led in Danbury. Near the fairgrounds, groups of
African American musicians, including Scott Joplin, performed in a new syncopated popular style that would soon become known as ragtime; we do not
know whether Ives heard it there, but in a few years at Yale and in New York
ragtime became another type of music that Ives had in his ears and under his
fingers and that would come out in his compositions.[33]

Most important to Ives were the classical concerts. He and his uncle
heard orchestral concerts by members of the Chicago Symphony Orchestra
and a series of organ recitals by various artists, all playing at a professional
level he had not experienced in Danbury. At a recital by organist and composer Alexandre Guilmant, whose music he had often played in church
and on recitals, Ives saw what a real international organ master could do.
Guilmant played pieces Ives knew well, including some of Guilmant's own
compositions alongside Mendelssohn's Organ Sonata No. 1 and Bach's
Toccata and Fugue in D Minor, as well as several pieces new to Ives by Di-
eterich Buxtehude, Liszt, Wagner, and Lemmens. He must have sensed the

gap between his own small-town training and the professional world, and it raised the level of his aspirations.[34]

Part of what distinguishes the classical tradition from others is its function: it is art music that one listens to closely, with attention. It is not entertainment music, like the band music and theater music Ives heard in Danbury; it is not used as part of family socializing, like parlor songs; it is not utilitarian music, like music for church services. It is listened to for its own sake, for the experience it offers. Concert etiquette by the late nineteenth century expected the audience to sit silently, and the room was often darkened to avoid any distractions. In Danbury, Ives was absorbing the sounds and styles of classical music, but he was not yet familiar with its ethos. His visit to the World's Fair helped to familiarize Ives with the demands and the potential of classical music. It seems to have inspired a new commitment to the classical tradition, a move away from the small-town musical world of George Ives and toward new dreams.[35]

From Danbury, Ives took his knowledge of popular music, Stephen Foster, band music, and fiddle tunes; his experience as a church musician; his familiarity with dozens of hymns that carried meaning for him because of the words and of how they were sung at the spirited revivals he had attended; his encounters with classical music, as a performer and an audience member; and his experimental approach and the novel sounds and techniques he had already developed. All of these echo in his mature compositions.

He also took what he had learned as an organist, reflected in his later music in many ways. His skill at improvising preludes and postludes is evident in keyboard writing that sounds like improvisation. His virtuosity as a player led him to expect that professional musicians should be able to play anything put in front of them, no matter how difficult. Organists often play a melody on one manual keyboard, the accompaniment on another, and the bass line on the pedals, linking each keyboard to a different group of pipes so that the simultaneous streams of music have contrasting colors and may sound like they are being played on different instruments; Ives often used similar layering effects in his mature music. Organists also alternate keyboards at different levels of loudness to suggest echoes, distance, and other effects that create a sense of space; use striking sounds to evoke events outside of music; hold down a bass note with a foot on the pedal keyboard while changing the harmony above it; set hymns or popular tunes in complex surroundings; introduce a hymn by presenting variants or fragments of the tune before stating it whole; and play music that features fugues and other types of counterpoint—all traits Ives used in his mature compositions.[36]

Ives came out of his Danbury years an exciting teenage musician. But he would not have become the Ives we know without the formative influences of his college years, described in the next chapter.

• *3* •

Apprenticeship

$\mathscr{T}$here is no composer more closely associated with his undergraduate college than Charles Ives is with Yale.[1] He wrote pieces at Yale, for Yale, and about Yale, depicting campus events and quoting Yale football cheers and songs of his fraternity and his senior secret society. Yale ran in the family, going back five generations from Ebeneezer White through his great-grandfather Isaac Ives and his uncles Joseph Ives and Lyman Brewster, and continuing with Ives's younger brother Moss, who graduated with a bachelor of laws in 1899, and Moss's son Richard (Yale 1925). Ives went to Yale because his family, especially Aunt Amelia and Uncle Lyman (who helped tutor him for the entrance exams), wanted him to go there as preparation for a career in business.[2] At Yale, still an all-male school, Ives took courses but also participated enthusiastically in the unofficial curriculum of student life that helped to forge social connections and develop skills useful for success in commerce. After graduation he lived with fellow Yale graduates for his first ten years in New York, returned for reunions, married the sister of a Yale classmate whose father was also a Yale graduate, and stayed in touch with Yale friends and mentors for decades. Almost by accident, he also encountered at Yale his most important teacher of classical music, who provided a model Ives absorbed, emulated, and ultimately rejected but without whom he could never have become a great composer. As is true for many of us, college changed Ives for good.

CLASSES AND ACTIVITIES AT YALE

Ives passed his entrance exams and matriculated at Yale in September 1894, taking required courses in Greek, Latin, mathematics, German, and English literature, the standard fare of nineteenth-century liberal arts colleges though

49

old-fashioned by the 1890s. Figure 3.1 shows Ives in the room at 76 South Middle (now Constitution Hall) where he lived all four years with his roommate Mandeville Mullaly. Just weeks after classes began, on November 4, his father unexpectedly died of a stroke, leaving Ives without the guiding light of his Danbury years and heightening the sense that he was now on his own and entering a new world. He was never a top student. His grades that first year

Figure 3.1.   Ives (right) and Mandeville Mullally in their room at Yale.
MSS 14, The Charles Ives Papers in the Music Library of Yale University, Series VI, Item 59.

averaged 223 on the 400-point scale then used at Yale, roughly equivalent to a D in the 1960s or a C today (allowing for grade inflation). His four-year average was only a notch higher at 238. In later years he completed his required courses in Greek, Latin, math, English literature, modern languages (switching from German to French), logic, psychology, ethics, and philosophy, and took electives his junior and senior years in political science, European history, American literature, and music.[3]

Other than music, Ives's favorite courses seem to have been the five semesters of English and American literature he took with William Lyon Phelps (1865–1943), shown in Figure 3.2. His grades in Phelps's classes were better than his usual marks, and he spoke fondly of his experience in a letter to Phelps in 1937, almost four decades after graduation:

> I can't close without telling you something that I know you know. All Yale men . . . have the same feeling of affection and gratitude to you that I have. Mine reaches far back. I can never forget you behind that white teacher's desk (probably once a pulpit) in the little classroom under Old Chapel. It was not only the natural and unusual way you had of stirring the mind and arousing enthusiasm that stands out in my memory, but—you always looked as if you thought everybody knew just as much as you did.[4]

Ives retained a lifelong interest in literature, and his taste was deeply influenced by Phelps's teaching. Ives set to music excerpts from Shakespeare's *The Tempest* and Milton's *Paradise Lost*, both assigned reading in Phelps's sophomore English class, and poems by many of the writers Phelps discussed enthusiastically in print and presumably taught in his courses, including Keats, Wordsworth, Browning, Matthew Arnold, Kipling, Emerson, Whitman, and John Greenleaf Whittier. Ives also wrote instrumental music on literary figures Phelps wrote about

Figure 3.2. William Lyon Phelps, Ives's professor of English and American literature at Yale.

Yale University Library, Manuscripts and Archives Digital Library, Image 3826 (Images of Yale Individuals, RU 684, Box 53, Folder 2021).

and taught, notably the *Robert Browning Overture* and three movements of the *Concord Sonata* on Emerson, Hawthorne, and Thoreau. In his senior year, Ives submitted an essay on Emerson to the *Yale Literary Magazine*, probably adapted from a paper for Phelps's course on American literature. Although it was "promptly handed back" and never published, that Ives made the effort shows how much he was enchanted by the world of words and ideas to which Phelps was introducing him.[5] Phelps kindled Ives's enthusiasm for literature and nurtured his tastes in ways that echo throughout Ives's career, making him Ives's most important teacher outside of music.

Another formative experience came through negotiating the unofficial curriculum outside the classroom. As Ives's biographers have documented, activities at Yale from sports teams to the *Yale Literary Magazine* prepared students for success in their careers by offering opportunities to compete, to demonstrate their work ethic and organizational skills, and to develop a network of friends and allies who could serve as future business contacts. Frank Rossiter points out the "curious ambivalence" among Yale students of Ives's day:

> The students thought of themselves as irresponsibles and hedonists, drinking away their nights at Mory's and enjoying themselves for a brief time until they had to enter the world of work. They created a mood of romance and nostalgia and sang of "bright college years." This mood, however, was largely an illusion, for they were actually caught up in an intensive round of activities . . . not undertaken for the pleasure they gave in themselves, but in order to secure the tangible honors that the system offered. . . . Competition was the lifeblood of Yale; and as with the football team, so with all other activities, the purpose of competition was to win.[6]

In this contest for status, the students themselves chose the winners by selecting them as members of the sophomore societies, junior fraternities, and senior secret societies that were at the center of campus life. Foreshadowing his later success in business, Ives was a favorite, chosen for the leading sophomore society, Hé Boulé; for one of the top three fraternities, Delta Kappa Epsilon; for the secret society Wolf's Head (only fifteen percent of the senior class were admitted to secret societies); and for the prestigious Ivy Committee, elected with the most votes from his classmates.[7] Ives would later pay tribute to these groups by incorporating songs of DKE and Wolf's Head into pieces about college life at Yale.

One of the ways Ives stood out was through music. Yale had a strong tradition of student music-making, staffed primarily by students preparing for careers in business, law, or medicine. Ives's musical skills, honed in Danbury, gave him a head start in this race. He sang in the Freshman Glee Club, wrote the music for shows put on by Hé Boulé and DKE, and composed three marches that incorporated college songs. In his junior year, the *Yale Courant* published two of his pieces to words by a classmate: *A Scotch Lullaby*, a parlor song in dialect; and *A Song of Mory's*, a piece for men's chorus. The Yale Glee Club sang several of his choral works; a special favorite, which celebrated the sound of the bells of Battell Chapel, was *The Bells of Yale* or *Chapel Chimes*, included on their December 1897 concert tour of fourteen cities and later published in a 1903 book of *Yale Melodies*.[8]

All of this music is in the popular styles of the time and served the purpose of creating comradeship through group participation. The program for the Delta Kappa Epsilon show *Hells Bells, or The Fight That Yaled* captures the spirit:

> Mr. C. E. Ives has furnished much original music for this play; his latest masterpiece will be sung at the close of the 3rd Act. The words were written by F. G. Hinsdale. You are all requested to join in the chorus, but kindly wait until it sounds familiar.[9]

Ives also found wider outlets for his music in popular genres with his first professional publications, printed in 1896 by publishers in New York and Philadelphia: *For You and Me!* for male chorus or quartet; *William Will*, a song for William McKinley's presidential campaign; and *March "Intercollegiate"* for band. Perhaps as a reward for the campaign song, Ives's march was performed in Washington for McKinley's inauguration on March 4, 1897, by the combined New Haven Band and Washington Marine Band, giving Ives his first performance outside his home region.[10]

While he was finding new success in the realm of popular music, he was writing a different kind of music for his coursework.

STUDIES WITH HORATIO PARKER

Ives did not go to Yale to focus on music. In March 1894, while studying at Hopkins in preparation for his entrance exams, he wrote to his father:

> There is some kind of music course in college which I will look up. I think it can be taken with out any extra charge and may be substituted with other things.[11]

This letter makes clear that Ives did not know what the "music course" included, and that both he and his family considered it ancillary to the main event at Yale, the training in liberal arts that would prepare him for a life in business.

**Figure 3.3.   Horatio Parker,
Ives's music professor at Yale.**
MSS 32, The Horatio Parker Papers in the Music
Library of Yale University, Box 40, Folder 2.

At this point, six months before matriculation, Ives could not have known that his principal teacher in music would be Horatio Parker (1863–1919), shown in Figure 3.3. Parker was appointed Battell Professor of the Theory of Music later that spring and began teaching at Yale in September, the same month Ives entered Yale as a freshman. Like Ives, Parker was an experienced church organist, serving as organist and choirmaster at New York churches and since fall 1893 at Trinity Church in Boston, a post he held throughout Ives's years at Yale. Parker had gained prominence as a composer with his church music, orchestral music, and choral music, especially the oratorio *Hora novissima*, premiered in May 1893. Although Parker had a huge impact on Ives's development, providing the training and craftsmanship he needed, Ives appears to have become his student by sheer luck rather than design.

That good fortune gave Ives an enviable pedigree. As a composer of classical music, Ives had a distinguished family tree with roots on both sides of the Atlantic. His teacher Parker had studied composition with George Whitefield Chadwick (1854–1931), a composer, conductor, pianist, and organist from Massachusetts who taught at the New England Conservatory in Boston and was its director from 1897 to 1930. Parker and Chadwick were among the leading American composers of classical music when Ives was at Yale. Chadwick had studied organ and composition at the New England Conservatory with Dudley Buck (1839–1909), one of the most prolific and popular composers of church music in the United States, and with Eugene Thayer, a student of John Knowles Paine (1839–1906), the most famous American composer of classical music of the previous generation. Paine, Buck, Chadwick, and Parker had all studied in Germany: Paine in Berlin, Buck and Chadwick at the Leipzig Conservatory, and Chadwick and Parker at the Munich Hochschule für Musik with Josef Rheinberger, one of the most respected composition professors in Europe. Among Chadwick's teachers at the Leipzig Conservatory were Carl Reinecke (1824–1910), who had been taught by Liszt, Mendelssohn, and Schumann, and Salomon Jadassohn (1831–1902), who had also studied with Liszt. Liszt studied with Carl Czerny, who was Beethoven's most famous student. So through Parker, Ives was in a direct line from Beethoven, as well as from Liszt, Mendelssohn, and Schumann. He also had connections to Dvořák: Ives's organ mentor Harry Rowe Shelley had studied with Dvořák, and Parker had taught at the National Conservatory of Music in New York in 1892–1893, Dvořák's first year as head of the conservatory.

In the nineteenth century, training in music composition consisted of two main kinds of assignment. On the one hand, there were exercises to learn and practice the basic techniques of tonal music, akin to learning the vocabulary and grammar of a foreign language by translating texts and writing sentences. On the other, students were challenged to compose original pieces of music, starting with small forms and working up to longer and more complex ones, like gaining fluency in a foreign language by writing paragraphs, essays, and stories. In both cases, students were given examples to follow, models of how to do it well, that they could learn from and imitate. All of these exercises and compositions were coached and corrected by a master composer. Students were like apprentices in an artisan's workshop, learning each step in the process of manufacturing a piece of music and developing their craft under strict supervision. Creativity was important for success as a composer, but that could hardly be taught; what was central to the teacher-student relationship was mastering the craft.

When Parker arrived at Yale, he reorganized the music curriculum into six year-long academic courses as well as lessons in performance. Parker taught all the academic courses, which could be taken as electives by juniors and seniors. The History of Music traced its development from medieval times through Beethoven. The other five courses were oriented toward technical training in the materials and procedures of tonal music. First was Harmony, in which students learned about intervals and chords, how to add chords to a given melody or bass line, and how to move into a new key and return to the home key. Next was Counterpoint, learning to combine two, three, or four melodic lines so the parts sound well together, including how to use imitation, in which the parts have similar melodies but start at different times, each entering in turn. That was followed by Strict Composition, practicing more complex counterpoint and composing pieces in particular forms, including canon, which he had studied in Danbury, and fugue, in which the parts enter one by one with the fugue subject (its main theme), and then move more freely. Instrumentation covered the capabilities of each instrument in the orchestra and gave students practice in arranging music for different combinations. The capstone was Free Composition, where students with "an unmistakable talent for original composition" wrote original pieces and produced "an extended work, probably in sonata form." In all of these courses, students wrote exercises and compositions to demonstrate their command of each concept, and as they advanced from course to course their compositions grew longer and more complex.[12]

Ives took Counterpoint and Instrumentation his junior year and Strict Composition his senior year, along with Instrumentation again. The official enrollment was always small, between one and three students, and Ives got to know his teacher well. His grades in these courses were far above those in his other classes. He never registered for Harmony or the History of Music, probably because he audited them informally during his first two years in college, when as an underclassman he was not allowed to enroll for music electives. In his *Memos*, Ives refers to "the music courses at Yale (four years with Parker)" and mentions showing pieces to Parker as a freshman, implying that indeed he sat in on courses his first two years.[13] The level of work he was doing in his senior year matches the description of Free Composition; Gayle Sherwood Magee has suggested that Parker allowed him to take the class despite lacking one prerequisite (Strict Composition), and signed him up for a second year of Instrumentation as a way to give him credit and record his grades.[14]

In *Memos*, written more than three decades after graduation, Ives complains about having to repeat some of his training from his Danbury years:

> Father had kept me on Bach and taught me harmony and counterpoint from [when I was] a child until I went to college. And there with Parker I went over the same things, even the same harmony and counterpoint textbooks ([both written by Chadwick's teacher Salomon] Jadassohn), and I think I got a little fed up on too much counterpoint and classroom exercises (maybe because, somehow, counterpoint gradually became so much associated in my mind as a kind of exercise on paper, instead of on the mountains).[15]

Yet the exercises and compositions that survive show that Ives learned a great deal from Parker, especially about counterpoint, fugue, instrumentation, and form. The canons and counterpoint exercises he wrote in college are at a higher level than those from his teens. Two classroom fugues, though not without infelicities, are beyond what he attempted for his father. For his Instrumentation class with Parker, Ives arranged a piano sonata movement by Beethoven for string quartet and piano pieces by Schubert and Schumann for orchestra. These arrangements show sensitivity to what works best in each medium. Ives does more than simply assign notes to various instruments;

in several passages he reworks the material to suit the new instrumentation, adding, omitting, and redistributing notes, weaving new lines into the counterpoint, enriching the texture with new accompanimental figures, and updating some aspects to fit the style of the late nineteenth century rather than of sixty to one hundred years earlier.[16] He also arranged for orchestra one of his own compositions for organ, Postlude in F, and noted on the manuscript that it was "tried over by [the] New Haven Orches[tra conducted by] Prof. H W Parker"—quite an honor for an undergraduate, and very useful to a student learning how the instrumental combinations he worked out on paper would sound in performance.[17] All of this was necessary preparation for Ives's later chamber and orchestral music.

Focused on teaching the techniques of tonal music, Parker was not sympathetic to Ives's experimental music that violated those rules. In *Memos*, Ives recalled showing Parker

> a couple of fugues with the theme in four different keys, C-G-D-A—and in another, C-F-Bb-Eb [instead of the expected series of entrances on C, G, C, and G that would begin a fugue in the key of C]. It resulted, when it all got going, in the most dissonant sounding counterpoint. Parker took it as a joke (he was seldom mean), and I didn't bother him but occasionally after the first few months. He would just look at a measure or so, and hand it back with a smile, or joke about "hogging all the keys at one meal" and then talk about something else.[18]

Ives contrasted Parker's attitude with the openmindedness of his father, whom he remembered saying, "If you know how to write a fugue the right way *well*, then I'm willing to have you try the wrong way—*well*. But you've got to know what [you're doing] and why you're doing it."[19] Parker's lack of encouragement for Ives's experimental ideas led generations of writers to regard him as a negative influence on Ives.[20]

Yet Ives respected Parker for his idealism and his craft, and he learned an enormous amount from him, from compositional technique to an understanding of what classical music can do and is for. He wrote in *Memos*, just after the passage quoted above,

> I had and have great respect and admiration for Parker and most of his music. It was seldom trivial—his choral works have a dignity and depth that many of [his] contemporaries, especially in the [field of] religious and choral composition, did not have. Parker had ideals that carried him higher than the popular but he was governed too much by the German rule.[21]

The ideals Parker articulated in his writings and teaching were ones that Ives would share for the rest of his life: self-discipline, integrity, service to others, reliance on intuition, commitment to progress, and faith in the moral, spiritual, and expressive power of music while rejecting the merely sensual.[22] Most important, Ives absorbed from Parker the idea of art music, music that is listened to for its own sake, offering an experience that can be conveyed in no other way. The concept of music as an art, of the composer as an artist with a distinctive personality, and of each piece as a unique artwork that speaks directly to the spirit and intuition of each individual listener, was far removed from the utilitarian music Ives had been composing since his teens, music that served to entertain an audience or accompany a church service. Without the lofty aspiration to write music that would earn a listener's total attention and communicate something of substance, a purpose for music that Ives learned from Parker, Ives could never have written his mature music.[23]

ART SONGS: *FELDEINSAMKEIT* AND *ICH GROLLE NICHT*

Among the genres Ives learned to compose at Yale was the art song, a song in the classical tradition intended to be performed in song recitals like the one in chapter 1. In an art song, a composer seeks to create an experience that will engage listeners on a high artistic level, fitting the music to the text in ways that reflect its accentuation, its meaning, the emotions it suggests, and the images in the poetry. Both the vocal melody and the accompaniment (usually for piano) are written out exactly and meant to be performed as written—quite different from folk songs or popular songs, which can be arranged with various accompaniments and freely altered by performers.

At Yale and during the four years after graduation, Ives composed more than a dozen songs to German poems, using as models art songs on the same texts by composers including Schubert, Schumann, Robert Franz, Peter Cornelius, and Brahms. John Kirkpatrick suggested that "Parker may have considered the re-setting of famous song texts as part of strict composition," the course Ives took in his senior year, and scholars long assumed that Parker assigned Ives to write these songs. But Bryan Simms has recently shown that Parker's papers do not include such assignments, and none of his other students made it a practice.[24] Apparently Ives came up with the idea himself as a way to learn the craft of writing an art song, using the Romantic, tonal musical language of the composers he was imitating. After college, he continued the habit, setting texts from famous French art songs by Jules Massenet and Benjamin Godard. Ives included almost all of his German and French songs in his 1922 collection of *114 Songs*, either in their original language or with new English words, showing that he valued the music as more than an exercise in composition. In *114 Songs*, after a series of four French songs and four German songs, he included a footnote regarding these songs to familiar texts, writing in typical feisty yet self-deprecating fashion:

> The writer has been severely criticized for attempting to put music to texts of songs, which are masterpieces of great composers. The song above and some of the others, were written primarily as studies. It should be unnecessary to say that they were not composed in the spirit of competition; neither Schumann, Brahms or Franz will be the one to suffer by a comparison,—another unnecessary statement. Moreover, they would probably be the last to claim a monopoly of anything—especially the right of man to the pleasure of trying to express in music whatever he wants to. These songs are inserted not so much in spite of this criticism as because of it.[25]

Yet "the spirit of competition"—inviting a comparison to the masters of art song—was exactly the point. When Ives set a poem that was well known in another composer's setting, he assumed that listeners would know that song and would compare it to his own, just as they would do if someone was bold enough to write new music for *Silent Night* or *The Star-Spangled Banner*. It was a way for Ives to develop his abilities and test them against the best composers in the business. If he could find something new to say, a different but equally satisfactory way to treat the familiar words, he could demonstrate his command of the craft of composition.

Ives's desire to compete with the masters on their own turf comes through in an anecdote he recorded on a copy of his song *Ich grolle nicht*, to a poem by Heinrich Heine that was well known in a setting from Schumann's *Dichterliebe* (1840). On March 31 of Ives's senior year, Parker conducted his New Haven Symphony Orchestra in a concert that included George Chadwick's orchestral piece *Melpomene*, named for the muse of tragedy. It was probably that week that Chadwick sat in on Parker's composition class and commented on two songs Ives had brought in, *Ich grolle nicht* and *Feldeinsamkeit*. The latter used a poem by Hermann Allmers set by Brahms around 1882 and later translated as *In Summer Fields*.

> Geo[rge] W. Chadwick came into class this afternoon. . . . Parker [was] objecting to the too many keys in the middle [of *Feldeinsamkeit*]—Geo. W. C. grinned at it and [at] H. W. P[arker]. Of this song [*Ich grolle nicht*], Prof. Horat[io] P[arker] said it [was] nearer to the G[rolle] of Schumann than the *Summerfields* was near to Brahms.
>
> But Chadwick said the *Summerfields* was the best. C[hadwick] said, "The melodic line has a natural continuity—it flows—and stops when [rounded out]—as only good songs do. And [it's] different from Brahms, as in the piano part and the harmony it takes a more difficult and almost

opposite [approach] to Brahms, for the active tranquillity of the outdoor beauty of nature is harder to express than just quietude. In its way [it's] almost as good as Brahms." He winked at H. W. P. and said "That's as good a song as you could write."[26]

In Ives's account, what Parker praised was staying close to the model and not straying too far from the key. Chadwick recognized that departing from the model and doing something new, even "almost opposite" from the original, was more difficult and creative, and felt that Ives's ability to carry it off showed he was capable of composition at the same high level as Parker or Brahms.

Comparing Ives's songs with his models, we find that he simultaneously followed them closely, demonstrating his command of the craft Parker was teaching him, and found a new approach, earning Chadwick's praise. In a paradox familiar to connoisseurs of any art, noticing what Ives takes from his predecessors throws into relief what is new and highlights his originality.

In *Feldeinsamkeit*, the poet describes an experience of solitude in an open field, lying on the ground and watching the sky:

> I rest silently in the tall green grass
> and for a long time cast my gaze upward,
> as around me crickets buzz unceasingly,
> wonderfully enveloped by blue skies.

> And beautiful white clouds pass by
> through the deep blue, like splendid silent dreams.
> I feel as if I have died long ago
> and move blissfully with them through eternal space.

Brahms's setting is soft, slow, and calm. Gently pulsing bass notes and chords in the piano project stillness and groundedness, counterpointed by a languidly moving inner part. Above this the voice rises repeatedly, capturing the image of looking up at the sky, and then gradually coasts back down to earth. The texture in the piano accompaniment changes subtly for each phrase in the voice, as is Brahms's usual approach. Both stanzas of the song begin and end alike, but the second verse diverges in the middle, wandering to more distant harmonies before returning to the home key.

Ives takes a very different approach. Instead of pulsing bass notes and chords in a slow tempo that suggest the unmoving poet, the piano has a quickly flowing line throughout, evoking the breeze in the tall grass, the constant whirring of crickets, and the majestic motion of the clouds. This is "the active tranquillity of the outdoor beauty of nature" Chadwick said was "harder to express than [the] quietude" in Brahms's song. Ives's song also differs in form and harmonic plan. Instead of making the second verse a variant of the first, Ives introduces new musical material for the poem's second stanza, reflecting its change of imagery, and then adds an abbreviated restatement of the first half of the song. The result is a form in three parts, with statement, contrast, and return, known as *ternary form*. In the middle of the first stanza, at the words "ohn' Unterlass" (unceasingly), Ives briefly wanders from the key, using parallel descending minor harmonies to create a sense of ceaseless, undirected motion. Throughout the second stanza, he moves rapidly through far distant keys—provoking Parker to object "to the too many keys in the middle"—and surges to an ecstatic climax on the words "ziehe selig mit durch ew'ge Räume" (move blissfully with [the clouds] through eternal spaces), louder than anything in Brahms's song.

Yet for all these differences, there are enough subtle parallels to show that Ives used Brahms's setting as a model, even while deliberately departing from it. Brahms repeats several phrases of the text, and Ives adopts all these repetitions and adds some more. Some moments in Ives's vocal melody, especially at "nach oben, nach oben" (upward) and "schöne stille Träume" (splendid silent dreams) parallel Brahms's so closely that they seem like purposeful allusions, a wink to the listener acknowledging that despite the obvious contrasts Ives is aware of the earlier song. Other moments are more subtle, using similar elements in the melody or harmony but rearranging them: for instance, echoing Brahms's alternation of even and uneven rhythms in the opening melody, but putting an uneven pattern where Brahms had an even one and vice versa. Throughout, the comparison shows Ives evoking his model while simultaneously putting forth a contrasting interpretation. Competition was the point: he wanted the listener to hear his song as an alternative to Brahms's setting and to recognize both his craftsmanship and his originality.

The same goal is evident in the other song discussed in class that day. Schumann's *Dichterliebe* is a cycle of songs that traces the course of a love affair from initial yearnings through joy, jealousy, separation, and resignation. *Ich grolle nicht* comes at the halfway point, as the lover turns bitter. Speaking to his "forever-lost love," he claims not to be resentful, although his heart may break, but then describes seeing her true nature in a dream, with vivid images of the dark void in her heart and of a serpent feeding on her heart. Schumann reshaped Heine's poem, repeating several phrases of text and returning to the opening words "Ich grolle nicht" (I am not resentful) at the middle and end of the song, like a refrain. Despite these repeated denials, the lover's resentment and anger come through in the music, with pulsing chords and pounding bass notes in the piano and a vocal line that starts strong, grows louder as he recounts his dream, and rises to a powerful climax as he says he sees how miserable she is. When he repeats "Ich grolle nicht" at the end, loud and assertive, it is apparent that his resentment has twisted into a kind of triumph at seeing her in misery.

Ives clearly used Schumann's song as a model: he follows Schumann's reshaping of the poem, repeats phrases of text and music in the same ways, uses similar rhythms and melodic contours at many points in the song, changes key or character in several of the same places, and begins to intensify at the same spot, leading toward the climax. Yet the overall mood is entirely different, and Ives offers a different interpretation of the poem. Instead of the pounding chords that create an ironic tension with the text from the very beginning of Schumann's song, Ives begins softly and slowly, with a gentle turning figure, lyrical melody, and sighing gestures followed by enigmatic dissonant harmonies in the piano. This tender music repeats as the voice enters, singing the opening words to the gentle melody and the words "und wenn das Herz auch bricht" (even though my heart may break) to the figure with the enigmatic chords. Here there is no ironic tension: the lover's statement seems entirely sincere, as if he is already resigned to the end of the relationship and wishes his former love no ill. Unlike Schumann, who keeps exactly the same rhythm and texture in the piano throughout the song, Ives changes the figuration frequently (as Brahms typically does), alternating new ideas with earlier ones. Each time the enigmatic figure recurs, it reminds us of the heartbroken words to which it was initially linked; when it returns at the end of the next phrase, now paired with the opening words "Ich grolle nicht," we feel at once the resignation in the words and the heartbreak in the music, two contradictory emotions that are felt at the same time.

Having set the opening lines of poetry with utter sincerity, only now does Ives reveal the lover's complaint. As the poet speaks of his beloved's radiant beauty obscuring the dark night in her heart, the music grows louder and faster, and Ives reverses the sighing gesture from the piano introduction into an accented rising figure, building to a peak at "deines Herzens Nacht" (your heart's night). Here the bitterness emerges suddenly and strongly—quite a contrast to the apparently sincere resignation expressed in the song so far. Grudgingly, the lover admits "das weiss ich längst" (I have known this for a long time); when he softly repeats these words to the enigmatic figure, we are reminded again of his breaking heart and may understand that part of his heartbreak comes from realizing that his love for her was based on an illusion, even his own self-deception.

After a piano interlude, the opening music and words return, with all their tenderness. When the poet describes the dream in which he saw his love, Ives begins by varying the warm, sad music he had used for the "forever-lost love," setting up an expectation that the dream will be loving, even if wistful and shaded by loss. But the music quickly turns louder and faster, suddenly bursting forth at the words "deines Herzens Raume" (the void in your heart) in a dramatic climax: the loudest music so far, with the highest note in the voice, the lowest notes in the piano, and the harmony that is both most dissonant and most distant from the key. Unlike in Schumann's setting, where anger is the constant undertone, here the poet's vision of his beloved's depravity is shocking, unexpectedly emerging from the tender surroundings. The outburst calms almost as fast as it began, and at the words "Ich sah, mein Lieb, wie sehr du elend bist" (I saw, my love, how miserable you are), the music slows and becomes gentle again, suggesting pity rather than anger—or both emotions at once. Final repetitions of "Ich grolle nicht," first with its original music and then set to the enigmatic figure, recall the resignation and heartbreak from the beginning of the song, folding what resentment the lover may feel into the sadness he feels not only for his lost love but for how far she was from what he had imagined her to be. Ultimately, in Ives's song the feelings of the lover seem much more complex, nuanced, and conflicting.

In both *Feldeinsamkeit* and *Ich grolle nicht*, Ives used a well-known work as a model, drawing elements from it while deliberately diverging from it in other ways to create a distinctive reading of the poem, convincingly conveying its moods and images through music. We saw in chapter 1 how vividly Ives can set English texts in an art song. Here we see him learning how to write such a song by competing with master composers on their own ground. In these songs he shows his command of the nineteenth-century Romantic idiom, absorbing lessons from his predecessors while extending their musical language to incorporate more irregular phrasing, greater dissonance, and unexpected chord progressions, all deployed to reflect the meanings and emotions of the poetry. Although they sound very different from Ives's mature music, these songs helped to lay the groundwork for his later success.

SYMPHONY NO. 1 IN D MINOR

In a similar way, Ives's Symphony No. 1 in D Minor laid the foundation for his orchestral music. He chose as his primary models four of the most popular symphonies of the nineteenth century: two of the most recent, Dvořák's *New World* (Symphony No. 9 in E Minor) and Tchaikovsky's *Pathétique* (Symphony No. 6 in B Minor), both premiered in 1893, and two from the 1820s, Beethoven's Ninth Symphony and Schubert's *Unfinished Symphony*. As with his songs, he drew elements from his models and intensified them, seeking to demonstrate his mastery of the craft of composition, his command of symphonic form, and his ability to create something new and individual in the musical language of the 1890s.

Ives wrote in *Memos* and on his manuscripts that he composed the symphony during his senior year at Yale and that Parker accepted the second and fourth movements as his thesis. For that reason, the symphony is typically dismissed as a student piece; one writer commented, "Ives was doing his homework."[27] Yet the situation is more complicated. Parker usually kept the work students submitted to him, but neither of these movements is in Parker's collected papers, and the versions we have of them were apparently composed after Ives left Yale. Sketches and drafts for the first movement date from around 1898 (this was apparently the "extended work ... in sonata form" for Ives's course in Free Composition), and the remaining manuscripts were written between 1898 and 1902. Whatever shape the symphony was in by the time Ives graduated in June 1898, he continued to work on it, completing it around 1902, and had an ink score prepared by a professional copyist around 1908–1910.[28] We may best regard the symphony in its final form, not as a student piece, but as an attempt to establish his professional credentials as a recent graduate and to claim a place in the symphonic tradition alongside his models.

A nineteenth-century symphony typically features four movements: a fast first movement in sonata form; a slow movement; a scherzo or dance movement; and a fast finale (final movement). Each movement is a self-contained musical statement, separated from the surrounding movements by pauses. Usually all are in the same key except the slow movement, which is in a closely related key. Each movement conveys a distinctive overall mood, while containing internal contrasts of key, mood, theme, and figuration. Ives follows this formula to the letter.

Sonata form, the form of Ives's first movement, is like an oration in tones: there is an *exposition* (often played twice) that introduces the main themes, each typically a series of ideas rather than a single melody; a *development*, where the ideas are developed, varied, parsed into fragments, and combined in new ways; a *recapitulation*, where the themes return, restated again in full; and often a *coda*, a wrapping-up that offers a strong conclusion. In the exposition, the first theme is followed by a transition that leads to a new key. A second theme of contrasting character appears in that key, setting up a conflict between themes and between keys that must be resolved by the end of the movement. The drama is heightened in the development, which moves to still more distant keys before preparing the return to the main key. The resolution comes in the recapitulation, where both themes appear in the home key, sometimes altered in ways that reflect the experience of the intervening music. Throughout, themes may appear complete or may be broken into *motives*, short melodic or rhythmic ideas that are repeated or varied. Indeed, most themes are themselves made out of motives, so the interplay between motive and theme, fragment and whole, original idea and variant, is continuous, operating at every level from the theme itself to the movement as a whole. Ives follows this traditional pattern, while introducing subtleties and complexities along the way.

In addition, his symphony is *cyclic*, meaning that themes from earlier movements reappear in later ones, binding the separate movements together into a more unified statement. The first famous cyclic symphony is Beethoven's Ninth, whose finale recalls themes from the first three movements before introducing its own main theme. Dvořák's *New World Symphony*, in which every movement after the first includes material from earlier ones, is one of the best-known examples from Ives's own time. In Ives's First Symphony, the clarinet melody that opens the first movement and the second melodic idea of the second movement both return in each subsequent movement, often in new guises and combined with other themes. Moreover, a melody that appears in the first three movements in relatively long notes as a countermelody—a secondary melody that accompanies the main material in counterpoint—returns in the finale transformed into a climactic march. Here Ives outdoes his models by making the symphony cyclic in two ways: not only recalling themes from earlier movements in later ones, as Beethoven and Dvořák do, but also foreshadowing a theme in the finale with hidden references in every movement.

As you listen to the orchestra warm up and tune, you glance at your program. The first item is a symphony you have never heard before, Ives's First, and you wonder what to expect. The orchestra quiets, and the conductor comes onstage to loud applause, bows, and steps onto the podium.

First Movement

The first movement begins softly, with murmuring strings accompanying a clarinet solo, at once lyrical and restless, that establishes the home key of D minor, then wanders through distant harmonies. The first theme continues with a brightly rising violin melody, answered by flutes, and a dramatic climbing figure in the wind instruments that alternates with the strings. Each new phrase picks up and varies rhythmic and melodic motives from the preceding one, in a constantly developing stream of thought. The entire theme then repeats with modified orchestration: the violins take up the clarinet tune, and the strings and winds trade places at the end. Ives's treatment of the orchestra here, layering one instrumental sound over another and juxtaposing groups of instruments in succession, is characteristic of his music; it is a habit he first learned from playing the organ, where the various keyboards are often given distinctive sounds to create an effect of two or three simultaneous layers of music or of different instruments in alternation.[29]

Ives starts his transition by repeating, varying, and fragmenting the opening theme, heightening the drama, then relaxing. The music moves through several keys while interspersing new melodic ideas with familiar ones. Bits of the first theme appear in the horn and the trumpet, then a swell in the orchestra leads to the second theme in the closely related key of F major. It begins with a sprightly melody featuring large leaps over running scales, tossed back and forth between strings and winds. The theme continues with a calmer phrase that combines a downward scooping flute melody, first heard in the transition, with two new ideas, a delicate dance-like figure in the violins and a gently turning melody in flute and oboes. The entire second theme repeats, then starts to repeat again, but instead leads into the exposition's closing section, where the various ideas in the theme play against each other in counterpoint. Especially striking is a louder, suddenly faster passage where Ives treats the dance-like figure in imitation, passing it between wind instruments, horns, and strings. A quick sleight of hand leads back to the beginning of the movement for the repetition of the exposition (omitted in some performances and recordings).

So far the movement has unfolded as you might expect. Yet as the development begins, you hear something quite extraordinary: a quiet, mysterious series of rising minor chords that seem to change key from one chord to the next, like the passage on "ohn' Unterlass" from *Feldeinsamkeit*. The harmony is constantly moving yet seems directionless, making it feel like we are floating in space. As this sequence of chords repeats, fragments of the second theme appear in counterpoint with it, joined by a slowly moving tune in the horn—the first two phrases of the countermelody that will be transformed into the triumphant march in the finale. In a soft, sweet episode, the chord sequence dissolves, bits from the second theme continue in the winds, and the horn countermelody is taken up and completed by the strings. The music gently swells and subsides again as the strings extend the countermelody. Then the rising chord sequence returns, now in the trombones and horns, while other instruments play segments from both first and second themes. The full orchestra swells to a climax, we magically return to the home key, and the recapitulation begins.

Rather than repeat themes verbatim in the recapitulation, Ives continues to vary them. The first theme appears softly in the violins over a steadily walking bass, a texture different from anything heard so far. The transition is shortened, omitting the scooping figure that foreshadowed the second theme, and leads back around to the home key of D. The second theme now sounds in D major, resolving the conflict between keys in favor of D while keeping the theme's distinctive major-key character. Instead of repeating as in the exposition, both themes are heard only once, lending a sense that events are moving more quickly. The second theme leads right into a long, dramatic coda, almost like a second development, where elements from both themes and from the development—including the horn countermelody—appear in new variants and contrapuntal combinations and culminate in a powerful, affecting climax in D minor.

Second Movement

The slow second movement in F major begins quietly with a beautiful tune in the English horn over soft, sustained chords in the strings. The violins answer with a gorgeous, yearning melody of their own; this idea will return in later movements, joining the first movement's opening clarinet tune and horn countermelody as cyclic recurring themes. The wind instruments interject a new motive, and the English horn tune returns, closing out the first section of the movement. The overall effect is calm, a serene respite after the activity of the first movement.

A new section begins in D minor, with a passionate, arching melody in the violins that is a subtle reshaping of the English horn tune. This melody repeats in the winds, then returns to the violins in a new key, accompanied by the horns playing the countermelody from the first movement. The strings build in intensity, reach a fervent climax, and gradually fade to quiet.

After this contrasting section, you expect a reprise of the first section, to create a traditional ternary form. Indeed, the opening material returns, but it is completely transformed in character. Instead of a soft English horn over strings, the entire orchestra bursts in at full volume. Horns and trombone majestically proclaim the tune that originally was in the English horn, joined in counterpoint by the violins playing the passionate arching melody from the middle section. When the violins take up their phrase from the first section, now ardent, grand, and pulsing with energy rather than gently yearning, the winds simultaneously play that same melody four times as fast, while the horns recall the first movement's opening clarinet melody. The orchestra builds to a peak of emotional intensity, then drops back. The English horn returns with its tune, joined by two solo violins, over the same sustained harmonies in the strings as at the beginning. Overall, the movement traces an arc of successively more intense climaxes, ultimately relaxing back to serenity.

Third Movement

The third movement, in D minor, is a scherzo, a fast dance in triple meter with a contrasting central section called a trio. The lively opening tune in flutes and clarinets leaps down, rises by step, and skips down again, then continues with fast runs and other figures. This melody is treated in canon, imitated by the violins and then by the lower strings and bassoons, each overlapping the others. The same pattern of entrances recurs in a new key. As the strings and bassoons comically continue the running figures, wisps of melody alternate between flutes and violins, the violin phrases hinting at the yearning violin melody from the second movement. The opening tune of the scherzo returns, again in canon, and the first section softly comes to a close.

The trio begins in F major with a quiet theme in the violins, played twice, that again echoes the yearning melody from the second movement, more in melodic contour than in character. New ideas bounce between winds and strings, leading the music through distant keys. The trio's opening theme returns, now luxuriant rather than quiet, joined by the horns playing the countermelody from the first movement development. The harmony leads back to the home key, and the first section of the scherzo repeats exactly to conclude the movement.

Fourth Movement

After the light, airy scherzo, the finale begins with a burst of energy. Over a fast walking bass in the low strings, the violins present the dynamic first theme in D major, a remarkably diverse series of ideas: a bold opening gesture, a leaping figure in march-like rhythm, a quick dialogue between instruments, then rushing up and down the scale. The theme repeats in the winds, then its segments appear in counterpoint with each other, varied and tossed back and forth. Hearing this, you recognize the same strategy as in the first movement: repeating the first theme in varied orchestration and then developing its elements in the following transition. One thing that leaps out at you is the horns, playing the march-like leaping figure from the theme, slowed down to half speed. Near the end of the transition, amid swirling strings and descending lines in the winds, four solemn chords in the brass offer a hint of things to come, as the trumpet sounds the opening notes of the horn countermelody from the first movement.

The second theme, in the contrasting key of A major, is warm, genial, quiet, and supple, with arching figures in violins and winds, skipping up and floating down. As these ideas continue, you hear the violin tune from the second movement, now stately instead of yearning, soon joined by trombones playing the first four notes of the first movement countermelody. After a quiet episode, a new idea appears, an angular melody treated in canon between winds and violins, which serves as a closing theme for the exposition.

Your expectations for sonata form are that the exposition will repeat, followed by a development and a recapitulation, as in the first movement. And indeed after the full orchestra swells to a climax you hear the energetic first theme again, exactly as it was at the beginning. You are well into the transition, building up to the second theme, when—surprise!—the horns and violins start loudly trading ideas from the first movement's opening clarinet melody. What you are hearing cannot be a repetition of the exposition—so what is it? Just as suddenly as it began, the interruption is over and we are back in the transition, but instead of leading to A major as before, it takes us back to D major, and the genial second theme appears in that key. What you thought was the repetition of the exposition turns out to be the recapitulation, where both first and second themes appear in the home key instead of in different keys. But what happened to the development? The answer: in this movement, Ives is using a variant of sonata form sometimes called "sonata form without development," where the end of the exposition leads right on to the recapitulation. In truth, there is no need here for a separate development section, since Ives has been developing, varying, fragmenting, and recombining ideas from his themes all along.

The second theme unfolds exactly as before, complete with its references back to the second movement violin tune and the first movement countermelody, except for the change of key. When the canonic closing theme enters, new events start to pile on. The first movement's opening clarinet melody appears in the winds, faster than before, while the horns play the first two phrases of their countermelody from the first movement. The finale's canonic closing theme returns, now twice as fast as before. Fragments of the horn countermelody sound in the brass, also twice as fast. The music builds, then suddenly bursts forth in sweeping waves of scales, quickly alternating between winds and strings. Out of this comes a triumphant march whose melody in trumpets and horns is the transformed countermelody from the first movement, now taking center stage. Bits of the finale's first theme mix with the march tune, the music builds in a series of successive peaks, and the symphony ends in a spirit of exultant celebration.

Models and Methods

Throughout the symphony, Ives adapts structural features from his models and alludes to their themes, deliberately signaling the relationship. The most audible references are to Dvořák's *New World Symphony*. Anyone familiar with the theme of Dvořák's slow movement is likely to hear Ives's as a near cousin, with the same texture of English horn over sustained strings and a similar mood and melodic contour. Ives also follows a form similar to Dvořák's, a modified ternary form in a major key with the middle section in minor and a climax that combines in counterpoint themes from the first and second movements. Such contrapuntal combinations of themes occur in every movement of the Ives, paralleling similar moments in Dvořák's symphony. Ives borrows elements from Dvořák's other movements as well, including details of form in the first movement (such as foreshadowing the second theme in the preceding transition) and the rhythm and sound of the finale's closing chords.

Ives's first movement is modeled on that of Schubert's *Unfinished Symphony*, which is also in a minor key and triple meter, features a soft first theme in clarinet over murmuring strings, immediately repeats both first and second themes, and ends the exposition by treating part of the second theme in imitation. Ives hints at his model by echoing portions of Schubert's second theme in his first theme and vice versa. Ives's D minor scherzo recalls another in the same key, that of Beethoven's Ninth Symphony. Both scherzos present the principal theme as a canon, and both themes have a similar melodic contour. The model for Ives's finale is the fast third movement from Tchaikovsky's *Pathétique Symphony*, which has a similar tempo, character, and form. The sweeping scales in Ives's coda closely resemble a passage from Tchaikovsky's coda, and both lead to a march-like melody over a bass line that descends by step. Again, Ives signals the relationship to his model through melodic resemblance; the leaping figure from his first theme echoes the rhythm and melodic shape of the march motive in Tchaikovsky's movement.

All of these references seem deliberate. It is not that Ives cannot think of anything else to do but rather that he wants to draw our attention to what he is taking from his models and therefore to what he is doing that is new and different. Whenever he borrows an idea, he takes it further; for instance, where Dvořák combines two themes in counterpoint in the coda of his first movement, Ives combines as many as four at once and carries on the combination for much longer. The sense of competition is palpable. This does not mean that Ives's symphony is better than his models—in music, often a simpler texture is more effective—but it does show that already in this work from his twenties he had mastered the craft of composing a late-nineteenth-century symphony, with a sure command of development, counterpoint, and form.

While he sought to establish himself as a part of the European symphonic tradition by invoking European models, he also included subtle nods to his status as an American. The first movement's first theme alludes to two American hymn tunes. In the second of the theme's three segments, the violins paraphrase a phrase from *Shining Shore* ("My days are gliding swiftly by") by George F. Root, and the flutes respond with a figure from John R. Sweney's *Beulah Land* ("I've reached the land of corn and wine"). In the third segment of the theme, the winds repeat a longer snippet from *Beulah Land*. In the finale, the march-like figure in the first theme sounds like a relative of the bugle call *Taps* or the patriotic song *Columbia, the Gem of the Ocean*. These subtle references imply that for all its connections to the European tradition, this symphony could only have been written by an American.

Ives was clearly interested in weaving his four movements into a unified whole through recurring keys and themes. The first movement introduces its first and second themes in D minor and F major and recapitulates them in D minor and D major respectively. The overall keys of each movement follow the same sequence: D minor, F major, D minor, D major. Moreover, the F major second movement has a contrasting middle section in D minor, and the third movement does the reverse, with a D minor scherzo framing a trio in F major. Such key relationships between movements help to bind the symphony together. We will see similar connections of key in some of Ives's later works.

The thematic links are strong as well. The opening clarinet melody reappears in all three later movements, often at moments of climax and in counterpoint with other themes. The yearning violin phrase from the second movement is echoed in two melodies in the third movement and returns in original form in the finale, again in counterpoint with other material. The theme first heard in the first movement development as a countermelody in the horn returns in all later movements in counterpoint with other themes and then bursts forth as the culminating march. Such connections, binding multiple movements into a cycle through common themes, became typical of Ives's later music, heard in most but not all of his multimovement instrumental works.

In this symphony, Ives designed his themes to work in counterpoint with each other, showing a compositional bent that was nurtured by his experience as an organist and by his studies with Parker, as well as by following the example of Dvořák (another organist turned composer). Textures with simultaneous melodies in different instruments became characteristic of his music, something he never lost even as he moved far beyond the musical language of the nineteenth century.

In these and other ways, the First Symphony paved the way for later developments. Though it sounds little like Ives's mature works, he could not have written them without the tools he learned through writing this piece. Yet it is more than a step along his way and a clue to his character: it is also a powerful Romantic symphony in its own right.

A Read-Through

After getting the score and parts copied, Ives arranged for Walter Dam-rosch, a friend of Parker and conductor of the New York Symphony Or-chestra, to try out the last three movements with his orchestra at a rehearsal on March 19, 1910.[30] Ives and his wife attended, and Ives recounted the read-through in *Memos*:

> He started with the second movement (adagio), an English horn tune over chords in the strings. When he heard the pretty little theme and the nice chords he called out "Charming!" When the second themes got going to-gether, and the music got a little more involved (but not very involved), he acted somewhat put out, got mad, and said it coul[dn't] be played without a great deal of rehearsing. . . .
>
> So, after playing these three movements of Symphony No. 1, Wally turned to Mrs. Ives and said, "This instrumentation is remarkable, and the work-manship is admirable." But even at that, he said it is too difficult in places, and will take too much rehearsal time—for his pocketbook.[31]

Ives's sarcastic reference to "the pretty little theme and the nice chords" sug-gests that as he wrote this two decades later he was still miffed by Damrosch's obvious preference for the English horn theme over the parts of the second movement of which Ives was apparently most proud: the complex counterpoint, combinations of themes, and emotional peaks of the middle and final sections.

Because of the performance difficulties, Damrosch did not program the symphony. It went unheard for another forty-three years, until its premiere on April 26, 1953, by the orchestra of the National Gallery of Art in Washing-ton, D.C., conducted by Richard Bales. Ives might have had a very different career if the First Symphony had been performed in 1910 to positive reviews.

CENTER CHURCH

While Ives was studying with Parker, he continued his career as a church musician. The same month he entered Yale, he began his new job as organist at Center Church on the Green in New Haven, playing his first Sunday ser-vice on September 30, 1894, and remaining through graduation in June 1898. It was a socially prominent Congregationalist church, the middle of three churches on the New Haven Green, close to Yale. The position was one of the most prestigious organ posts in town; indeed, Ives's predecessor was Harry B. Jepson, who became the organ instructor at Yale in 1895, and his succes-sor was a future dean of the Yale School of Music. The choirmaster was John

Cornelius Griggs (1865–1932), a sensitive musician and supportive colleague who became something of a father figure to Ives after George Ives's death.[32] Ives kept up his organ studies for a time as well, taking lessons with two of the most esteemed organist-composers in the New York region: Dudley Buck, whose *Variations on "Home Sweet Home"* Ives had played at the Baptist Church benefit concert in 1890, and Buck's student Harry Rowe Shelley, whom Ives had met in Danbury, where Shelley conducted the Danbury Choral Society.[33]

The music Ives wrote for services at Center Church shows increasing skill and finesse in comparison to his earlier church music. As in many other Protestant churches at the time, the performers included a quartet of trained singers—soprano, alto, tenor, and bass—who sang as a group, in trios or pairs, or as individual soloists. They were supported by an amateur choir who could alternate with or double the soloists. Lewis Bronson, a Yale student (class of 1901) and member of the choir, recalled in a 1969 interview that when he began attending Center Church in 1896 it

> had the best church quartet that I knew about. . . . The organist was Charles Ives. I can still see him sitting up on the old organ stool. He was thin and tall and dynamic in his handling of the organ—he was all over the thing.
>
> The chorus sang only at the four o'clock [Sunday] service, but we had choir rehearsals and gave some fairly substantial pieces with Mr. Ives playing the organ and the quartet and chorus directed by Dr. Griggs. We had a rehearsal every week, and the members of the chorus received [voice] lessons [from Griggs] in return. We had a good quartet, so that we could really do some pretty elaborate pieces.[34]

One of these elaborate pieces was Ives's *Easter Carol* (1896), which has extensive passages for organ alone and for the quartet of soloists as well as for the full chorus. The quartet has the most difficult music, notably a long passage in imitation that would have challenged amateur singers. Ives's other anthems from this period include *Crossing the Bar* (1894), to a text by Alfred Lord Tennyson; *The Light That Is Felt* (1898), to words by John Greenleaf Whittier; and *Turn Ye, Turn Ye* (1896), *I Come to Thee* (1896–1897), and *All-Forgiving* (1898), on texts taken from hymns. These could have been sung by the solo quartet or by the choir, and most are accompanied by organ. With close and colorful chromatic harmonies (familiar today from barbershop quartet singing), they are closer in style to the church anthems of Buck and Shelley, whose accessible and attractive music for quartet and choir was widely sung, than to the more elevated and demanding church music of Parker. Yet Ives also incorporates ideas learned from Parker, such as alternating different meters as Parker did in one movement of *Hora novissima*, resulting in a blend of influences.[35]

In addition to his music for quartet or choir, Ives also composed songs for voice and organ that were performed by Griggs or the other soloists, as well as improvising—and sometimes writing down—preludes, postludes, and other service music for organ. While still an apprentice in the classical realm, Ives was already composing for church at a professional level, in the language and genres of his time.

PROGRESS AND CHANGE

During his Yale years, Ives immersed himself in the European classical tradition in his studies with Parker. At the same time, he grew more sophisticated as a composer of church music in the American Protestant tradition and continued to write music in popular styles and genres, from fraternity shows to glee club songs to marches, including his first publications. In a sense, he served three simultaneous apprenticeships: in the classical tradition with a master composer; in church music with a supportive choirmaster and fellow organist-composer mentors; and in popular music by producing music for his Yale friends and for a wider public.

Ives had begun to learn all three traditions during his youth in Danbury. There the church music and popular traditions absorbed most of his attention, outside his organ lessons and recitals and his *Variations on "America."* But at Yale, especially in his senior year, the balance began to reverse. Church music is utilitarian, serving to bring worshipers into closer contact with God and with each other. Popular music also serves utilitarian purposes, entertaining listeners and building camaraderie among the groups Ives wrote for in college. But art music invites a deeper engagement, not for a religious or social purpose but for its own sake. Once Ives encountered that idea, that listening to music could be all-absorbing and could carry deep personal meanings, he seems to have been drawn inexorably into the world of art music, the music that held out that promise. Ultimately, he abandoned every genre he had tried in his Danbury years, other than songs, and committed himself entirely to those he had learned at Yale. What is remarkable, and made Ives the composer he became, is that he never gave up on his other musical worlds. Instead, he brought them along with him as he became a composer of art songs, sonatas, chamber music, and symphonic works.

In June 1898, Ives graduated and moved to New York City. The next ten years saw an end to writing popular music and to his career as a church musician, a renewal of his experimental music, and the beginnings of a synthesis of traditions within his music in classical genres. As we will see in the next chapter, what he had learned at Yale was crucial to what he did next.

• 4 •

Weaving the Threads

$\mathcal{I}$n his first four years after graduating from Yale, Ives moved to a new city and embarked on a new career, but he kept many ties to his past. Like his great-grandfather Isaac Ives, he sought his fortune as a businessman in New York—not in hats, but in insurance. At the same time, he continued to work as a church musician, now as both organist and choirmaster, and to compose art music and church music in an essentially Romantic musical language. He lived in a communal apartment with other Yale graduates, extending the camaraderie of college life. He began to explore synthesizing the four musical traditions he had learned at Danbury and Yale, blending art music with church music in his First String Quartet, church music with experimental music in a series of psalms for chorus, and experimental music with popular music in a short orchestral work about Yale. In these pieces he began to weave together the threads of his varied experiences with music, creating new variations on American music.

FINDING WORK

Even before graduation in June 1898, Ives had secured a new church position in the New York area, at the First Presbyterian Church in Bloomfield, New Jersey, a town of about ten thousand easily accessible by train from Manhattan. His first Sunday service there was on May 1 (when his contract began) or May 8 (when he was first listed in the church bulletin). The hundred-year-old church on the Bloomfield town green boasted a new steeple, built in 1896, with a large bell that sounded the hours and a set of Westminster chimes that marked the quarter hours; the Westminster chimes melody stuck in Ives's mind, and he used it later during majestic moments in the Second String Quartet and the Fourth Symphony. The organ, shown in Figure 4.1, was also relatively new, having been installed in 1883 in a prominent position at the

Figure 4.1. The organ at the First Presbyterian Church in Bloomfield, New Jersey, in the 1890s.

front of the church behind the pulpit. After almost a decade of working as a church organist, Ives was now for the first time both organist and choirmaster, in charge of all the music presented at services. His duties included recruiting, rehearsing, and conducting the choir and choosing the music they would perform, as well as playing the organ. He also occasionally gave concerts, recalling in a 1949 letter that he played his *Variations on "America"* at organ recitals in New Jersey (presumably at the Bloomfield church) and in Brooklyn in 1899.[1]

In May 1900, Ives moved to another position as organist and choirmaster at Central Presbyterian Church in Manhattan, then on 57th Street between Broadway and Seventh Avenue, near Central Park. His new post was more prestigious, serving one of the most prominent and wealthy congregations in New York, and more convenient, a quick walk from his apartment. There too he led all the music for services and also gave recitals, playing some repertoire that was new to him alongside pieces he had been performing since he was a teenager. A new, larger organ was installed in 1901 during Ives's time at the church.[2]

These positions carried more responsibilities and paid better than his post at Center Church in New Haven. They provided continuity, a routine that was familiar, along with some new challenges, and they kept him in regular contact with performing music, including opportunities to play or conduct his own. But they were not full-time jobs, and he could not make a living from them alone.

Just as the idea of going to Yale was to further Ives's prospects in business rather than in music, the same was true of moving to New York. Yet apparently what kind of businessman Ives would become was decided not by a predetermined plan but by the connections he had and could use. Granville White, from the White family of Danbury and a second cousin of Ives's father, was a doctor serving as medical examiner for the Mutual Life Insurance Company of New York, and he helped to secure a job for Ives in the actuarial department at Mutual Life's office at 32 Nassau Street, near Wall Street.[3] Ives started sometime in the summer after graduation. He was not a natural at the work of an actuary, given his failing grades in mathematics his freshman year at Yale. In the spring of 1899, Ives changed jobs, moving over to Charles H. Raymond & Co. at 32 Liberty Street, general agents for Mutual Life. There he met Julian S. Myrick (1880–1969), his future partner, shown in Figure 4.2. As Myrick told the story seventy years later,

I was an applications clerk, and he came in to relieve me. I'd been doing a poor job, but his handwriting was so bad that they preferred mine, so I got the job back, and he went out to handle the agents. That's just the way it happened. Charlie and I became fast friends from then on. We divided the work that way not only in the Raymond Agency but later on. I handled the financial part of the business, and Charlie handled the agents.[4]

That division of labor would become the secret of their success, both at Raymond and in the agencies they would later found together.

Figure 4.2.   Julian S. Myrick, Ives's business partner.

MSS 14, The Charles Ives Papers in the Music Library of Yale University, Series VI, Item 121.

POVERTY FLAT

Ives apparently spent much of the summer after graduation at home in Danbury, commuting to his church job in New Jersey and sometimes staying in New York at the Yale Club. By September, he and two other members of the class of 1898 had moved in with a group of fellow graduates from Yale in a pair of apartments on the fourth floor of 317 West 58th Street, near Central Park and just north of Hell's Kitchen. A tradition went back several years of Yale graduates sharing the apartments while studying at Columbia University's College of Physicians and Surgeons. Some time before Ives joined them, they had dubbed their living quarters "Poverty Flat," in ironic acknowledgment of their current income level but with full awareness that their future prospects were rosy. Most were from well-to-do families, and they had enough money between them to afford the rent and employ a maid who cleaned the apartment and cooked their meals. Each year some moved on and a new batch moved in, including law students as well as medical students, plus a few who were already working, as was Ives. Typically they left when they finished school or got married; Ives would stay with the group for ten years, until his own marriage. In fall 1901, Ives and five flatmates moved their part of Poverty Flat farther north to 65 Central Park West at 66th Street, a more upscale address across from Central Park. In September 1907, he and another group moved south to relatively posh quarters at 34 Gramercy Park, a nine-story red brick building across from Gramercy Park at 20th Street.[5]

The common connection to Yale meant that the spirit of college life continued in some respects. Some of Ives's apartment mates became close, long-lasting friends. One of his best friends from college, David Twichell (1874–1924), joined the group in October 1899 after serving in the Spanish-American War. A letter from Ives to Twichell in September or October 1903, after Twichell had graduated from medical school and was a physician at a tuberculosis sanatorium at Saranac Lake in the Adirondacks, suggests the tone of the banter among the denizens of Poverty Flat, including quick references to six current or former inmates and humorous allusions to the punchline of a scatological joke, to the sanatorium, and to drinking whiskey and tonic water:

> Dear Dave,
> Why don't you occasionally write damn you anyway I hear good reports from time to time and hence the pyrimids [*sic*]. Willis Wood spent a day with us recently & tells us you're in good form and an able foreman in the "wheez factory." Del Wood took me to Keene Valley over Labor Day. We didn't seize any panthers, but had an agreeable time though I am afraid I was a disturbing element being full of malaria . . . quinine and *whisky* at the

time. YES. The flat is filled with 2 new dogs. Harry Farrar of Bart's class and Walter McCormick, a cousin of Vance.[6]

There was a piano in the apartment, and Ives played it, improvised on it, and composed at it evenings and weekends when he was not working at the office or at the church. In *Memos*, he recalled "trying out sounds, beats, etc., usually by what is called politely 'improvisation on the keyboard'—what classmates in the flat called 'resident disturbances.'"[7] Some of his manuscripts include memoranda recording reactions of his flatmates to whatever he was working on, and they are in a similar jesting spirit; for instance, on an early sketch for *Country Band March*, Ives wrote, "Geo[rge Lewis,] Bart [Yung,] Tony M Bill [Maloney]—3 quite right critics!! say I haven't got the tune right & the Chords are wrong—Thanksgiving 1905."[8] A few pieces were inspired by experiences he shared with his apartment mates. In *Memos*, he describes *The Cage* (heard in chapter 1) as "a result of taking a walk one hot summer afternoon in Central Park with Bart Yung [whose father was Chinese] and George Lewis.... Sitting on a bench near the menagerie, watching the leopard's cage and a little boy who had apparently been a long time watching the leopard—this aroused Bart's Oriental fatalism—hence the text ['Is life anything like that?'] in the song."[9] The sound of Ives composing must have been a familiar part of life in the apartment. George Lewis wrote in 1933 that he was "brought back to memories of long ago by hearing over the radio a few days ago Charlie's *Ah! 'Tis a Dream* [*My Native Land*], which I heard him compose in Poverty Flat."[10] But recollections of Ives focus more often on his conviviality than on his music, which was apparently regarded as part of his personality rather than as his vocation. As Edwards Park (known as Ned, although Ives, ready with the obvious pun, nicknamed him "Central" Park) recalled, "I had not the slightest intimation that Charley was a musical genius.... I regarded him as a most delightful man and companion, completely unpredictable.... One never knew what to expect next."[11]

That last comment came to fit Ives's music even better than it fit his personality. It was in his Poverty Flat years that he began to interweave his influences in unexpected ways.

THE APPRENTICE BRANCHES OUT

In New York, Ives continued to soak up the music around him. Church music and organ works were his bread and butter, and he constantly was learning new repertoire. On the classical side, there were concerts of chamber music by the Kneisel and Kaltenborn String Quartets, among others; recitals and other events at Carnegie Hall, including the annual visits of the Boston Symphony Orchestra; and performances by the New York Philharmonic under Emil Paur and the New York Symphony led by Walter Damrosch. The orchestral repertoire was dominated by Romantic composers from Beethoven through Wagner, Brahms, Tchaikovsky, and Dvořák, but gradually came to include younger composers such as Richard Strauss, Nikolai Rimsky-Korsakov, and Claude Debussy. Meanwhile, in restaurants, cafés, bars, and theaters, Ives heard the most current styles of commercial popular music: the stick-in-your-head melodies churned out by the popular song industry nicknamed Tin Pan Alley, and the jaunty syncopated style known as ragtime. He may never have encountered piano rags like those of Scott Joplin, but he recalled hearing blackface minstrels sing ragtime syncopations as early as the 1890s in Danbury and New Haven, and in New York he heard ragtime songs such as Joseph E. Howard's *Hello! Ma Baby* (1899) and Harry Von Tilzer's *Alexander* (1904).[12] Having absorbed popular styles from Stephen Foster and Civil War songs to band music from his father at home in Danbury, Ives learned these more recent styles as an adult. The older and newer kinds of popular song would come to carry different associations for him, and the contrast between them became part of his expressive toolbox.

In his compositions from his first four years in New York, Ives assimilated the lessons of his apprenticeship under Parker while at the same time he started to move beyond them.

He kept working on the First Symphony and completed it around 1902. During these years the symphony grew from a student piece to the calling card of a young independent composer seeking to establish himself in the symphonic tradition.

He continued writing art songs in a Romantic style, including a few more German songs, the French songs *Élégie* and *Chanson de Florian*, and several songs in English. He also adapted some songs originally written to German poetry, altering them to fit English words that were not a translation of the original texts—for instance, recasting *Frühlingslied* (Spring Song), composed around 1898 to words by Heinrich Heine, as *I Travelled among Unknown Men* (ca. 1901) to a poem by William Wordsworth. Ives often reworked one piece into another, including remaking instrumental music as a song, as he did in recasting the opening theme of the First Symphony into the song *On Judges' Walk* in about 1901–1902. Around this time he seems to have first conceived of the idea of gathering some of his songs into a collection, a project not to be fulfilled until two decades later with *114 Songs*. He paid a professional copyist who worked at the Tams Copying Bureau, George Price, to prepare good copies of four songs, which Ives had bound as a book along with blank sheets of music paper that he and other copyists later filled in with four more songs.[13] All of these songs were tonal, using a personal idiom that drew on the harmonic and melodic practice of his primary models from the late nineteenth century, including Brahms, Franck, Dvořák, Tchaikovsky, and his teachers Horatio Parker and Dudley Buck.

The last two were the direct models for a new work from this period, *The Celestial Country* (1898–1902), a church cantata in seven movements that Ives premiered in a Friday evening concert at Central Presbyterian Church on April 18, 1902. The subject, a vision of the afterlife as a heavenly city, resembles that of Parker's oratorio *Hora novissima*. So does the disposition of movements, including opening and closing movements for chorus, arias for solo singers, and movements for vocal quartet and for double vocal quartet. At times Ives drew closely on Parker. Ives's movement for two unaccompanied vocal quartets echoes a movement in *Hora novissima* for two choruses with orchestra, in the way the two groups of singers alternate in dialogue and in several striking rhythmic ideas. Ives's third movement, for solo vocal quartet with accompaniment, is modeled on Parker's third movement, an aria for bass and orchestra that Ives had heard Parker conduct in 1897 at a concert of the New Haven Symphony Orchestra. Both are in the same moderate tempo and in the key of D minor; both begin in triple meter; both have a middle section in the key of F major; and in that middle section, both feature a distinctive rhythmic pattern that alternates between measures of three and four beats, creating a very unusual effect. Characteristically, Ives extends the idea to twice the length, as if to show that he could surpass his teacher. The melodies in this passage are also similar in shape and rhythm to the parallel passage in Parker's oratorio, and the accompaniment has similar syncopation and counterpoint. In these respects, Ives seems to have been seeking to match the success of the masterpiece that made Parker's reputation, competing with his teacher in the same way that he evoked and sought to outdo Brahms and Schumann in his German songs and Schubert, Dvořák, Beethoven, and Tchaikovsky in his First Symphony.[14]

But in other ways *The Celestial Country* is closer in style and conception to the church music of Dudley Buck. As Gayle Sherwood Magee has pointed out, *Hora novissima* is a grand oratorio in the tradition of the Handel, Haydn, and Mendelssohn oratorios, pieces for chorus, soloists, and orchestra that were performed by large amateur or professional choruses like the Church Choral Society of New York that premiered Parker's work in May 1893. It is in Latin, on a twelfth-century poem, scored with full orchestra plus organ, and lasts over an hour. By contrast, Ives's *The Celestial Country* is a cantata in English, on a hymn text, for a smaller group of singers and players (organ, string quartet, and two horns), and lasts about half an hour, on the scale of

Buck's church cantatas. Instead of taking up the whole evening's program, as *Hora novissima* did at its premiere, *The Celestial Country* was performed as the second half of a concert that included several pieces Ives played on the organ; three movements from Beethoven's String Quartet in F Major, Op. 18, No. 1; and a duet for soprano and alto from Gioachino Rossini's *Stabat Mater*. The vocal counterpoint in *Hora novissima* is much more challenging than that in Ives's cantata, which is closer to the level of difficulty in Buck's cantatas, well suited for the solo quartet and amateur choir typical in American Protestant churches at the time.[15]

Ultimately, *The Celestial Country* is a blend of Ives's influences, bringing the prestige of the oratorio and the ethos of the art music tradition Ives had learned from Parker into the functional music of a church cantata. It represents one of Ives's attempts around this time to synthesize two of the traditions he knew—in this case, the classical tradition and the music of the Protestant church. The result may sound conservative to our ears today, but it shows Ives's interest in weaving together the threads of his experiences with music.

His other attempts at the same time are even more interesting. Their diversity—"one never knew what to expect next," as Edwards Park said—reflects the differences between the traditions he was trying to interweave, and the various ways he tried to bring them together.

STRING QUARTET NO. 1

Ives's String Quartet No. 1 was his first substantial piece of chamber music and his first thoroughgoing synthesis of American music with the genres and styles of European art music. In it he married two traditions to which he felt the deepest commitment: the classical tradition, which had the loftiest goals for music as a deep and engaging experience for its own sake, and the hymn tradition, which embodied and expressed deeply felt sentiments for millions of people.

The string quartet as a standard grouping of four instruments—two violins, viola, and cello—became popular in the second half of the eighteenth century, initially as an outlet for amateurs to play music for their own pleasure, joined in the nineteenth century by professional quartets who performed in concerts. The core of the repertoire consists of pieces (called simply "string quartets") by Haydn, Mozart, and Beethoven that include the same types of movements as in a symphony: typically a fast first movement in sonata form, a slow movement, a dance movement or scherzo, and a fast finale. Romantic composers from Schubert, Mendelssohn, and Schumann through Brahms,

Tchaikovsky, and Dvořák added their own flavors to the string quartet literature, which has a prestige second only to the symphony among connoisseurs
of classical instrumental music. This was the tradition Ives sought to join by
composing a string quartet. You might expect him to base his first foray on
famous models already in the repertoire, as he did in his First Symphony. It
is remarkable that instead he chose to create his First String Quartet entirely
around themes paraphrased from American hymn tunes.

The piece represents in one sense the integration of his coursework at
Yale with his activities as organist at Center Church. As he originally conceived it, the quartet has four movements, like most string quartets, yet the
movements carry titles associated with organ music that might be played
during a service: *Chorale*, *Prelude*, *Offertory*, and *Postlude*. Ives later reworked
the *Chorale* as a movement in his Fourth Symphony and removed it from
the quartet, but it was restored when the quartet was published after Ives's
death, and almost all performances and recordings include all four movements. According to Ives, he adapted the *Chorale* from a "Fugue for Parker" he
composed in 1897–1898, while he was taking Strict Composition, and played
as a postlude at Center Church; the *Prelude* and *Postlude* from a prelude and
postlude he played on the organ at "a 'Revival' Gospel Service" at Center
Church in 1896; and the *Offertory* from an organ prelude he played in February 1898.[16] Thus the four-movement version joins together music originally
written for class with music intended for church.

Yet the quartet, in either the three- or the four-movement version, is
ultimately not an arrangement for strings of music conceived for church but
the opposite: a string quartet that brings the atmosphere of Protestant church
music, and particularly hymn tunes, into a genre that is quintessentially part
of the classical tradition. The nature of the piece is confirmed by its compositional history. Ives's pencil sketch for the fugue can be dated about 1898,
but no sources survive from Ives's Yale years for the other movements, whose
extant sketches are on music paper that was not available before 1900. He
finished the quartet and copied it out in ink around 1902, making it a work
more of his early New York years than of his time in college.[17] Whether the
pieces he remembered playing at Center Church were improvised, worked out
at the keyboard and played from memory, or written down and later lost, they
must have differed in ways large and small from the quartet as we have it, for
we can see in the sketches that Ives was creating some themes and extended
passages for the quartet from scratch, at least two years after leaving New
Haven. The music throughout is conceived for four instrumental lines, the
texture native to the string quartet, not for the textures typical of Ives's organ
music. Whatever he played in church services, the final version is a piece of
concert music, a string quartet infused with the sound and spirit of hymns.

Ives created all the themes in the quartet by paraphrasing hymn tunes he had learned as a child and played as an organist. Some themes are based on a single hymn tune, and others combine elements of two or three tunes. In each case, Ives reshaped the melodic material into a theme appropriate for a string quartet in a style similar to Brahms or Dvořák. This took some effort. Hymn tunes are perfect for their function: songs that can be easily sung and remembered, usually in four, six, or eight short phrases that fit a poetic text and can be repeated for as many verses as are printed in the hymnal. Most hymn tunes are built around a recurring rhythm or melodic idea, and many repeat full phrases, often creating an AABA form or another pattern of repetition and contrast. The plain, foursquare shape and the repetitiveness of hymn tunes make them useful for congregational singing. A string quartet theme, however, needs to be more varied and less predictable and should not be complete in itself; it has to set out problems to be solved, material to be developed in what follows. Ives recasts each hymn tune as a theme suitable for a quartet, keeping the most characteristic elements of the melody while changing its structure, trimming repetitions, emphasizing motives he wants to focus on, and omitting others. After presenting each theme, he varies, fragments, and develops it like any other, so that each movement unfolds as a logical series of musical events even for listeners who do not know the hymn tunes on which it is based. The effect is ingenious: the whole is suffused with the character of Protestant hymns while fulfilling the expectations for a string quartet, and it fits neatly into the classical tradition while offering a new and distinctively American sound.

Although the First String Quartet is perfectly coherent without recognizing any of the source tunes, it can be a more rewarding experience for those who know them and can follow Ives's transformations as he plays with the melodic ideas. You can familiarize yourself with the tunes used in each movement, and hear those transformations more readily, by listening to each hymn at the Charles Ives Society website (charlesives.org/borrowed-tunes/hymns).

First Movement: *Chorale*

The first movement, *Chorale*, is based on *Missionary Hymn* ("From Greenland's icy mountains") by Lowell Mason, a hymn in AA'BA" form whose first, second, and last phrases start alike but have different endings.

The movement begins as a fugue in C major, using as a subject (main theme) the hymn's majestic first phrase. You hear the cello enter with the subject, which gently arches up, sinks back down, and ascends again. The other instruments enter in turn, from lowest to highest—viola, violin II, violin I—each stating almost all of the hymn's opening phrase, then changing to free counterpoint as the next one takes up the tune. The texture shifts to pairs of voices, the violins against the lower instruments, in a serene episode. A gentle turning motive leads to a more spirited dialogue among the parts in imitative counterpoint; in what seems like an in-joke for organists, this passage quotes from Bach's *Dorian* Toccata and Fugue in D Minor, which Ives had been playing for over a decade.

The opening subject returns, now joined by a countermelody adapted from the final phrase of another hymn: Oliver Holden's *Coronation* ("All hail the power of Jesus' name!"), at the words "Bring forth the royal diadem, And crown Him Lord [of all]." When you hear this melody, if you recognize the tune, you may realize in retrospect that the turning motive you heard earlier is from this phrase of *Coronation* (at "diadem"), although it also resembles turning figures at the end of the second phrase of *Missionary Hymn* and in the counterpoint from Bach's fugue. This kind of interrelationship between melodies, where one thing becomes another—a sort of musical punning—is typical of how Ives works with his borrowed tunes.

The texture shifts again to pairs of voices, and the instruments gradually build in intensity, then pause. When they resume, they develop the ideas presented so far, mixing ideas in new orders and juxtapositions, then once again grow more intense. At the magnificent climax, the cello descends to its lowest note, low C, and holds it like an organ sustaining the lowest note on its pedal keyboard as violin I dramatically paraphrases the hymn tune's third phrase, which begins by leaping up and down a fourth. The phrase is imitated by the viola and repeated by the violin, and echoes in other instruments. After more development and a pause on a dissonant but resonant chord, we hear the final phrase of *Missionary Hymn* played in long notes by violin I, harmonized by the other voices in a style akin to a Bach chorale. Bach's settings in four-voice harmony of chorales, the hymns of the Lutheran church, are a mainstay of instruction in harmony classes and for organists; no doubt this closing passage is the reason Ives titled this movement *Chorale*.

Although the movement starts like a fugue, it really takes its shape from the hymn tune itself, presenting all four phrases of *Missionary Hymn* in order, each paraphrased and presented in a different manner and texture. A fugue that turns out to be an elaboration of a hymn tune, and a hymn setting that moves from a fugue-like opening to a chorale-like ending, this movement is a compelling demonstration that the classical and church hymn traditions have a great deal in common.

Second Movement: *Prelude*

The second movement, *Prelude*, begins with a sprightly theme in G major whose playful character contrasts markedly with the majestic first movement.

Here, instead of presenting the most obvious allusion to the source tune at the outset, as in the first movement, Ives lets the tune sneak up on you, playing with his listeners by paraphrasing the tune at varying levels of recognizability. Even if you know the main source melody, the opening phrases of the quartet movement merely hint at its rhythm and contour, until the source is unveiled when you hear the end of the verse of *Beulah Land* and the beginning of its refrain ("O Beulah Land, sweet Beulah Land"). Its appearance creates a metric disturbance: the quartet theme paraphrased from it is in quadruple meter (four beats to the measure), while the hymn tune itself is in triple meter (three beats to the measure), gently contradicting the accents of the prevailing meter. As Ives develops his material, the musical ideas and meters contend and interweave in unpredictable ways. The key changes, the harmony wanders, and the music grows more fragmented and syncopated. Then the cello restores order, plucking instead of bowing (an effect called *pizzicato*) to emphasize a regular four-beat rhythm, then returning to bowing with an arching line as the music gradually slows and quiets.

The contest between groups of four beats and three beats in the movement's first section sets up a contrasting middle section in triple meter. Here a vibrant new theme in D major enters, paraphrased from *Shining Shore*. Once again, Ives plays with the listener: he leaves off the most recognizable part of the tune, its opening motive (which we heard in the First Symphony's first movement as the middle phrase of its first theme), and instead follows the overall contour of the hymn tune while freely interpolating or omitting notes and changing some rhythms. Even a churchgoer who has sung *Shining Shore* from childhood is more likely to hear this theme as sounding vaguely familiar than to identify it as the hymn tune. But after repeating and varying ideas from his theme, Ives tips his hand, playing the opening phrase of *Shining Shore* in violin I over a fragment of *Beulah Land* in the viola and cello, as if to point out the two main source tunes for this movement. The middle section theme repeats, then leads into a more extensive development. The texture thins and the first violin presents a new idea in C major, a melody that repeatedly skips up and down by fourths and thirds, over a flowing countermelody in the viola. The skipping melody repeats in the viola and in the cello, then Ives combines fragments of it with bits of the middle section theme, changing keys and mixing motives as in the development section of a sonata form movement.

A series of resonant chords brings the middle section to a close, and the opening material repeats in G major, slightly varied, creating a ternary form. This time around, you may notice a brief allusion to *Shining Shore* that served the first time as a hint of what is to come and now serves to recall the middle section. A burst of new energy leads into an extensive coda. After a pause, the pace increases, and you hear a varied statement of the complete refrain of *Beulah Land* interrupted with phrases from *Shining Shore* and the middle section theme. The music builds to a climax, suddenly stops, then comes to a quiet close. Whether you recognize the hymn tunes or not, the effect is like a Beethoven quartet movement, presenting themes that are full of interesting ideas, developing them through fragmentation and counterpoint, constantly introducing new variants, and alternating moments of tuneful clarity with dramatic juxtapositions and climaxes until everything resolves at the end.

Third Movement: *Offertory*

After such an active movement, you expect a slow one, and Ives obliges with the serene and appealing third movement, *Offertory*. The opening theme in D major is adapted from *Nettleton* ("Come, Thou Fount of ev'ry blessing") by Asahel Nettleton or John Wyeth. Anyone who knows the hymn melody will recognize its opening notes at the beginning of the movement. But Ives reshapes this AABA hymn tune, evading closure at the end of the first phrase, eliminating the repetition of A, extending the B phrase with interpolated material, and condensing the final A phrase to a motive that combines its opening and closing gestures. The result is a theme that foregrounds the hymn tune's most familiar moments but reshapes it into an irregular, continually unfolding melody like a theme by Brahms. Like Brahms, Ives immediately develops the theme, spinning out new versions of the material, especially the descending gesture that begins the hymn.

The music slows to a pause amid vague harmonies, then the cello and viola pluck a gentle accompaniment in a distant key. Over this, the violins present a charming new theme that knits together melodic and rhythmic elements from *Nettleton*, *Shining Shore*, and *Beulah Land*, using innate similarities between these tunes to weave a supple, beautiful melody with something of a folk-like character. This theme repeats, then moves into a development that includes more-direct references to *Shining Shore* and *Nettleton*. After a pause, the harmony leads back to D major and a reprise of the movement's opening theme, followed by a brief coda that recalls portions of both themes. Although very different in mood, this movement resembles the second in its ternary form: ABA' plus coda, with the theme of the B section repeated and followed by a development.

Fourth Movement: *Postlude*

The vigorous final movement, *Postlude*, begins like a fast march. The opening theme in G major starts with a phrase from *Coronation*, the same phrase Ives used as a countermelody in the first movement fugue. Yet the tune is hard to recognize because Ives has transformed its accentuation. In the hymn tune and the fugue, the accents fall on the second and fourth notes of the phrase, but here the first and third notes get the stress (as if singing "BRING forth THE roy-AH-al di-a-DEM"). That utterly changes the melody, making it difficult to hear as the hymn tune. Ives then elides this phrase with two snippets from *Webb* by George J. Webb: its initial motive ("Stand up, stand up for Jesus") and the end of its B phrase (at the words "His army shall he lead"), interweaving parts of the two hymns to make a coherent whole.

Once again, having presented the theme Ives immediately begins to develop it, traveling through several keys and building rhythmic intensity until the music slows and pauses on a rich chord. Then, quietly and in a distant key, the middle section from the second movement returns, its mood now calm rather than vibrant, its triple meter once again contrasting with the quadruple meter of the first section. As the middle section unfolds, somewhat varied, you notice that in the latter part of the section Ives has replaced part of the skipping melody with the opening motive of *Webb*, changed to fit into triple meter. A rapid buildup and a return to quadruple meter lead back to G major and a complete reprise of the finale's opening section, again creating a ternary form.

As the reprise comes to completion, the cello bursts into song with a full statement of *Webb*, accompanied by the middle-section theme in violin I and by bits of *Shining Shore* (the source for the middle-section theme) in violin II and viola. The combination of these melodies in counterpoint is unexpected and impressive. *Webb* is in quadruple meter, the middle-section theme in triple meter, and Ives just lines up the beats, laying four measures of triple meter over every three measures of quadruple meter. Magically, the melodies fit together harmonically—Ives clearly designed his middle-section theme to work in counterpoint with *Webb*, making some adjustments to smooth the fit—but their rhythmic accents conflict, as the strong beats in the two simultaneous meters occur at different places. What began in the second movement as a conflict between a theme in quadruple meter and its source tune in triple meter, then expanded to a contrast between sections in quadruple and triple meter, here in this coda becomes a layering of triple over quadruple meter, a climax of counterpoint and of conflicting meters. Such layering of material in different meters is an effect Ives returned to in many of his later works. When the cello completes its statement of *Webb*, all four instruments converge on the hymn tune's final notes and come together in a closing passage very like the rousing culmination of the First Symphony.

Integrating Traditions

The reminiscence of the First Symphony may remind us of the similarities between the two works. Both are in a late-nineteenth-century Romantic style like that of Brahms or Dvořák. Both use the hymn tunes *Beulah Land* and *Shining Shore*, though Ives makes much greater use of them in the quartet than the brief references in the symphony. Both are unified by key relationships, with the keys of the four movements (C, G, D, and G major in the quartet) also serving as the main keys within one movement (in the quartet, the second movement has extensive passages in G, D, C, and G major). Both combine themes in counterpoint. And both are cyclic: in the quartet, the middle section of the second movement returns in the finale; the second and third movements both draw on *Beulah Land*; the last three movements all use elements of *Shining Shore*; and the third phrase of *Coronation* features prominently in the first and last movements.

Yet the First Symphony and First String Quartet differ in one major respect, besides their genres and performing forces. In the First Symphony, Ives alludes throughout to European symphonies that served as his models, while making only passing reference to hymn tunes. In the quartet, the situation is reversed: he briefly cites a Bach fugue, but the whole quartet is suffused with material from hymn tunes, which serve as sources for the main themes of every movement. In the First Symphony, he showed that he could compete with the masters of Europe on their own ground. In the quartet, such competition seems beside the point. He takes the language of Brahms and Dvořák as a given and uses it to work with American hymns in a new way. This represents a true integration of two traditions, a new variation on America.

EXPERIMENTAL CHURCH MUSIC: *PSALM 67*

While in *The Celestial Country* and the First String Quartet Ives found different ways to bring together the classical tradition with that of Protestant church music, he was also exploring ways to merge church music with experimental music. At both Bloomfield and Central Presbyterian Church, he was choirmaster as well as organist and had at his disposal a choir led by a professional vocal quartet. This may have given him the idea of writing for unaccompanied choir or for choir and organ a series of pieces that use a variety of experimental techniques, setting psalms in the King James translation of the Bible. He may have tried them out with his choir—his *Memos* and manuscripts include recollections of doing so, although it is unclear whether

Ives is referring to complete pieces, parts of them, or individual sonorities—but there are no documented performances until decades later. Although John Kirkpatrick suggested that several of these psalms were composed as early as 1894, based on comments in Ives's *Memos*, Ives himself never dated any of them earlier than about 1898, and Gayle Sherwood Magee has persuasively argued that he composed them between 1898 and 1903, roughly contemporaneous with *The Celestial Country* and the First String Quartet.[18] Although the psalms sound very different from the cantata and quartet, they show a similar interest in blending traditions.

Psalm 67 for unaccompanied chorus was the first to be publically performed and published, in the late 1930s. In a note on the piece, Ives described it as if it were a continuation of his experiments with polytonality in his teen years:

> This is a kind of enlarged plain chant, the fundamental of which is made of two keys (but to be felt [or] heard as one)—G minor, with C major superimposed. The chords standing for the other relations [to these] fundamentals keep a similar tonal relation.[19]

The opening sonority—"the fundamental"—is indeed a combination of a G minor chord (the home chord in the key of G minor), sung by the lower voices in the choir, with a C major chord (the home chord in C major) above it, sung by the upper voices. But what follows is much more sophisticated than Ives's earlier settings of *London Bridge* with the melody in one key and the accompaniment in another.[20]

In the first section of *Psalm 67*, Ives devised a new musical language to evoke the style of Anglican chant, used in Anglican and Episcopal churches for performing psalms and canticles, poetic texts from the Bible. Anglican chant is a style of group recitation for choir, with a melody in the soprano, harmonized by a simple chord progression in the other voices. The melody is in two musical phrases, sung respectively to the two halves of each verse of the psalm, and all the voices declaim the text in the same rhythm. Since psalms and canticles have variable numbers of syllables in each verse, the melodies are designed to accommodate a wide range of texts, allowing notes to be repeated as often as necessary to fit in all the words. Ives encountered Anglican chant in 1893–1894 when he was organist at St. Thomas Episcopal Church in New Haven, and he wrote several canticle or psalm settings in the traditional style during that time.[21]

Psalm 67 has seven verses, given here in the modernized King James translation Ives used:

1. God be merciful unto us, and bless us; and cause his face to shine upon us.
2. That thy way may be known upon earth, thy saving health among all nations.
3. Let the people praise thee, O God; let all the people praise thee.

4. O let the nations be glad and sing for joy: for thou shalt judge the people righteously, and govern the nations upon earth.
5. Let the people praise thee, O God; let all the people praise thee.
6. Then shall the earth yield her increase; and God, even our own God, shall bless us.
7. God shall bless us; and all the ends of the earth shall fear him.

The opening pair of verses offers a group prayer for mercy and blessings; the third and fifth verses are identical, calling the people to praise God; the central verse appeals to all the nations of the world; and the final two verses look to the future for blessings. The poetic structure is symmetrical, like an arch, with the fourth verse as the capstone, and Ives echoes that structure in the music.

Ives sets the first two verses in a way that closely resembles Anglican chant, with an altered harmonic language. The melody in the soprano is in two phrases, beginning on the note C, rising above it, and returning to C at the end of the first half of each psalm verse, then dipping below C and rising up again in the second half. Each time the sopranos sing C, it is harmonized with "the fundamental," the combination of a G minor chord and C major chord Ives mentions in his note. This chord is dissonant, yet it serves as the home base for the music, the point of resolution as well as the beginning. When the melody moves to a different note, the accompanying sonority changes as well. In almost every case the new sonority is a transformation of "the fundamental," raising or lowering it to a different pitch level and then reordering the notes from top to bottom to create a new but closely related sound. In the first phrase, Ives arranges the notes to give the lower voices a minor chord and the upper voices a major chord, but in the second phrase he reverses this, giving the lower voices a major chord and the upper voices a minor chord, and adds one slightly contrasting sonority just before the end to create a stronger sense of resolution. Ives's explanation that "the fundamental . . . is made of two keys (but to be felt [or] heard as one)" is a bit misleading; neither the upper voices nor the lower ones have a chord progression that defines a key, and the piece is not really polytonal, since the relationship between the upper and lower parts changes with every phrase. Instead, the chords that combine to make up each sonority should be "heard as one" chord: each new sonority is a variation on the fundamental, and as we listen we hear a consistent sound at every moment, more dissonant than Anglican chant but equally convincing and smooth.

For the third verse of the psalm, Ives continues evoking the style of Anglican chant but changes the melody and introduces new variants of the fundamental sonority. Then for the fourth verse he introduces a contrasting style: imitative counterpoint. Much sacred choral music uses imitation and other forms of counterpoint. There are very few pieces—and none that Ives is likely to have known—that include both imitative passages and Anglican chant, since the purpose of the latter is to present the text as simply and comprehensibly as a choir can do, while imitation usually means that different voices sing the text at different times, making the words harder to hear. But it is not unusual for pieces to contrast sections where all the voices declaim the text in the same rhythm with sections in imitative counterpoint. Ives had used that same effect in his *Easter Carol* and other earlier church music. As we have seen in *Memories, Variations on "America,"* and many other works, using contrasts of style to differentiate sections of a piece or for expressive purposes is very common in Ives's music.

The contrast here highlights the imagery in the text. In the first three verses, the effect of the choir chanting the words together carries the sense of a group pleading for mercy and blessing and offering praise. In the fourth verse, the imitation between parts of the choir evokes the idea of many nations, and the faster motion and rising gestures in the melody suggest the multitudes singing for joy. After the initial point of imitation, the counterpoint becomes more dissonant than usual, matching the dissonance of the first section of the piece while differing greatly in texture.

Having explored various tonal regions, the fourth verse ends on "the fundamental" chord. In the rest of the piece the music retraces its steps: the fifth verse repeats the text of the third verse, and the music follows suit; the sixth verse reprises the music of the first; and the final verse of the psalm is chanted in free rhythm, beginning and ending on the fundamental chord heard at the beginning of the piece.

In most ways, *Psalm 67* is a traditional piece of church music. The music unfolds in an arch form, fits both the structure and the meaning of the text, refers to familiar styles of church music, and returns to the opening sonority at the end, paralleling the return to the home key in a piece of tonal music. These traditional elements highlight what is new: an innovative approach to harmony in the outer sections, and dissonant counterpoint in the middle section.

Ives's experiments from his teen years were mostly brief exercises that try out one or two novel ideas to see what happens. But *Psalm 67* is a finished, polished piece that can be performed and is logical and satisfying on its own terms. Despite its unorthodox musical language, we can see in it the influence of Horatio Parker. The canons, fugues, and other works Ives wrote for Parker had to be complete, polished pieces to demonstrate his mastery of technique. Ives adopted the same approach in creating his experimental choral psalms: each systematically works out specific compositional devices, in a way that parallels the training in strict composition he received in college. Playing around with chords by stacking one on top of another to make a more complex and dissonant chord was one thing; showing how one could use this procedure to create a coherent, logical, and compelling piece of music is a much more difficult task. As Ives wrote in *Memos*, "What started as boy's play and in fun [in his teen years] gradually worked into something that had a serious side to it that opened up possibilities." The same is true for the expanding and contracting wedges in *Psalm 24*; the parallel chords in *Psalm 100* and *Psalm 150*; the whole-tone scales and dissonant counterpoint in *Psalm 54*; and the many other innovative techniques Ives used in these and other choral psalm settings. All of these pieces show a level of craft, sophistication, and ability to realize a procedure through composition that Ives owed to Parker, however distant their musical language may be from Parker's.[22]

EXPERIMENTAL PROGRAM MUSIC: *YALE-PRINCETON FOOTBALL GAME*

After graduation, Ives stopped composing the marches, fraternity show songs, glees, and other types of popular music he had kept up at Yale, having no outlet for it. He then began to incorporate the sounds and sometimes the very melodies of popular music into his other works.

An early step along this path was *Yale-Princeton Football Game*, a short piece for orchestra he sketched around 1899 and revised around 1914–1919.[23] This is apparently his first work of program music, music that attempts to tell a story or depict a series of events, as in Berlioz's *Symphonie fantastique* or Richard Strauss's *Till Eulenspiegel's Merry Pranks* and *Don Quixote*. The idea of program music comes from the art music tradition, but in every other respect *Yale-Princeton Football Game* represents a synthesis of experimental music with popular music. In it Ives sought to capture the sounds, events, and feelings of a football game in New Haven on November 20, 1897, which became famous for the Yale quarterback's electrifying run down the field, zig-zagging around the opposing Princeton team. To keep the piece brief—about two minutes long—Ives condenses the game to a series of plays for each team. He marked in the score the events he was trying to picture.

Ives understood that if you want a concert audience to hear your piece as representing something outside music, it is helpful to contradict their expectations and even to break the usual rules of music. If listeners cannot make sense of your piece in purely musical terms, they will likely seek explanations for it in a story or program. As Ives comments in *Memos*,

> When once one [is] using "tones" to take off or picture a football game for instance, [how] natural it is to use sound and rhythm combinations that are quite apart from those that would be a "regular music." For instance, in

picturing the excitement, sounds and songs across the field and grandstand, you could not do it with a nice fugue in C.[24]

The opening movement of the First String Quartet is "a nice fugue in C," and it could hardly be farther from evoking a football game. But in *Yale–Princeton Football Game*, Ives combines experimental sounds with tunes everyone at Yale would have known to convey everything from the noise of the crowd to the action on the field. Like *Memories* and *The Circus Band*, this piece is an example of fictional music, inviting you to imagine yourself at a football game hearing these sounds and songs. As we saw with the First String Quartet, knowing the tunes can help you catch their appearances in the music. You can familiarize yourself with the college songs by listening to them at the Charles Ives Society website (charlesives.org/borrowed-tunes/songs).

The piece begins with murmuring in the strings, dissonant repeating figures that convey the buzz of the crowd, gradually growing faster and more intense to suggest their increasing excitement. Over this come cheers and songs, representing groups of students in the bleachers chanting and singing before the game begins. The cheers are in clusters of dissonant notes, sounding like the cluster of voices in a crowd:

> Winds, trumpets, and bass drum shout "Rah, rah, rah! Rah, rah, rah, rah! Rah rah! Yale! Yale! Yale!" as they grow faster, louder, and more dissonant.
> Bassoons, trombones, and snare drum intone the chorus of frogs from the ancient comedy *The Frogs* by Aristophanes, which every Yale student read in the original Greek ("Brekeke-kex, brekeke-kex, brekeke-kex ko-ax ko-ax").

College songs are heard in fragments, just long enough for a Yale student from the 1890s to catch them, coming from all directions as if different groups are contending for who can sing out the loudest:

> Flutes play the Princeton song *Old Nassau*, representing fans for the opposing team.
> Clarinets shout them down with the Yale song *Hy-Can Nuck a No*.
> The piccolo and oboes add *Harvard Has Blue Stocking Girls*, a Yale song that taunts their ancient rival Harvard ("Harvard has blue stocking girls, Yale has blue stocking men; / We've done fair Harvard up before, we'll do her up again").

In the midst of this the brass band comes in, playing the *Second Regiment Connecticut National Guard March* by David Wallis Reeves, an old favorite both in Danbury and at Yale. Then, as the band plays and the strings continue to depict the murmuring of the crowd, more songs pile on:

> Trombones and bassoons add a phrase from *Bright College Years*, also known as *Dear Old Yale* ("How swiftly are ye gliding by, / Oh why doth time so quickly fly").
>
> The horns chime in with the football song *Hold the Fort, McClung Is Coming* (to the tune of Philip Bliss's gospel hymn *Hold the Fort*).
>
> The brass respond with *Old Nassau*, showing that Princeton will not be silenced.

Suddenly a shrill trill high in the piccolo interrupts, representing the whistle of the referee calling for the game to begin. There is a brief hush in the crowd, then the murmuring resumes in the strings. A loping trombone and a thump in the bass drum depict the kickoff from Yale to Princeton, and running scales in the winds and brass portray the players running around the field. The referee's whistle marks off a series of downs for Princeton, each launched by bassoons that imitate the sound of the quarterback calling out numbers before the ball is hiked, followed by motions in the brass and winds that evoke the offensive and defensive lines pushing against each other. Princeton makes little progress, and Yale gets the ball.

Once again the referee's whistle punctuates the plays. Three quick downs go by, with the Yale team using a flying wedge formation suggested by a musical wedge, dissonant chords contracting to a tighter group of notes, as if the moving lines of music represented the motions of players on the field piling together to push through the defensive line. Then comes the play that made the game famous. As every instrument plays at peak volume and in constant motion, the trumpets zig-zag up and down, embodying the Yale quarterback's broken-field run. At the climax—touchdown!—the winds and brass sustain a loud dissonance as the violins, percussion, and kazoo chorus go wild; Ives marks their parts "improvise," expecting that each line will be as loud, active, and independent as possible, producing a sound of joyous chaos. Then the winds and brass cut off, and the strings return to their murmuring, softer and slower as at the beginning. The game is over, and the crowd starts to file out of the stadium. We hear the cheers once again, and the music fades to a quiet close.

The result is not a literal reproduction of how the game sounded, but an evocation in music of the crowd through the noises they make, the cheers they chant, and the songs they sing; of the band through a popular march; and of the game through notes that move around like players on the field or that imitate the referee's whistle or the thump of a foot kicking the ball. By including the songs, cheers, and march, this work shows just how vital music is to the experience of a football game.

GIVING UP MUSIC

Yale-Princeton Football Game was never performed in Ives's lifetime. Ives recalled copying out the full score in ink in 1899 and sending it to a college classmate, but that score disappeared. He revised the sketch in about 1914–1919 but did not complete another full score. The piece had to be reconstructed after his death, and it was first played in the 1970s in two different realizations, by Gunther Schuller and by James B. Sinclair.[25] Yet it is significant because in it Ives explored ideas he would pursue more completely in many of his most important works: blending popular and experimental traditions; using innovative techniques to depict an event by imitating its characteristic sounds and suggesting physical motion through musical gestures; and representing in music itself how people in America make and respond to music as an integral part of everyday life or special celebrations. It was also the first of several pieces to capture a memory and portray it in sound.

Psalm 67 was premiered in 1937 in New York, in a concert of American choral music conducted by Lehman Engel; two years later it was published and appeared on a Columbia recording, the first recording of an Ives piece issued by a major label. *Psalm 24* was first performed in 1951 and published in 1955. All the other experimental psalms had to wait until the mid-1960s, when they were sung and recorded by the Gregg Smith Singers, followed by publication in the 1970s to 1990s.[26] It would be wonderful to know whether Ives led his church choirs through them and, if so, how the singers reacted to these difficult, dissonant works. Their significance for Ives's development is twofold: they exemplify his interest in synthesizing the various traditions he knew (here blending experimental and church music), and they demonstrate a much higher level of compositional craft than the experiments of his teen years, showing how serious he had become in his exploration of new musical resources. They led to further syntheses and more experiments in the years to come.

The First String Quartet is also significant for its blending of traditions, in this case filling a classical music genre with material from Protestant hymnody, a combination he would revisit in many future works. He may have intended it for the Kaltenborn Quartet, a professional string quartet he knew who had played other music of his, but there is no record that they performed it or even read through it. The only confirmed performance in Ives's lifetime was in an arrangement of the last three movements for string orchestra, played over the radio in March 1943 by the Columbia Concert Orchestra conducted by Bernard Herrmann, though the Roth Quartet may have played the same movements five years earlier. The four-movement version of the quartet was premiered by the Kohon Quartet at the Museum of Modern Art in New York on April 24, 1957, three years after Ives had passed away.[27]

All of the pieces discussed in this chapter illustrate Ives's attempts in the four years after college to integrate ideas from different traditions. The only one to be performed at the time was *The Celestial Country*, and it proved to be the only dead end. Its premiere at Central Presbyterian Church on April 18, 1902, was the biggest musical event of Ives's entire career so far, a concert that showcased his skills as an organist, as a choirmaster, and as a composer. The typefaces, wording, and list of performers on the front of the program booklet, shown in Figure 4.3, set a serious tone for the evening. He highlighted the church's four vocal soloists and named everyone in the choir, perhaps the largest group he had ever conducted. He hired the Kaltenborn Quartet to play the string parts and featured them by including in the cantata a movement for string quartet alone, an unusual feature in a vocal work; they returned the favor by playing that movement in their own concert in New Haven on May 7. He sent out notices to the newspapers and music journals, identifying himself as a student of Horatio Parker. The cantata itself embodied influences from Parker, joining his command of compositional craft and his high aspirations for music with the more practical church style of Dudley Buck. In every respect, Ives seems to have sought through this concert to establish a reputation like Parker's, as a distinguished organist, choirmaster, and composer, worthy of a prestigious position.[28]

Ives knew that he could never make a living by composing symphonies, orchestral works, chamber music, and art songs, even in the Romantic style of his First Symphony and First String Quartet. Parker himself supported his activities as a composer by working as an organist, choirmaster, conductor, and college professor, and in a 1911 book about the music business he bluntly described the predicament facing composers of art music in the United States:

> The money rewards of a serious composer are slender at best, and most precarious, especially in this country. Excepting a few men who devote themselves chiefly to light opera or dance music, the writer knows not one composer in America who can possibly live by the exercise of his chosen vocation. One who aspires to compose music must therefore be prepared to content himself with little beyond his work.[29]

Concert

And Presentation of a New Cantata,

"The Celestial Country!"

WORDS BY HENRY ALFORD.
(*Latin Text from St. Bernard.*)

MUSIC BY CHARLES E. IVES.

For Solo, Quartet, Octet, Chorus, Organ and String Orchestra.

MISS ANNIE WILSON	Soprano
MISS EMMA WILLIAMS	Contralto
MR. E. ELLSWORTH GILES	Tenor
MR. GEORGE A. FLEMING	Baritone

The Kaltenborn String Quartet:

MR. FRANZ KALTENBORN	First Violin
MR. WILLIAM ROWELL	Second Violin
MR. GUSTAVE BACH	Viola
MR. LOUIS HEINE	'Cello

MR. CHARLES E. IVES	Organist

Assisted By

MRS. SPRINGER,

MRS. DULANY,

MISS CAROLINE ANDRESEN,

MISS MARTHA SNEAD,

MISS CHARLOTTE SNELL,
[Soprano.]

MISS MARY GROUT,

MISS MANSFIELD,
[Mezzo-Soprano.]

MISS SARAH EDWARDS,

MISS MINA ANDRESEN,

MISS DOLORES REEDY,
[Contralto.]

MR. JOHN W. CATCHPOLE,

MR. A. C. EADIE,

MR. HARRY B. MOOK.
[Tenor.]

MR. EDWIN F. FULTON,

MR. FREDERICK BALLANTYNE,
[Basso.]

MR. HERMAN TROST,

MR. THOMAS.

Horns: { In B flat (Euphonium) . . MR. W. S. PHASEY
{ In A . . . . . (Player to be Announced)

Central Presbyterian Church,

New York

Friday,

April 18, 1902.

Figure 4.3. Program booklet for the premiere of *The Celestial Country*.

MSS 14, The Charles Ives Papers in the Music Library of Yale University, Series VII, Box 50A, Folder 1, April 18, 1902.

If Ives envisioned a career in music, it would have been to continue his current work as organist and choirmaster while seeking additional opportunities as a composer and perhaps as a teacher—in sum, a career like Parker's. He seems to have planned *The Celestial Country* as a major step toward securing such a career.

If so, it had the opposite effect. The reviews were favorable, but they were not glowing. The *New York Times* reviewer complained about the lack of a full complement of singers for the chorus, then said the cantata was "scholarly and well made . . . also spirited and melodious." The *Musical Courier* reviewer identified Ives as "a Yale graduate and pupil in music of Professor Parker" and described each movement of the cantata in some detail, noting the thematic links between movements, praising the string quartet movement as "full of unusual harmonies and pleasing throughout," and commenting that the finale "shows some original ideas, many complex rhythms and effective part writing." Overall, he concluded, "the work shows undoubted earnestness in study and talent for composition." The review ends by reflecting the positive response from those present: "An audience completely filling the church listened with expressions of pleasure, and at the close the composer was overwhelmed with congratulations, which he accepted in modest fashion."[30] The praise was sincere, but saying that the work was "scholarly and well made" or "shows undoubted earnestness in study" made it sound like a school assignment, not the music of a composer with a distinctive voice who was about to become famous—not at all like the premiere of *Hora novissima* nine years earlier that made Parker's reputation.

Although we cannot know for sure, it seems likely that Ives had been keeping his options open, working in insurance while hoping that he could make his way in music. Now, with his best effort earning only tepid reviews, he must have concluded that those hopes would never be fulfilled.

Less than a week after the reviews appeared, Ives resigned his post at Central Presbyterian Church, his last paid position in music. His resignation was reported in the *Danbury Evening News* on April 26—he was still making news in his hometown paper—in an announcement that sounds like a member of his family wrote it:

A DANBURY COMPOSER.
Charles E. Ives Resigns Organ to Devote His Time to Composition

Charles E. Ives, the Danbury young man whose recent composition, "The Celestial Country," brought him suddenly into fame as a musical composer, has given up his position as organist of the Central Presbyterian church, New York city, and will in future devote his time entirely to composition.[31]

Despite the bravado in these words, Ives knew they were not true: reviews in the *New York Times* and *Musical Courier* did not constitute fame, and he would be spending most of his time at work at the Raymond Agency, not composing. He played his last Sunday service on June 1. When he packed up his belongings, he left some of his choral and organ music at the church, having no more use for it. He was stepping away not only from his job but also from the purposes his church music had served and the genres he had cultivated.[32] After that, he played no more recitals and wrote no more music for church services or for organ. He later described this as the time "when I resigned as a nice organist and gave up music."[33] At twenty-seven years old, Ives had been a professional church musician since he was fourteen, almost half his life. He was giving up his identity as a working musician, his weekly regimen as a performer, any dream of a career in music, and very likely any expectation that anyone would ever think of him as a composer.

That door had closed. He would make his fortune in insurance, becoming one of the most innovative and successful people in the business.

Seeking and Finding

$\mathcal{T}$he years after resigning his last paid position as a musician were a time of seeking and finding for Ives, in work, music, and love. He left behind any dreams of a career in music and committed himself fully to a career in insurance. As a composer, he lapsed into relative silence for a while, then took up the ideas of experimentation and of synthesis with new determination. His new energy for music was stimulated by courting his future wife, Harmony Twichell.

LIFE INSURANCE: SCANDAL AND SUCCESS

When he left his post as organist and choirmaster at Central Presbyterian Church in June 1902, Ives continued to live in Poverty Flat at 65 Central Park West and to commute downtown to work at Charles H. Raymond & Co., general agents for the Mutual Life Insurance Company of New York. There he supervised agents who sold life insurance policies, although he did no direct selling himself.

Ives might have had an unremarkable business career, if not for a crisis in the insurance industry. In July 1905, the New York state legislature established a committee chaired by Senator William W. Armstrong to investigate questionable practices of several insurance companies based in New York. The committee held hearings from September through December. The investigation did not implicate Ives, but Michael Broyles has argued that it profoundly affected his future path, leading to the establishment of his own agency and inspiring his idealism about insurance as a service to humankind.

As Broyles explains,

> Mutual, Ives's company, came under fire for serious actuarial and accounting practices involving insurance policies as well as favoritism and

nepotism. Richard A. McCurdy, Mutual's President, drew an extraordinarily high salary and had established his son Robert McCurdy as manager of the Raymond agency, to which Mutual not only channeled many large policies but paid unusually high commissions. . . .

. . . Because of his relatively junior position [Ives] was not directly in the line of fire from the investigating committee. But as the investigation unfolded it came closer than has been realized. Coming under particular attack were the manner and extent of compensation for agents and agencies, with the Raymond Agency of Mutual singled out as the most egregious of abusers. Ives not only worked for the Raymond Agency but was assigned to the section that dealt with agents. [Although] his level of management is unknown, . . . he was not only in the house but in the very room under heaviest attack.[1]

The focus on nepotism may have caused Ives to worry, as he had gained his initial position at Mutual through his father's second cousin Granville White, whose name came up during the hearings. The Raymond Agency where he worked was threatened, and the entire industry was in danger of being tainted by the scandal. Meanwhile, Ives was having issues with his health, apparently exacerbated by the Armstrong investigation. A health crisis in the summer of 1905 prompted an extended vacation with his Yale friend David Twichell and family at Saranac Lake in the Adirondacks, and a recurrence in late 1906 led to another rest cure that December at Old Point Comfort, Virginia. Although earlier biographers, following Ives's lead, identified the illness as heart troubles, Gayle Sherwood Magee has demonstrated that the likely diagnosis was neurasthenia, also called nervous exhaustion. Associated with anxiety and overwork, especially among businessmen, its symptoms included heart palpitations, rapid heartbeat, weakness, and depression. The standard treatment was a rest cure.[2]

Yet out of this crucible Ives emerged in a stronger position. The Raymond Agency was dissolved on January 1, 1907, the day the new laws prompted by Armstrong's investigation came into effect. On that same day Ives launched a new agency, Ives & Co., with his friend from the Raymond Agency, Julian S. Myrick (known as "Mike"), as his assistant. The office manager at Mutual had asked Myrick to accompany Ives to Old Point Comfort, where they worked out details of the new arrangement. Their agency represented the Washington Life Insurance Company, which was closely related to Mutual; it had been established as a subsidiary of Mutual, was headed by a former officer from Mutual, and served to handle excess insurance, providing a means for Mutual to respond to the Armstrong Committee's demand that companies limit the amount of insurance they carried. By 1908 the crisis was over. No longer useful to Mutual, Washington Life was sold to Pittsburgh Life and Trust, which

Figure 5.1.   The office of Ives & Myrick at 38 Nassau Street around 1918, with Julian Myrick standing at the far left.
MSS 14, The Charles Ives Papers in the Music Library of Yale University, Series VI, Item 118.

did not sell insurance in New York, and Ives and Myrick returned to Mutual as agency managers. Their new agency, Ives & Myrick, began operations on January 1, 1909, with the two as equal partners, each earning a $2,500 salary from Mutual. By 1919, their agency was the second largest in the nation in volume of insurance, with sixty full-time agents. By 1929 it was the largest, and it continued to grow throughout the 1930s, even during the Depression. Figure 5.1 shows the Ives & Myrick office around 1918, with Myrick at the far left; Ives is not in the photograph.[3]

In a 1969 interview, Myrick recalled the secrets of their success and summarized Ives's distinctive contributions. His comments are worth unpacking, for they point to how the partners made their fortunes and what was so remarkable and creative about Ives's work in insurance, which was as innovative as his work in music.

> We had a good plan, and it worked out satisfactorily, so we were successful from the start. We got our business from general insurance brokers and got them to put in life insurance departments, and as a result they sold a great deal of life insurance, which they placed through our agency. Charlie used

a formula for the amount of insurance to carry and how to carry it. It was so successful, nearly everyone in the business used it eventually.

Ives never did direct selling, but he was a very good trainer of agents and taught them how to sell. . . . He had a great conception of the life insurance business and what it could and should do, and he had a powerful way of expressing it. He did a great deal of writing, much of it published and widely used. Charlie was responsible for the material that went to make up the classes, more than I was. . . . Our agency was the first to have a school for insurance agents. . . . Ives's contribution to the business was very great, and he worked continuously to improve it. He felt that the protection of the family and the home was a great mission.[4]

Myrick's recollections highlight four key factors. First was the way the partners organized their agency. Instead of keeping everything in-house, they assembled a large group of agents, in part by working with brokers of other kinds of insurance (such as fire and casualty) who were based all around the city, offering the agency's help at no cost to the brokers. At Ives's suggestion, they also recruited agents from New York's ethnic and immigrant groups, who could more easily sell policies to people in those communities. The more agents, the more sales through their agency, which earned them a manager's commission on each new policy sold and the opportunity for further commissions on policy renewals, split between the two partners. The rewards were considerable: by 1913 Ives was earning more than $10,000 a year as reported on his income tax return, equivalent to around $270,000 in 2020, and his total reported income between then and his retirement in 1930 equaled roughly $14 million in 2020 dollars. After retirement, Ives's share of the manager's commission gradually declined, but he still had an annuity from Mutual plus income from investments. His wealth made it possible for Ives from 1920 on to subsidize performances and publications of his own music as well as music by other American composers, and he became one of the most important patrons of modern music.[5]

The second factor Myrick's account highlights was Ives's "formula for the amount of insurance to carry." Ives laid it out in his pamphlet *The Amount to Carry and How to Carry It*, first published in 1912 and later revised and frequently reprinted, and in a training document he called *Broadway*, a story of two agents and their different sales pitches. The formula is straightforward, couched in *Broadway* as a series of questions to a man—a family's breadwinner—who wants to provide for his family. If anything happens to you, how much income will continue from your business and investments? How much income *should* continue to your family to supply everything they need? If the need is higher than the expected income, you need to make up the difference with life insurance, which will provide an income if you are disabled and, if you die, a lump sum to your family large enough to support your wife for her life and your children until they can support themselves. As Ives explains, the precise amount of insurance coverage you need is "only a simple matter of mathematics," which the agent can work out. This approach allowed the prospective client to convince himself of the need for life insurance, and indeed for a higher level of coverage than he would purchase from a salesman who did not make the pitch in these terms. As Myrick observes, this approach—now known as "estate planning"—became the standard in the industry, and it is still used today. Frank Rossiter notes that "the idea [of estate planning] was not original with [Ives], but he was the first to apply it on a large scale in practical agency work." His efforts to promote the idea and make it systematic forever changed the way agents sold life insurance.[6]

The third factor Myrick highlights is the training Ives offered their agents. Myrick notes that their agency "was the first to have a school for insurance agents." The idea of classes for businessmen was still new in 1909, when Ives set up the first classes for agents at Mutual Life; the first school of business in the United States, the Wharton School at the University of Pennsylvania, had opened only in 1881, and most businessmen learned their skills through a kind of apprenticeship system. Ives did not teach the classes himself, but trained and supervised the teachers, prepared curricular materials, and met with students individually. In these classes, agents learned Ives's formula for calculating the amount of insurance each client needs, along with other strategies for making sales and finding prospective clients, as well as family trusts, taxation, and other issues. As a result, the agents for Ives & Myrick were the best trained and most up-to-date in the business.[7]

Finally, Myrick mentions Ives's idealism, his "great conception of the life insurance business and what it could and should do," his belief that "the protection of the family and the home was a great mission." Ives wrote in *The Amount to Carry* of life insurance as "supplying a need which had been long intuitively sensed" and "doing its part in the progress of the greater life values." "To carry life insurance is a duty," both to one's family and to society as a whole; "a life insurance policy is one of the definite ways of society for toughening its moral muscles, for equalizing its misfortunes."[8] Those who purchase life insurance not only protect their own families from financial catastrophe but also contribute to a pool of funds that protects the families of other policyholders, to everyone's mutual benefit. Thus life insurance serves to improve human happiness and prevent suffering, and the more who participate the better. This idealism about life insurance was inspiring to agents and helped to fuel Ives & Myrick's success.

As Michael Broyles points out, Ives's views echo the 1905 testimony of Richard McCurdy, president of Mutual Life, to the Armstrong Committee. The *New York Times* printed a daily transcript of the hearings, and Ives very likely read McCurdy's words in the October 11 issue:

> Every person ought to understand when he takes a policy of life insurance
> that he is not doing it solely for his own benefit, but he is participating in
> a great movement for the benefit of humanity at large and for every other
> person who comes in and takes a policy in that company, and in that way
> joins the great brotherhood.

McCurdy described Mutual Life as a "great beneficent missionary institution"
whose purpose was "to extend the benefits of life insurance as far as possible
within the limits of safety and as far as practicable into every town and hamlet
of this country." Broyles notes that McCurdy's testimony "was greeted with
laughter and derision," and that he may have put forward these ideas as a way
to defend himself from allegations of unscrupulous business practices.[9] But
whether they were part of the institutional culture at Mutual Life or not, Ives
took these ideals to heart, and from them he built his vision of life insurance
as a moral enterprise and a force for good.

Thus from the crisis of 1905–1906 Ives emerged as a leader in the life
insurance business, one who articulated its goals, inspired his colleagues, organized a remarkably successful agency, created a school for training agents,
wrote the curricular materials for those classes, and popularized what he
called a "scientific" method for calculating the right amount of insurance and
for convincing prospects to purchase it that became standard in the field. As
Myrick wrote in a tribute after Ives's retirement in 1930, he was

> a guiding spirit whose impress upon his fellows was stimulating, uplifting
> and of untold value to life insurance production. His creative mind, great
> breadth of culture, intensive sympathies and keen understanding of the
> economic as well as of the material needs of the community made it pos-
> sible for him to evolve literature which paved the way for additional sales
> of life insurance. . . . The passing years will demonstrate that his philoso-
> phy will ever hold good.[10]

This was a talented and committed man, highly successful in his profession, rewarded both financially and with the esteem of his associates. Why
would he want to write music, a field where success, esteem, and financial
rewards eluded him?

HARMONY

Part of the answer is no doubt because composing had become a habit, too
long-standing and powerful to give up just because he no longer had an outlet
for it in church. But perhaps the greater part can be found in his relationship

with the woman who became his wife and life partner, who believed in him, encouraged him to compose, and reconnected him to memories of his father and to his aspirations in music.

Harmony Twichell (1876–1969) was the sister of Ives's college friend David Twichell and the daughter of Joseph Hopkins Twichell, a leading Congregationalist minister in Hartford, Connecticut. Ives heard Reverend Twichell speak at Yale during his first semester there. Harmony was then at Miss Porter's School, a private school for girls ten miles from Hartford in Farmington, Connecticut, where she took singing lessons alongside courses in science, mathematics, Latin, modern languages, and history. In August 1896, David Twichell invited Ives up to Keene Valley in the Adirondack Mountains for a vacation with the Twichell family, and Ives stayed with them for two and a half weeks. This was probably his first opportunity to spend time with Harmony and may have been when they met. She came to New Haven at least once to visit her school roommate Sally Whitney, and they attended Center Church on the Green where Ives was organist. According to Ives's nephew Bigelow Ives, in spring 1897 Ives took Harmony to the junior prom at Yale: "Harmony was the queen of the Yale prom that year. The wonder to me was that he worked up the courage to ask her."[11] But in the next few years the relationship progressed no further.

After two years at home in Hartford studying painting and accompanying her father on his travels to preach or speak, Harmony entered the Hartford Hospital Training School for Nurses in 1898, graduating in October 1900 as a registered nurse (RN). At graduation, she read an essay articulating her ideals for the profession of nursing and counting it a great blessing, "for it is proved that the fullest development individually comes from altruistic effort, and fullest development means in the end the greatest usefulness and happiness." That idealism never left her, and it became central to her marriage. She worked as a visiting nurse during 1901–1902 in the slums of Chicago, then alongside her brother David at the Saranac Lake tuberculosis sanatorium in 1903–1904, followed by a position as personal nurse and companion to a wealthy elderly woman in Albany, New York. Figure 5.2 shows her in her nurse's uniform in about 1902. She was briefly engaged to a minister in the fall of 1904 but broke it off. As Myrick recalled, "Harmony was a beautiful girl, and lots of men were chasing her. Ives had a lot of competition."[12]

In 1905 she and Ives met up again. In January and July, she was in Hartford when Ives came up to visit David and his family, and on July 30 she and Ives attended a concert together where they heard Dvořák's *New World Symphony*. In August, she was in New York as a nurse at the Henry Street Settlement, a not-for-profit agency on the Lower East Side providing immigrants and the poor with health care, social services, and education. David

Figure 5.2.   Harmony Twichell in
her nurse uniform around 1902.
MSS 14, The Charles Ives Papers in the
Music Library of Yale University, Series VI,
Item 77.

invited Ives to vacation with
the Twichells at Saranac Lake
that month, and Harmony
joined them for the first week
of September. Their friendship grew slowly, sustained by
correspondence and occasional
encounters, since she was still
working in Albany. By sometime in 1906 she was in love
with him, and no doubt he felt
the same, although neither felt
ready to disclose their feelings.
In summer 1907 she was again
at the Henry Street Settlement, and Ives took her to concerts and plays. On
October 22, two days after Ives's thirty-third birthday, during a walk near
Farmington and her family's home in Hartford, they declared their love and
pledged their lives to each other. The tone of Harmony's letters instantly
changed from friendly to impassioned. Her next letter to him begins "I never
wrote a love letter & I don't know how," then avows, "I love you & love you
& love you and no numbers of times of saying it can ever tell it. But *believe*
it and that I am yours always & utterly—every bit of me." Ives's many letters
from the time do not survive, but a month later he wrote, "This is Nov 22—a
month after Oct 22 and the greatest event in the history of this Country!"[13]

On Sunday, November 17, Ives and Harmony asked her parents for their
permission to marry, and they readily consented. David Twichell also approved,
writing his sister, "You know how I have always loved Charlie. He is real and has
a character of solid gold." But there was one last hurdle: Reverend Twichell was
Mark Twain's closest friend, immortalized as his traveling companion Harris in
A Tramp Abroad, so Harmony took Ives to introduce him to her "Uncle Mark."
As Ives told the story later, Twain looked him over and said, "Well, the fore
seems to be all right; turn him around and let's see the aft!"—and then gave his
assent. Charlie and Harmony were married by her father in Hartford on June 9,
1908, and the whole Twichell family posed with their new in-law on the lawn
of the parish house for the picture in Figure 5.3. After their honeymoon, they
moved into their new apartment at 70 West 11th Street in New York.[14]

Figure 5.3. Wedding photograph of Harmony Twichell and Charles Ives with the Twichell family on June 9, 1908. The newlyweds are fourth and fifth from the left in the back row, and her brother David Twichell is at the far right; her parents are seated in the middle of the front row.

MSS 14, The Charles Ives Papers in the Music Library of Yale University, Series VI, Item 78.

Harmony rekindled Ives's confidence. They became reacquainted as the Armstrong investigation was heating up, and by the time he proposed he had weathered that crisis and established his own thriving agency. Her belief in his capabilities and integrity as a businessman shines through in her letters during their courtship. He wrote to her that receiving her letters "gives me courage and more ability all day long," and he looked forward to having her with him "to get your encouragement in the morning and your sympathy at night."[15]

They shared an interest in music, attending concerts together and discussing music in their letters, and she encouraged his composing. He sent her songs (his own and by others), she sent him her poetry, and he set several of her poems as songs in a Romantic, accessible style. *The World's Highway* was probably the first, in 1906, followed by *Spring Song* in August 1907 and *Autumn* that November, on a view they shared from a cliff the day they became engaged. John Kirkpatrick called these Ives's "courting songs, that he wanted

Harmony and her family to like and understand." She did, writing in December, "Charlie, I think you are a wonderful person to have made these songs—I know some of them are lovely."[16]

She was surely complimented by Ives's settings of her poetry, and she genuinely liked them. But she also supported his composition in general, during their courtship and during their entire marriage. She wrote in February 1908 of their future life together in New York, hoping for "quiet hours & solitude" with "times for leisure of thought . . . & we will have your music." Ives wrote her in October 1910, when she was visiting her family, "How much I love to work when you're by me & how hard it is to without you." Myrick remembered that "Ives was writing music all the time when I first knew him. There was a piano at Poverty Flat. His friends joked about it, and he just took that good naturedly. But Harmony encouraged him all the time in his writing. . . . He would take his music home with him and work on it over the weekends." According to John Kirkpatrick, "Ives seldom told her much about the music he was working on," but she believed in what he was doing.[17] In the 1930s, Ives paid tribute to her consistent support:

> One thing I am certain of is that, if I have done anything good in music, it was, first, because of my father, and second, because of my wife. What she has done for me I won't put down, because she won't let me. But I am going to put this down at least: . . . she never once said or suggested or looked or thought that there must be something wrong with me—a thing implied, if not expressed, by most everybody else, including members of the family. She never said, "Now why don't you be good, and write something nice the way they like it?"—*Never!* She urged me on my way—to be myself! She gave me not only help but a confidence that no one else since father had given me.[18]

Barbara MacKenzie, who met the Iveses in 1944, said of Harmony, "She was never in doubt that Charles Ives was a genius, and so he was never in doubt." Lucille Fletcher, who interviewed Ives in the 1940s for an article that never appeared, wrote that he regarded her as "his greatest source of inspiration."[19]

One aspect of that inspiration was the confidence she had in him, but equally important is that they shared similar ideals for what music could achieve. Her attitudes toward music appear to have influenced Ives's own, and her interest in Ives's family, in American history, and in reading literature helped to guide him to the subject matter of some of his greatest works.[20]

Her letters show a sensibility typical of nineteenth-century Romanticism, conceiving of music as an art that can convey feelings and speak directly from the composer to the individual listener. In September 1907, after reading an obituary for the Norwegian composer Edvard Grieg that Ives had recommended to her, Harmony wrote that "it seemed to me very true that his music is individual rather than National or general—lyric rather than epic. It generally seems as if the song of [Grieg] I hear is meant exactly for me."[21] In February 1908, she wrote about artistic inspiration, expressing her hope that Ives would write music that would capture their love and their happiness together:

> It seems to me too, dearest that inspiration ought to come fullest at one's happiest moments—I think it would be so satisfying to crystallize one of those moments *at the time* in some beautiful expression—but I don't believe it's often done—I think inspiration—in art—seems to be almost a consolation in hours of sadness or loneliness & that most happy moments are put into expression after they have been memories & made doubly precious because they are *gone*—I think that is what usually happens tho' I don't see *why it should*. I think, as you say, that living our lives for each other & for those with whom we come into contact generously & with sympathy & compassion & love, is the best & most beautiful way of expressing our love—and the Bravest way too, dear love, but to put it too into a concrete form of music or words would be a wonderful happiness wouldn't it? I think you will & that will be doing it for both of us.[22]

Her views reinforced the Romantic notions of music as an art of feelings and as the personal expression of the composer, ideas Ives had already absorbed from Parker and elsewhere and stayed true to throughout his career. But in this letter she also articulates two concepts that hint at music he had yet to write: putting into expression specific moments or experiences that carry deep personal meaning, and doing so in retrospect, through memory. The music Ives wrote from this time on shows an increasing trend toward representation of memories and of specific remembered experiences, both recent events, as in *The Housatonic at Stockbridge* and *From Hanover Square North*, and idealized memories of childhood, as in *Decoration Day* and *The Fourth of July*.

Several of his mature works are linked in some way to his father, George Ives. To judge from the recollections of Ives by his friends at Yale and in Poverty Flat, or by Myrick and other business associates, Ives seldom spoke to them about his father or the rest of his family. But Harmony immediately took an interest in them, encouraging him to share his memories and regarding his family with reverence. The Sunday after their engagement, she wrote that "in church I thought all of a sudden of your Father—so intensely that the tears came into my eyes and I thought how much I love him—actually as if I'd known him—I almost *felt* him and I am sure he knows all about this and how dearly I love you and that your welfare is my happiness." The following January and February she visited Danbury and met Ives's mother, brother Moss, aunt Amelia Brewster, uncles Joseph and Isaac Ives, and other relatives, and on the train back to Hartford she wrote,

"It has been very sweet to me to be in your home & be so happy there. They all love you . . . your Uncle Joe said how proud your father would be of you two boys if he were here now. . . . I feel sure that your father knows your lives & sees what his love & thought has meant to you."[23]

Harmony's reverence for Ives's father seems to have rekindled Ives's own, reviving his interest in the popular music, patriotic songs, Civil War songs, band marches, outdoor revivals, and open-minded experimentation he associated with George Ives. All of these are prominent in his music from 1905 on, in several experimental works, in his pieces that incorporate popular songs and hymns from the Second Symphony through the Fourth Symphony, and in pieces that celebrate music-making in places like Danbury, such as the *Holidays Symphony* and *Putnam's Camp*.

Harmony also may have stimulated Ives's interest in writing music on subjects from American history and from literature. At Saranac Lake in September 1907 and in several subsequent letters, they discussed collaborating on an opera set in North America during colonial times, but in January 1908 Harmony suggested a change of focus: "Charlie, of course the place for the good man in *our drama* to come from is *our country ennobled*—our own country, as our forefathers planned her, and as Mr. Lincoln desired her in his Gettysburg speech, and as we hope she will be in the good process of time—don't you think so?"[24] The idealism she expresses here has echoes in the view of America's ideals and potential Ives later wrote about in *Essays Before a Sonata* and represented in his pieces on American subjects, such as *Three Places in New England*. In a February 1908 letter envisioning their life together in New York, she wrote, "We must plan to have times for leisure of thought & we must try & read a lot, the best books—we can live with the noblest people that have lived that way."[25] Indeed the Iveses spent much of their time together reading literature, and several of the works Ives wrote in the first decade of their marriage are about the writers they read, including the *Robert Browning Overture* and the *Concord Sonata* (on Emerson, Hawthorne, the Alcotts, and Thoreau).

We will see Harmony's influence at work throughout the rest of this book. For now, let us turn to the music Ives completed between the time he "resigned as a nice organist" in 1902 and their marriage in 1908.

COURTING SONGS

As Gayle Sherwood Magee has pointed out, based on the revised dating of his manuscripts, Ives apparently composed relatively little in the years just after leaving his post at Central Presbyterian Church.[26] Following concentrated work between 1898 and 1902 on the First Symphony, the First String Quartet, *The Celestial Country*, numerous sacred choral works, and a raft of songs, the only securely dated pieces from 1903–1904 are a song, *The Sea of Sleep*; a couple of short experimental sketches for the Kaltenborn Quartet to try out, later combined in a brief Scherzo for String Quartet; and a pencil sketch titled *Overture and March "1776,"* later incorporated into *Putnam's Camp*.

Courting Harmony seems to have unleashed his energies. One current was his "courting songs," written to please her and therefore set in an accessible tonal language. *The World's Highway* (1906 or 1907) may have been their first collaboration, and Harmony later told John Kirkpatrick that "it was the only one of his songs she learned to sing—'not in public of course—his other songs were beyond me.'" Her poem tells of wandering the world, finding joy and laughter but also rough patches stained with blood that bring sadness and fear. At last she comes to a garden, ends her wandering, and finds contentment. As Jan Swafford comments, the poem is an obvious metaphor for her own situation: "The poem practically shouts, I'm tired of this life, of being a saint to the sick! I have made up my mind among all these men. You're the one I want!"[27] No wonder she learned to sing it for him.

Ives's setting changes styles to match the changing moods. He begins in a style and format not far from a Stephen Foster parlor song. The piano plays a lyrical four-measure prelude that breathes glad contentment. The singer enters with an arching melody accompanied by sweet chromatic harmonies that suggest her wandering and continues with the contented prelude music as she expresses her love for the new and far away. It sounds like the song will follow the conventions of popular music, with two or three verses set to the same music and little contrast along the way. But suddenly it turns into a drama, painting each scene with new music. Happy people dance and laugh, evoked by light music in a dance-like triple meter. When the road gets rough and bloodstained, the music turns dark and agitated, with large leaps in the voice and a running bass in the piano. She grows tired and sad; the music returns to the triple meter and rhythm of the dance, but now it is quiet, slower, and in a minor key to reflect her emotions. As she admits fear of the far away, the music grows loud and chromatic, with a threatening bass line and leaps in the voice. Then she comes to a garden, and her opening music returns; the music first used to express her happiness in wandering now conveys her gladness in finding refuge. A voice calls her in, and she answers the call and leaves her wandering, reaching the highest note in the vocal line and the climax of the song. As her garden blooms with sweet contentment, we hear the contented music of the prelude, now showing her love for what is nearby, not the far away.

By invoking the style and conventions of popular song, breaking them with unpredictable drama, and then returning to the opening music, Ives creates a narrative like a tiny opera, reflecting the conflicts in the poem with conflicting musical styles. This is not the Ives who became famous for modern sounds, but this song shows his craftsmanship and his skill at using styles and their associations to convey meaning, one of his most characteristic traits.

EXPERIMENTAL CHAMBER MUSIC

Alongside his "courting songs," from late 1905 through 1908 Ives produced a number of short pieces, mostly for small groups of instruments, that took up again the exploration of new techniques he had begun in the experimental music of his teen years and continued in his psalm settings of 1898–1902. In most of these experimental instrumental works, there is an extramusical idea—a visual image or a narrative program—that helps to explain the musical events and gives listeners a way to grasp why such extraordinary things are happening in the music. Whether the image or program was Ives's original inspiration or was added later is not always clear; sometimes Ives seems to have started with the musical technique he wanted to explore and then matched it with an idea outside music, and sometimes—as in *Yale-Princeton Football Game*—a particular event or image prompted a search for appropriate musical means to represent it.

From the Steeples and the Mountains

From the Steeples and the Mountains (ca. 1905–1906) combines Ives's interests in layering, in polytonality, and in the traditional technique of canon with creating an image of the outdoors. There are four sets of orchestral bells, imitating the sound of church bells, and a trumpet and trombone that echo back and forth like bugle calls heard from a distance, then play lines that jump up and down in craggy patterns, metaphorically representing "the Rocks on the Mountains." The bells are in different ranges and keys (high bells in C and B major, low bells in D-flat and C major), to suggest the sounds of bells from the steeples of four different churches.

The piece begins with bells jangling softly. Each set of bells in turn plays a descending scale in its key, while the trumpet and trombone trade leaping figures like the first three notes of the bugle call *Taps*, constantly changing key. Then the bells enter one by one in a canon, each repeating its own descending scale and playing it faster and louder each time. At the peak of noise and density, the bells change to a new pattern, sounding the same notes but in a different order, skipping down by thirds twice (for instance, shifting from C-B-A-G-F-E-D-C to C-A-F-D, B-G-E-C). Both the descending scales and this new pattern evoke the tradition of change-ringing, in which bellringers on church bells start with a descending scale and systematically change the order the bells are rung to create new patterns. From the point the pattern changes to the end of the canon, the rhythm of each bell part is exactly backwards from what it had been up to that point, gradually growing slower instead of faster. This creates a rhythmic palindrome in each bell part: whether read front to back or back to front, the rhythm is the same, like the letters in the palindrome about Napoleon, "Able was I ere I saw Elba."[28]

Accompanying the canon in the bells is a canon between trumpet and trombone, with a craggy melody that uses all the notes in the chromatic scale and constantly seems to change key—or defines no key whatsoever, an effect later called *atonal* music (music that is not in a key and has no central pitch). The chromatic, atonal music for the brass sets them apart from the major scales of the bells, heightening the difference in instrumental color between the two layers. At the point the bells reverse their rhythms, the brass instruments also start going backwards, but in a different way. It is as if Ives cut up the music he had written for them so far and then stitched the measures together in reverse order, creating a palindrome in the brass to parallel the one in each set of bells. When the canons and palindromes are over, the music grows louder and more active, and after an even more powerful climax the piece ends with a kind of polytonal "Amen" in the bells.

This piece is an experiment that extends the idea of counterpoint to create simultaneous layers of sound that are independent from each other. As in his previous instrumental works like the First Symphony, Ives spins out his initial material—here the very simple ideas of a descending scale in the bells and a jumping fourth in the brass—into a longer span through repetition and variation. The piece is unified by the use of canon, one part echoing another, and of palindrome, the second half reflecting the first. Its coherence is assured by the process of gradual change, so that we can hear each moment proceding logically from what came before. Yet despite these parallels to earlier music, it sounds radically new.

Scherzo: All the Way Around and Back

Another experimental chamber work from around this time is *Scherzo: All the Way Around and Back* (ca. 1907–1908). This is even more explicitly a palindrome: the second half of the piece is the first half played in reverse, note for note, with a brief coda added at the end. Here there are no canons, but there are layers, as Ives gradually builds up the number of different instruments playing (piano, bugle, violin, bells, and finally clarinet) and the number of independent rhythms sounding at once. At the peak, there are seven different rhythms heard simultaneously. Six are equal divisions of the measure: the first six prime numbers—1, 2, 3, 5, 7, and 11—expressed as evenly spaced notes within each measure, as if six different meters were sounding at once. The only place these rhythms coincide is at the beginning of each measure. Over this dense web of notes a bugle plays a fanfare in a more normal meter of four beats per measure, changing rhythms from each measure to the next. The bugle plays on the notes of a C major chord, but all the other lines are dissonant, over a repeated low C in the piano.

As is true for *From the Steeples and the Mountains*, the piece is coherent in its own terms, introducing the different equal divisions of the measure in turn, combining them, building to a climax, reversing the process, and briefly repeating the climax for a coda. Yet here too Ives offered a non-musical parallel, hinted at in the title: building up the complex musical texture and then reversing course suggests the excited noise of a crowd at a baseball game as the batter hits, the base runners take off, the hit goes foul, and the runners have to retrace their steps, running "all the way around and back" to the base where they began.[29]

In this case, it seems clear that the musical idea came first, as the overlay of conflicting divisions of the measure fits Ives's description in *Memos* of the way he practiced playing and hearing different rhythms simultaneously:

> I have with much practice been able to keep five, and even six, rhythms going in my mind at once, so that I can hear each one naturally by leaning toward it, changing the ear in each measure—and I think this is the more natural way of hearing and learning the use of and feeling for rhythms, than by writing them and playing from them on paper, which shows the exact position of each note in relation to each other, in the eye. The way I did it was to take, for instance, in the left hand a 5—with the left foot, beat a 2—with the right foot, beat a 3—with the right hand, play an 11—and sing a 7. Start with two, gradually add the others—perhaps to begin with, have a slow metronome with a bell play the one-beat, and think of the [number of equal notes in the measure] as a 2, then a 3, then a 5, then a 7, then an 11.[30]

This is almost exactly what happens in *Scherzo: All the Way Around and Back*, which is a musical embodiment of Ives's exercise in keeping conflicting meters going against each other, a study in rhythm for players and listeners. The superimposition of conflicting rhythms and meters became part of Ives's toolkit, useful for representing the many simultaneous sounds we may hear at moments in our lives.

CENTRAL PARK IN THE DARK

Ives used his experimental techniques to capture one such moment in *Central Park in the Dark* for chamber orchestra. He wrote on the pencil sketch the original inspiration and the date: "Runaway smashes into fence, heard at 65 C P W [Central Park West] July—finit Dec 16 1906, with J S M [Julian S. Myrick]. Old Pt. Comfort."[31] When he revised it in the 1930s, he added a program note:

> This piece purports to be a picture-in-sounds of the sounds of nature and of happenings that men would hear some thirty years ago [around 1906] (before the combustion engine and radio monopolized the earth and air), when sitting on a bench in Central Park on a hot summer night. The strings represent the night sounds and silent darkness—interrupted by sounds from the Casino over the pond—of street singers coming up from [Columbus] Circle singing, in spots, the tunes of those days—of some "night owls" from Healy's whistling the latest or the Freshman March—the "occasional elevated [train]," a street parade, or a "break-down" in the distance—of newsboys crying "uxtries"—of pianolas having a ragtime war in the apartment house "over the garden wall," a street car and a street band join in the chorus—a fire engine, a cab horse runs away, lands "over the fence and out," the wayfarers shout—again the darkness is heard—an echo over the pond—and we walk home.[32]

Like *Yale-Princeton Football Game*, this is fictional music, inviting us to imagine ourselves in Central Park around 1906, listening to the music and other sounds around us. Ives cast the piece in two principal layers: the string instruments, representing the sounds of nature, and the rest of the orchestra, representing sounds—mostly music—made by human beings. Like layers in the organ music he played and in his own *Variations on "America,"* these layers are set apart by sound color and other factors.[33]

At first we hear just the strings, softly playing a series of dissonant chords that rise and fall in waves, gently changing in rhythm and sound. Like nature itself, the music representing nature is systematically organized in ways a listener is more likely to sense than to notice, but worth describing here to illustrate how this piece grew from Ives's experimentation with new techniques. The chords move together, up and down in parallel motion, like the chords in *The Cage* (discussed in chapter 1), another experimental work from 1906, and like dissonant sonorities in some experimental organ pieces from his college years.[34] Every chord has at least six different notes in it instead of the usual three or four (out of the twelve possible notes in the chromatic scale), giving the harmony a clouded sound, like the buzz of insects, frogs, and other natural sounds in summer. The rhythm ripples faster and slower, each successive measure divided into a different number of equal units (as in *Scherzo: All the Way Around and Back*), following a numerical sequence like the cresting and subsiding of successive waves (2–3, 2–3–4, 3–4–5, 4–3). After each rhythmic crest, the bass note moves and the structure of the underlying chords changes, from whole-tone chords to chords made of fourths, chords of mixed fifths and tritones, and chords of fifths. A tritone is an interval bigger than a fourth and smaller than a fifth, and quite dissonant, so overall the harmony gradually increases in dissonance and then relaxes, like a wave of intensity that swells and passes. All of these details illustrate Ives's systematic thinking, but at the same time they perfectly suit what he wants to portray. The gradual, wavelike motions in every parameter of the music evoke the gentle ebb and flow of the sounds of nature. They also prevent us as listeners from sensing a regular beat, a meter, familiar harmonies, or clear phrasing—elements that are typical of the music of humankind. And this music is not tonal; Ives thought of tonality as "a man-made thing," so by implication music that represents nature must not be tonal.[35] By *not* being like everyday music, this series of dissonant chords can symbolize nature.

This music of nature repeats ten times over the course of the piece, forming a background to human activity, represented through music. Evoking "sounds from the Casino over the pond," a clarinet plays a waltz melody paraphrased from *Ben Bolt*, a popular song from the 1840s. A flute and oboe play a little tune in canon, and a muted violin plays part of *Violets*, an up-to-date song from 1900, representing "street singers coming up from [Columbus] Circle" and "some 'night owls' from Healy's [a nearby tavern] whistling the latest." A piano plays some ragtime figures, at first soft, irregular fragments like a pianola (a player piano) heard from "the apartment house 'over the garden wall,'" then the chorus of the ragtime song *Hello! Ma Baby* from 1899. Each of these scraps of music has a different instrumental color and comes from a different spot in the orchestra, creating an effect of three-dimensional space with sounds coming from all directions.

The tempo of the human-made music grows faster and faster, but the sounds of nature are unaffected, continuing at their own pace; such an idea, having two parts of the orchestra play at different speeds, was an innovation that Ives used again in *Putnam's Camp*, the Fourth Symphony, and other works. As the piano repeats *Hello! Ma Baby*, a high clarinet echoes it. The third time through the song, a second piano comes in with a different tune, marked in the first sketch "another piano from another floor pushes Freshmen in Park" (perhaps a Yale song). Thus begins the "ragtime war" between pianos that Ives mentions in the program. Meanwhile, other instruments pile on, taking up these tunes or adding new ones, including part of the fiddle tune *The Campbells Are Coming* in the flute and a phrase from John Philip Sousa's *Washington Post March* in the second piano, evoking the "street band" in Ives's program. The noise reaches a climax of intensity, with high trills in the wind instruments suggesting the fire engine and wildly running figures in the trumpet, trombone, and bassoon portraying the runaway horse.

All of a sudden everyone stops playing but the strings. The sounds of humankind cease, and "again the darkness is heard"; we hear the sounds of nature, reminding us that they were there all along, unheard or unnoticed behind the noises of people. Nicolas Slonimsky called this effect "sonic exuviation"— "the shedding of old skin of instrumental sonority," "a cut-off of sonic matter, leaving a soft exposed bodily shape." Ives learned this effect from playing the organ as a teenager; it appears in Mendelssohn's Organ Sonatas Nos. 1 and 2, which Ives performed in 1890.[36] In *Central Park in the Dark* and several other works, Ives uses it to represent a loud, prominent, nearby stream of sound suddenly stopping so that a quieter or more distant sound can be heard. The sudden contrast reinforces the sense that we are outdoors, in a three-dimensional space, hearing sounds from many directions and distances.

As the music of nature repeats its cycle twice more, we hear again "an echo over the pond"—the clarinet waltz from the Casino—and then the flute melody and the violin playing *Violets* from up the street. The strings complete their cycle, "and we walk home."

In this piece, the experimental ideas—rhythms generated by number patterns, new kinds of chords, processes of gradual change, layering contrasting streams of music on top of each other—are all used to fulfill a program, creating a "picture-in-sounds" that is both Romantic in intention and modernist in execution. This combination of Romantic goals with new tools, techniques associated with the dissonant modernist music of the early twentieth century, becomes typical of Ives's later music. So does the integration of elements from the classical tradition, popular music, and experimental music: here, an orchestral tone poem that incorporates popular tunes and experimental devices. As we will see, many of Ives's later pieces are like this one, representing a scene in which he is both an observer and a participant.

THE UNANSWERED QUESTION

A companion piece to *Central Park in the Dark* is *The Unanswered Question*, about an imagined experience rather than a real one. Ives dated it "some time before June, 1908," the month of his wedding—a date confirmed by the handwriting—and revised it in the early 1930s.[37] Ives took the title from a line in

Ralph Waldo Emerson's poem *The Sphinx*, a dialogue between the Sphinx of ancient Greek mythology and a poet. Near the end, the Sphinx ends the discussion with these words to the poet, representing humankind:

> Thou art the unanswered question;
>   Couldst see thy proper eye,
> Alway it asketh, asketh;
>   And each answer is a lie.
> So take thy quest through nature,
>   It through thousand natures ply;
> Ask on, thou clothed eternity;
>   Time is the false reply.

What this stanza, or the whole poem, means is cryptic and still disputed by critics and literary scholars. Ives picked up on the idea of humans as "the unanswered question," eternity in clothing, always asking, never satisfied with the answers, and devised this piece, adding his own program note when he revised it in the 1930s. As in *Central Park in the Dark*, there are two main layers, the strings and everyone else, but here it is the strings that play tonal music while the others are atonal. *The Unanswered Question* is usually played with the various groups of instruments widely spaced from each other, enhancing the effect of independent layers being heard simultaneously. The effect in performance can be electric.

As the concert audience quiets, four flutes take the stage. Unexpectedly, they sit silent and unmoving. Quietly, almost imperceptibly, an ensemble of string instruments begins to play offstage, sounding a widely spaced, ethereal, brightly consonant major chord for about twenty seconds. Slowly, some instruments move while others hold their pitches, and the chords gradually change, making resonant consonances with occasional passing dissonances or smoothly moving lines against the sustained chords. Despite this gentle motion, the strings never grow louder, remaining at the softest possible level, giving their music a sense of effortlessness. In Ives's program for the piece, the strings represent "The Silences of the Druids—Who Know, See, and Hear Nothing." They maintain their music unchanged by anything else that happens, as if in their own world.

After the strings return to their opening chord and begin to repeat, you hear a soft trumpet coming from another direction, perhaps up in the balcony or out of sight behind a curtain. In an irregular rhythm unrelated to the strings, the trumpet plays a melody of five different notes, all of them dissonant against the chord in the strings. The effect is not like a melody played over an accompaniment that supports it; it is a completely separate stream of music, set off from the strings by pitch, tone color, meter, and rhythm as well as space. Ives says in his program that this melody represents "The Perennial Question of Existence." He does not tell us what the question is, but from the arching contour of the five-note melody, you can imagine a voice asking, "What are we here for?"

The strings do not respond, maintaining the Druids' silence. They keep moving slowly, undisturbed in their calm, beautiful progressions of chords. But now the four flutes on stage finally rouse themselves to action, searching for the answer to the trumpet's question. They enter softly, one by one, each new note dissonant with the others and with the strings. Then the top and bottom flutes move inward, their chromatic motion—using the half step, the smallest interval in music—a stark contrast with the large leaps of the trumpet and the mix of whole and half steps in the diatonic music of the strings.

Again and again the trumpet asks its question, each time in the same way, only changing its last note to make it dissonant against the slowly moving chords in the strings. Again and again the flutes respond, each time faster, louder, more active, more dissonant, and always in a tempo entirely independent of the strings. The second and third answers are like more energetic variants of the first, the fourth turns the question into a ragged march, the fifth tries rapid, spiky notes and syncopations—but none of them works, no answer is satisfactory. The flutes hold a "secret conference," gathering together in a chromatic cluster at the bottom of their range, each softly sustaining one of the four lowest notes on the flute, as if discussing among themselves what to do next. The trumpet asks the question again, and the flutes burst forth with the fastest, loudest, most active, and most vehement answer yet, mocking the question by imitating and varying it at a much quicker pace, and climaxing on a shrill dissonance near the top of their range. They have given up hunting for an adequate answer and impatiently try to cut off debate. But their attempt to shout the question down is not the final word. Over the undisturbed solitude of the strings, sustaining the same chord on which they began, the trumpet sounds its question one last time. As it hangs in the air, unanswered, the strings fade to silence.

Layering Contrasting Streams of Music

The Unanswered Question and *Central Park in the Dark* were premiered on May 11, 1946, in a concert of Ives's works that was part of the Second Annual

Festival of Contemporary American Music at Columbia University in New York. They were played by students from the Juilliard School, with Edward Schenkman conducting the onstage instruments and Theodore Bloomfield conducting the strings offstage.[38] The score for *Central Park in the Dark* does not call for such spatial separation of the two main layers of music, but the conductors decided to present them as a pair (Ives had grouped them together at one point as *Two Contemplations*) and placed the strings offstage as called for in *The Unanswered Question*. The *New York Times* reviewer, Olin Downes, complained about the sound:

> The music for the divided orchestra failed to go over the footlights, because of bad acoustical arrangements which made the orchestra back of the stage practically inaudible to any but those who sat in the front seats.... This work is really an extreme experiment in impressionism, needing a far more sensitive balance and coordination of all elements than it received to bring it off.[39]

Downes astutely recognized both pieces as experiments, exploring the effect of simultaneous layers of music that differ from each other as much as possible yet somehow cohere into a single experience. He also recognized a link to impressionism, the style identified with Claude Debussy, in whose works for orchestra and for piano there are often multiple layers set off by tone color, rhythm, range of pitches, and other qualities. Ives knew some of Debussy's music, beginning as early as 1902; although he criticized Debussy's choice of subject matter, he never criticized Debussy's style and appears to have been directly influenced by him, especially in the ways he creates musical textures and juxtaposes contrasting layers of sound.[40] The greatest difference between the two composers is that, unlike Debussy's *Nuages* (Clouds, 1899) or *La mer* (The Sea, 1903–1905), Ives's musical representations of a scene always contain human beings, represented through their music.

Despite its apparently inauspicious premiere, *The Unanswered Question* became one of Ives's most famous and most frequently played works, probably due to its intriguing program, crystal-clear structure, and paradoxical combination of simultaneous tonal and atonal streams of music. The score was printed in a Uruguayan music journal in 1941, then published in New York in 1953, followed by *Central Park in the Dark* in 1973. The two appeared together on the first recording of each, by the Polymusic Chamber Orchestra, issued in 1951.[41] They make a good pair, exploring similar ideas but with opposite effects: an atonal layer superimposed on a tonal one, or vice versa; a layer that gets faster and louder atop a quiet layer that moves at its own slow speed throughout; playing the juxtaposition of disparate elements for comedy in *Central Park in the Dark* and more seriously in *The Unanswered Question*.

A PRIVATE KIND OF MUSIC

The songs Ives wrote for Harmony during their courtship were a kind of private music, something for them to do together and for her to share with her family and friends. The experimental pieces were also private, like the experiments Ives had written in his youth and shared with his father. They were now more professionally polished, using the skills Ives had learned from Parker and from his growing experience as a composer to go beyond trying out a new technique for its own sake and to craft a real piece of music that is internally coherent, feels complete, has emotional content, and can convey an image or a series of events. Even more than the experimental psalms of 1898–1902, the experimental instrumental works of 1905–1908 represent the coming together of influences from George Ives and from Horatio Parker, his two most important mentors, and the synthesis of the experimental tradition Ives pioneered with the classical tradition he had increasingly absorbed since playing Bach and Mendelssohn as a teenager twenty years earlier. But they were still essentially private, compositional studies in how to use new musical resources, pieces he wrote for himself more than for an audience. Although he recalled that a theater orchestra tried out *Central Park in the Dark* in 1906 or 1907 between the acts of a play, the other experiments waited a long time for their public debuts. *The Unanswered Question* and *Central Park in the Dark* were premiered forty years after their first versions were sketched, and after the *Concord Sonata* and other works had already made Ives's reputation. *From the Steeples and the Mountains* and *Scherzo: All the Way Around and Back* were not performed or published until the 1960s, after Ives's death.[42]

The courting songs were aimed at Harmony and easy for her to understand. These experimental works were something else again. At some point, probably during their courtship but perhaps in the 1930s when he revised them, Ives explained to her what he was trying to accomplish in *The Unanswered Question* and *Central Park in the Dark*. As John Kirkpatrick reported, "Ives seldom told her much about the music he was working on, though she does remember his showing her *The Unanswered Question* and *Central Park*—'he fixed it so I could understand it somehow.'"[43] It may have been the programs that made these pieces comprehensible to her despite their radical new language.

It is perhaps no surprise that as Ives regained confidence, after the hiatus that began when he "resigned as a nice organist and gave up music," the first pieces he would write would be essentially private, the courting songs like a conversation with Harmony, the experiments like a conversation with himself and a reengagement with the experimental streak he identified with his father. But before long, Harmony's confidence in him as a composer also inspired Ives to return to composing music of greater ambition, aimed at a wide public: another symphony.

· 6 ·

Synthesizing American
and European Music

𝒥n his youth and college years, Ives kept his four musical traditions separate. Each genre and style he composed in served a specific purpose and audience, and he avoided mixing them. The few exceptions, such as his fugue based on *Missionary Hymn* and the First Symphony theme that borrowed from two hymn tunes, suggest an interest in integrating his experience as a church organist with the classical tradition he was studying with Parker.

During his first years in New York, Ives explored ways to blend elements across genres and traditions, bringing experimental ideas into church music in *Psalm 67*, hymn tunes into a classical genre in the First String Quartet, and popular music and experimental techniques into orchestral program music in *Central Park in the Dark*. In his Symphony No. 2, Ives continued down the same path, synthesizing what he had learned from Parker and from composing his First Symphony with the American popular music and hymns he had grown to love as a child. Encouraged by Harmony's confidence in him as a composer, he returned to the aspirations his two main mentors had inspired in him, bringing the music he identified with George Ives into the symphonic genre he studied with Parker. As in his First Symphony, he drew on European composers as models for symphonic style and structure. But every theme is paraphrased from an American popular song or hymn tune, and many transitional passages blend elements from Europe and America, with familiar snippets constantly turning in new directions. The overall effect is of American melodies reshaped to fit the mold of a late Romantic symphony. The result is one of Ives's most winning works, a masterpiece that appeals to listeners as diverse as America itself.

SYMPHONY NO. 2

Ives began his First Symphony as part of his coursework for Parker, and from the start he knew he was working on a symphony. The origins of his Symphony No. 2 are more uncertain because Ives's account and the surviving sources tell conflicting stories.

According to Ives, he finished the Second Symphony in 1901 or 1902, drawing on at least six other pieces dating back to college or beyond: *Down East Overture* (1897–1898), an organ sonata (1897), a rejected slow movement for the First Symphony (ca. 1898), a piece for string quartet played in a revival service at Center Church (ca. 1897–1898), an overture called *The American Woods* (1889), and a set of overtures *In These United States* (1896–1898), including *Overture: Town, Gown and State* and perhaps *Down East Overture*. Of these, only the rejected slow movement for the First Symphony survives, and that only in part. Ives added that the third movement was revised and scored around 1909–1910, and the whole symphony was then professionally copied.[1] The picture Ives paints is of a piece assembled from earlier works in a variety of genres, mostly written during his last two years at Yale, and completed by 1902.

Yet the sketches that exist for the Second Symphony strongly suggest that he composed it several years later, around the time of his engagement and marriage, and that most of it was new. According to Gayle Sherwood Magee, except for material based on the rejected slow movement from the First Symphony, almost all of the remaining sketches are written on music paper that was printed no earlier than 1907 and are in Ives's handwriting from about 1907–1909.[2] A few themes in these sketches, such as the finale's second theme, are complete in their first draft, suggesting that Ives may have taken them from earlier pieces or worked them out at the keyboard. Everywhere else, we can see Ives inventing the themes, replacing first thoughts with better ideas, elaborating those ideas in transitions and developmental passages, and deciding how to string together these segments of music to create each movement. Nearly every stage of the compositional process is represented in these sketches, making clear that the symphony as we know it was a product of about 1907–1909 and that no movement was taken in its entirety from an earlier work. The professional copy made around 1909–1910 was thus of a relatively recent composition, not one that was almost a decade old.[3]

Perhaps the best way to reconcile Ives's recollections with the extant sketches is to imagine his perspective, the problems he faced and was trying to solve. When he resigned from his position at Central Presbyterian Church in 1902, he had recently completed three multimovement works: the First Symphony, *The Celestial Country*, and the First String Quartet. He probably had begun to think about writing a second symphony, and if so he would likely have seen the rejected slow movement of his First Symphony as a place to start. Like all four movements of his First String Quartet, it was based on themes paraphrased from hymn tunes, and he may have envisioned a symphony along similar lines. His resignation from his last church job broke his weekly connection to religious music and greatly reduced his compositional activity, so that whatever progress he may have made toward a new symphony must have ceased.

When his deepening relationship with Harmony renewed his interest in composition, he started by writing songs and instrumental pieces in one movement, but as his confidence grew he returned to the high level of ambition embodied in composing a symphony. At the same time, Harmony's desire to hear and share Ives's memories of his father, family, and home town apparently stimulated him to reengage with the music he associated with home: not only hymns but also Stephen Foster songs, fiddle tunes, patriotic songs, Civil War songs, and band music. Rather than write another symphony like his First, he saw a way to celebrate these kinds of music in the context of a symphony. According to his recollections, he turned back to ideas he had tried before in overtures on American topics, commemorating life and music "in these United States." What he took from these overtures we can only guess, since none of them survives, and some or most may have been no more than ideas for pieces rather than works committed to paper. But they must have contained the seed of the idea that flowers in the Second Symphony, which is ultimately *about* American music.

What's New in the Second Symphony

Comparing Ives's first two symphonies highlights other novel aspects of his Second.

In his First Symphony, Ives followed the traditional four-movement plan, with a fast first movement in sonata form, a slow movement, a scherzo, and a fast finale. For the Second Symphony, he dropped the scherzo and added a slower introductory movement before each fast movement, resulting in five movements:

First Symphony	*Second Symphony*
	1. Slow (introduction)
1. Fast sonata form	2. Fast sonata form
2. Slow movement	3. Slow movement
3. Scherzo	
	4. Slow (introduction)
4. Fast finale	5. Fast finale

Numerous symphonies from Haydn through Dvořák's *New World* and Tchaikovsky's *Pathétique* begin with a slow introduction to the first movement, and a few have a slow introduction to the finale. Some, like Brahms's Symphony No. 1 in C Minor, have both. Ives is unusual in numbering these introductions as separate movements, but he follows tradition—and makes their introductory function clear—by linking each of them directly to the following fast movement, without pause. Indeed, he originally planned his last two movements as a single movement modeled on the finale of Brahms's First Symphony. Ives's fifth movement features the same unusual form Brahms used for the fast portion of his finale, and Ives alludes to Brahms's symphony at several points in his own to signal the relationship to his model.

Like Ives's First Symphony, his Second is cyclic, with thematic ideas from earlier movements returning in later ones, and passages from every previous movement show up in the finale. What is more unusual is that the two introductory movements are both based on the same material, so that the fourth movement is a shortened and intensified reprise of the first.

Both symphonies are unified by their key schemes, but again the Second is more elaborate. In Ives's First Symphony, the contrast in the first movement between D minor and F major—two keys a minor third apart—returns in the two middle movements and is resolved in the finale in favor of D major. In the Second Symphony, the idea of keys a minor third apart expands to encompass four keys: B, D, F, and A-flat. Ives contrasts B minor and D major in the first and fourth movements, and F major and A-flat major in the other three, ending the symphony in F.

The cyclic repetition of material and the unifying key structure make clear that he conceived of the Second Symphony as a whole, as fully integrated a symphonic statement as his First Symphony. Whatever Ives may have drawn from the overtures and other earlier pieces he mentions must have been reworked to fit that overall scheme.

It seems evident that in his Second Symphony Ives was trying to outdo himself, writing a symphony that surpasses his First while standing in the same tradition. The pattern of movements, the cyclic thematic structure, and the key scheme are all more complex in the Second Symphony than in the First, while still building on past precedents. As in the First Symphony, themes—whether from the same movement or different ones—often appear in counterpoint with each other, showing that Ives designed them to fit together and conceived them in relation to each other; this is another sign that he imagined the Second Symphony from the start as a unified totality. He was still trying to compete with the major figures of symphonic music—now adding Brahms to the mix as the most important model for the Second Symphony—but was also seeking a more individual voice than he had achieved in his First Symphony.

He created that individual personality by extending the idea at the heart of his First String Quartet, of blending a classical genre and classical forms with the vernacular music of the United States. All the themes in the First Quartet were paraphrased from hymns, and the first movement borrowed an episode from a Bach fugue. In a similar way, all the themes and several countermelodies in the Second Symphony are paraphrased from American songs, hymns, or fiddle tunes, while at least one transition in each movement is based on a transitional passage from Bach, Brahms, or Wagner. The result is steeped in tradition—indeed, three traditions, the European symphony, Protestant hymnody, and American popular music—and yet like nothing ever heard before in combining all three so completely and overtly.

Like the First Quartet, the Second Symphony is musically coherent without recognizing any of the sources from which Ives drew. He reshaped each borrowed element into material that makes sense in its context, proceeding logically from what precedes it and leading elegantly to what follows. Even the contrasts between American vernacular styles and the European framework in which they appear can be readily heard without knowing the source tunes; the style of a hymn is quite different from that of a patriotic song, a fiddle tune, or a band march, and they all differ markedly from the style of a transition, a development section, or a rousing coda in a symphony. All of this makes it possible to enjoy the Second Symphony and derive meaning from it without knowing a single source it borrows from. As always, if you want to experience this music directly, listen to it now, before reading the explanations and interpretations offered here.

Yet, as for the First Quartet, recognizing the sources of the themes can make listening to the Second Symphony a more rewarding experience, making it possible to follow how Ives transforms his sources and integrates them with each other. Again, you can familiarize yourself with the tunes he uses by listening to them at the Charles Ives Society website (charlesives.org/borrowed-tunes), where the hymn tunes appear on the page for Hymns, other types of song under Songs, and the fiddle tunes under Instrumental Pieces.

A Delayed Debut

After completing the Second Symphony and having it copied around 1909–1910, Ives tried to get it performed. He sent the copyist's score to Walter Damrosch, who had sightread through most of the First Symphony with his New York Symphony Orchestra, but Damrosch never tried it out and did not return the score. Ives was more successful with Edgar Stowell, who played violin in Damrosch's orchestra and directed the orchestra at the Third Street Music Settlement School, a school for poor immigrant children. Ives recalled showing the first movement to Stowell, who liked it and conducted that movement in a school concert. Years later, in the late 1930s, Ives gave a photostat of his pencil score to Bernard Herrmann, staff conductor at CBS radio and a champion of Ives's music, but no performance resulted. In 1943, he tried to interest conductors Artur Rodzinski of the New York Philharmonic and Serge Koussevitzky of the Boston Symphony Orchestra in performing the symphony, to no avail. In 1949 Ives found his pencil score again in a pile of manuscripts and gave it to Henry Cowell. Cowell prepared a full score with the help of Lou Harrison, and it was published in 1951.[4]

On Thursday, February 22, 1951, more than four decades after Ives completed it, his Second Symphony was premiered at Carnegie Hall in New York by the New York Philharmonic led by Leonard Bernstein, a rising star even younger than Ives had been when he finished the symphony in his mid-thirties. The symphony was greeted with rapturous applause, and the concert was repeated each of the next three days. Harmony Ives attended the premiere along with their daughter and son-in-law and other family members, but Charles Ives did not. He was already famous, after the success of his *Concord Sonata* and Third Symphony and his Pulitzer Prize for the latter. He had told Cowell that "if his Second Symphony were ever performed in Carnegie Hall, he would go to hear it, for it was full of nostalgic references to music of the period when his father was still alive, and he thought he could enjoy listening to it." Yet having experienced negative reactions to his music for decades, he was apparently too nervous to go, and he pleaded ill health. Instead, he and his wife went over to their West Redding neighbors' house on Sunday afternoon ten days later to listen to the symphony when it was rebroadcast nationwide on the radio.[5]

What must it have been like for Ives to sit and listen to this piece he had finished more than forty years earlier, played by one of the nation's leading orchestras in the grand hall where he had attended concerts since he was a teenager? If you were the composer, what would have been going through your mind? Better than anyone, you would have heard the many references you made to other music, both to pieces you knew in Danbury and to the classical works you tucked into the symphony. And if the audience, so many decades later, missed most of these references, so what? They would at least catch the way the piece evokes familiar American styles—of Stephen Foster songs, fiddle tunes, hymns, marches, and patriotic songs—and makes them at home in a symphony, the most prestigious genre in European musical culture.

That is what this symphony is about: making a place for American music in the European classical tradition.

First Movement

The first movement opens quietly in B minor, with a gracefully curving melody in the cellos over a walking bass in the string basses. The violas take over the melody, then pass it on to the second violins as the first violins add a slower, gently descending line above it. The texture is like the counterpoint in a Baroque trio sonata, and the rising bass line and melody resemble the opening of the Prelude in B Minor from Book 1 of Bach's *Well-Tempered Clavier*. But the first violin line is a phrase from Stephen Foster's song *Massa's in de Cold Ground*, and the melody in the other instruments is paraphrased from that same Foster phrase, tracing similar contours while adding notes, changing the rhythm, and reordering events. Right from the beginning, elements from the European classical tradition and the American vernacular tradition are interweaving and interpenetrating, virtually inseparable.

The basses begin to syncopate their rhythm and the upper parts start to move more quickly, initiating a transition that builds on the figuration introduced in the opening theme. The use of strings alone throughout the first theme and transition evokes the sound of a Baroque string orchestra spinning out the initial ideas. After swelling to a climax, the transition leads to a new key of A major, where the violins introduce a sparkling second theme. The style changes from rich, continous counterpoint to country fiddling at a barn dance, as playful bits of melody ricochet between instruments in the string section. True to its sound, this theme is based on the opening phrase of a traditional American fiddle tune, *Pig Town Fling*.

As the second theme is varied and changes key, a brief, elegantly arching melody appears in the cellos and basses, reinforced by bassoons—the first wind instruments heard so far. This lyrical phrase is part of the final movement's second theme, a foreshadowing of what is to come. The texture of strings alone returns and leads back to the opening theme, now in F-sharp minor, a fifth above its original key. A sprightly idea in the violins—a repeated motive of a skip down, a leap up, and a repeated note, played higher each time—suggests something new, but leads instead to the transition that followed the opening theme at its first appearance. This sprightly idea also foreshadows a theme to come, one that will appear in the middle of the third movement and return in the finale. The transition steers us to the second theme in the new key of D major, a fifth below its initial statement, balancing the rise of a fifth in the key for the first theme. While the second theme begins in the violins, another family of orchestral instruments—the brass—is heard for the first time, as the horns join in with a ponderous tune in a low register. This is the first phrase of the patriotic song *Columbia, the Gem of the Ocean,* and it again anticipates events in the finale.

The interweaving of American and European traditions begun in the opening theme continues in the rest of the movement. Figures from the second theme develop into an intense transitional passage, as a three-note motive incessantly repeats, rises through the chromatic scale, and builds to a peak. This passage, which emerges so naturally from the fiddle-tune figuration, is paraphrased from a transition in the finale of Brahms's Symphony No. 1 in C Minor. It culminates in a climactic return of the movement's first theme, back in the opening key of B minor but now in a higher register, played with full force by the entire string section. As a new transition begins, the pace accelerates and another three-note motive appears, tossed back and forth between the bass and a middle line in the counterpoint as it gradually crawls up the scale. This too is borrowed, from an episode in Bach's Three-Part Invention in F Minor for keyboard.

By echoing transitions and episodes from European masterworks in his transitional passages, Ives makes the point that European genres such as inventions and symphonies *have* transitions and episodes, which the American popular songs and fiddle tunes paraphrased in his themes do not. At the same time, developing a fiddle tune into a passage from a Brahms symphony, like creating a Bach-like theme from a Stephen Foster melody, shows how much the European classical and American popular traditions have in common. Throughout the symphony, Ives integrates the two traditions by highlighting both what they share and how they differ.

After one last climax, the movement relaxes into a charming coda, recalling the opening theme in violin, viola, and oboe solos, now reharmonized in D major. Rather than come to a close, the oboe jumps up to a note outside the key, then is joined by the other wind instruments as they begin the next movement, linking the first two movements together.

Second Movement

The second movement is in sonata form. The jaunty first theme in A-flat major is full of bouncy figures in dotted rhythms, so called from the way they are notated. The theme's main idea appears in the winds, repeats varied in the strings, then is developed and again varied, resulting in an AA'BA" form for the entire first theme. This theme is paraphrased from Henry Clay Work's 1864 song *Wake Nicodemus,* celebrating the liberation of enslaved African Americans during the Civil War. Without alterations, Work's song would be too repetitive to use as a theme, so Ives varies the rhythm and harmony and adds engaging twists to the melody. These changes introduce the variety and interest typical of a theme by Brahms, in which each new phrase varies and extends elements from the previous one in a continuing process of developing variation.[6] Yet the song's American character comes through in the paraphrase, which preserves its dotted rhythms, most striking motives, and AABA form.

The transition begins with a vigorous new theme over an active walking bass. Linked to the first theme through dotted rhythms and some similar melodic gestures, this melody repeats in a new key, then leads to new variants of the first theme. This transitional theme is also paraphrased from an American tune: the refrain of the gospel hymn *Bringing in the Sheaves* by George A. Minor. The harmony moves through several keys, then settles into F major as the rhythms become more even and flowing.

A pair of oboes introduces the serene and songlike second theme. Since the eighteenth century, solo wind instruments and the key of F major have been used for music of a pastoral character, like a pleasant and restful country scene, and the simple, shapely melody reinforces the bucolic mood. Following themes based on a Stephen Foster song, a fiddle tune, a Civil War song, and a gospel hymn, this theme is adapted from yet another type of popular music, the college song *Where, O Where Are the Verdant Freshmen?* (The answer? The freshmen, once green and inexperienced, have completed their first-year courses and are "Safe now in the sophomore class.") After the oboes state the tune with just a few alterations, the strings present a more distant paraphrase of it, replacing its repeated notes with gentle wavelike motion, and then two flutes repeat the tune. The ABA form of the second theme contrasts with the constant variation of material in the first theme, and the placid, pastoral mood seems worlds away from the bouncy first theme and transition.

As in the first movement of the First Symphony, the second theme leads without a break into a closing section where motives from the theme are juxtaposed with other motives in alternation and in counterpoint with each other. The exposition ends with a melody in the violin that descends chromatically and rises up again. This is another sly allusion to Brahms, a figure from the first movement of his Symphony No. 3 in F Major. (The repetition of the exposition, marked in the 1907–1909 pencil score of the Second Symphony, was omitted in the 1951 score and in most recordings.)

After repeating and varying the Brahms figure, the development section continues with a stately and majestic new theme in F major in the trombones, in counterpoint with the first theme in the violins, slowed to half its original speed. The new theme is stated in long notes like a solemn hymn, and indeed it alternates phrases from two hymn tunes by Lowell Mason, taking its first and third phrases from *Hamburg* ("When I survey the wondrous cross") and its second and fourth from *Naomi*. The last phrase of this composite hymn repeats three more times in the horns, alternating with its first phrase in the violins, played twice as fast and in soft, rapid pulsations. This long episode on F major is extraordinary for a development section, which normally moves rapidly through a number of keys.

Having begun with an allusion to Brahms, the development section culminates with another, borrowing a restless figure from the first movement of Brahms's Symphony No. 1 and spinning it out at length. Meanwhile a bass drum and a snare drum join in, for the first time in the symphony. They play a version of a drum pattern often used for marching, called *Street Beat*, growing louder as the music builds in intensity. The combination of Brahms with a marching band drum pattern, hymns by Lowell Mason, and a theme based on a Civil War song, all in the development of a symphony movement in sonata form, creates a thorough blending of elements from European classical and American vernacular music.

After such an extraordinary development section, the recapitulation is unusual as well. We hear the first theme, transition, and second theme, as we would expect, but something is amiss. Usually the recapitulation marks the point in a sonata form where the music returns to the home key and presents both the first and second themes in that key. This resolves the conflict set up in the exposition, where the two themes appeared in different keys. But in this movement, the entire recapitulation is in the "wrong" key: F major, the key of the *second* theme. We should be in A-flat major, the key of the first theme.

All is resolved in the coda. After a quick change of key, the second theme appears in A-flat major in the violins, in counterpoint with the trombones playing the first phrase of the new theme from the development. Both of these themes were introduced in F major, and now for the first time they appear in the movement's home key. Brief development of these ideas leads to the opening phrase of the movement's first theme in winds and strings, back in A-flat major, combined with the second theme in the horns in the same key. Now all the main themes have been restated in the home key of the movement. The culminating passage from the development returns, played twice as fast (though without the drums), and fragments of all three themes bring the movement to a brilliant conclusion.

Third Movement

The third movement is the symphony's slow movement, a moment of respite at the center. It begins in a restful, pastoral F major with a brief introduction of soft, slowly changing chords, like an awed silence. The sense of quiet contemplation continues with the movement's principal theme, a gently rocking melody in the strings that slowly meanders up to a pinnacle, then quickly falls to a close. Like themes from the First Symphony and First String Quartet, this one is paraphrased from the gospel song *Beulah Land,* adding a gesture from Samuel A. Ward's hymn tune *Materna* at the peak of the phrase. (The latter tune, originally sung to the hymn "O Mother dear, Jerusalem," had become familiar as the melody for *America the Beautiful* by the time of the Second Symphony's 1951 premiere.) There follows a contrasting episode that repeats and varies a descending figure, changing keys, building to a climax, and then ebbing away. Part of the opening theme returns in a solo cello, and a new conclusion draws the first section of the movement to a close.

Tucked into the music are hints of the classical tradition nestled among the hymns. At the climax of the contrasting episode, the strings twice rise to a peak in successive waves, and at the very end of the section a chromatic turning figure appears in the violins. Both are brief passages borrowed from the prelude to Richard Wagner's opera *Tristan und Isolde,* famous for its evocation of intense yearning, an emotion that strongly contrasts with the serenity of the hymnlike principal theme.[7] Here in the symphony's central movement it is Wagner who represents the European tradition, rather than Bach and Brahms, although the latter two will return in the next two movements.

A slightly faster tempo and a change of character mark the beginning of the movement's middle section. Horns, winds, and strings exchange bits of melody that coalesce into a lyrical theme. Like the movement's principal theme, this one threads together elements from two hymn tunes: the opening motive of Charles Zeuner's *Missionary Chant* ("Ye Christian heralds, go proclaim") and an abbreviated paraphrase of *Nettleton* ("Come, Thou Fount of ev'ry blessing"), the hymn tune that was paraphrased in a different way for the theme of the First String Quartet's slow movement. The music grows louder and slightly slower. Over constantly moving figuration in the strings drawn from the preceding material, the winds and brass present a theme based on melodies heard in the symphony's first movement: the phrase from Stephen Foster's song *Massa's in de Cold Ground,* sounding out in full harmony like a grandiose chorale, and the sprightly idea that followed that tune's second appearance. The strings repeat this theme more softly.

As they come to a close, the movement's first section returns, with its main ideas in reverse order: the intense contrasting episode first, followed by the gentle principal theme. A coda weaves together phrases from *Beulah Land* with fragments of *Missionary Chant* and *Materna,* linking the source tunes for the main themes of the first and middle sections of the movement.

Fourth Movement

After the quiet ending of the third movement in F major, the fourth begins with a shock: a return to the opening theme of the first movement, in the distant key of B minor. The theme's initial motive is played loudly in the horns, answered by a descending figure in the basses, then repeated in the horns and joined by a twisting countermelody in the violins and violas. The appearance of this motive in the horns over a descending bass parallels the very opening of the finale of Brahms's Symphony No. 1 in C Minor, the first of many references signaling to listeners that Brahms's finale was Ives's principal model for the last two movements of his symphony. The fourth movement continues as a varied and abbreviated reprise of the first movement. The transition, now scored for winds as well as strings, leads to the second theme in D major, combined with the first phrase of *Columbia, the Gem of the Ocean* as it was in the first movement. Once again the fiddle-tune figures of the second theme develop into the passage paraphrased from a transition in the finale of Brahms's First Symphony. The climactic return of the first theme in B minor in the strings, with the twisting countermelody added in the winds, is cut short, and the music starts to change keys rapidly. The climbing episode adapted from Bach's Three-Part Invention in F minor returns, followed by two more quick allusions to classical works: the twisting countermelody becomes a phrase from one of Brahms's *Vier ernste Gesänge* (Four Serious Songs), and that blends into another passage from the finale of Brahms's First Symphony, a figure that skips up and down as it climbs upwards above a sustained note in the bass. The music quiets and slows as a horn rocks between two notes, a dissonance waiting to resolve.

Fifth Movement

The fast finale in F major begins with a rush in the violins, launching a theme that constantly changes rhythm while emphasizing figures that alternate two notes a whole step apart. The horns break in with a rising arpeggio, and the strings respond with a descending chromatic figure that leads back around to the movement's opening phrase. The climbing episode from Bach's Three-Part Invention in F Minor pops up again, recalling the first and fourth movements. Drums, flutes, and piccolos interrupt with a march, sounding like a fife and drum corps with *Street Beat* in the drums.

The rising arpeggio returns, mixing with motives from the initial violin melody. Suddenly these melodic scraps coalesce into the chorus from Stephen Foster's *Camptown Races* ("Gwine to run all night! Gwine to run all day!"), played in the trombone with fragments in other instruments. From the beginning of the movement to this point, the whole first theme teases the listener with hints of that tune, verse and chorus, which only gradually emerges into recognizability. For the second time in the symphony, a theme has been revealed to be paraphrased from a Stephen Foster song, only this time the unveiling happens more gradually and the effect is more surprising and thrilling because the tune is one of Foster's most famous.

As the trombone plays *Camptown Races*, the violins join in with a coun-termelody in fiddle-tune style. Even for listeners familiar with the tune, it takes a moment to recognize this as *Turkey in the Straw*, because it first appears rhythmically displaced, the beats on the offbeats and vice versa. Throughout the finale's first theme, the music plays like this with levels of recognition, hinting at something that sounds vaguely familiar and then becomes more recognizable over time.

A brief transition tosses around fragments of the first theme and rapidly changes keys. As the music quiets, slows, and settles into the key of A-flat major, the violins take up motives from the fiddle tune *Pig Town Fling*, heard in the second theme of the first and fourth movements, and combine them with bits of *Turkey in the Straw*. This blend of two fiddle tunes continues as a countermelody to the second theme in the horn, a noble, soaring melody foreshadowed in the first movement. It has the character of a slow Stephen Foster song, in the mold of *Old Black Joe*, and its middle section is partly based on the phrase from *Massa's in de Cold Ground* used in the first and third movements. (Ives described this theme as "suggesting a Steve Foster tune, while over it the old farmers fiddled a barn dance with all of its jigs, gallops, and reels.")[8] Like the second movement's second theme, this is in the songlike form of ABA. After the first part of the theme repeats, the music grows louder and more active as both parts of the theme are developed.

Soon we return to the opening tempo, theme, and key of F major. The fi-nale appears to be a movement in sonata form, this being the repetition of the exposition before the development begins. But clues begin to emerge that this is not a simple repetition, as some minor cuts and changes in orchestration have been made to the first theme. Perhaps this is the recapitulation, having skipped the development, as in the sonata form without development in the First Symphony finale.

Yet after the first theme concludes and the transition begins, it suddenly cuts off, replaced by what sounds like a real development with all the usual hallmarks: frequent changes of key, a rapid kaleidoscope of events, and frag-mentation and juxtaposition of material from the exposition. It starts with a quiet bustling in the violins, which shares the character of the quickly moving first theme and fiddle-tune countermelodies but turns out to be an episode from another Bach keyboard piece, the Fugue in E Minor from Book 1 of *The Well-Tempered Clavier*. Material from the fugue intermixes with elements from the first theme, and they fuse together when an arpeggiated motive in Bach's fugue is transformed into the rising opening figure from the chorus of *Camptown Races*. Such mixing of high and low culture—fugue and minstrel song—evokes the range of music Ives played on the organ as a teenager, from Bach fugues to his own *Holiday Quickstep*.

Into the mix comes the first phrase of *Columbia, the Gem of the Ocean* in the brass, joined in the violins by the countermelody based on *Pig Town Fling*, recalling the similar combination of tunes in the first and fourth movements. The Bach fugue episode returns, the two main themes of the second movement make a cameo appearance at twice the speed and in counterpoint with each other, more motives pile in as the music grows more agitated—and then suddenly everything stops. After a brief pause, the countermelody based on *Pig Town Fling* and *Turkey in the Straw* gently leads back to the majestic second theme, now in F major and played by a solo cello. The movement is sort of a sonata form after all, but with the development pushed back to come between the recapitulation of the first theme and that of the second theme in the home key—exactly the form of Brahms's First Symphony finale, showing that in his Second Symphony Ives was still drawing directly on European models, as he had in his First.

This time the extension after the second theme leads not to the first theme but to a long, spectacular coda filled with reminiscences of earlier movements and new developments and combinations. Up first is the episode from the middle of the third movement based on *Massa's in de Cold Ground*, highlighting its melodic relationship to the finale's second theme. Next, part of the second movement's first theme appears in trumpet and winds, in combination with itself twice as fast in the violins. Fragments of the finale's first theme and of *Columbia, the Gem of the Ocean* lead to the passage that ended the fourth movement, adapted from the finale of Brahms's First Symphony and now in a similar position as in that movement.

As the orchestra swells, the trumpet sounds out the bugle call *Reveille*, and then everything comes together in a climax of themes in counterpoint: the complete verse of *Columbia, the Gem of the Ocean* in the trombones; the opening idea of the second movement's first theme in the trumpet; the finale's first theme in the strings; and the fiddle-tune countermelody to the finale's second theme in the winds. A few final chords and fragments of themes, with a bit of *Columbia* in the trombones and *Reveille* in the trumpet, and the symphony crashes to a close.

Reception

What was Ives's reaction to hearing his symphony on the radio? His neighbor Luemily Ryder recalled the moment:

> Mr. Ives sat in the front room and listened as quietly as could be, and I sat way behind him, because I didn't want him to think I was looking at him.

After it was over, I'm sure he was very much moved. He stood up, walked over to the fireplace, and spat! And then he walked out into the kitchen. Not a word. And he never said anything about it. I think he was pleased, but he was silent. I was thrilled to think that he came here to hear it. It was my privilege. He was pleased to have the Pulitzer Prize [awarded to the Third Symphony in 1947] and to be elected to the National Institute of Arts and Letters [in 1945], and yet he didn't brag about it. Speaking of it, you had to drag it out of him.[9]

Ives's modesty in front of his neighbors is characteristic, as is the New England manner of not speaking out loud about one's deepest emotions.

Harmony Ives summarized his feelings, and hers, in a letter to Leonard Bernstein on March 11:

Dear Mr. Bernstein:
It was a wonderful and thrilling experience to hear Mr. Ives['s] 2nd Symphony as you conducted it on February 22nd. I have been familiar with it—in snatches—for forty years and more and to hear the whole performed at last was a big event in my life. People did like it, didn't they? Someone wrote in the New Yorker recently of Mr. Ives['s] music that its hearers are participants in it.

Mr. Ives has had many letters and he wants me to say to you that "the enthusiasm with which it was received was due so much to your devoted interpretation and wonderful conducting." Mr. Richard Bales, conductor of the orchestra at the National Gallery of Art in Washington [who would premiere the First Symphony two years later], wrote that he "just wanted to yell when he wasn't on the verge of tears."

Mr. Ives heard the broadcast tho' he does not hear well over the radio and it took him back so to his father and his youth that he had tears in his eyes. You will be interested to know that his comment on the allegro [fast] movements was "too slow"—otherwise he was satisfied.

He thanks you from the bottom of his heart for getting this symphony played and for your skillful and artistic and masterly conducting.

I am so glad I had the pleasure of meeting you. . . .

With all our good wishes

Sincerely yours

Harmony T. Ives[10]

Her question, posed partly on her husband's behalf—"People did like it, didn't they?"—speaks volumes about the negative comments his music had received over the previous forty years, in public and in private, and suggests how moved she and he were at the positive reception. Her remark that "it took him back so to his father and his youth" testifies to the emotional importance of the tunes and types of music he had woven into the piece, and the connection he felt they established with his father's music-making in Danbury, and no doubt with his own. And his observation that the fast movements were "too slow" hints at other objections he may have had to the performance: among them, that Bernstein made some cuts (for example, omitting the passage based on the Bach invention from the first movement, which weakened the links between movements) and held the last chord too long.

Shortly before the work's performance and publication, Ives altered the ending, which in the 1909 score resembled that of the First Symphony, by adding *Reveille* and changing the final chord from a sustained F major chord to a very short accented cluster with eleven of the twelve notes of the chromatic scale. According to Henry Cowell, Ives told him that a dissonant chord like that "was the formula for signifying the very end of the last dance of all: the players played any old note, good and loud, for the last chord. It was the common practice in the days of the Danbury Band conducted by Ives's father."[11] Played short and loud, as Ives wrote it, it produces the right effect. By holding this dissonant chord out for a couple of seconds, Bernstein turned it into a raspberry, completely out of character with the rest of the symphony. Maybe that is why Ives spat into the fireplace.

Ives's nephew Bigelow Ives also heard the broadcast at his home in Danbury. He wrote his aunt and uncle on March 10 to report on the reactions there, which testify to the town's pride in their native son and to the piece's accessibility and broad appeal.

> The broadcast was heard here in Danbury under the best conditions—it came in so well over our set that we found it remarkably comparable to a seat at Carnegie. Immediately after its conclusion the phone started ringing and we were kept busy listening to the exuberant expressions of appreciation from a host of friends and strangers alike. I felt a deep pride in our old home town—that it could still be roused to an awareness of its great Yankee heritage. One fellow told me that his whole family—grandparents, parents, and children—gathered around the radio which was placed on the kitchen table. Sunday dinner had been swept aside. The older men had just returned from church (Congregational) where they had been singing in the choir. Before the symphony was half way through—Grandfather had jumped to his feet to pound his fists on the table and shout with joy, "By god, that's the kind of music I always knew there was in America—but I've never heard it before!" Everyone who called us said about the same thing in substance. So as long as Uncle Charley's music is played the spirit of New England will continue to live and maintain real vitality.[12]

The reviews were glowing. Olin Downes in the *New York Times* praised "the composer's originality[,] . . . complete conviction in his art, and audacity in expressing himself," and wondered what impression the symphony "would have made if it had been heard when it was completed at the beginning of the century." Virgil Thomson wrote in the *New York Herald Tribune* that "orchestrally, harmonically and melodically the symphony is both noble and plain. It speaks of American life with love and humor and deep faith. It is unquestionably an authentic work of art, both as structure and as composition." Robert Sabin in *Musical America* described it as "a wholesome and natural expression of American life before the world wars and the triumph of the machine age."[13]

A SYNTHESIS OF TRADITIONS

These reviews reflect back to Ives the affection with which he composed the piece: affection for the tunes and types of music he had learned in Danbury and associated with his father, and affection and admiration as well for the European tradition, from the keyboard music of Bach to the operas of Wagner and the symphonies of Brahms. He had learned the symphonic tradition while studying with Parker and writing his First Symphony, but he had also played transcriptions of symphony movements by Dvořák, Brahms, and others on the organ, and he recognized a religious element in them.[14] Wagner had been one of his father's favorite composers. The intertwining of Bach with Stephen Foster in the first and last movements reflects Ives's own experiences with music as a boy, as he recalled in a 1930 letter:

> [My father] had a belief that everyone was born with at least one germ of musical talent, and that an early application of great music (and not trivial music) would help it grow. He started all the children of the family—and most of the children of the town for that matter—on Bach and Stephen Foster (quite shortly after they were born—always regardless of whether [they] had, would have, or wouldn't have any musical gifts or sense, etc.). He put a love of music into the heart of many a boy who might have gone without it but for him.[15]

That love of music, encompassing Bach and Foster as part of a complete experience, never left Ives. He played preludes and fugues from Bach's *Well-Tempered Clavier* at the piano almost every day, and he used Foster's *Massa's in de Cold Ground* in over a dozen other pieces composed over two decades, so much so that he could use it as a symbol for his own presence in some of the events he depicted.

Ives's affection for Foster can be hard to understand today—not because of the melodies, which are world-famous and beautiful, but because of the texts and other associations. Many of Foster's songs are linked to the offensive practice of blackface minstrelsy, in which white performers smeared their faces with burnt cork and impersonated African Americans in ways that reinforced stereotypes of blacks as inferior to whites. Excoriated by Frederick Douglass and other abolitionists, minstrel shows were already seen as racist in the nineteenth century, but they were among the most popular forms of entertainment in the United States and Europe from the 1840s through the 1950s and beyond; George Ives performed with touring minstrel groups, Yale clubs put on minstrel shows in Ives's day, and *The Black and White Minstrel Show* played on British television from 1958 through 1978.[16] Foster wrote *Camptown Races* (1850) and *Massa's in de Cold Ground* (1852) for the Christy Minstrels, one of the most prominent minstrel groups, and both songs use dialect that supposedly reflected the way African Americans spoke. *Massa's in de Cold Ground* even depicts enslaved people mourning the death of the person who kept them in bondage. The melody Ives uses in the Second Symphony is the first half of the chorus, whose whole text is this:

> Down in de cornfield
> Hear dat mournful sound:
> All de darkeys am a weeping,
> Massa's in de cold, cold ground.

They might have reason to weep if the next master was more cruel, yet the implied message that enslaved African Americans felt affection for their oppressors ("Massa made de darkeys love him, / Cayse he was so kind") was more comforting to white audiences than it was close to the truth.

Despite this history, Ives clearly did not consider Foster's songs racist. Ives supported the rights of African Americans, in line with family tradition. Ives's grandfather and grandmother were abolitionists before the Civil War, his father served in the Union Army, and Ives himself celebrated abolitionists in his music and was committed to racial equality in his writings and in his business.[17] *Wake Nicodemus*, the source for the first theme of the symphony's second movement, was an abolitionist song, celebrating "the great Jubilee," the emancipation of enslaved African Americans, and calling one of them "the salt of the earth." It is unthinkable that Ives would have set this song next to Foster's if he had regarded the latter as carrying racist messages. Indeed, when he wrote about the symphony to Rodzinski and Koussevitzky in 1943, he described the second theme of the finale as expressing "Stephen Foster's sadness for the 'Slaves.'"[18]

Most of Foster's songs were parlor songs, like *Jeanie with the Light Brown Hair* (1853), with no connection to minstrelsy. Foster stopped using dialect by 1853 and quit writing songs for minstrel shows the next year. *Old Black Joe* (1860) is not in dialect, and it presents its African American subject with great empathy; indeed, except for their use of dialect, Foster's minstrel songs depict African Americans sympathetically, as the subjects of their own stories. Foster's songs were the most widely sung body of popular songs by one composer in the United States throughout the nineteenth century and beyond, unchallenged until the era of Irving Berlin and George Gershwin in the 1920s. They were part of Ives's heritage, known to almost all Americans. It would never have occurred to him to reject them as racist.

And Ives was not alone in seeing Foster's songs as great American music that could be used in a symphony. Dvořák proclaimed in 1895 that composers in the United States should turn to "Negro melodies" as "inspiration for truly national music," saying that "the so-called plantation songs are indeed the most striking and appealing melodies that have yet been found on this side of the water, [and] this seems to be recognized, though often unconsciously, by most Americans." By "Negro melodies," Dvořák meant both authentic African American spirituals, several of which he learned from an African American student of his, and the "plantation songs" of Stephen Foster—songs that included *Old Black Joe* and *Massa's in de Cold Ground*. Dvořák loved Foster's minstrel songs, considered them an offshoot of African American music, and arranged *Old Folks at Home* for chorus and orchestra and conducted it at Madison Square Garden in New York. For Ives, these Stephen Foster tunes represented African Americans and their struggle for freedom and equality, embodied in the first movement of *Three Places in New England*, just as the Irish tunes he used in *Washington's Birthday* and *The Fourth of July* signified the inclusion of Irish immigrants and their descendants in Danbury and in its holiday celebrations.[19]

The Second Symphony presents a broad panorama of musical life in the United States. Foster's songs, dance tunes, an abolitionist song, gospel hymns, a college song, traditional hymns, a marching band drum pattern, and a patriotic song—plus Bach keyboard pieces, Brahms symphonies, and a Wagner opera excerpt, all staples for American piano students and orchestras—all show up in the symphony, representing the people and activities associated with each type of music.

The specific tunes may no longer be recognized, and some have changed their associations; *Materna* now inevitably sounds like *America the Beautiful*, and part of *Missionary Chant* coincidentally resembles the opening motive of Beethoven's Fifth Symphony (a resemblance Ives puns on in his *Concord Sonata*, but not in this symphony). Yet it does not matter if people do not know the tunes, or if they hear references that Ives did not intend. The charm of the Second Symphony is that the themes all sound American in some way, reflecting the diverse music and people of the United States, and are presented in a European frame, with classic forms, dramatic transitions, and intricate counterpoint that mark this piece as coming from the European art music tradition. If we recognize the specific sources he is reworking, we can follow Ives's mind through the labyrinth of transformation and integration that made this piece happen. But anyone who has heard music before can hear the styles change and the melodies morph into new ones. The interpenetration of diverse musical sources, and the fascinating play with familiar material that is constantly being made new, make the Second Symphony one of Ives's best and most widely appealing pieces.

The integration of European and American music is complete in this symphony. Yet ultimately Europe dominates. Except for *Columbia, the Gem of the Ocean*, foreshadowed from the first movement and finally unfurled at the end of the finale, the American tunes have all been smoothed out to fit into their new symphonic home. In Gayle Sherwood Magee's words, "Ives dresses them up in a new suit, combs their hair, and restricts their behavior to match the profile of a bona fide symphonic identity."[20] His next step was to figure out a way to put American tunes into the context of art music without compromising their identity.

What he needed was a new form.

· 7 ·

A New Form

*I*n their first years of marriage, Charles and Harmony Ives established new routines, endured personal tragedies, and welcomed their daughter Edith into their family. Encouraged by Harmony, Ives composed often in the evenings, on weekends, and especially during vacations, making the decade between 1908 and 1918 his most prolific. Increasingly he explored ways to bring together the American popular music and hymns he loved with the genres and procedures of European art music. One of his key innovations was a new form that he would use more than twenty times, from symphonies and sonatas to tone poems and songs.

In his First String Quartet and Second Symphony, Ives paraphrased American tunes, reshaping them to work as themes in European forms like sonata form and ternary form. In his Third Symphony and four sonatas for violin and piano, Ives turns the tables, adapting the procedures of European music but reshaping its forms to place American melodies at the center of the listener's experience. Instead of beginning with the main theme and varying or developing it, as in the standard forms of classical music, he begins with fragments and variants of the theme and gradually develops them into a complete statement near the end of a movement—a cumulative form that draws on European techniques but allows Ives to use American melodies as themes without having to rework them to fit standard European forms. By mulling over their most beautiful moments and gradually piecing them together, Ives invests great meaning in these tunes and helps us hear them in entirely new ways. In these pieces, for the first time, music recognizable as American participates as an equal in the international tradition of classical music.

A NEW LIFE

After their wedding and honeymoon in June 1908, the Iveses settled into their first home together, an apartment in lower Manhattan at 70 West 11th Street near Sixth Avenue, where they stayed for three years. They moved in on June 25. Harmony recorded in their joint diary that evening was their "first night at home" and June 30 was their "First meal at our own table—breakfast," the start of "a Vita Nuova"—a new life. Half a year later she wrote on January 1 that it was the first New Year's Day "in our married life & our home. A very happy one." At some point in their first months of marriage, she became pregnant with their first child. As Stuart Feder writes, "Both were poised for it, Harmony eagerly and fervently, Ives quietly, deeply."[1] His brother Moss, who had married in 1900, already had four boys (soon to be followed by a fifth boy and a girl); Ives loved them and enjoyed their visits, but he was ready for his own.

But that spring, less than a year after their wedding, the Iveses suffered a grievous loss. Harmony was taken to the hospital on April 20, 1909, because of a difficulty with the pregnancy (perhaps a miscarriage, ectopic pregnancy, stillbirth, or late-term loss) that may have threatened her life. She was given an emergency hysterectomy. Thus ended their hopes of having children of their own, of bringing new life into the world. She remained hospitalized until May 15, while her sister Sally came and helped with care and housekeeping.[2]

The ordeal seems to have brought the Iveses even closer together. Harmony's mother wrote on May 10,

> My heart is full of joy and gratitude over you, over Sally, and I must say over dear Charley with his great loving heart. I thought myself so happy in my trust in him, but now, after the revelations of tenderness in him through the great trial that has come to you, I feel that I did not half appreciate what was in him. With him to protect you, life cannot bring you any thing you cannot bear—and still have in your heart abiding happiness.[3]

A year and a day after Harmony's hospitalization, her "Uncle Mark" Twain passed away. Three days later her mother died suddenly in the night after attending Twain's funeral. Once again, shared grief intensified the bond between Harmony and Charles Ives.

During the next decade, they moved frequently, living in six different residences in Manhattan and two homes in suburban Hartsdale, twenty miles north of New York City and a convenient commute by train to the Ives & Myrick office in downtown Manhattan. For their first few years of marriage they continued to take vacations in the Adirondacks in the late summer or early fall. In August 1912, they purchased almost fifteen acres of land, half

Figure 7.1. Charles and Harmony Ives outside their West Redding house in the 1920s.

MSS 14, The Charles Ives Papers in the Music Library of Yale University, Series VI, Item 130.

in meadow and half in woods, on Umpawaug Road in West Redding, Connecticut, about eight miles from Ives's childhood home in Danbury. Over the next few months, they had a summer house and barn built plus a small cottage near the road. Figure 7.1 shows them outside their West Redding house in the late 1920s. Each year from 1913 on they lived there from late spring through early fall, a rural retreat from the cityscape of New York, with Ives commuting by train. In the six colder months of the year they lived in the city, changing their residence almost every year until 1917, when they began a nine-year stay in a rented house at 120 East 22nd Street. In 1926 the Iveses moved uptown to their last New York address, buying a four-story townhouse at 164 East 74th Street, three blocks east of Central Park between Lexington and Third Avenue, where Ives's music room was on the top floor.[4]

By then they had a daughter. In July and August 1915, while at their summer place in West Redding, the Iveses opened the little cottage on their property to families from poor neighborhoods in New York spending time in the country through the Fresh Air Fund. The second family to visit was Mrs. Charles Osborne, Jr., with five of her children, including fourteen-month-old Edith (known as Edie). When the Osbornes returned to New York in mid-August, Edie was apparently too sick to go home and stayed with the Iveses. They doted on her, as is clear from the picture of her with Harmony in Figure 7.2. She met their need to be parents, and by the end of the year they both felt what Harmony wrote in a letter: "I feel as if I *couldn't* let her go from us. . . . She is a love." It is unclear what arrangements were made, but they found a way to keep her, adopting her legally on October 18, 1916, and continuing to give money to the family for years. Jan Swafford captures Edith's importance to the Iveses perfectly: "She was the angel of the house and played the role instinctively." When she was fifteen, Ives wrote to John Griggs, "No child has ever given her family more than she has us." A dozen years later, she wrote

Figure 7.2.   Harmony and Edith Ives around 1915.
MSS 14, The Charles Ives Papers in the Music Library of Yale University, Series VI, Item 108.

him on his birthday to say "you are, and ever have been, the dearest, sweetest father a girl could ever have."[5]

Amid all their moves, wherever they were, Ives seems to have been almost constantly writing music when he was not at work downtown. He and Harmony sometimes went to concerts or hosted friends, but most of their time at home was spent alone together, reading and conversing, as she had imagined their life together, or with him playing, improvising, or composing at the piano. An acquaintance who knew them in the 1940s related that

> Mrs. Ives told me about earlier times when Mr. Ives would come home from a strenuous day in the insurance business, have his meal, and then go to the piano and forget all about time until the wee hours. He would be completely absorbed in his music. And she told me about how their little girl had learned to adjust. He couldn't take any interruptions because he was listening to what was inside him. He'd play, and the little girl was allowed to sit there underneath the piano and play with her dolls, but she must not make a sound.[6]

Ives typically began composing a new piece by trying things out at the piano or writing down initial ideas, such as working out a theme or fitting a countermelody to it. Most often he notated his sketches on two staves, as for piano: sometimes just a melody, or melody and bass line, other times several parts in counterpoint. Some passages he sketched repeatedly, trying alternatives, each one just below the previous one on the same page, drawing lines to show what follows what, until it seemed right. He usually worked on a piece in chunks, then put the segments together in a continuous draft of a section or movement. For an orchestral work, next would come a score-sketch as he assigned parts to particular instruments or groups, strings on two staves and woodwinds and brass on two or three staves above the strings. A full pencil score would follow, with each instrumental part on a separate staff. Ives would then prepare an ink score or send out his score to be copied in ink by a professional copyist. Often, each version of the score would get annotated with further revisions, replacing, deleting, or adding notes or passages.[7] Since Ives had time to compose only evenings, weekends, and vacations, and worked on many pieces simultaneously, it could take years for a piece to progress from initial sketch to final fair copy. In many cases it appears from the surviving manuscripts that Ives had already worked out ideas by memory at the piano before committing anything to paper, so that we often cannot trace the earliest versions of a piece or passage.

Among the pieces Ives worked on in the decade after his marriage are the Third Symphony and the four violin sonatas, compositions that take a new approach to the problem of how to integrate American hymn tunes with the sounds and procedures of the European classical tradition.

SYMPHONY NO. 3: *THE CAMP MEETING*

After the grand statements of his First and Second Symphonies, Ives's Symphony No. 3 seems modest by comparison. Gone are the references to European symphonies and any sense of a young composer competing with his elders and elbowing his way into the concert repertoire. Instead of four or five movements, there are only three, and each begins and ends quietly. The first and last movements are slow and majestic, the middle one fast, the opposite of what one expects. The orchestra is smaller: only one each of the wind instruments (flute, oboe, clarinet, and bassoon) instead of the usual pairs; just two horns (instead of four) and one trombone (instead of three) for the brass, with no trumpets or tuba; and no percussion but for a touch of bells at the end. The material is less extroverted, with few of the bouncy themes and loud climaxes scattered throughout the previous two symphonies. The quiet sense of inner contemplation makes this symphony seem more personal, more deeply felt.

In essence, the Third Symphony is a meditation on a small number of hymn tunes Ives identified with the outdoor revivals around Danbury that he had attended as a boy and played for as a teenage organist. Although there is no program, no series of events like those he had represented in *Yale-Princeton Football Game* or *Central Park in the Dark*, he sought to capture the spirit and character of those outdoor meetings and to suggest the feelings of the participants. As a clue to his intentions, he subtitled the symphony *The Camp Meeting* and titled the movements *Old Folks Gatherin'*, *Children's Day*, and *Communion*. The sense of gathering and of joining in communion suggested by the titles of the outer movements is embodied in the new form they share.

Ives recalled that he completed the symphony in 1911 and adapted its three movements from an organ prelude, postlude, and piece for communion that he played for services at Central Presbyterian Church in 1901–1902. Like most of Ives's organ music, these pieces are lost or—more likely—were improvised or worked out by memory and never written down. They must have been quite different from the symphony movements as we know them, since the sketches for all three movements are on music paper not available before 1907 and in Ives's handwriting from around 1908–1911, and they show Ives inventing several themes and drafting most of each movement from scratch, which he would not have had to do if he were writing down music he had played years before. Like the First String Quartet, this is concert music *about* hymn tunes, not an arrangement of music conceived for church services.[8]

Despite the smaller scoring and shorter duration, the Third Symphony is still clearly in the symphonic tradition, using procedures familiar from the first two symphonies: tonal harmony, with B-flat major as the main key of the outer movements and the closely related E-flat major for the middle movement; themes that are presented, varied, fragmented, and developed; ternary form for the middle movement; two contrasting themes in each outer movement; the combination of themes in counterpoint; and cyclic unification of all three movements through shared motives and themes. Ives's musical language throughout is similar to that of his prior symphonies: tonal, with a few chords spiced with added dissonance and some surprising moves from one chord to the next, tendencies that are more pronounced in the third movement. (In some performances, you will hear "shadow parts"—soft dissonant melodies in solo instruments that cloud the harmony—which Ives added years later, then crossed out, and are sometimes played at the discretion of the conductor.)[9]

Cumulative Form and How to Listen to It

What is new in the Third Symphony is the structure of the first and last movements. Instead of presenting the main theme at the outset as in a sonata or ternary form, Ives gives us hints, fragments, and variants, providing more as the movement unfolds, and finally states the theme in full, for the first and only time, near the end. This process, of developing material that gradually accumulates until it comes together into the complete theme, gives the form of these movements its name: *cumulative form*. In addition to the main theme, there is in both movements a countermelody, which undergoes a similar cumulative process and then appears in counterpoint with the full statement of the main theme.[10]

Adopting this form allowed Ives to use as the main theme of his first and last movements a hymn tune, as it is, unaltered. For the First String Quartet and Second Symphony, Ives reshaped hymn tunes into themes suitable for classical forms, because if he left them in their original shape they would be too repetitive in rhythm, too foursquare in their phrasing, too plain and unvaried in melody and harmony, and too complete in themselves to make good themes. But the features of a hymn tune that would be faults in an opening theme are perfect for the conclusion of a movement, where you *want* there to be no more problems to solve, no more variations or rhythmic jolts or hidden potentials that call for further discussion and resolution. The modernist composer Arnold Schoenberg, Ives's exact contemporary, complained about composers who attempted to use folk and popular songs as themes for symphonic works, writing that "there never remains in popular tunes an unsolved problem, the consequences of which will show up only later. . . . There is nothing in them that asks for expansion."[11] Ives resolves this dilemma. By developing his hymn tune themes *before* presenting them whole, Ives makes them into the solution of the problem posed by the fragments and variants we hear from the beginning. These movements feature the continuous development of ideas that Ives had learned from Brahms, only in reverse; as he would later write about another movement in cumulative form, the finale of his Third Violin Sonata, "the working-out develops into the themes, rather than from them."[12]

The form works whether we know the hymn or not, but it can be especially affecting for someone who recognizes the tune, since the process of gradual revelation can give the melody new depth and suggest new meanings. This also solves another problem, one of reception. A hymn tune is in a very different category from a symphony, at home in a different place and with different people. Those who attended symphony concerts in the 1910s would likely have looked down their noses at hymns, particularly those associated with revivals and camp meetings, and starting a movement with a tune like that could get your piece laughed off the stage. But if the motives that make up the hymn's melody are hinted at first, introduced gradually, and developed in the manner of a symphony or sonata, they become interesting in their own right, and we are drawn in, wondering what will happen next. When it turns out that this profound and fascinating process of musical development culminates in a simple American hymn tune, the hierarchy of musical values is turned on its head; the developmental procedures familiar from Beethoven and Brahms symphonies lead to a commonplace bit of American music, ennobling what might otherwise have been beneath notice. Instead of dressing up his American tunes, combing their hair, and making them behave according to the norms of art music, as in the Second Symphony, in his Third Symphony Ives uses the techniques of European music to lead us step by step to the American hymns and then presents them just as they are.

Thus a hymn tune, unaltered, can serve as a main theme for a movement in cumulative form. The countermelody, on the other hand, has to fit in good counterpoint with the theme. In the Third Symphony, the countermelodies are themselves adapted from hymn tunes, which must be paraphrased and reshaped to fit well with the tunes they accompany. In this way, the art of paraphrase, a craft Ives mastered in creating the themes for his First String Quartet and Second Symphony, is still present.

As in those earlier works, Ives often plays with his listeners, making his source tunes now more and now less recognizable for those who know them, often keeping recognition just out of reach until the *aha!* moment when all is revealed. For those who want to play along, the tunes can be heard on the Charles Ives Society website (charlesives.org/borrowed-tunes/hymns).

Yet there is another way to listen to this symphony (and to the violin sonatas later in this chapter), one that is easier to do when you do not know the source tunes at all. All movements in cumulative form are based on themes: a main theme and often (though not always) a countermelody or subsidiary theme. Like other forms based on themes—such as sonata form, ternary form, or variations—cumulative form can be understood without knowing the themes before you listen, because the piece itself presents them. What makes cumulative form distinctive is that the main theme is presented near the end, rather than at the beginning; instead of hearing the theme first and *then* the fragments, variants, recombinations, and contrasting material the composer adds to it, these things come at us in the opposite order. It can be a powerful experience to *not* know which of the bits of music one hears will develop into the main theme or the countermelody, or how everything will come together at the end. It is like thinking through a problem, or trying to solve a puzzle: what is this? what matters? how does this bit relate to that one? how does everything fit together? The theme becomes the solution, and it comes at us like a revelation after a long struggle. That experience is worth having, and it may come most easily for you if you listen to the music with no preparation, no clues about what will happen.

If you have the time and the curiosity, consider listening to the Third Symphony before you read the following description or listen to the source tunes. Then skim the account of each movement, listen to the tunes Ives uses in it, and listen to the movement again, following the description as you listen. Finally, listen to the whole symphony again. A movement that waits until the end to present its theme invites—even requires—repeated listenings, because knowing the theme puts everything else in a different context. Each time you listen, you will hear new things in the music, as you grow more familiar with the theme and its permutations.

It is your choice. If you want to encounter the symphony this way, stop reading now, and come back later. If you want more guidance—if you prefer to put the jigsaw puzzle together knowing the picture on the box—read on.

It is spring in New York, May 1946. You have come to the concert to hear Ives's Third Symphony, written long before the war that just ended, even before the previous world war. You saw the glowing reviews from the symphony's premiere last month, and a friend enthusiastically recommended you hear the piece. It's right up your alley, he said: given your religious upbringing, you'll know all the tunes. The other pieces on this all-Ives concert have stretched your ears, so you are hoping for something more familiar from the symphony.

First Movement: *Old Folks Gatherin'*

The first movement, *Old Folks Gatherin'*, begins with wisps of melody in the violins over rich chords in the strings. The brass take over for a moment, then the strings drift back in, grow more active, and build. You hear what sounds like a fugue, the subject in the violas over a faster countersubject in the cellos and basses. The fugue subject has a distinctive rhythm—long-*short*-short-long, long-*short*-short long, with the emphasis on the first short note—and the melody climbs up gradually, then descends, alternating repeated notes with downward skips, like carefully stepping down a ladder. Violins, horns, and cellos take up the idea in turn, and as various instruments toss it around you hear the cellos and basses bring in a second countersubject, a variant of the first.

Juxtaposing and varying ideas like this sounds like a symphony in the middle of a development section. But your friend was right: the ideas themselves are drawn from hymn tunes you recognize. The fugue subject is the first three phrases from *Azmon* by Carl Gotthelf Glaser and Lowell Mason, which you know to the words "O for a thousand tongues to sing." Both countersubjects seem to be rather distantly paraphrased from the tune you know for "What a friend we have in Jesus": *Erie*, by Charles Converse.

Next is a brief interlude, with a soft melody in the horn, played twice, accompanied by the violins playing the second countersubject based on *Erie*. The horn melody is another hymn tune, the first phrase of "Just as I am"—*Woodworth*, by William B. Bradbury. Then the orchestra continues to develop the fugue subject and its countersubjects, leading to a climax and a brief pause.

Now the oboe, accompanied by strings, begins a slower, softer section. The flute echoes what the oboe just played and extends it into a long-breathed, arching, beautiful melody. You recognize that this is also paraphrased from *Erie*, drawing on its most distinctive motives but linking them in new ways to create a supple and ever-varied melodic line. As it nears its end, you hear in the violins bits of *Azmon* that were missing from the fugue subject.

After this lovely episode, the orchestra quietly resumes developing ideas presented so far, focusing first on the melodies adapted from *Erie* but soon weaving in fragments of *Azmon* and mixing everything together. The pace picks up, then relaxes as the basses and cellos settle on a long sustained note, like an organ pedal. The upper strings reach for a peak, then slow and quiet. Now comes the moment. Softly, the first violins play the complete melody of *Azmon*, pulled together for the first time from the partial statements you have already heard, while above it the flute plays its lovely melody paraphrased from *Erie*, assisted at times by the oboe. The violins repeat the last notes of *Azmon*, and the final chord fades to nothing.

You realize only in retrospect that *Azmon* is the main theme of this movement, and the flute line based on *Erie* is its countermelody. Each is developed before it appears complete, including in the fugue near the beginning, and at the end they appear together in counterpoint. The way they gradually come together from fragments is a lovely musical parallel to the image in the movement's title, of the "old folks" gathering, greeting each other warmly, and settling down to worship. Words you remember from the hymns reinforce the sense of gathering for worship, "to sing my great Redeemer's praise" (*Azmon*) and to "carry everything to God in prayer" (*Erie*).

Second Movement: *Children's Day*

The energetic second movement, *Children's Day*, opens quietly in E-flat major with a texture of three simultaneous layers: pulsing violas and cellos, a slowly moving melody in the horns and bassoon reinforced by the violas, and a rapidly unfolding theme in the violins that repeatedly rises to a peak, falls, and rises again. The violin theme commands your attention, constantly changing its rhythm, never settling into a regular pattern of phrases, and never pausing to take a breath. Its faster pace and irregular shape distract you from the slow and very regular melody in the horns, bassoons, and violas, but at some point you realize they are playing Lowell Mason's hymn tune *Naomi*. You also figure out that the violin theme is paraphrased from *Fountain* ("There is a fountain filled with blood"), another Mason tune. *Fountain* shares some motives with *Erie*, the source for the countermelody in the first movement, and the first phrase of *Naomi* is remarkably similar to the first phrase of *Woodworth*, heard in the first movement. These and other melodic echoes bind the movements together, as in other cyclic symphonies. When *Naomi* is complete, the horns, bassoon, violas, and cellos take over the violin theme, weaving new variations on motives from *Fountain*, then pass it back to the violins. The strings slow and build in intensity, bringing the first section to a close.

The middle section begins in B-flat major (the main key of the outer movements) with a jaunty theme that jumps between winds and strings, like bits of conversation or a children's game. The main melody is paraphrased from yet another hymn tune by Lowell Mason, *There Is a Happy Land*, starting with its second half and continuing with the first half. An extension plays with rhythmic and melodic ideas from the theme, and gradually the dotted rhythms from the theme become more and more prominent. The theme and extension repeat, and the dotted patterns lead into a kind of development section, with comical stops and starts, a march in a distant minor key, and other surprises, wandering farther and farther afield.

When the first section returns, it is in the wrong key—A major, a tritone away from where it should be—with the theme in cellos, violas, and bassoon and *Naomi* in the flute and pulsating violins. An interjected fragment of the middle-section theme in the horn and winds puts things to right, jerking the key back to E-flat major, giving the pulsating *Naomi* to violas and cellos, and returning the theme to the violins. In an expansive coda, the violin theme turns more recognizably into an almost complete statement of *Fountain*. Over descending bass lines, bits of the middle-section theme return, gradually growing more and more prominent as the music slows and comes to a quiet close.

This movement has a more traditional shape than the first movement: ternary form rather than cumulative form. The hymns used in this movement—*Naomi*, *Fountain*, and *There Is a Happy Land*—are not specifically directed to children, and Ives probably chose the title *Children's Day* after writing the music. Yet the energy and occasional mischief of children are neatly suggested by the energetic rush of the outer sections and the light-hearted theme and surprising events in the middle section.

Third Movement: *Communion*

The last movement, *Communion*, is the slowest of the three. It begins with a rising figure of three notes stepping up the scale, played quietly by the cellos and quickly imitated by violas and violins. The cellos continue with a meandering line, the rising figure echoes in the other strings, and the violins soar up to a peak and descend. You recognize these gestures as fragments and variants of the hymn tune *Woodworth*, foreshadowed in the first movement, and usually sung to words by Charlotte Elliott:

> Just as I am, without one plea,
> But that Thy blood was shed for me,
> And that Thou bidd'st me come to Thee,
> O Lamb of God, I come! I come!

Suddenly the winds break in with a figure that climbs up, falls back, and climbs again, marked as important by its loud accents and full harmonization. The strings return with new variants on motives from *Woodworth*, at first soft and gradually becoming more intense. The climbing figure returns in the oboe and violas, the first violins carry it up to a climax, and as they relax back down you hear a segment of *Azmon* you remember from the first movement, alternating repeated notes and downward skips in the distinctive rhythm long-short-short-long, long-short-short-long. Throughout this first section, the harmony moves fluidly, passing quickly between the home key of B-flat major and several other keys, some quite distant.

After a brief pause, an angular, hesitant melody in the strings leads to the first extended tune in the movement, beginning a new section. Over a pizzicato (plucked) line in the basses and arpeggios in the violas, the first violins sing out a melody that links together the climbing figure introduced by the winds with the melodic peak and phrase from *Azmon* just heard in the violins, then climbs again. This first violin melody is all paraphrased from *Azmon*, borrowing the middle segment exactly and surrounding it with more distant reworkings of the climbing figures that begin and end *Azmon*. You hear bits of *Woodworth* sneak back in, leading to a moment of temporary repose.

The third section begins with a horn playing a distorted version of *Woodworth*, soon picked up by the violins. The hymn tune's rhythm and general shape are easily recognizable, but some of the intervals are stretched so that the melody keeps changing keys as it climbs ever higher. The music grows louder and more intense, juxtaposing fragments of *Woodworth* and the melody paraphrased from *Azmon* that you heard a few moments ago in the first violins. You begin to wonder: is one of these hymn tunes going to be the theme, like *Azmon* was in the first movement, and the other a countermelody? And if so, which will be which? The music swells to a climax, then subsides, rocking between two rich chords that guide us back to the home key of B-flat major.

Now comes the final section, the moment of resolution, when everything joins together. As the first violins play the melody paraphrased from *Azmon* and the violas and basses accompany it as they did before, a solo cello and flute, joined by the rest of the cellos below them, play the complete tune of *Woodworth*. Well, almost complete: the last phrase cuts off before its last three notes, and there is an unexpected pause. The second half of *Woodworth* begins in the violins, in a higher key, then shifts back to B-flat major to conclude. Finally you hear the last two notes of the hymn, on the words "I come," played twice in the solo cello, softly harmonized by the rest of the strings.

Quietly in the background, you hear orchestral bells (marked in the score "as distant church bells") echoing the last notes of the hymn. They imitate the sound of church bells by highlighting the harmonics that give large bells their distinctive peal, and they produce an effect like bells playing "I come!" three times at a great distance. The sense of distance is created by key—the bells are a tritone away from the solo cello, as distant as it gets in tonal music—as well as by their very soft level of sound. The suggestion of wide outdoor spaces is the symphony's last evocation of the open-air camp meeting in its title, as strings and bells fade to silence.

As you wait in the hushed moment before the applause begins, you realize how neatly this movement fits its title, *Communion*. The hymn that is its theme, *Woodworth*, was often used for a central moment of the revival service, inviting the faithful to come forward and share communion or recommit themselves to Christ. The movement's cumulative form aptly conveys a sense of coming together, coming into clarity, and—after much thought—arriving at a profound personal commitment. The words of the hymn reinforce these ideas, and the opening phrase—"just as I am"—is beautifully embodied in the presentation of the hymn tune in the final section, just as it is.

Meaning and Roots of Cumulative Form

The Third Symphony is an extended meditation on hymn tunes, wringing from them meanings that we, Ives's listeners, would not have found in them without his musical ruminations. The treatment of the hymns in the outer movements is like a sermon on a Bible verse, or a process of thinking through a problem where the ultimate revelation is a simple truth, a realization that is hard won and especially meaningful because it has been lived through. That sense of a truth being earned is the essence of cumulative form.

The new form had roots both in Ives's experiences as an organist and in his training in the classical tradition. In nineteenth-century Protestant churches, the organist accompanied the hymn singing and would typically introduce each hymn by playing a short prelude, usually improvised. One common approach was to develop motives and phrases from the hymn tune, play the whole tune in varied or embellished form, and then play it unaltered as the congregation joins in to sing. The sequence of events, leading from fragments to variation to direct statement of the tune, resembles cumulative form. In the late nineteenth century, it was also common to add a countermelody above the hymn tune, as Ives does in many cumulative form movements. In addition to these influences from the improvisatory practice of church organists, a few of the organ pieces Ives played, such as the first movement of Mendelssohn's first organ sonata, anticipate aspects of cumulative form.[13]

Ives also drew on his experience with classical forms and genres. In cumulative form, there is constant development of the material. Ives applied in his Third Symphony the procedures he had learned in writing sonata-form movements for his earlier symphonies: working with motives, spinning out material, creating variations and paraphrases, and devising themes that work well in counterpoint with each other.

In his earlier big pieces, he had clearly been thinking of music that would build from fragments to wholeness. Examples include the march theme that emerges in the coda of the First Symphony finale after being anticipated in every previous movement, and the borrowed tunes that appear in full in the codas of the First String Quartet and Second Symphony finales, accompanied by themes already heard, after partial statements earlier in the work. These finales still use traditional forms, either sonata or ternary, and the climactic theme appears in a coda, only after a repetition of large amounts of material from the first section of the movement. Ives's inventiveness lay in taking that repetition away and relying on the techniques of development and of building toward wholeness as the foundations of his form. This kind of thinking—giving up on routine expectations to focus on what is most important—undergirds his musical innovations as much as it does his innovations in the insurance business.

THE VIOLIN SONATAS

Ives's symphonies and string quartets reflect the extraordinary diversity of his music; the two string quartets could hardly be more dissimilar, and each of the five completed symphonies represents a different vision of what a symphony should be and do. By contrast, the four violin sonatas, multimovement works for violin and piano, resemble each other in many ways, and all seem to spring from a single impulse, like variations on the same idea. All four have three movements, in either the traditional sequence for violin sonatas, with fast first and final movements around a slow central movement, or the opposite, with the fastest movement in the middle. All four include movements in cumulative form (sometimes blended with other forms) using themes based on hymn tunes; the Third and Fourth Violin Sonatas feature such movements exclusively, and the other two use them for the first and final movements, as in the Third Symphony.

The presence of hymn tunes in ten of his twelve violin sonata movements can be surprising for performers and listeners, because sonatas are rarely religious and are typically based on newly composed themes. But Ives came to know the genre of the sonata in part through Mendelssohn's organ sonatas, which were the sonatas he most often played, and four of the six use Lutheran chorale tunes as themes in at least one movement. He may have regarded religious tunes as native to the sonata, rather than as something unexpected.[14]

The violin sonatas also share a history, spanning two decades. Ives worked on his first attempt at a violin sonata, which Henry Cowell later dubbed the "Pre-First" Violin Sonata, for several years (around 1901–1903 and 1907–1909 by Ives's recollection, although the manuscripts date from around 1908–1913). He wrote a first movement, two different tries at a slow movement, the beginnings of a scherzo, and a finale before apparently deciding that they did not fit together into a coherent whole. The only movement in cumulative form is the finale, which he seems to have begun last (around 1910 or 1911) and completed by 1913. Roughly contemporaneously with that movement, he sketched two others that use cumulative form, and around 1914 he assembled the First Violin Sonata using these two as its first and final movements and repurposing as its middle movement his second try at a slow movement for the "Pre-First" Sonata. Around 1914–1917 he put together the Second Violin Sonata, with the revised finale of the "Pre-First" Sonata as its first movement, a middle movement based on the scherzo and part of the first movement of the "Pre-First" Sonata, and a new finale in cumulative form composed in about 1915–1917. Both sonatas were subsequently revised and put in final form in the early 1920s. Meanwhile, Ives composed all three movements of the Third Violin Sonata in 1914 and of the Fourth Violin Sonata between 1914 and 1916.[15] While the impulse to write a violin sonata may stretch back to 1901, the pieces as we know them are products of his maturity, composed between 1908 and 1917, with revisions to Nos. 1 and 2 over the next few years.

Cumulative form traces an arc from relative complexity to simplicity, and the same may be said for Ives's four violin sonatas as a group. The First is the most difficult, the Fourth the easiest to play and the most direct, and the Second and Third in between. Thus it makes sense to encounter them in reverse numerical order. This is exactly how violinist Stefan Jackiw and pianist Jeremy Denk have played them in a recital they have given many times in concert halls around the world, with Nos. 4 and 3 before intermission and Nos. 2 and 1 after. In their recital, each sonata but the Fourth is preceded by vocalists singing the hymns and other songs that Ives incorporated into it, so that the audience has the source tunes in their ears, can hear the way Ives played with them, and can recognize them coming into focus over the course of each movement.[16] We can trace the same path through the sonatas, taking them up from Fourth to First and hearing the tunes at the Charles Ives Society website (charlesives.org/borrowed-tunes).

Of course, as is true for the Third Symphony, each movement unfolds logically and is thematically coherent without recognizing a single tune, and many of Ives's listeners have learned these melodies from his music, rather than from a hymnal. If you would like to experience these sonatas without the foreknowledge of the tunes he uses or the shape each movement takes, stop reading now. Listen to each sonata for yourself, first. Then go through each movement—read the description given here, listen to the source tunes, and listen to the movement while following the description—and then listen to the whole sonata again, taking note of how different the experience feels to you.

SONATA NO. 4 FOR VIOLIN AND PIANO: *CHILDREN'S DAY AT THE CAMP MEETING*

In his *Memos*, Ives described the Fourth Violin Sonata as

> an attempt to write a sonata which [his brother Moss's youngest son] Moss White [Ives] (then about twelve years old) could play. The first movement kept to this idea fairly well, but the second got way away from it, and the third got about in between. . . . It is called "Children's Day" because it is based principally on the church hymns sung at the children's services.[17]

Like the Third Symphony, and like all the violin sonatas, this is not a piece of program music (although twenty-five years later Ives added a program note to the published score) but rather a character piece, one that captures from the perspective of the children the flavor of the outdoor camp meeting revivals Ives had witnessed in his youth. Unlike the Third Symphony, there are no thematic links between movements, nor are the movements unified by a key scheme; rather, as with many of Ives's later works, the piece makes sense as a whole because its three movements contrast greatly in mood yet share a common perspective and approach. All three use cumulative form, but each does so with a twist.

The fast first movement is based on Ives's astonishing discovery in his teens that the refrain of William H. Doane's hymn tune *Old, Old Story* ("Tell me the old, old story") combines well in counterpoint with one of the fugues his father wrote while studying music theory and composition in the 1860s. The only surviving sketches for this movement are Ives's notations, written in about 1892 on an ink copy of his father's Fugue in B-flat Major, showing how to fit the hymn tune together with the fugue.[18] The hymn refrain is the movement's main theme, the first portion of the fugue its main countermelody. A secondary theme, heard at the beginning and end as a kind of framing device, is derived from part of the hymn tune's verse.

The movement opens with resonant chords in the piano, and the framing theme enters in the violin, then shifts to the piano as the violin plays the main theme's opening motive. The piano introduces the fugue subject, the violin joins in with the framing theme, and the two instruments trade ideas, including fragments of *Old, Old Story* that are in neither theme. Soon both instruments collaborate in playing the entire countermelody, the first dozen measures of George Ives's Fugue in B-flat Major. The development resumes, the violin focuses more and more on the main theme's opening phrase, and the music grows faster and louder. At the climax, the violin plays the main theme, the refrain of *Old, Old Story*, over the fugue as countermelody in the piano. The framing theme returns quietly in the violin, and with one last reminder of the fugue subject the music fades to a close.

The slow second movement is a ravishing cumulative form, blended with variations and ternary form. The theme is the refrain of *Jesus Loves Me* ("Yes, Jesus loves me, / The Bible tells me so"), about as simple a tune as there is in the hymnal. It uses the *pentatonic scale*, which has only whole steps and minor thirds, without any half steps, like playing only the black keys on a piano. The countermelody is one of Ives's most beautiful melodies, paraphrased from the same hymn refrain but spun out in a supple, unpredictable, and wide-ranging line. A contrasting middle section is based on yet another motive paraphrased from part of *Jesus Loves Me*.

The piano begins slowly and quietly with the opening motives of the countermelody, the hymn tune theme, and the middle section over vague harmonies. The violin responds with the same three ideas in a different order, then plays a distorted version of the theme, jumping between high and low notes. Over rolling chords in the piano, the violin spins out parts of the theme and countermelody in a free fantasia. Settling into E major, the first clear key in the movement, the violin presents the complete countermelody for the first time over the piano's gentle arpeggios. As the countermelody concludes, the piano bursts in with the dissonant middle section, faster and louder and marked "*conslugarocko*"—a made-up word meant to evoke, as Ives wrote in the note he added to the published score, a break in the service that would "give the boys a chance to run out and throw stones down on the rocks in the brook!"

What follows is a kind of reverse variations, growing closer to the theme rather than further from it and progressively returning to the opening slow tempo and to E major. The violin reenters with hints of the countermelody, while the piano plays a variation of the theme in a high range in D major. The tempo relaxes, the key changes to A major, and the violin plays the entire countermelody against the theme in the piano. Finally, the violin plays the whole theme at last, slowly and in E major, with the countermelody and rolling chords in the piano, ending with a soft "Amen."

With these closing variations after the interruption of a contrasting middle section, the movement combines variation form and ternary form with the overall process of cumulative form, gradually piecing together the theme and the countermelody from fragments and presenting them at last complete and in counterpoint. The whole movement is an extended rumination on the hymn tune, like mulling over a Bible verse, exploring its meanings, and finding in it riches one scarcely suspected were there. Listeners who might have found *Jesus Loves Me* too simplistic or treacly to take seriously as a theme, if it were presented at the outset, may by the end hear it as beautiful and profound, the culmination of a gradual process of revelation and decorated by a gorgeous countermelody and accompaniment.

After such a rich meditation, the fast finale is lighter and more straightforward. A motive that circles around a note, touching the notes just below and above it, appears in the piano, then in the violin, and begins to coalesce into a longer melody. The music quiets and slows, then picks up strength and speed again as a contrasting idea is heard in the violin over dissonant chords in the piano. Variants of the first motive return and lead into a full-blown tune in the violin saturated with that motive: the complete gospel hymn *The Beautiful River* ("Shall we gather at the river") by Robert Lowry, verse and refrain. The verse is accompanied by the contrasting idea in the piano, and both verse and refrain are slightly altered in their last phrase. Here the hymn tune is the theme, the contrasting idea its countermelody. The piece ends with a brief final reference to the beginning motive of each; instead of concluding with the affirmation in the refrain ("Yes, we'll gather at the river . . . That flows by the throne of God"), Ives takes us back to the question in the verse: Shall we gather at the river? For the hymnist, that meant in heaven, but for the children at the camp meeting, it might mean running down again to the brook.

Each of these movements uses cumulative form, each in its own way, so that each is an individual, unique in some respects while sharing a common approach to form. The diversity here parallels the varied ways Beethoven used sonata form and Bach wrote fugues; as much as they relied on a paradigm, all three composers sought variety, and they never wrote two movements that present exactly the same sequence of events. The moods and feelings conveyed vary as well, from the peppy outer movements to the slow and meditative central movement.

SONATA NO. 3 FOR VIOLIN AND PIANO

That same variety is evident in the Third Violin Sonata. Here the outer movements are slow, surrounding a fast middle movement, and all three offer different takes on cumulative form and on their hymn-tune sources. Ives described the sonata in a program note for the first performance in 1917 as "an attempt to express the feeling and fervor—a fervor that was often more vociferous than religious—with which the hymns and revival tunes were sung at the Camp Meetings held extensively in New England in the [18]70's and 80's." Although long sections of each movement are in a key, particularly when the themes are being presented, none of the movements begins and ends in the same key, and many passages are harmonically fluid; as Ives commented, "the tonality throughout is supposed to take care of itself."[19]

The first movement is a striking blend of cumulative form with verse-refrain form. Ives described it as "a kind of a magnified hymn of four different verses, all ending with the same refrain."[20] The refrains are always slow, as are the first and last verses, but the second and third verses grow progressively faster. The theme of the refrains is partly new and partly paraphrased from the refrain of *Beulah Land*. The melody is essentially the same each time it appears, as befits a refrain, but each presentation differs in some ways from the others, like a series of variations. The theme of the verses, presented in its definitive form at the end of the last verse, is paraphrased from the refrain of *Need* ("I need Thee ev'ry hour") by Robert Lowry. Several recurring motives are in turn derived from the verse theme. The words sung to the refrain of *Need* convey the intensity of prayer:

I need Thee, O I need Thee;
Ev'ry hour I need Thee!
O bless me now, my saviour,
I come to Thee.

The whole movement is a meditation on this urgent prayer, which will return as the theme of the finale.

Verse I opens with arpeggios in the piano that later return to signal the beginning of each verse. The violin enters with a variant of the verse theme, lingering on motives that will suffuse the movement. A meandering figure in the piano launches a lyrical fantasy on motives from the theme, growing more rhapsodic. After a pause at a high point, the arpeggios and meandering figure return in the piano, and over them the violin plays a paraphrase of the verse theme. The piano states the refrain alone, stopping on a dissonant chord, and pauses.

The arpeggios return to begin Verse II. The piano plays a new paraphrase of the verse theme, then develops motives from it with occasional comments from the violin. Both instruments join in a faster episode, an extensive exploration of motives from the refrain theme and its source *Beulah Land*. A brief reappearance of the last part of the verse theme concludes the verse, and the refrain returns, its melody divided into short segments that alternate between violin and piano.

Verse III again begins with arpeggios in the piano and motives from the verse theme in the violin. Soon the violin introduces a faster, more distant variant of the verse theme, adapted from the variant that appeared at the opening of Verse I, that is immediately imitated by the piano. Part of Verse I returns in varied form, and the faster variant mixes with other motives derived from the theme. The last part of the verse theme again closes the verse. Now the violin states the refrain melody, while the piano recalls the faster variant of the verse theme, much slower than before.

The final verse opens with the piano playing its arpeggios and yet another new paraphrase of the verse theme, followed by a varied reprise of part of Verse II. At last the verse theme appears in full in the violin, completing the cumulative development of that theme, over accompanimental figuration in the piano that appeared once before in Verse I. The refrain includes the contrapuntal combination of themes we have come to expect from cumulative form: the violin again states the refrain theme, while the piano plays the variant of the verse theme we heard in the violin at the very beginning of the movement. For the first time, the dissonant chord left hanging at the end of each prior refrain is allowed to resolve, and the movement comes to a quiet close.

The fast second movement has the character of "a meeting where the feet and body, as well as the voice, add to the excitement," as Ives described it in his note.[21] The ragtime-like theme is paraphrased from parts of Ira Sankey's gospel song *There'll Be No Dark Valley*, the first half of the verse overlapping the first half of the chorus, with the second phrase from *The*

Beautiful River tagged on at the end. The countermelody begins with the same rising gesture as the theme and shares elements with *There'll Be No Dark Valley* and with *Need*.

Over a repeating note F in the bass, the piano introduces and develops several quickly rising figures in F major, including fragments of what will become the theme and countermelody. The violin enters with the opening notes of the theme followed by new motives, then drops out again. In an extended interlude that wanders through a variety of keys, the piano develops ideas that gradually coalesce into a paraphrase of the countermelody. The violin drops in fragments of the theme, and then presents the entire theme in F major together with the countermelody in the piano. In most movements in cumulative form, this combination of theme and countermelody would bring the movement to a close, but here development resumes until the theme and countermelody come back again in E-flat major, followed by a climactic varied statement in D major and a brisk coda. The unexpected repetitions combine with the almost constant rhythmic motion to create a feeling of excitement quite different from the sober prayer of the first movement.

The slow third movement is the most straightforward. The theme is the refrain of *Need*, and the countermelody is paraphrased from the same tune, drawing elements from the first half of the verse and the last part of the refrain. The use of this hymn tune recalls its paraphrases and variants in the first movement, and a middle portion of the countermelody echoes the beginning of the countermelody in the second movement, drawing the movements together through motivic links as in the cyclic structure of Ives's first three symphonies. Just as the movement itself moves from fragments to wholeness, and from free fantasy to increasing clarity, so the sonata as a whole traces an arc from the complexity of the first two movements, each based on a paraphrased theme, to simplicity in the final movement, ending with a direct statement of the refrain from *Need*.

The movement falls into three large sections, which focus respectively on the motives that make up both themes, on the countermelody, and on the theme. Each section begins with a long passage for piano alone.

At the outset, the piano introduces motives from the verse of *Need*, from the countermelody, and from the theme, linking them in our minds from the start. The piano adds a recollection of the meandering figure from the opening of the first movement, again linking the movements. The violin enters, and rhapsodic development of these ideas continues, the key constantly changing. After quite some time, both instruments grow quieter and play with more detachment between each note and the next. The piano presents a ghostly paraphrase of the theme under descending scales from the countermelody in the violin; the violin plays the final few notes of the theme in a high range;

and the piano repeats its paraphrase louder and with the descending scales in the bass to bring the first section to a close.

The second section again starts with the piano playing fragments of the theme and countermelody. The violin enters with the entire countermelody over sonorous arpeggios in the piano, then both instruments develop the countermelody with occasional references to the theme, and the piano ends the section with a free, rapturous passage.

After a pause, the piano softly begins the final section, gradually weaving motives from the theme into a paraphrase of the entire theme. The violin sneaks back in and joins the development of the theme, with occasional bits of the countermelody. Both instruments grow louder and pick up speed, climaxing in a complete presentation of the theme in the violin, with the countermelody and its arpeggiated accompaniment in the piano. They slow and quiet, then very softly repeat the theme, countermelody, and accompaniment, their quiet intensity perfectly embodying the sense of urgent prayer.

SONATA NO. 2 FOR VIOLIN AND PIANO

In the Second Violin Sonata, the outer movements are in cumulative form, and the central movement is a fast ternary form. All three movements have titles, but there is no program or overall title for the work as a whole.

The first movement takes its title from the hymn tune on which it is based: *Autumn*, by François-Hippolyte Barthélémon. An altered and abbreviated version of the hymn melody, missing its third phrase, serves as the theme. The countermelody is paraphrased from the middle of the hymn tune, including the material omitted from the theme. A slow introduction presents the opening motive of the countermelody low in the piano, followed by the beginning of the theme as the violin echoes and continues the first part of the countermelody. A moderately fast section varies and develops elements from both theme and countermelody. Suddenly softer and slower, the violin states the countermelody's first half in varied form, with part of the theme in the piano. Development resumes, once again moderately fast, then gradually slowing. At last the theme appears majestically in the violin over the countermelody in the piano, and both fade to a quiet close.

The second movement, *In the Barn*, evokes country fiddling for a barn dance, starting with an original theme in fiddle-tune style and later incorporating bits of familiar fiddle tunes such as *College Hornpipe* (also known as *Sailor's Hornpipe*), *Money Musk*, *The White Cockade*, and *Turkey in the Straw*. Suddenly a contrasting middle section breaks in with part of George F. Root's

Civil War song *The Battle Cry of Freedom* in the violin, followed by a wild fantasia on ideas drawn from that tune. Bits of fiddle tune drift back in, and elements of the first and middle sections mix it up in an even wilder final section that barrels to a precipitous conclusion.

The finale, *The Revival*, uses *Nettleton* ("Come, Thou Fount of ev'ry blessing") as its theme, with no countermelody. It opens softly and slowly, passing hints of the hymn tune between instruments. The first phrase of *Nettleton* appears in the piano, imitated by itself a beat later and a tritone away, creating a mysterious effect tinged with whole tones; then, more quickly and briefly, the piano varies the third phrase of the hymn tune. These ideas repeat, now with the violin taking part. The next section is faster, developing motives from *Nettleton* in both instruments and building in intensity. At last, over noisy, incessantly pulsing chords in the piano, the hymn tune theme appears in the violin, but the last phrase is left incomplete, and the movement closes quietly and without finality. The gradual rise in speed and volume to a peak of excitement captures the emotional shape of a revival meeting, and the ambiguous ending poses a question akin to the end of *General William Booth Enters into Heaven*: having witnessed the growing fervor of a religious experience, are we moved in the same way?

SONATA NO. 1 FOR VIOLIN AND PIANO

In a note written long after the piece itself, Ives described the First Violin Sonata as "a general impression, a kind of reflection and remembrance, of the peoples' outdoor gatherings ... of holiday celebrations and camp meetings in the [18]80s and '90s—suggesting some of the songs, tunes and hymns, together with some of the sounds of nature joining in from the mountains in some of the old Connecticut farm towns."[22]

The First Sonata begins like the Second: with a slow introduction, starting with a variant of the very same motive, low in the piano. Since the opening movement of the Second Violin Sonata began life as the finale of the "Pre-First" Sonata, perhaps Ives once planned the two movements as the first and last of a sonata, linked by a common motive. The motive plays an important role throughout, initiating the fast main section of the movement and the varied reprise of the slow introduction at the end, and returning at other times.

Yet in the course of events *Shining Shore*, used earlier in the First Symphony and First String Quartet, emerges as the main melodic material of the movement. This hymn tune is in AA'BA' form; the A phrase is the theme of the cumulative form, the B phrase the source for the countermelody. Fragments and variations of the countermelody, a pentatonic melody marked by a repeated falling gesture, permeate the slow introduction and the first half of the fast section. After a variant that sounds a bit like *Bringing in the Sheaves* (but isn't), we hear bits of the theme in both instruments, and then the piano pounds out the theme with the countermelody in the violin. The music quiets, and the violin recalls the theme. The slow introduction returns in varied form as an epilogue, and it gently fades away while the violin foreshadows the melody that will open the next movement.

The second movement is a rhapsody in ternary form. The slow first section is based on the opening phrase of George Kiallmark's nostalgic popular song *The Old Oaken Bucket* ("How dear to this heart are the scenes of my childhood"), and the faster middle section on George F. Root's equally nostalgic Civil War song *Tramp, Tramp, Tramp*, which depicts a captured Union soldier far from home ("In the prison cell I sit, / Thinking, Mother dear, of you"). The two songs share some rhythmic and melodic similarities that Ives exploits to interweave them, and again at the end the violin anticipates the next movement's opening motive.

The finale combines two cumulative forms, one inside the other. Both are based on hymn tunes by Lowell Mason, which are linked by subtle motivic similarities and by texts that mention the image of night. The movement opens with the principal motive of Mason's hymn *Work Song* ("Work, for the night is coming"). The piano develops this and other motives from the hymn, soon joined by the violin. The music is active and mostly loud, reflecting the text's emphasis on working while one can.

Both instruments slow and grow softer, signaling a change of mood and material. From short, dreamy fragments of melody, rising and falling by step, gradually emerges the first phrase of Mason's *Watchman* ("Watchman, tell us of the night"). Picking up speed, the violin presents more parts of the hymn, and the piano adds a repeated descending figure that will serve as the countermelody. Further development leads to a quiet statement of the complete theme in the violin and countermelody in the piano. The theme is based on *Watchman* but reworks the tune, especially its second half.

A soft transition puns on a resemblance between the end of the first phrase of *Watchman* and the opening motive of *Work Song*, leading us back to that tune. Development continues, and at a climax the violin paraphrases *Watchman* while the piano slowly pounds out the main motive of *Work Song*, linking the two together. We reach the culmination with the complete presentation of the theme, the first half of *Work Song*, in the violin. As a countermelody, we hear the opening motive from the first movement repeated several times in the bass of the piano, a final link binding the sonata movements together.

THE NEW FORM FINDS AN AUDIENCE

For a composer whose music is as diverse as Ives's, the violin sonatas are a remarkably coherent group, sharing approaches to form, a similar complex yet still tonal harmonic language, and a common fund of source material in the hymns Ives knew from childhood, especially those he identified with camp meeting revivals. Yet each violin sonata is an individual, as different from its siblings as are the sonatas of Beethoven or Brahms. Each cumulative form movement is unique in some way, while all follow the same general pattern of stating the principal theme in complete form (with its countermelody if any) only near the end of the movement, *after* the fragmentation, variation, and recombination typical of development sections in a sonata form. Ives used cumulative form so often, in some two dozen movements, because he found it a rich and flexible way to create profound and beautiful music based on simple hymn tunes. As we have seen, he often uses the tunes as themes essentially as they are, while in some cases he reworks them to create a theme that remains closer to the original tune than are most of the paraphrased themes in his First String Quartet or Second Symphony.

During the period that Ives was working most intensively on the violin sonatas, he tried to interest performers in playing them. Around 1914 he invited Franz Milcke, a professional violinist Harmony knew from her Hartford days, to play through the First Sonata. As Ives recounts in *Memos*, Ives and Milcke started the first movement, but

> he didn't even get through the first page. He was all bothered with the rhythms and the notes, and got mad. He said, "This cannot be played. It is awful. It is not music, it makes no sense." . . . I remember he came out of the little back music room with his hands over his ears, and said, "When you get awfully indigestible food in your stomach that distresses you, you can get rid of it, but I cannot get those horrible sounds out of my ears."[23]

On another occasion around the same time, Edgar Stowell, who had conducted the first movement of the Second Symphony at the school where he taught, came over to the Hartsdale house.

> We played over the Second Violin Sonata and started the First, but Stowell said it was too difficult and stopped. He said there were too many ideas too close together. We then played Daniel Gregory Mason's Violin Sonata [in G Minor, Op. 5 (1913)]. . . . Stowell said Mason's was better than mine because it was Geigermusik [German for "real violin music"], but he did say that one page of mine had more ideas than Mason's whole sonata. Whether he meant this as advice in restraint and prudence I don't know.[24]

Ives had more success with David Talmadge, who was Moss White Ives's violin teacher.

> Talmadge, in his nice way, always liked to kid me more or less about those funny sounds, but he said that, the more he learned and studied the music, the more he thought there was something in it. He played the First Violin Sonata, and also most of the Second, I think, and all of the Third, with me in 1914–15. He gave them serious, hard, and intelligent study, and played them well and in a kind of big way.[25]

In 1917, Talmadge and Stuart Ross (piano) played the Third Violin Sonata at a private concert in Carnegie Chamber Music Hall in New York. Over the next quarter century, the sonatas gradually had their public premieres: the Second by Jerome Goldstein and Rex Tillson in March 1924 at Aeolian Hall in New York; the First in November 1928 by Dorothy Minty and Marjorie Gear at a San Francisco concert sponsored by Henry Cowell's New Music Society; the Fourth in June 1939 in Los Angeles by Orline Burrow and Frances Mullen, followed in January 1940 by Eudice Shapiro and Irene Jacobi at a concert sponsored by the League of Composers at the Museum of Modern Art in New York; and the Third in Los Angeles by Sol Babitz and Ingolf Dahl in March 1942. The Fourth Violin Sonata was published in 1942, the others in 1951 and 1953.

The premieres earned a few mostly positive reviews. The *New York Herald Tribune* described the Second Sonata, because of its movement titles, as "program music, of what might be called an advanced French post-romantic type, but with a certain American flavor"; the *Christian Science Monitor* said that it "describes rural America 70 years ago" and that "the several divisions seemed to me to be built largely out of New England ballad and sacred tune material, some serious, others trivial, and all characteristic of the period under contemplation." Of the Fourth Sonata, the *New York Herald Tribune* wrote that its title, "Children's Day at the Camp Meeting," is reflected by "the melodic character of the musical ideas, whose treatment, while not conventional, is consonant with their prevailing vein. The principal theme of the brief first movement is extensive and articulated rather than pronounced in profile; the peaceful close of the large [slow movement] presented a tune of a Fosteresque character."[26]

Getting the Third Symphony performed took more time but bore a rich reward. After completing the work and having a professional copy made in 1911, Ives tried again to interest Walter Damrosch, who had conducted a reading of three movements from the First Symphony and then had ignored the Second; once again, Damrosch did nothing with it and never returned the score. In *Memos*, Ives mentions a tantalizing possibility: Gustav Mahler, in New York as conductor of the New York Philharmonic, saw the Third Symphony at the copyist's shop "and asked to have a copy—he was quite interested in it."[27] Mahler died in May 1911; had he conducted a performance, Ives might have gained a reputation as a composer while still in his thirties.

Three and a half decades later, Lou Harrison conducted the premiere with the New York Little Symphony on April 5, 1946, with Harmony but not Charles Ives in attendance. The orchestra played it a second time at the end of the concert so listeners could absorb it. The piece caught fire. Both audience and critics responded enthusiastically. Noel Straus in the *New York Times* praised it as "music close to the soil and deeply felt," marked by "a richness of orchestral sonorities," a "richness of imagination abounding in every page," "a freshness of inspiration, a genuineness of feeling and an intense sincerity that lent it immediate appeal and manifested inborn talents of a high order."[28] It was played again by other performers that May in an all-Ives concert at Columbia University and in July on a radio broadcast—more performances in a short time than any other piece by Ives had been given to that point—and earned a special citation by the New York Music Critics' Circle. The next year, it won the Pulitzer Prize for Music, the highest honor Ives ever received.[29]

Having explored American songs in a European context in the Second Symphony, and having placed American hymns at the center of the Third Symphony and violin sonatas, Ives turned to the American experience. How to capture in music what is distinctive about life in the United States, specifically in Ives's home region of New England? One way is to portray American holidays, and to show how Americans use music to celebrate them.

· 8 ·

American Holidays

In the Third Symphony and four violin sonatas, Ives celebrated the camp meeting revivals he remembered from his youth and the hymn tunes that were central to them. Around the same time, he began to compose a series of orchestral tone poems that reflected his memories of holiday celebrations during his childhood in Danbury and especially the role of music in them. In the late 1910s, he gathered four of these tone poems into "a kind of Holiday Symphony, each movement based on something of the memory that a man has of his boy holidays."[1] In this piece, the four traditions Ives learned as a child and young man come together: the marches and songs of popular music, the hymns of the Protestant church and camp meetings, the procedures and ideals of the European symphonic tradition, and the toolbox of innovative techniques he had honed over two decades of writing experimental music, now utilized for their rhetorical power and ability to depict events. Especially prominent is his overlay of many distinct layers of music in different rhythms, tone colors, and levels of audibility to represent the sounds of the environment surrounding the event, creating a three-dimensional effect. In two of these movements, Ives creates a collage of familiar tunes, representing the many memories that rush in unbidden as we remember experiences of our youth. Two are in cumulative form, the other two organized by a specific program. All four movements convey the place that music holds in American celebrations and how important music is to our memories, whether of yesterday or of long ago.

A SYMPHONY: NEW ENGLAND HOLIDAYS

A few months before their wedding, Harmony wrote to Ives that although "inspiration [in art] ought to come fullest at one's happiest moments," she

173

thought that "most happy moments are put into expression after they have been memories & made doubly precious because they are *gone*."[2] The idea of putting memories into music became increasingly a focus for Ives during the decade after their marriage. Some were recollections of recent experiences, such as the walk by a river the Iveses took the summer they were married, or the response of a crowd of commuters to the sinking of the *Lusitania* in 1915. Others were somewhat idealized memories of his childhood, especially of holidays where music-making, often featuring his father as leader of the Danbury band, was a central part of the festivities. During the fiftieth anniversary of the Civil War in 1911–1915 and the Great War of 1914–1918, his thoughts turned as well to stories of the Civil War he had heard from his father, his father-in-law, and other veterans of the conflict.[3] From this fount of memories, Ives created a number of songs, mostly to his own poems, and a series of movements for orchestra, symphonic poems in the tradition of Franz Liszt, Richard Strauss, and Claude Debussy.

Sometime around 1917–1919, Ives gathered four of the orchestral tone poems into what he called *A Symphony: New England Holidays*, or *Holidays Symphony* for short. (Most of the others he grouped into two orchestral sets, described in chapter 9.) He continued to revise all four movements over the next decade or so, and they reached final form between the middle 1920s and the early 1930s, completed in the order they appear in the symphony. They depict uniquely American holidays as they were celebrated in New England during Ives's youth: *Washington's Birthday* on February 22; *Decoration Day* (the predecessor of Memorial Day) on May 30; *The Fourth of July* on July 4; and *Thanksgiving and Forefathers' Day* combining two holidays, Thanksgiving in late November and Forefathers' Day on December 22. As Ives observed in *Memos*, the order he chose created a cycle of the four seasons:

> In putting these movements together as a kind of a symphony, the *Washington's Birthday* (winter) would go first, the *Decoration Day* (spring) second, *The Fourth of July* (summer) third, and *Thanksgiving* (autumn) last. But these movements have been copied and bound separately, and may be played separately.[4]

His comments reveal Ives's ambivalence: is this a symphony, or just a collection of single-movement works like Bedřich Smetana's *Má Vlast* (My Country), a set of six tone poems of which *The Moldau* is the most famous? Each movement is scored for a different group of performers, from a small orchestra for *Washington's Birthday* to a large orchestra with extra percussion and chorus for *Thanksgiving*; in a performance of all four, many performers would only be needed for one or two movements, sitting idly through the others. The movements were premiered, published, and first recorded separately, and as Ives pointed out in *Memos*, "there is no special musical connection among these four movements"—that is, no cyclic sharing of themes between movements as in all his other symphonies, nor any unification through a key scheme as in the first three symphonies.[5]

Yet, put together in the order Ives indicated, they not only trace a cycle of the seasons through the calendar year but also follow in many respects the typical sequence of movements in a nineteenth-century symphony: a first movement with ideas of contrasting character; a somber slow movement; a sort of a scherzo, here more of a march than a dance; and a weighty finale that culminates in a hymn-like closing statement, even bringing in a chorus as Beethoven did in the finale of his Ninth Symphony. As movements in a symphony tend to do, they contrast with each other in mood and form, yet share a great deal in common. All of them represent music-making in a New England town, with popular songs and fiddle tunes in the first and third movements, patriotic songs and marches in the middle two, and hymns in the second and fourth. All of them include contrasting sections in different tempos, meters, moods, and styles; Jan Swafford notes that all four include both "introverted slow music and extroverted fast music" and use "the mingling of stylistic voices, the meta-style, that had become second nature to Ives."[6] All end softly, like each movement of the Third Symphony, and all but the last begin softly as well. And they all draw on a similar range of procedures for expressive purposes, from the thematic development and noisy climaxes of his earlier symphonies to techniques he had explored in experimental works like *Central Park in the Dark.*

Ultimately, Ives saw both alternatives as valid: play them as a symphony, or perform individual movements as works that are complete in themselves. He had played single movements from symphonies on the organ, including the slow movement of Dvořák's *New World Symphony*, and suggested that "quite a number of the larger forms of instrumental music (symphonies, sonatas, suites, etc.) may not always necessarily form, or were originally intended to form, such a complete organic whole that the breath of unity is smothered all out if one or two movements are played separately sometimes."[7] Indeed, the four holiday movements have been performed separately more often than as a symphony. His openness to different possibilities reflects both his experience with bands, who often program excerpts from longer works, and his eagerness to get his music played.

Whether performed as individual movements or as a whole, the *Holidays Symphony* celebrates American people, life, and culture by depicting how we use music in our holidays. It combines the techniques of European symphonic music, and the European genres of the symphony and symphonic poem, with tunes that represent an American identity, using the innovative techniques and ideas Ives had developed in his experimental music and the meanings associated with American styles and specific tunes to create a narrative that conveys how we value music as part of American life.

WASHINGTON'S BIRTHDAY

According to *Memos* and his early work lists, Ives completed *Washington's Birthday* in 1913 and paid professional performers to try it out on several occasions between 1913 and 1919. The surviving manuscripts suggest that he worked on it throughout that period, then in the mid-1920s revised it and had it copied.[8] As Ives recalled, the players he hired in the late 1910s

> were supposed to be the best men in the [New York Symphony] orchestra, and they were good musicians—but . . . they made an awful fuss about playing this, and before I got through, this had to be cut out, and that had to be cut out—and in the end the score was practically emasculated. . . .
>
> This score (. . . with no simplifications) was played in San Francisco in September 1931 [at a concert sponsored by Henry Cowell's New Music Society], Nicolas Slonimsky conducting. It was given after three rehearsals, and [judging by] the reports from Henry Cowell (who looked over the score while they were playing), and [by] what the critics in the newspapers said . . . , it was well played. This shows what fifteen years of a little study and practice can do in turning impossibilities into possibilities.[9]

Cowell published the piece in his quarterly *New Music* in 1936.

Washington's Birthday is not about the first president of the United States but is a picture in sounds of the holiday as Ives remembered it from his childhood in the late nineteenth century. Although he worked on it during the same time as some of his violin sonatas, from the start it was a very different kind of piece, structured not by cumulative form but by a series of events Ives detailed in a program he attached to the copyist's ink score. In it he quotes from *Walden* by Henry David Thoreau and from John Greenleaf Whittier's poem *Snow-Bound*.

> "Cold and solitude," says Thoreau, "are friends of mine. Now is the time before the wind rises to go forth and see the snow on the trees."
>
> And there is at times a bleakness, without stir but penetrating, in a New England midwinter, which settles down grimly when the day closes over the broken hills. In such a scene it is as though nature would but could not easily trace a certain beauty in the sombre landscape!—in the quiet but

restless monotony! Would nature reflect the sternness of the Puritan's fibre or the self-sacrificing part of his ideals?

The older folks sit

"... the clean winged hearth about,
Shut in from all the world without,
Content to let the north wind roar
In baffled rage at pane and door."
—Whittier

But to the younger generation, a winter holiday means action!—and down through "Swamp Hollow" and over the hill road they go, afoot or in sleighs, through the drifting snow, to the barn dance at the Centre. The village band of fiddles, fife and horn keeps up an unending "break-down" medley, and the young folks "salute their partners and balance corners" till midnight. As the party breaks up, the sentimental songs of those days are sung half in fun, half seriously, and with the inevitable "adieu to the ladies" the "social" gives way to the grey bleakness of the February night.[10]

Ives wrote that the program is necessary for understanding the piece:

If this piece is played separately, without outlining the program, it may give (and it has given) a wrong idea of what it is and what it was made for. These three holiday movements (perhaps less in *Thanksgiving*, which has some religious significance) are but attempts to make pictures in music of common events in the lives of common people (that is, of fine people), mostly of the rural communities. That's all there is to it. . . . So if *Washington's Birthday* were put on a [concert] program with no program-[notes], the D.A.R. [Daughters of the American Revolution] would think it pretended to have something to do with Washington, or his birthday, or "These United States"—or some speech by Senator Blowout![11]

There are three sections, depicting in turn the "New England midwinter" outdoors with the older folks indoors around the warm hearth; "the barn dance at the Centre"; and the trip home by sleigh or foot, singing a sentimental song and remembering the dance. The first of these is the hardest to portray, and probably the main reason Ives felt it was necessary for listeners to read the program to understand the piece. How does one depict a cold landscape and the old folks sitting around the fire?

As the movement begins, soft, dissonant, rapidly trembling chords in the strings suggest shivering in the cold, and then slower, irregular pulsations, ever so slightly louder, give a sense of gradually warming up. Above these come little wisps of melody—a bit of *Home! Sweet Home!* by Henry R. Bishop in the first violins, fragments of Stephen Foster's *Old Folks at Home* in the horn and later in the violins, each more hinted at than stated. Both of these are popular songs from earlier generations (around 1820 and 1850 respectively) that were favorites of the older folk, and both are full of nostalgia for home, neatly evoking the indoors. Just as snow softens a landscape, both visually by rounding its shapes and literally by muting sounds, the first section stays soft for the most part. The rhythm is uneven, changing speeds and often differing between the parts, making the meter unclear and undercutting any motion that would break the calm silence of winter. After a while, soft orchestral bells add bright sounds that may suggest the glint of light off the snow. At last the music begins to grow louder and faster—"to the younger generation, a winter holiday means action!"—as dissonant chords rise and fall in parallel to depict the hills and snowdrifts on the way to the barn dance. Bits of dance tunes in the flute—*Turkey in the Straw* and *College Hornpipe*—suggest the fife in the village band, heard through the walls and doors of the barn as we approach. The music slows and pauses, like the slowing of a horse and sleigh as we come to a stop outside the barn.

Suddenly we are indoors, at the dance. The band strikes up with loud chords in D major (mostly—a few off-key notes sneak in), the strong sense of tonality contrasting greatly with the ambiguous, almost atonal music of the first section. As in the "In the Barn" movement from the Second Violin Sonata, Ives begins his portrayal of a barn dance with his own theme in the style of a fiddle tune, and then adds other tunes to it. In the violin sonata movement, working with just two instruments, he stitched bits of fiddle-tune melodies together in a kind of patchwork. Here, with the resources of an orchestra, he layers dance tunes on top of each other as well, in a kind of musical collage.

Just as in a visual collage scraps of paper or other objects are pasted on a surface to create interesting juxtapositions, in his musical collages Ives juxtaposes ideas by adding scraps of borrowed tunes on top of a musical fabric that would be logically coherent without them. He keeps these added layers distinct by placing them in different instruments, keys, rhythms, or levels of loudness, making them sound like separate streams of music.[12] Over his fiddle-tune theme, we hear bits of a waltz in the flute and violins, *College Hornpipe* in the flute echoed by violins, *Camptown Races* in the horn and cellos, and even *For He's a Jolly Good Fellow* in flute or horn. The band loses momentum and comes to a stop, then starts up again with *The White Cockade*, joined by the distinctive sound of a Jew's harp (or jaw harp), a mouth instrument Ives remembered men playing along with the band as they stood on the side of the dance floor.[13] More fragments of tunes drift by, with the flute and piccolo playing American, English, and Scottish tunes (*Turkey in the Straw*, *Massa's in de Cold Ground*, *Fisher's Hornpipe*, and *Money Musk*) and the horn adding Irish and Scottish ones, reflecting more-recent immigrants to New England (*Irish Washerwoman, The Campbells Are Coming, Garryowen,* and *Saint Patrick's Day*). The noise and confusion increase to a peak of loudness and dissonance.

The noise cuts off in a sonic exuviation, revealing a softer layer of music underneath. The party is breaking up, and the young folks are on their way home, singing as they go. "The sentimental songs of those days" are represented by a melody in the first violins that sounds like a compilation of all the tricks nineteenth-century songwriters put in their melodies, from lilting rhythms and ornamental turning figures to expressive leaps and chromatic neighbor notes. Softly and in a conflicting key, one solo violin plays a much quicker line strung together from bits of fiddle tunes (*Pig Town Fling* and *Turkey in the Straw*). This is one of Ives's patented "shadow lines," hovering in the background like something heard from a distance. Here it represents the dancers' memories of the dance, flitting through their minds as they go home. The young men say goodbye to their dates, suggested by Edwin P. Christy's *Goodnight, Ladies* in the flute and violin. As "the 'social' gives way to the grey bleakness of the February night," we hear again the soft shivering chords from the beginning.

Representing Memories of Music and of Holidays

In his description of *Washington's Birthday* in *Memos*, Ives suggested a reason for including several tunes at once in the barn dance:

> In some parts of the hall a group would be dancing a polka, while in another a waltz, with perhaps a quadrille or lancers going on in the middle. Some of the players in the band would, in an impromptu way, pick up with the polka, and some with the waltz or march. Often the piccolo or cornet would throw in "asides."[14]

But this music does not realistically depict how a barn dance sounds, even one with three bands going at once. It is more like an entire evening's worth of dance music, telescoped into two minutes. What Ives is trying to represent is not the experience of actually being at a barn dance in the 1880s, but what it is like to *remember* it thirty years later. When we remember, one memory leads to another, through some kind of association. Here, as Ives recalls the dances of his youth, one dance tune suggests another in the same style, or with a similar rhythm or melody, or from the same national tradition. The collage of fragmentary tunes represents the way our memory works, recalling things as they come, often altered, even distorted, and jumbled up together. This is a piece about memory: remembering the barn dance as we go home that evening, but also, decades later, remembering the whole day's experience, and many days like it, including our memories of remembering. It is a beautiful and moving fulfillment of what Harmony wrote to Ives, that "happy moments are put into expression after they have been memories & made doubly precious because they are *gone*."

And memories are fickle. If you know these dance tunes—say, you play in a contra dance band, and all of these are in your repertoire—you still may not catch them all as they fly by. Some are prominent, others harder to hear amid the overlapping simultaneous lines; some are easy to recognize, others shifted to offbeats or otherwise distorted, making them hard to place. The seeming chaos reflects the randomness of memory, and the way some memories are more vivid than others. On the other hand, you may not know any of these tunes. The music still makes sense: like Ives's own theme for this section, they sound like dance tunes, inviting you to tap your foot or get up and dance, and especially like the tunes you might hear at a square dance or contra dance. The associations may be more specific for someone who knows the tunes, which is one reason Ives carefully avoids melodies with the wrong associations—a Tin Pan Alley song, for example, even if equally bright and perky, would suggest urban life or a street scene, not a dance in a barn in rural New England. But recognizing the tunes is not a requirement. If it were, in the opening section he could have made *Home! Sweet Home!* and *Old Folks at Home* instantly recognizable and unmistakable. His subtle hints of them fit the wispiness of memory better than a flat-out statement. That he is picturing memories of *home* and of the *old folks* we will know only if we recognize them and recall the words, in the same way that we have to know *Goodnight, Ladies* to catch "the inevitable 'adieu to the ladies'" at the end.

Program music has its limits. Ives asked at the beginning of his *Essays Before a Sonata*, his book-length explanation of what he was after in his *Concord Sonata*,

> Can a tune literally represent a stone wall with vines on it or even with nothing on it, though it (the tune) be made by a genius whose power of objective contemplation is in the highest state of development? Can it be done by anything short of an act of mesmerism on the part of the composer or an act of kindness on the part of the listener?[15]

The answer, of course, is no. A piece of program music is not just music; like a song, choral work, opera, or movie, it is a combination of music and words. One understands the music in relation to the program, and vice versa. The first section of *Washington's Birthday* represents winter because Ives says it does in the program, and knowing the program helps us understand, for example, that the softly trembling strings at the beginning may suggest shivering in the cold, and slowly warming as the trembling eases. If the program were about frightful happenings in the dark, we would interpret the same music to mean something quite different.

The barn dance is easier: it sounds like a barn dance from the start. In a classic example of fictional music, it invites us to imagine ourselves at the dance, hearing the band play. And the sense that the fiddle tune in the last section is a memory, or perhaps a tune heard from a distance, is clearly conveyed by its being much softer, echoing a technique Ives had learned as an organist, and in a different key.[16] What Ives is after in this movement, and in the other movements of the *Holidays Symphony*, is to portray both the holiday itself and how music plays a role in it. It may be hard to write a tune that represents a stone wall, but representing a barn dance, or "the sentimental songs of those days," or any other kind of music, is something music is born to do. Ives's pictures of American holidays can be wonderfully evocative and specific because they are pieces of music that are *about* music itself, about the associations music brings, about the joy and exuberance and sentiments and tears music gives us. They work magic for a listener who knows the particular tunes he cites and who carries similar memories of them, but they also work for anyone who can hear the difference between a fiddle tune and a hymn— and that is just about everyone.

DECORATION DAY

The next movement, *Decoration Day*, is a product of roughly the same span of years as *Washington's Birthday*. Ives usually dated it 1912 or 1913, but the surviving manuscripts are on music paper from 1915 or later. The pencil score was ready by about 1919, followed by further revisions in the 1920s and a final copyist's score by 1929.[17]

In *Memos*, Ives describes a disastrous read-through in the spring of 1920 by the New Symphony Orchestra conducted by Paul Eisler at Carnegie Hall. The orchestra "had offered to give an invitation rehearsal-concert playing American manuscript compositions," and after initially objecting that "it is absolutely impossible for us to play this composition at our rehearsals, as it is much too difficult to read at sight," Eisler relented and agreed to try it. In his account, Ives refers to letters marked in the score and parts, used during rehearsals to help everyone find the same place in the music quickly; the conductor must have called out the rehearsal letters as they went by.

Mr. Eisler . . . stood up and started them off with a nice baton in his hand. At the end of each section, one little violinist in the back row was the only one playing, all the others having dropped by the wayside. When they got to letter B, they all started together, and the back-line violinist was again the only survivor reaching C. Section C was started in the same way, and so on till the march at the end came. At the end of that, a bass drum and the fiddler were the two survivors. I doubt if there was a single measure that was more than half played. . . . After the "performance," at which some of the audience laughed, some of them cussed, and some did something else, Mr. Eisler was mad, came up, and handed me back the score saying, "There is a limit to musicianship." . . .

This is a good example of how much water can run under the bridge in a few years time. This "performance" was . . . thirteen years ago, yet today this score could be picked up and played readily by any symphony orchestra with only a few rehearsals, and it has been. It was recently played by the Havana Symphony Orchestra [Orquesta Filarmónica de la Habana, conducted by Cuban composer Amadeo Roldán in the public premiere], December 27, 1931, and with apparently little difficulty.[18]

Given his own skills as an organist, Ives clearly expected professionals to be able to play anything set before them. He writes that he wanted to tell Eisler that "the greatest limits to musicianship are your [own] limitations."[19]

The disappointing read-through was doubly unfortunate, for in several ways *Decoration Day* was the most personally meaningful movement for Ives in the *Holidays Symphony*. It depicts the day set aside each year to decorate with flowers the graves of Union soldiers who died in the Civil War. (After World War I, the day was renamed Memorial Day and broadened to commemorate soldiers from all wars and eras.) The Civil War ended less than a decade before Ives was born. During his childhood many of the men around him, including his father, had served in the war, and memories were fresh of those whose graves their families were decorating. Central to the day's events in Danbury was the town band, led by his father, who was a bandleader in the Union Army and played *Taps* many times for memorial observances at the town cemetery.[20]

This movement has the most specific program of any in the *Holidays Symphony*, and the music closely follows the program. This shows how important it was for Ives to convey the events and feelings of Decoration Day as commemorated in Danbury, inviting his listeners to imagine ourselves there, back then, hearing these sounds.

In the early morning the garden and woods about the village are the meeting places of those who, with tender memories and devoted hands, gather the flowers for the day's memorial. During the forenoon, as the people join each other on the [village] green, there is felt at times a fervency and intensity—a shadow, perhaps, of the fanatical harshness—reflecting old abolitionist days. It is a day, Thoreau suggests, when there is a pervading consciousness of "Nature's kinship with the lower order—man."

After the town hall is filled with the spring's harvest of lilacs, daisies, and peonies, the parade is slowly formed on Main Street. First come the three marshals on plough horses (going sideways); then the warden and burgesses (in carriages!!), the village cornet band, the G.A.R. [members of the Grand Army of the Republic, the association of Union veterans] two by two, and the militia (Company G), while the volunteer fire brigade, drawing the decorated hose-cart with its jangling bells, brings up the rear—the inevitable swarm of small boys following. The march to Wooster Cemetery [just outside Danbury] is a thing a boy never forgets. The roll of muffled drums and "Adeste fideles" answer for the dirge. A little girl on the fence-post waves to her father and wonders if he looked like that at Gettysburg.

After the last grave is decorated, "Taps" sounds out through the pines and hickories, while a last hymn is sung. Then the ranks are formed again, and we all march back to town to a Yankee stimulant—[David Wallis] Reeves's inspiring *Second Regiment [March]*—though to many a soldier the somber thoughts of the day underlie the tunes of the band. The march stops, and in the silence the shadow of the early morning flower-song rises over the town, and the sunset behind West Mountain breathes its benediction upon the day.[21]

Reeves's *Second Regiment Connecticut National Guard March*, which earlier served as the model for Ives's youthful *Holiday Quickstep* and makes a brief appearance in *Yale-Princeton Football Game*, was both George Ives's and Charles Ives's favorite march; Ives called it "as good a march as Sousa or Schubert ever wrote, if not better!" The appearance here of its entire Trio, the longest borrowed passage in any Ives piece, is a clear reference to George Ives and his band. This movement about a memorial service is Ives's most direct and profound memorial to his father.[22]

The piece begins soft and poignant, a perfect picture of early morning on a day of tender memories. The strings sustain a major chord, made more open by large spaces between the notes, suggesting the open spaces of "the garden and woods about the village." Above it the first violins play a slowly arching melody in a completely different key; almost every note forms a dissonance, more sweet than harsh, against the chord below, evoking the gentle sadness of the day. The people gathering flowers are represented by a tune—"the early morning flower-song"—first played by English horn and then traded back and forth between the violins and the flute, always beginning the same way and then veering in a different direction as if depicting individuals working together on a common task but each with thoughts of their own.

A brief pause prepares a shift of scene. A somewhat faster and more varied section suggests "the people join[ing] each other on the [village] green." Their memories of the Civil War and the intense abolitionist struggle against slavery are invoked by phrases from Henry Clay Work's song *Marching Through Georgia*, about General William T. Sherman's 1864 march "from Atlanta to the sea," whose chorus (divided between flute and bassoon) begins "Hurrah! Hurrah! We bring the Jubilee!" As the parade slowly forms, only some of the images in Ives's program seem to be pictured in the music; leaping fourths sound like bugle calls, perhaps summoning groups to line up, and quiet bells may represent "the decorated [fire]hose-cart with its jangling bells."

"The march to Wooster Cemetery" begins with dissonant chords in the strings that suggest "the roll of muffled drums," an orchestral parallel to the piano-drumming in Ives's songs *The Circus Band* and *General William Booth Enters into Heaven*. *Adeste fideles*, slightly altered and played by strings and horns with afterbeats in the flutes, is known today as a Christmas song ("O come, all ye faithful") but was also sung in the nineteenth century with other texts that suited it to "answer for the dirge" played by "the village cornet band." The range of feelings the Civil War evoked is hinted at by phrases from two other songs: *Tenting on the Old Camp Ground*, Walter Kittredge's 1864 song of soldiers who are "weary tonight, wishing for the war to cease," and George F. Root's rousing *The Battle Cry of Freedom* from the first months of the war, which begins, "Yes we'll rally round the flag, boys, we'll rally once again." Quiet, trembling notes in the basses reflect the awe and emotion of the crowd as the marchers arrive at the cemetery.

An offstage trumpet plays *Taps*, sounding from a distance as if "through the pines and hickories." Meanwhile "a last hymn is sung": Lowell Mason's *Bethany* ("Nearer, my God, to Thee"), a regular at funerals and memorial services, its first phrase played softly in the trembling violins. Then the strings again imitate drums, faster now and playing the marching pattern *Street Beat* to begin the "march back to town." The band strikes up the Trio of Reeves's *Second Regiment Connecticut National Guard March*, made even more vivid and vibrant as Ives adds instruments, running scales, and new figuration. Yet "the somber thoughts of the day underlie the tunes of the band": *Taps* in bells and solo viola and twisted variants of *The Battle Hymn of the Republic* ("Mine eyes have seen the glory of the coming of the Lord") in a flute and clarinet. These probably go unheard amid the noise of the march, but in a live performance the audience can see these performers playing in their own rhythms, separate from the rest of the orchestra, as if in their own private worlds. A better musical image for inner thoughts, unspoken in the midst of a crowd, is hard to imagine.

Then "the march stops," and the loud music dissipates in another trademark sonic exuviation. Hanging in the air is the English horn (now off-stage to create a sense of distance) with "the shadow of the early morning flower-song," symbolizing the thoughts of those who gathered flowers, still thinking of their loved ones in the cemetery. The piece ends quietly with an "Amen" in high strings and *Taps* in bells and viola, two ways "the sunset behind West Mountain breathes its benediction upon the day."

Music and Program

As in *Washington's Birthday*, the program illuminates the music and vice versa. Ives mentions in the program the music he wants to make sure we notice: "the early morning flower-song," *Adeste fideles*, *Taps*, and Reeves's march. *Taps* is crucial; it is the bugle call played when a soldier or veteran is buried and at the annual Decoration Day (or Memorial Day) ceremony, and the piece could not be a true picture of the day without it. If we do not catch "Nearer, My God, to Thee" playing alongside it, the soft, trembling string sound is enough to suggest the inner feelings of those at the cemetery, a mix of sadness and prayer. That the village band plays a dirge on the way to the cemetery and a quickstep on the way home is just what the band would do, and their presence in this movement puts the band at the center of the experience. The particular music Ives includes makes the memory of the day more specific to Danbury and to his father, but if we do not recognize those tunes, we still get the point. The Civil War songs are more subtle; Ives only hints at them in his program (mentioning "a fervency and intensity . . . reflecting old abolitionist days" and referring to the G.A.R. and Gettysburg), and if we recognize the tunes and know their connection to the war they can deepen our understanding of the meaning of the holiday for those observing it so soon after the war ended. Once again, the piece is not just about the holiday but about the part music plays in commemorating it and in Ives's memories.

THE FOURTH OF JULY

The third movement of the *Holidays Symphony* captures the spirit of festivities on the most patriotic of American holidays. Ives composed *The Fourth of July* around the same time as the first two movements; he dated it 1912 or 1913, and according to Gayle Sherwood Magee the sketches are from around 1914, the score-sketch around 1919 (on paper from no earlier than 1917), and the pencil score around 1919–1923, with further revisions before the copyist's score was prepared around 1930–1931.[23] In a 1969 interview, Julian Myrick recalled a moment when the piece was almost destroyed:

> Once when we were moving from one place to another, we had a little safe. Charlie had one part, and I had another. He'd cleaned out his part, and I went to clean out my part, and there was a stack of music. And I said, "Charlie, you want me to throw this away?" And he looked and said, "Why, Mike! God, that's the best thing I've written!" And it was *The Fourth of July* about to be thrown away. That was dedicated to me, and his wife was responsible for that.[24]

The Fourth of July was premiered on February 21, 1932, soon after the first two movements of the *Holiday Symphony* were first played in late 1931. For a piece about celebrations of Independence Day in the United States, it seems ironic that the first performance was in Europe, at the Salle Pleyel in Paris, by an orchestra of French musicians drawn from the Orchestre Symphonique de Paris, conducted by a Russian emigré, Nicolas Slonimsky, who had conducted the premiere of *Washington's Birthday* the previous fall (and of *Three Places in New England* in early 1931). Slonimsky repeated the piece in Berlin on March 5 with players from the Berlin Philharmonic, and in Budapest on April 2 with the Hungarian Symphony Orchestra. Later that year it became Ives's first piece to be published in Europe, issued simultaneously in Berlin by Edition Adler and in San Francisco by Cowell's *New Music*.[25]

Ives wrote in *Memos* that *The Fourth of July* "is pure program music—it's also pure abstract music—'You pays your money, and you takes your choice'" (quoting Mark Twain's *Huckleberry Finn*).[26] His program for the piece captures its overall spirit:

> It's a boy's 4th—no historical orations—no patriotic grandiloquences by "grown-ups"—no program in his yard! But he knows what he's celebrating—better than most of the county politicians. And he goes at it in his own way, with a patriotism nearer kin to nature than jingoism. His festivities start in the quiet of the midnight before, and grow raucous with the sun. Everybody knows what it's like—if everybody doesn't—Cannon on the Green, Village Band on Main Street, fire crackers, shanks mixed on cornets, strings around big toes, torpedoes, Church bells, lost finger, fifes, clam-chowder, a prize-fight, drum-corps, burnt shins, parades (in and out of step), saloons all closed (more drunks than usual), baseball game (Danbury All-Stars vs. Beaver Brook Boys), pistols, mobbed umpire, *Red, White*

and Blue, runaway horse—and the day ends with the sky-rocket over the Church steeple, just after the annual explosion sets the Town-Hall on fire. All this is not in the music—not now.[27]

A few events in this program are depicted in the piece, yet most are not. This movement is not "pure program music" in the way that *Washington's Birthday* and *Decoration Day* are movements whose structure and musical material are almost entirely determined by their programs. Nor is it "pure abstract music," music whose form and contents have no associations outside music. Rather, it combines an "abstract" form—cumulative form, in which fragments and variants of the theme and countermelody gradually build up to a complete presentation of the two together—with musical material whose associations fit the Fourth of July holiday. The main theme is *Columbia, the Gem of the Ocean* (which Ives calls by its alternate title, *The Red, White, and Blue*), and the countermelody is paraphrased from *The Battle Hymn of the Republic* and a phrase from *Marching Through Georgia*. Around this basic structure is a collage of melodic scraps from patriotic songs and dance tunes. Like the collage in the barn dance episode in *Washington's Birthday*, this represents a swirl of memories: the sounds, sights, and people Ives remembered from childhood celebrations of the Fourth of July.

The movement begins in a way very like *Decoration Day*, with a soft, sustained, open-spaced major chord in low strings under a melody in the first violins in a different key, every note in the melody dissonant against the chord below. The soft yet haunting music and the motionless harmony convey "the quiet of the midnight before," while the first violin melody—the opening notes of *Columbia, the Gem of the Ocean*, echoed in distorted form by the second violins—suggests the boy's dreams of "his festivities" to come. The dreamy atmosphere is continued by a soft dissonance held by two violins while another violin, barely heard in the background, plays a repeating chromatic figure that creates more dissonances against them. The opening phrase of *Columbia*, still soft, repeats slowly in the basses, then basses and tuba together. Above it in the strings are chords based on fourths, on whole tones, or on fifths, all intervals taken from the tune itself. These chords, sonorities Ives had explored in his experimental music, are static, without the forward propulsion of tonal music, and they seem here like changing colors in the cool stillness of the early morning.

Gradually new instruments are heard from, and the pace picks up as the day begins. A cuckoo's call in the piccolo is followed by fragments and partial paraphrases of *Columbia, the Gem of the Ocean*, with occasional bugle call figures and bits of two Civil War tunes, *The Battle Cry of Freedom* and *Marching Through Georgia*. Two flutes and a piccolo play variants of *Columbia*, sounding like fifes. A sudden loud chord marked "like a gun-shot!" may represent the "pistols" or "fire crackers" in the program. We hear the cuckoo's call again, softer now, as the sounds of human activity begin to overwhelm the sounds of nature.

The tempo picks up again and a new section begins, throwing out more scraps of melody, like memories coming too fast to track. For those who recognize the tunes or the styles of music they represent, they evoke the combination of partying and patriotism typical of the Independence Day holiday. Bits of the dance tunes *College Hornpipe* and *Fisher's Hornpipe* in the winds are answered by military and patriotic music: part of the countermelody based on *The Battle Hymn of the Republic*, with *Street Beat* in the drums, *The Battle Cry of Freedom* in the horns, and *Reveille* in the brass. The beginning of the countermelody in flutes and oboes is paired with the first phrase of *Columbia, the Gem of the Ocean* in trombones, both melodies beginning to sound like they will when combined at the end of the movement. A tune from George Washington's era, *Hail! Columbia*, appears in clarinets and bassoons. Then a fife and drum band marches across the musical landscape in a faster tempo, disconnected from everything else like the "parades (in and out of step)" in the program, playing a tune made of bits of the fiddle tune *The White Cockade*, the Civil War song *Tramp, Tramp, Tramp*, and the British soldiers' song *The Girl I Left Behind Me*, mixing together strands from different eras and with diverse associations. The fifes start *London Bridge Is Falling Down*, picked up by flutes, oboe, and bassoon, and—

BANG! Suddenly the "Cannon on the Green" goes off, represented by music that wonderfully captures the blast and quick decay of an explosion: a gigantic splat of sound containing almost every note the orchestra can play from lowest to highest, followed by rapidly rushing figures that gradually slow and return to quiet.

As the music resumes, fragments of *Columbia, the Gem of the Ocean* reappear, joined by *Hail! Columbia* in horn and trumpet (and later cello and clarinet), the dance tunes *Garryowen* and *Saint Patrick's Day* in the xylophone, and *Reveille*, *Irish Washerwoman*, and *Marching Through Georgia* in the trumpet. Again, the hailstorm of tune scraps comes too quickly to hear them all but aptly suggests memories pouring in of holidays past. The density of sound builds and builds.

At last, the trumpets and trombones blast out *Columbia, the Gem of the Ocean* at full volume, with a cornet, clarinets, oboes, and flutes playing the countermelody based on *The Battle Hymn of the Republic* and a bit of *Marching Through Georgia*. The instruments on each melody do not play exactly the same thing, as Ives affectionately imitates the mishaps of an amateur band. These include playing wrong notes or rhythms, getting out of step with each other, and "mixed shanks on cornets": when brass players on the same part mistakenly use different shanks—extension tubes that alter the pitch of the instrument—so they are playing in different keys. *Street Beat* in the drums makes it sound like a parade, and the upper strings add the roar of the crowd, playing all the notes from three different keys simultaneously while running up and down their scales in a wash of total dissonance. A brief pause, a distant bell, and then comes another, even louder roar as "the annual explosion sets the Town-Hall on fire." The noise vanishes in a sonic exuviation, and soft falling figures in high solo strings portray the descent of "the sky-rocket over the Church steeple."

"Profoundly National"

Of some twenty different tunes that appear in this movement, the only one Ives mentions in the program is *The Red, White, and Blue*—that is, *Columbia, the Gem of the Ocean*, the theme of the piece, the culmination of the cumulative form. The others give the piece a special character, embodying the variety of music one might hear during the course of Independence Day, from patriotic songs to fiddle tunes and popular songs, and thereby representing Ives's memories of the holiday in his youth. The meaning is more specific for listeners who can recognize the borrowed tunes as they go flying by, but the types they represent are sufficient to suggest the roles music played in late-nineteenth-century small town celebrations of the Fourth of July.

When the piece was premiered in Paris, critics were generally positive. Among the most sympathetic was Boris de Schloezer, who wrote that Ives

> is not an imitator; he has something to say. Ives is a musical painter, if one may use such an expression, an impressionist; he is, however, not without moments of naive realism. His art is at times coarse and clumsy, but in him there is genuine strength and inventiveness, thematically as well as rhythmically, in no way taking fashion or authority into consideration. . . . *The Fourth of July* (the American national holiday) is based on national motifs; in this regard Ives is, perhaps, the only one among the composers of North America whose work is profoundly national, and in him there is something reminiscent of Walt Whitman.[28]

The comparison to Whitman must have pleased Ives, who had set Whitman's poetry as a song and as a choral work and had considered writing an orchestral piece about him.

THANKSGIVING AND FOREFATHERS' DAY

The final movement of the *Holidays Symphony* is the least programmatic, has the earliest roots, and was the last to be finished. It links two holidays: Thanksgiving, celebrating the Pilgrims' first harvest in the New World in the fall of 1621, and Forefathers' Day, a regional New England holiday that commemorates the Mayflower Pilgrims' reaching land and coming ashore at the future site of Plymouth Colony on December 21, 1620. Ives did not give this movement a written program as he did the others, but meant it to convey something of the character of the Pilgrims, the work of the harvest, and the determination to cross the sea and build a new life.

According to Ives's *Memos*, the movement was derived from a pair of pieces he wrote while at Yale,

> an organ *Prelude and Postlude for a Thanksgiving Service* played in Center Church, New Haven, Conn., in November 1897. . . . Parker made some fairly funny cracks about it, but Dr. Griggs said it had something of the Puritan character, a stern but outdoors strength, and something of the pioneering feeling. He liked it as such, and told Parker so. Parker just smiled and took him over to Heublein's for [a beer].
>
> . . . The *Postlude* started with a C minor chord with a D minor chord over it, together, and later major and minor chords together, a tone apart. This was to represent the sternness and strength and austerity of the Puritan character, and it seemed to me that any of the major, minor, or diminished chords used alone gave too much a feeling of bodily ease, which the Puritan did not give in to. . . . There is a scythe or reaping Harvest Theme, which is a kind of off-beat, off-key counterpoint.[29]

Only one page of these early pieces still exists, the first page of the *Postlude* in a copy from about 1899. Like the orchestral movement, it starts with a C major (not minor) and a D minor chord superimposed and includes a motive marked "Harvest Work Theme," which mimics the repeated sweeping motion of a scythe cutting grain with a repeating figure of a long note, quick motion down a step and back up, and big downward leap. How closely the rest of the organ pieces resembled *Thanksgiving and Forefathers' Day* we cannot know. Ives said the organ prelude and postlude "were put into a single piece for an orchestra . . . some time around 1904," but the surviving sketches date from around 1913–1919, and he prepared the full score in the winter of 1932–1933, after the other three movements of the *Holidays Symphony* had already been premiered. This movement was first performed at the premiere of the full four-movement symphony by the Minneapolis

Symphony Orchestra conducted by Antal Dorati on April 9, 1954, less than six weeks before Ives passed away.[30]

Ives's comments in *Memos* make clear how he sought to represent the Pilgrims' character and the work of harvesting through musical imagery. This comes near to the question he raised elsewhere about whether music can represent a stone wall; without his explanation, we might never understand what the opening sonority stood for, or what the sweeping motions in the music were meant to evoke. The arrival of the Pilgrims in the New World as the culmination of a great journey is suggested, not through programmatic imagery, but through the form of the movement and the hymn tunes he used for his main themes. Like the middle movement of the Fourth Violin Sonata, this piece blends cumulative and ternary forms, with two outer sections that together comprise a cumulative form and enclose a contrasting middle section.

The cumulative process reaches its goal near the end when a choir, reinforced by trumpets and bassoon, sings the main theme, a hymn suitable for Forefathers' Day: John Hatton's *Duke Street* with these words by Leonard Bacon, written in 1833 for the bicentennial of the 1638 founding of New Haven (Ives's ancestor William Ives was one of the founders):

O God, beneath Thy guiding hand
Our exiled fathers crossed the sea;
And when they trod the wintry strand,
With prayer and psalm they worshipped Thee.

The tune, composed in the 1790s, is as stirring as the words. Unlike many other hymn tunes Ives used, every phrase is different, each rising to a peak, then stepping down to close. Ives slightly alters both the tune and the words, syncopating the rhythm in places, starting the third phrase early, and changing "when" to "as" and "psalm" to "praise" in the last two lines. He uses as a countermelody another hymn tune, *Federal Street* by Henry K. Oliver; Ives replaces its third phrase with the third phrase from *Duke Street* so that the countermelody briefly imitates the main theme when the two appear together. Both tunes share a repeating rhythm (long-short-short long-short-short) but have very differently shaped melodies: *Duke Street* marches up and down in broad arches, while *Federal Street* begins with repeated notes and stays in a narrow range.

The middle section is itself a small ternary form (ABA'). The A theme is *Shining Shore*, slightly varied, and the lively B theme is paraphrased from the same hymn tune in a way that resembles the paraphrased themes in the First String Quartet and Second Symphony. The words of *Shining Shore* look forward to the afterlife using images of traveling across the water that parallel the Pilgrims' voyage to the New World:

> My days are gliding swiftly by,
> And I, a pilgrim stranger,
> Would not detain them as they fly,
> Those hours of toil and danger.
>
> *Refrain*
>> For now we stand on Jordan's strand;
>> Our friends are passing over;
>> And, just before, the shining shore
>> We may almost discover.

The last verse ends with lines that would especially resonate with New Englanders convinced that God led their forebears over the ocean to the new land:

> Our King says "Come!" and there's our home,
> Forever, and forever.

The other movements of the *Holidays Symphony* illustrate the roles music plays in celebrating Americans holidays. This movement does too—not by means of a program, but by centering the music on these hymns that could be used in a church service on Thanksgiving or Forefathers' Day, and by drawing on organ pieces that were.

<hr />

The movement opens dark and bold, reflecting the stern strength of the Pilgrims with loud, dissonant chords. Amid the impressive blocks of sound, bits of melody emerge like plants from the rocky soil, all foreshadowing events to come: the opening of *Federal Street*, a repeated note followed by a half step up and down; the swooping motive of the Harvest Work Theme; the first phrase of *Shining Shore*. In a quieter moment, the first phrase of *Federal Street* passes between instruments, while other hymn tunes float softly in the background in "shadow" lines, marked "Faintly, as choir practicing before church [as heard from] the distance," in a kind of collage of remembered hymns. Again the music swells, growing darker and more dissonant. A noble tune rings out in the brass and low strings: the first phrase of *Duke Street*, the main theme, soon echoed in other parts and joined by bits of the countermelody. Things speed up, becoming more and more agitated. At the peak of confusion, the Harvest Work Theme appears in complete form for the first time, jumping between high and low to convey the sweeping motions of the scythe. The music slows and softens, and the sweeping scythe gradually becomes a gentle rocking back and forth in a transition to the middle section of the movement.

The stern dissonance of the first section dissipates, replaced by a gentle tranquillity. Over a soft bed of strings and bells, an oboe and flute quietly trade phrases of *Shining Shore,* the A theme of the middle section. The violins take over the tune and vary it over a light accompaniment, alternating at times with flute and oboe. After the loud, dissonant beginning, this is an oasis of spiritual calm. Sudden loud chords in a faster tempo announce the vigorous B theme, paraphrased from *Shining Shore* but sounding more like a contra dance tune. The full orchestra repeats the B theme, joined by more hymn tune shadow lines in the oboes. Suddenly everyone cuts off in a sonic exuviation—a real Ives trademark—and the A theme returns in varied form, restoring serenity.

A transition gradually grows more dissonant, louder, and more active, leading into the movement's third large section. This takes up where the first section left off, bringing back elements of the Harvest Work Theme, the countermelody based on *Federal Street,* and the main theme, *Duke Street.* As these intermix, the music grows more intense, moving through the darkness of the movement's opening section to find a greater dynamism, building toward a climax. Then the majestic moment we have been waiting for arrives: the chorus, trumpets, and bassoon burst forth with the complete statement of *Duke Street,* joined by the countermelody in the horns and trombones and portions of the Harvest Work Theme in the clarinet. From this peak, the music ebbs away, as the chorus repeats the last notes of the hymn and the brass and winds repeat the last phrase of the countermelody, slowly fading to nothing.

BRINGING IT ALL TOGETHER

In the *Holidays Symphony,* Ives brought together all four traditions he had learned as a boy and young man. American popular music is represented by popular songs and fiddle tunes in *Washington's Birthday* and *The Fourth of July* and patriotic songs, marches, and bugle calls in *Decoration Day* and *The Fourth of July.* Protestant church music appears through hymn tunes in *Decoration Day* and *Thanksgiving,* adaptations of organ music in *Thanksgiving,* and effects Ives learned as an organist, from counterpoint to sonic exuviation, in all four movements. The European classical tradition is evident in the genres of the symphony and symphonic poem, the concept of program music, and standard procedures of themes, form, contrasting sections, and orchestration. And techniques Ives learned through his musical experiments serve to convey images in his programs. Juxtaposing tonal music and atonal music sets off a barn dance from the winter outdoors and bands in parades from the sounds of nature or exploding fireworks. Layering disparate streams of music creates a sense of many things happening at once, conveying an outdoor scene or the whirl of memories. Simultaneous melodies in different keys, tone colors, and levels of prominence suggest remembered dance tunes, private thoughts, and music heard at a distance. Novel dissonant chords move in parallel to suggest snowdrifts, drum patterns, crowd noise, or the sweep of a scythe. All of these techniques, first tried out just to see what would happen, now serve a musical narrative, used not for their own sake but to tell a story. The most astonishing thing about these movements is the way Ives uses modernist means to achieve Romantic ends, depicting events or conveying thoughts or feelings, as nineteenth-century composers had done, but with spectacularly innovative methods.

What is the message of the *Holidays Symphony*? Not nostalgia for the past, as some have claimed.[31] First conceived as a medical diagnosis for homesickness, coined from combining the Greek words *nostos* (return home) and *algos* (pain), and later broadened to mean a longing for the way things used to be, nostalgia is a yearning for what was once familiar and is still beloved but is now impossibly remote or lost forever. Ives's affectionate images of small-town holiday celebrations in the 1880s are too cheerful to evoke pain. One gets instead a sense of a past that is still with us, still usable, embodying values that endure in the present: community, friendship, family, character, self-sacrifice, energy, fun, strength, dedication, perseverance, faith, respect for others and oneself, accepting each other's foibles and one's own, remembering those who came before us and seeking to do them proud. These are lasting values, ones Ives saw lived out in his hometown holidays and felt were needed still in twentieth-century America, and he brought them to life in his *Holidays Symphony*.

· 9 ·

American Histories

$\mathcal{A}$longside the four movements that became the *Holidays Symphony*, Ives was working on a number of other symphonic poems in the 1910s. After trying various combinations, he grouped six of them into two suites he called Orchestral Set No. 1 and No. 2. Each has three movements in the order slow-fast-slow, which he had used earlier in the Third Symphony and the Second and Third Violin Sonatas. Both sets celebrate the ways Americans use music in our lives, and both trace a similar arc, with a slow first movement incorporating Stephen Foster tunes, a fast middle movement evoking public gatherings of his youth, and a slow final movement that captures a recent experience of hearing a hymn outdoors. The First Orchestral Set is unified by its subject matter, focusing on particular places in Massachusetts and Connecticut; Ives gave it the title *Three Places in New England*, and it became one of his most famous works. Although the Second Orchestral Set includes a finale Ives thought was one of the best pieces he ever wrote, he never gave the set a more evocative title, and it has been performed much less often than the first, illustrating the power of a catchy name. Both sets include movements about specific moments in American history—in the Revolutionary War, Civil War, and World War I—giving these works a broader sweep and a wider set of associations than the *Holidays Symphony*. But in other respects, they are cut from the same cloth, using similar procedures and combining elements from the four traditions of American popular music, Protestant church music, European symphonic music, and experimental music in similar ways.

ORCHESTRAL SET NO. 1: *THREE PLACES IN NEW ENGLAND*

Three Places in New England continues a tradition of landscape pieces that includes Mendelssohn's *Hebrides Overture*, Smetana's *The Moldau*, and Richard

Strauss's *Alpine Symphony* among many others. As in those works, one has a sense of the composer observing the scene, taking it all in and trying to depict it in music. Denise Von Glahn remarks that in his many pieces that are about or refer to places, Ives is "always an observer and eyewitness, [and] sometimes he is a more active participant."[1] Yet Ives's focus is not primarily on the wonders of nature, as was true for most of his predecessors, but on the people he identified with each place: soldiers who inspired the war memorials in the first two movements, townsfolk gathered for a Fourth of July picnic with the town band in the second, a congregation worshiping in a church near a river in the third. As he does in the *Holidays Symphony*, he brings these people to life through the music he associated with them, from war songs and band music to a hymn.

The three movements had independent origins and compositional histories, but by around 1919–1921 Ives had grouped them together and completed a full score for large orchestra. In 1928, Henry Cowell introduced Ives to Nicolas Slonimsky, a Russian emigré who was working in Boston as an assistant to Serge Koussevitzky, conductor of the Boston Symphony Orchestra. Drawing on musicians from the BSO, Slonimsky had founded the Chamber Orchestra of Boston in 1927, a smaller group that specialized in music suited for fewer players. He was especially interested in conducting new music and wanted to perform one of Ives's works. Ives picked *Three Places in New England* and rescored it for chamber orchestra, taking the opportunity to make other revisions as well. Slonimsky conducted a private reading of the piece in New York on February 16, 1930, for the United States section of the International Society for Contemporary Music, but it was not accepted for performance at the Society's annual European festival. Instead, Ives underwrote a concert by Slonimsky and his Chamber Orchestra of Boston at Town Hall in New York on January 10, 1931, featuring recent works by American composers that included the premiere of *Three Places in New England*, making it the second of Ives's orchestral works to be played in public, after the first two movements of the Fourth Symphony four years earlier.[2]

Slonimsky later recalled that Ives came to the concert:

> The performance was excellent. After the last residual chord . . . I made an attempt to espy Ives in the hall, . . . [but] Ives never acknowledged his presence, and nobody in the audience knew that he was there except from the evidence of my trying to find him. . . . Ives told me that he liked the informal manner of the whole concert. He said that it was like "a town meeting" and that everyone seemed to enjoy it.[3]

Ives sent tickets to George A. Lewis, his old friend from Poverty Flat, who wrote the next day and ended his letter with a new form of the Yale cheer Ives had included in *Yale-Princeton Football Game*:

Many, many thanks for the tickets. I enjoyed your compositions very much.... There was genuine enthusiasm and prolonged applause after all of the numbers you had written.... Ives shone brightly and Mozart [whose *A Musical Joke* was on the concert] was eclipsed. Rah! Rah! Rah! Ives! Ives! Ives! a bas [down with] Mozart![4]

Slonimsky and his group performed *Three Places in New England* again in Boston on January 25 (with Ives again in attendance), in New York at the New School for Social Research on February 7, in Havana on March 18, and then in Paris on June 6, the first of a series of concerts financed by Ives and designed to introduce modernist American composers to Europe.[5] Reviews in the Boston papers were mixed. The *Boston Post* critic identified Ives with "the lunatic fringe of modern music" and said the first movement "bore no observable relation to its subject matter" while judging the second "an ingenious and sometimes humorous parody of the efforts of a country band." Stephen Somervel in the *Boston Herald* was more generous, writing that the piece

is modern in the exact manner of those painters whose canvases—so redolent of this chaotic age—are a patchwork of jagged fragments overlapping, dovetailing, with an added complexity which painting cannot rival, namely that of a bewilderingly crowded simultaneity, an extraordinary contrapuntal freedom.[6]

Critics in Paris were generally positive, drawing comparisons to Igor Stravinsky's ballet *The Rite of Spring*, still a modernist touchstone almost two decades after its premiere. Paul Le Flem wrote in *Comoedia* that Ives

seems to have created for himself, before the *Rite of Spring*, a style whose audacities place its author among the pioneers. Compared to his compatriots, he appears to be the most spontaneously gifted musician, whose savage daring, though sometimes awkward, is never in contradiction with the aspirations of his feeling....
    Charles Ives's *Three Places in New England* is by turns humorous, with an amiable sincerity, and at other times a little heavy. He is as knowledgeable as his colleagues and manipulates polytonality without letting it blow up in his hands. But he knows how to add to his craft something sensitive, fresh, and alive which is not a mere extravagance.[7]

Writing in *Les Beaux-Arts*, Boris de Schloezer set out what became a common view of Ives as isolated, unskilled in traditional composition, but a bold innovator, calling him

a true precursor, an audacious talent, who may lack technique and skill but who, sticking to his way and working absolutely alone—because we

are sure that, living alone in the country, he never heard a note of Stravinsky—discovered a number of rhythmic and harmonic processes in vogue
today. In his music, in spite of his awkwardness, or rather because of it,
modernism acquired a remarkably individual flavor.[8]

Ives had consummate training and skill as a composer, so that any awkwardness was deliberate, a part of how he represented the scenes and people he
sought to capture in his music. He indeed had anticipated "rhythmic and
harmonic processes" later taken up by others, from polytonality and chords
based on fourths or fifths to layers of music in conflicting meters and rhythms.
Yet what was and remains most important in his music is what Schloezer
called its "remarkably individual flavor," a distinctive personality that derives
less from being a pioneer than from having a remarkably broad range of techniques at his fingertips, drawn from four different traditions, and using them
to convey a deeply personal vision.

Slonimsky conducted the last two movements of *Three Places in New
England* with the Philharmonic Orchestra of Los Angeles in December
1932, and the complete set was published in 1935. Although more than a
decade passed before it was performed again in 1948, it eventually became
one of Ives's most widely played pieces. Two decades after Ives's death, James
B. Sinclair created a new version that restored the original scoring for large
orchestra while preserving the revisions Ives made for the chamber orchestra
score and first publication, and it is now performed and recorded in both
full orchestra and chamber orchestra versions.[9] It offers a diverse set of tone
poems, each movement with its own title, and each suffused with a sense of
a special place and the people who once were present there. Let us visit the
three places, one by one.

The "St. Gaudens" in Boston Common

As in many old New England towns, near the center of Boston is the Common, a grassy open area once used for grazing cattle that by the early nineteenth century became the city's first and most important public park. Near
its northeast corner, directly opposite the Massachusetts State House across
Beacon Street, stands the *Memorial to Robert Gould Shaw and the Massachusetts Fifty-Fourth Regiment*, dedicated in 1897 and shown in Figure 9.1. The
huge bronze relief sculpture, fourteen feet wide and eleven feet tall, is by Augustus Saint-Gaudens (1848–1907), one of the leading American sculptors of
his generation. Front and center on horseback is Colonel Robert Gould Shaw
(1837–1863), and behind him, marching rank upon rank in parade formation,
are the soldiers he commanded, the 54th Regiment Massachusetts Volunteer

Figure 9.1. Augustus Saint-Gaudens's bronze relief sculpture on the *Memorial to Robert Gould Shaw and the Massachusetts Fifty-Fourth Regiment* in Boston Common.
Royal Cortissoz and Bruce Rogers, *Augustus Saint-Gaudens* (Boston: Houghton, Mifflin, 1907), 58.

Infantry, one of the first regiments of African Americans in the Union Army during the Civil War.

The regiment was formed in early 1863 after the Emancipation Proclamation, issued by President Lincoln that January 1, freed slaves in the rebel states and authorized the recruitment of African American soldiers. Free black men from the Boston area and throughout the North enlisted in the regiment, encouraged by black leaders such as Frederick Douglass (two of whose sons joined the regiment) as well as by white abolitionists. The officers were white, most—including Shaw himself—from abolitionist families and already experienced in battle with other Union regiments. Officers and soldiers alike understood that the 54th Regiment would serve not only to bolster the Union Army but also to demonstrate to skeptics that men of African descent were the equal of white men in valor, discipline, and ability. After three months' training at nearby Camp Meigs, on May 28 the regiment marched through Boston, past the future site of Saint-Gaudens's memorial, and traveled to an area on the coast of South Carolina that was already under Union control. On July 18, in their most famous battle, Shaw and his regiment led an assault on Fort Wagner, near Charleston, breaching the walls and capturing part of the fort before being forced back. Shaw and about thirty of his men were killed, fifteen were captured, and almost half of the remainder were wounded or missing in action. The regiment's bravery was celebrated across the North and inspired many other African Americans to enlist, helping to tilt the war toward the Union.

Saint-Gaudens depicted the regiment on parade down Beacon Street, marching off to war. Shaw is in three dimensions, foregrounded for the viewer but riding beside his soldiers rather than in front of them. The soldiers closest to us are also fully sculpted, others in high or bas relief to create a sense of increasing distance. They march with a unified stride and bearing, showing their training and discipline; yet they are each individuals, with distinctive facial features and differences in their heights, in the look of their bedrolls and backpacks, and in the angle of the rifles they carry over their shoulders. This is not an undifferentiated mass but a group of human beings, marked by dignity and resolve. Flying above them is the allegorical figure of Liberty, giving her blessing to their cause of ending slavery and reuniting the nation.

Ives's unwieldy double title for his first movement, *The "St. Gaudens" in Boston Common (Col. Shaw and His Colored Regiment)*, makes clear that it is about both the monument and the people who inspired it. (The word "colored" in Ives's title was a respectful term for African Americans at the time; the nation's leading organization working to secure civil rights and justice for African Americans was founded in 1909 and named the National Association for the Advancement of Colored People.) Ives began to compose the movement sometime between 1911–1912 (his date) and 1914–1915 (the earliest possible date for the surviving sketches), during the fiftieth anniversary of the Civil War, and completed the full score by 1919–1921. He was drawn to the subject through his father's service in the war and his grandparents' strong support for the abolition of slavery. In a 1943 letter he described the movement as "emblematic of the fight against slavery."[10]

In his music, Ives echoes several aspects of Saint-Gaudens's sculpture: the regular rhythm of marching feet; a somber mood with a sense of dignity; layers of music from prominent to less fully rounded to distant background, creating a three-dimensional impression of depth like the rows of soldiers in the monument; melodies that are constantly varied rather than repeating exactly, reflecting the individuality Saint-Gaudens cast into every face. The shape of the movement parallels the story of the 54th Regiment, with bits of melody joining together at the beginning like volunteers for the regiment; a march-like passage, like the slow march to the south; gradually building in intensity to a loud climax, suggesting the battle for Fort Wagner; and a return to the quiet march, now tinged with mourning, and the opening wisps of melody.[11] The troops in the regiment are represented by two plantation songs by Stephen Foster, *Old Black Joe* and *Massa's in de Cold Ground*, and two Civil War songs, Henry Clay Work's *Marching Through Georgia* and George F. Root's *The Battle Cry of Freedom*. All four songs share elements in common that Ives uses to weave them together in a musical embodiment of men who are both black and Civil War soldiers.

———⌒———

You have scored tickets to hear Leonard Slatkin and the St. Louis Symphony Orchestra play a program of music by American composers, including Ives's *Three Places in New England*. You settle into your seat and wait with anticipation. As usual with Ives, you don't know what to expect. Anything can happen.

The first movement begins on a quiet, low, dissonant chord in the strings. Above it, you barely hear a scrap of melody, dropping a minor third and rising again, like the opening of the chorus of *Old Black Joe*: "I'm coming." After a brief pause, the first violins take up the idea, repeat it, and link it to other wisps of melody that sound like bits of other tunes: "Hear dat mournful sound" from the chorus of *Massa's in de Cold Ground*, and "Hurrah! Hurrah! we bring the Jubilee!" from *Marching Through Georgia*. As the melody arches higher, it paraphrases more of *Old Black Joe*: "I'm coming, I'm coming, for my head is bending low." You may hear all of these tunes or none of them, for the melodic fragments are woven together into a single sustained and expressive melody, like the individual recruits melded into a fighting unit. Bits of the source melodies appear in the horn, flute, oboe, clarinet, and piano, adding glints of contrasting colors around the strings, as the violins continue to stitch together their melody from scraps of these tunes. If you recognize these fragments of melody, the words they evoke may suggest the determination of the volunteers of the 54th Regiment, coming to serve in hopes of bringing "the Jubilee"—the end of slavery—to their brothers and sisters enslaved in the Confederacy. Throughout this opening passage, the music is quiet and reflective; the harmony is dissonant yet grounded in tonal music by recurring hints of a key; and the bass softly repeats a rising minor third, echoing the melodic idea.

A slight increase in activity leads to a slow march. It begins quietly, as if to suggest the steady but silent marchers in the Saint-Gaudens sculpture. Drums tap out the *Street Beat*, keeping the march pattern going for the rest of the movement. The basses repeat a figure of a falling whole step and minor third, found in all four source tunes. The violins paraphrase half the chorus of *Marching Through Georgia* ("Hurrah! Hurrah! we bring the Jubilee! Hurrah! Hurrah! the flag that makes you free!"); the subtle reference to the flag invokes at once the American flag visible to the left in Saint-Gaudens's sculpture, the flag Sergeant William Harvey Carney caught and carried into Fort Wagner when the flag bearer fell in battle, and the liberty that the flag represented and that Union soldiers brought to enslaved people everywhere they triumphed. Meanwhile, offbeat and hard to hear, the piano plays part of the chorus of *The Battle Cry of Freedom*: "The Union forever, Hurrah boys, Hurrah!"

As *Street Beat* continues softly in the drums, the music speeds up slightly and the other instruments change to syncopated rhythms suggestive of ragtime—an anachronistic reference (since ragtime first emerged three decades after the Civil War) to a kind of music that was rooted in African American culture. The march slows again, then winds and strings develop fragments from *Marching Through Georgia*, building to a series of climaxes like the successive waves of assault on Fort Wagner. The music at this point is much less loud than it could be, with less noise than one would expect in battle, as if we were observing from a distance, or remembering at a later time, or standing in front of Saint-Gaudens's monument thinking about the fate that lies ahead for these brave men with determined faces.

After the third climax, the music quickly quiets and soon pauses. The march returns, with *Marching Through Georgia* in the violins joined by *The Battle Cry of Freedom* in the flute. As the music slows, the violins add a line from *Massa's in de Cold Ground*, mourning for Colonel Shaw and his men lost in battle. Bits of *Old Black Joe* return, ushering in a partial reprise of the opening section. With a few last echoes of the promise, "I'm coming," the movement fades to a close.

<hr />

Putnam's Camp, Redding, Connecticut

The second movement, like the first, evokes both a place and the events it commemorates. The title *Putnam's Camp, Redding, Connecticut* refers to the oldest state park in Connecticut, Putnam Memorial State Park, the site where American soldiers under the command of General Israel Putnam camped during the third winter of the Revolutionary War. The park lies about seven miles from Ives's boyhood home in Danbury and about five miles from the Iveses' summer home in West Redding. Although it was private property until becoming a state park in 1887, when Ives was twelve, he may have visited the site in his youth, and it is a boy's perspective that he summons up in his program note published in the score:

> Near Redding Center, Conn., is a small park preserved as a Revolution-
> ary Memorial; for here General Israel Putnam's soldiers had their winter

quarters in 1778–1779. Long rows of stone camp fire-places still remain to stir a child's imagination. The hardships which the soldiers endured and the agitation of a few hot-heads to break camp and march to the Hartford Assembly for relief, is a part of Redding history.

Once upon a "4th of July," some time ago, so the story goes, a child went there on a picnic, held under the auspices of the First Church and the Village Cornet Band. Wandering away from the rest of the children past the camp ground into the woods, he hopes to catch a glimpse of some of the old soldiers. As he rests on the hillside of laurels and hickories, the tunes of the band and the songs of the children grow fainter and fainter;—when— "mirabile dictu" [wonderful to relate]—over the trees on the crest of the hill he sees a tall woman standing. She reminds him of a picture he has of the Goddess of Liberty,—but her face is sorrowful—she is pleading with the soldiers not to forget their "cause" and the great sacrifices they have made for it. But they march out of camp with fife and drum to a popular tune of the day. Suddenly a new national note is heard. Putnam is coming over the hills from the center,—the soldiers turn back and cheer. The little boy awakes, he hears the children's songs and runs down past the monument to "listen to the band" and join in the games and dances.

The repertoire of national airs at that time was meagre. Most of them were of English origin. It is a curious fact that a tune very popular with the American soldiers was "The British Grenadiers." A captain in one of Putnam's regiments put it to words, which were sung for the first time in 1779 at a patriotic meeting in the Congregational Church in Redding Center; the text is both ardent and moving.[12]

The music is in three main parts, closely following the sequence of events Ives describes in his second paragraph. The first section depicts the picnic at the park "some time ago" through an affectionate portrayal of "the Village Cornet Band" with all its energy and mistakes. The middle section captures the boy's dream, with two fife and drum corps leading groups of soldiers on the march, one faster and more distant than the other, until Putnam returns to rally them again. Then suddenly the dream ends, the village band resumes, and the music builds to a final climax. Like the *Holidays Symphony*, this is a piece about memories: here, both the town's collective memory of an incident from the Revolutionary War and Ives's personal memories of his father's band playing at picnics, outdoor concerts, and holiday celebrations.

The overall form and the strong contrast between the sections reflect the movement's compositional history. Ives began work on it around 1914 by combining two earlier pieces, inserting one into the middle of the other, and completed it by 1921. He adapted the middle section from *Overture and March "1776,"* which he had begun around 1903 as the overture to an opera set during the Revolutionary War, on a libretto by his uncle Lyman Brewster. The music of the village band in the outer sections is from *Country Band*

March, composed between about 1905 and 1914, a reminiscence of amateur music-making in the spirit of the barn dance from *Washington's Birthday* and roughly in the form of a march with two alternating strains. To create the effect in *Putnam's Camp* of a dream sequence about Revolutionary soldiers in the middle of a Fourth of July picnic, Ives interrupts the amateur band march with a transition leading to the material from the overture, then jumps back to the band march where it had left off, and ends with a noisy coda that combines material from both pieces.[13] The result is surprisingly satisfying and dramatically effective, like a movie that dissolves from one scene into another, framing it as a flashback or dream, and then without transition cuts back to the first scene and continues it, as if the protagonist had suddenly woken to reality in the present. For a composer who apparently rarely or never went to the movies, Ives's anticipation of later cinematic effects is haunting.

As you thought to yourself earlier, you never know what to expect with Ives. Unlike the quiet opening of the first movement and others you have heard, this movement starts with a bang, almost rocketing you out of your seat. The orchestra blares out a loud, intensely dissonant chord, which clambers down the scale in a gesture right out of Ives's experimental music and at the same time wickedly comic. Just as suddenly as it began, the noisy outburst vanishes. From pulsing strings and drums emerge the introduction and first strain of a march, begun by the strings and quickly joined by other instruments. The tune is Ives's own, like the opening themes of the barn dances in the Second Violin Sonata and *Washington's Birthday*, but it reminds you of the sound and spirit of marches from the late nineteenth century by David Wallis Reeves and John Philip Sousa. As the strain continues, you hear the flute, oboes, and clarinets throw in bits of *The British Grenadiers* and the bassoon add a bugle call. The extra beats, missing beats, offbeat accents, wrong notes, and apparently wrong entrances or improvised additions surprise you, but then you realize that this is fictional music: the St. Louis Symphony Orchestra is not making mistakes; it is playing the part of an amateur band from a country town whose members are slipping up or having fun, and you are magically transported to another place and time, listening to an outdoor concert of these fervent but fallible musicians.

After a short bridge where the bandleader seems to have trouble getting the drums to stay together and the horn to play in the right key, the opening strain repeats. Piled on top of it is a collage of other bits of music a band might play on the Fourth of July: *Street Beat* in the drums, Sousa's marches *Semper Fideles* in trombone and tuba and *Liberty Bell March* in violas and winds, the fiddle tune *Arkansas Traveler* in the trumpet, and Foster's *Massa's in de Cold Ground* in the winds (the same phrase used in the Second Symphony), soon followed by phrases from *Marching Through Georgia*, *The Battle Cry of Freedom*, and *Yankee Doodle*. As in *Washington's Birthday* and *The Fourth of July*, this collage of musical fragments does not reproduce how a country band might actually sound but represents the way you might recall their playing in memory, as hearing or remembering one band performance summons up memories of other occasions and tunes through association or resemblance.

Suddenly the music quiets and you hear a new tune, like a contrasting second strain or trio. Again motives from *Marching Through Georgia* pop up. The rhythm grows more irregular and gradually slows, ideas repeat, the harmony sinks lower, the music grows softer, and instruments drop out one by one, in a beautiful depiction of the band music fading from hearing as the boy in Ives's program wanders away from the others into the woods, rests on the hillside, and falls asleep.

A quiet, sweetly dissonant chord in the strings and piano marks the beginning of the boy's dream. A soft fanfare in the flute, like a distant fife, conjures up a military scene. A yearning melody in the oboe may stand for the Goddess of Liberty "pleading with the soldiers not to forget their 'cause' and the great sacrifices they have made for it." Beneath it, you hear two groups of instruments playing *Street Beat* at different tempos, representing two groups of soldiers on the march at different speeds and distances: the strings, moving more slowly and marking the rhythm by repeating dissonant chords; and the piano, snare drum, bassoon, and pizzicato violas, moving more quickly but also softer and thus seemingly farther away. This is a famous passage, inspired in part by Ives's experience as a boy watching his father's band and another band parade by each other playing different marches, each in their own key and tempo.[14]

In step with the more distant marchers, a trumpet plays fragments of *The British Grenadiers*, the "popular tune of the day" mentioned in the program. Soon after, hints appear in the violin of another late-eighteenth-century tune, not yet composed at the time of Putnam's encampment but familiar to late-nineteenth-century children like Ives and the boy in his program: *Hail! Columbia*, with words from 1798 by Joseph Hopkinson set to the melody of *The President's March*, written by Philip Phile in 1793 when George Washington was president. The distant march fades from your hearing and the music grows quieter. "Suddenly, a new national note is heard," a sprightly tune begun in the brass and picked up by the strings while above it the flute plays most of *The British Grenadiers*. This must be the moment when "Putnam is coming over the hills," returning to the encampment, and "the soldiers turn back and cheer." Irregular accents may suggest the cheers of the soldiers. Trumpets, clarinets, horns, and upper strings sound out a later phrase of *Hail! Columbia*, and other instruments pile on in raucous celebration.

At the peak of noise and confusion, the loud music suddenly cuts off in a trademark Ives sonic exuviation, and you hear again the trio strain of the march. The boy has woken from his dream and runs back to listen to the band. A brief episode in ragtime rhythms leads to a reprise of the march's opening strain, now louder than ever and with a countermelody in the upper winds cobbled together from parts of *The British Grenadiers*. Once again the drums and brass play their disorderly bridge—the bandleader seems to have even more trouble with them this time around—and the opening strain repeats one last time, louder still, with bits of *The British Grenadiers*, *Marching Through Georgia*, a bugle call, and themes from the middle section mixed into the counterpoint. Gradually all the tunes give way to an ever more dense and dissonant swirl of rising and falling lines in a loud and chaotic climax, capped off by the first few notes of *The Star Spangled Banner* and a huge final dissonance. Wow, what a ride!

The Housatonic at Stockbridge

Ives wrote in *Memos* that

> the last movement, *The Housatonic at Stockbridge*, . . . was suggested by a Sunday morning walk that Mrs. Ives and I took near Stockbridge [Massachusetts], the summer after we were married. We walked in the meadows along the river, and heard the distant singing from the church across the river. The mist had not entirely left the river bed, and the colors, the running water, the banks and elm trees were something that one would always remember. Robert Underwood Johnson, in his poem, *The Housatonic at Stockbridge*, paints this scene beautifully. I sketched the first part of this movement for strings, flute, and organ shortly after we got home that summer.[15]

In this movement Ives represents "the distant singing from the church across the river" through a melody paraphrased from a hymn tune and "the mist . . . and the colors, the running water, the banks and elm trees" through many layers of undulating lines in repeating patterns.

That same year of 1908, the second edition of Johnson's *Poems* was published, including his ode "To the Housatonic at Stockbridge." Ives apparently found the poem in that collection.[16] He must have had in mind from his early sketches the idea of combining a sound-picture of the scene he describes with a setting of rhyming couplets selected from the poem, for the hymn-based melody perfectly fits the poetic text, and he produced both a song for voice and piano using those words and a version for orchestra featuring the same melody. The gestation of the music shows that the orchestral movement and song were closely interrelated, for he seems to have gone back and forth between them: his first sketch in 1908 was for instruments alone, focused on capturing the scene; he sketched a version for voice and piano between 1908 and about 1914, getting the essential continuity of the melody and accompaniment but reducing the layered complexity of the undulating lines, which were too much to play on the piano; he then sketched out the orchestral movement between about 1913 and 1919, completing a full score around 1919; and in 1921 he finalized the song, published the next year in *114 Songs*.[17]

The melody of *The Housatonic at Stockbridge* is one of the most beautiful Ives ever wrote. He paraphrased it from Isaac Woodbury's brief hymn tune *Dorrnance*, repeating segments of melody and adding or subtracting notes to fit the text he drew from Johnson's poem, fourteen lines in four stanzas excerpted from the sixty-six lines of the original:

> Contented river! in thy dreamy realm—
> The cloudy willow and the plumy elm: . . .
>
> Thou beautiful! From every dreamy hill
> What eye but wanders with thee at thy will, . . .
>
> Contented river! and yet over-shy
> To mask thy beauty from the eager eye;
> Hast thou a thought to hide from field and town?
> In some deep current of the sunlit brown . . .
>
> Ah! there's a restive ripple, and the swift
> Red leaves—September's firstlings—faster drift; . . .
> Wouldst thou away, dear stream? Come, whisper near!
> I also of much resting have a fear;
> Let me tomorrow thy companion be
> By fall and shallow to the adventurous sea![18]

For each stanza Ives paraphrased the hymn tune, giving the entire movement the shape of a hymn in four verses. Each successive stanza reworks the melody in a new way, more distant from the original tune, more chromatic, with more inserted material, and accompanied by more restless harmonies, representing the constant changes of the river and its growing momentum as it advances toward the sea.[19] Except for the rippling water and the elm, the images in the poem do not match those in Ives's recollection, yet the music reflects both, beginning with the scene that Ives remembered and changing to follow the course of the poem.

After the loud ending of *Putnam's Camp*, the finale begins quietly, with a richly woven texture in the strings that creates a sense of great space through layers of rippling lines that seem to recede into the distance. Lowest and most audible, like the "deep current" in Johnson's poem, is a rich chord in the basses and cellos, the lower instruments sustaining an open fifth, the upper cello line slowly tracing a melody that after a few notes is joined by the bassoon and comes into focus as the last segment of the hymn tune *Dorrnance*. Above the cello melody, softer but more rapidly moving, is a line in violas that wanders among four closely spaced notes, dissonant against the lower strings, moving in irregular rhythm and repeating every seven beats so that it does not line up with anything else. Above the violas, and softer still, are four separate violin parts, adding further dissonance and constantly cycling through repeating patterns to create a sense of endless flow that yet remains the same. Each layer has its own rhythm, and the higher the layer the softer it sounds and the more rapidly it moves, producing an effect that captures in music the look and feel—rather than the sound—of the great, slowly flowing river and the lighter, less ponderous movements above it of gentle ripples, flitting leaves, and floating mists, each moving independently of the others.

Into this pastoral scene comes the hymnlike melody paraphrased from *Dorrnance*, passed between the horn and an English horn and doubled by half of the violas, in the same major key suggested by the low strings. Although Ives mentions in *Memos* "the distant singing from the church across the river," in the music it is this melody that sounds most prominent and closest to you, against the background of the swirling mists and gurgling river. You can tell from this melody's prominence that the subject of this movement is not just the river, but the people by the river, those singing in the church and those standing on the bank observing the scene. After the horn and English horn exchange phrases twice, the music in the strings shifts in new directions, as if to mark the end of the first "verse" of the hymn. The strings settle back into their opening ideas, and the English horn and horn return with the second, quite varied verse, sliding briefly into a slightly higher key before returning home, reflecting the "eye [that] wanders with thee at thy will," taking in the river's beauty as it meanders through the valley.

The background texture grows more diverse, with winds taking over some of the string parts and the harp and celesta adding rapid arabesques. Now violins sound out the third verse of the melody, more distantly paraphrased yet still recognizably derived from *Dorrnance*, repeating many of the same gestures while moving more continuously, more dissonant now against the background. The melody lies higher, sounding like a tune in a minor key over the drone fifth in the low strings. The music reflects the restlessness implied by Johnson's poem, which imputes human-like impulses to the river that turns shy and seeks to hide from observers.

The rippling figures return to the strings, then grow more turbulent as the fourth verse enters, shared by horn and trumpet. The melody moves more quickly now, with many added notes interspersed between motives from the hymn, ever more dissonant against the accompaniment and passing through many distant keys. The poem speaks of "a restive ripple" and autumn leaves drifting along, and the poet attributes to the river his own feelings of restlessness. The music grows in volume and density, an image for the swelling of the river as it heads to the sea—again, a musical effect that captures the look and feel of the river, not the sounds it makes. With everyone playing at maximum intensity, the orchestra swells to a climax of dissonant sound. It cuts off suddenly in a sonic exuviation, and you hear a quiet reminiscence of the beginning of the melody paraphrased from *Dorrnance*, recalling the beautiful scene depicted at the opening of the movement, the mists, leaves, and calmly rippling river far from the sea.

People are clearly at the center of the first two movements, despite their emphasis on place. Ives does not set the scene by depicting Boston Common or the woods around Putnam's campsite, but focuses on the experiences of the soldiers commemorated in Saint-Gaudens's sculpture and at Putnam Memorial State Park, on the village band, on the townsfolk hearing them play, and—by implication—on the one who is looking at the sculpture or remembering Fourth of July celebrations at the park. The title of *The Housatonic at Stockbridge* suggests that here the river is the focus.[20] Yet the river's deep current and restive ripples are the backdrop for the hymnlike melody paraphrased from *Dorrnance*, which represents both "the distant singing from the church across the river" and—because it is *not* distant but rather the most prominent element in the music, seemingly the closest to us—the feelings of the couple on the banks of the river, observing the scene. There is a reverence in this picture of the Housatonic River, a sense of the divine in this "dreamy realm," but it is those who observe the scene who commune with the divine in nature. The river is almost human in its feelings of contentment, shyness, restlessness, and willfulness, expressed in Johnson's poem. The hymn, a human construct for worshiping the divine, changes with each verse to capture the mood and activities of the river, and in that sense it comes to speak for the river. Throughout this movement, music, humans, nature, and the divine flow together and become inseparable. In this way, all *Three Places in New England* are ultimately about people and about how we fit into the world around us.

ORCHESTRAL SET NO. 2

Ives never heard a performance of his Second Orchestral Set, which was the last of his major orchestral works to be premiered—in 1967, thirteen years after Ives had died, by the Chicago Symphony Orchestra led by Morton Gould. But it captured the spirit of music he had heard and, in the last movement, a performance that took place all around him.

The first movement, *An Elegy to Our Forefathers*, was composed around 1914–1915 and orchestrated between 1923 and 1929.[21] In it Ives weaves together strands of melody paraphrased from Stephen Foster songs—*Massa's in de Cold Ground* and *Old Black Joe*—and from hymns—*Jesus Loves Me*, which has phrases that resemble both Foster tunes, as well as *Nettleton* and the chorus of Edward S. Ufford's gospel hymn *Throw Out the Life-Line*. This remarkable slow movement unfolds over a bed of repeating figures in the basses, percussion, and other instruments that continue throughout. It starts extremely softly, steadily adds layers, grows louder and more intense, then gradually becomes softer and thinner again and fades to silence. Rather than a typical symphony movement with contrasting sections, textures, and themes, what we experience is like a slow procession that comes into view, marches toward us, passes by, and continues on its way until it disappears in the distance.

The second movement, *The Rockstrewn Hills Join in the People's Outdoor Meeting*, captures the spirit of outdoor revivals by treating three gospel hymns with rhythms derived from ragtime, whose bouncy syncopations and shifting accents seem to reflect both the spirited singing of the congregants and the rocks and hills of the surrounding countryside. Sketched around 1914–1919 and scored between 1923 and 1929, the movement was adapted from an earlier set of four *Ragtime Dances* for theater orchestra, incorporating the third movement and parts of the first two.[22] Like each of the *Ragtime Dances*, this movement reflects the verse-refrain form of its source tunes, with a "verse" based on *Bringing in the Sheaves* and motives from *Happy Day* ("O happy day that fixed my choice") followed by a brief "refrain" on the refrain of *Welcome Voice* ("I am coming Lord!") by Lewis Hartsough. Ives uses motives the hymns share to weave the movement into a coherent whole. The refrain tune is anticipated during the verse, building up from brief variants to longer phrases until the complete statement at the end, as in cumulative form. Bits of other tunes flit by, creating a collage that heightens the sense of remembering a camp meeting from long ago.

The last movement, composed between 1915 and 1919 and fully scored in 1929, is one of Ives's masterpieces.[23] He wrote of it that "as far as I'm concerned, I think it's one of the best that I've done"—although, with characteristic modesty, he added, "that's not the same as saying that it's any too good."[24] He gave it the ungainly title *From Hanover Square North, at the End of a Tragic Day, the Voice of the People Again Arose.* Any marketing consultant could have told him that was no way to get the piece played, and indeed this orchestral set is performed much less often than the first. But the title captures something important to Ives. This piece memorializes a particular event, at a particular place, on a tragic day, when the voices of his fellow New Yorkers joined together to express their grief, showing the power of music to bring people sustenance and create community in times of need. There could be no more powerful testimony to Ives's longstanding belief, shared with his Romantic predecessors, that music can give voice to feelings that cannot be expressed in any other way. So it is no surprise that he sought to capture this experience *of* music *in* music.

It happened on Friday, May 7, 1915, in the late afternoon, as Ives was going home after work at his insurance agency. Earlier that day a German submarine torpedoed the British ocean liner *Lusitania* off the coast of Ireland, sending 1,198 passengers and crew to their deaths, including 128 Americans. Ives knew at least two victims personally from his years at Yale. The disaster hit New Yorkers particularly hard, especially those in the business district where Ives worked. The ship was a mainstay for wealthy travelers sailing between New York and England, and its sinking caused the stock market to dive and presaged losses for the insurance industry in which Ives worked.[25]

Ives recalled the scene in his *Memos*:

> Leaving the office and going uptown about six o'clock, I took the Third Avenue "L" [elevated train] at Hanover Square Station. As I came on the platform, there was quite a crowd waiting for the [northbound] trains, which had been blocked lower down, and while waiting there, a hand-organ or hurdy-gurdy was playing in the street below. Some workmen sitting on the side of the tracks began to whistle the tune, and others began to sing or hum the refrain. A workman with a shovel over his shoulder came on the platform and joined in the chorus, and the next man, a Wall Street banker with white spats and a cane, joined in it, and finally it seemed to me that everybody was singing this tune, and they didn't seem to be singing in fun, but as a natural outlet for what their feelings had been going through all day long. There was a feeling of dignity all through this. The hand-organ man seemed to sense this and wheeled the organ nearer the platform and kept it up fortissimo and the chorus sounded out as though every man in New York must be joining in it. Then the first train came in and everyone crowded in, and the song gradually died out, but the effect on the crowd still showed. Almost nobody talked—the people acted as though they might be coming out of a church service. In going uptown, occasionally little groups would start singing or humming the tune.
>
> Now what was the tune? It wasn't a Broadway hit, it wasn't a musical comedy air, it wasn't a waltz tune or a dance tune or an opera tune or a classical tune, or a tune that all of them probably knew. It was only the refrain

of an old Gospel Hymn that had stirred many people of past generations. It was nothing but—*In the Sweet Bye and Bye.*[26]

The incident as Ives relates it was ideally suited for the tools he had at hand as a composer. First, there was the urban setting. The same kind of musical texture he had deployed at the beginning of *The Housatonic at Stockbridge* to represent the swirling mists, fluttering leaves, and rippling river—overlapping, independently moving layers in constant motion, repeating their gestures with subtle variations—could be used here to represent the sounds of the city. Then there was the way the tune was introduced, taken up by the crowd phrase by phrase, and sounded out at last in all its glory by everyone coming together; this is exactly the shape and spirit of cumulative form, which by 1915 Ives had used so often that it was second nature, the form he deployed more than any other. Finally, there was the gospel hymn itself, often sung at funerals. Its tune, by James P. Webster, was widely known, and its words, by Sanford F. Bennett, were both consoling, through their vision of a peaceful afterlife, and ironic, in their imagery of a safe and distant shore, on a day when over a thousand souls had died at sea mere miles from land:

> There's a land that is fairer than day,
> And by faith we can see it afar;
> For the Father waits over the way
> To prepare us a dwelling place there.
>
> *Refrain*
> > In the sweet by-and-by,
> > We shall meet on that beautiful shore;
> > In the sweet by-and-by,
> > We shall meet on that beautiful shore.

The piece unfolds over a series of drones in the bass that slowly lead from D minor to F major. This harmonic foundation undergirds a dense fabric of overlapping streams of music, a kind of texture Ives had been exploring since *Central Park in the Dark* and had become one of his most characteristic sounds. The techniques and approaches he had honed over the previous two decades equipped him perfectly to capture this moment when people of all classes from workman to banker came together in a shared expression of grief.

After the ragtime-y second movement, you wonder what will happen next. All the musicians you can see are silent, waiting. The first sounds come from offstage: voices begin to sing, while piano, harp, solo strings, and chimes lay down a bed of constant motion. The instruments softly play figures that continually repeat with slight variations, each recurring in a different cycle so that you cannot hear any clear meter, weaving a musical tapestry that creates a sense of mystery and wonderfully evokes the rumble of distant traffic and city noises. Over this the voices chant in unison the first three phrases of the Anglican *Te Deum*:

> We praise Thee, O God:
> We acknowledge Thee to be the Lord.
> All the Earth doth worship Thee.

The solemn liturgical invocation sets a somber mood and lends what follows the atmosphere of a religious service. An offstage horn responds with a mournful melody of its own, subtly related to *In the Sweet By-and-By* in contour and melodic gestures but entirely different in mood.

As the horn melody ends and the other offstage instruments continue their soft murmurs, a few instruments in the main orchestra begin to play. The basses softly tremble on a low drone while the cellos slowly play the first phrase of *In the Sweet By-and-By*. A clarinet answers with a variant of the same phrase, like someone starting to sing along and not getting the tune exactly right. Both cellos and clarinet smooth out the melody, omitting the uneven rhythms that are part of the hymn tune. As if to remind them, the onstage piano pulses out the missing rhythm. The horn in the orchestra enters with a distant paraphrase of the hymn tune's first phrase, full of uneven rhythms and reminiscent of the offstage horn melody in tone color and melodic gestures. The horn comes to a close, and the cellos (now joined by violas), clarinet, and piano all return, each playing a different variant of the hymn verse, each starting at a different time and in a different key, like the crowd on the elevated train platform gradually joining in. The mood remains solemn, even as the music gradually grows louder and more active.

Over the offstage instruments and the continuing lines in the cellos, violas, piano, and clarinets, the violins enter with a long and winding melody drawn from the hymn verse. The orchestral horn returns, playing its paraphrase of the hymn, louder now and joined by the piano, flutes, clarinets, and percussion. As the horn settles into a more recognizable version of the hymn tune, the piano parallels it in a different key, and the violins play the last two phrases of the verse in yet another key. The layering of two rhythms and three keys at once, all playing versions of the same melody, reminds you of hearing a crowd singing when not everyone is in the same key or rhythm.

The mass of sound continues to grow, the texture thickens, and the melody shifts from the verse of the hymn to its refrain. The violins play most of the refrain in one key, while the trumpets play a rhythmically varied and offset version in another—as if two groups in the crowd were each singing at full voice, each group in its own key, unable to hear the others. Around them, rising and falling lines and chords in other instruments, often following melodic contours from the hymn tune, create a dense texture. Just as the final phrase is beginning, the hymn refrain stalls amid repeated dissonant chords.

Then the trumpets and other brass instruments drop out, and the violins play the refrain again, growing more spirited. Above the violins and a measure or two behind them, the flutes play the hymn refrain in a different key, in a polytonal canon reminiscent of Ives's early experiments but here representing different groups in the crowd. Other parts add repeating figures or counter-melodies. Hidden in the texture, softer and in another key, the violas play the phrase from *Massa's in de Cold Ground* ("Down in de cornfield, hear dat mournful sound") that Ives had already used in his Second Symphony, *Washington's Birthday*, and the first two movements of both orchestral sets, so often that you identify that phrase with Ives himself. In this movement, it seems to symbolize him and his presence in the crowd.

As they complete their separate but simultaneous statements of the hymn refrain, the violins and flutes converge on the same key and repeat several times the final notes of the tune. The music picks up speed and intensity, moving beyond solemnity to a deeper expression of mourning, a vociferous moment of catharsis. Strings, brass, and clarinets sound out the refrain of *In the Sweet By-and-By* in full harmony like a crowd singing at the top of their lungs, "as a natural outlet for what their feelings had been going through all day long" and "as though every man in New York must be joining in it." Adding to the sense of a crowd rather than a disciplined chorus of singers are extra notes added to the tune in some parts (often in the wrong key), accordions playing the hymn tune faster than everyone else, flutes and a clarinet playing it in a different key and meter, dissonant repeating figures in the background, and layers of melody that cannot be heard distinctly in the din. This climactic moment is a perfect New York mess, yet somehow it combines the passion of the crowd with its mix of backgrounds, the hopeful message in the words of the hymn, the reverent spirit set by the choral invocation that opened the movement, and the constant hum of life in the city, maintained throughout by the offstage instruments. It is both a consummate outlet for grief and a celebration of the way strangers can come together through music to express their shared feelings.

When the hymn refrain is complete, the music quickly quiets down, and instruments drop out or turn to gentle undulations or repeating figuration. Now once more you can hear the offstage instruments, which have been playing all along, obscured by the main orchestra. The onstage violins continue to play the hymn refrain for a while, but after a couple of phrases it begins to disintegrate into repeating figures, and even the offstage instruments fade to silence. This gentle final passage reflects the effect Ives describes in *Memos*, that the hymn stayed in people's minds as they rode uptown, sometimes humming it to themselves, as the vibrant, deeply emotional event faded into memory.

MUSIC ABOUT AMERICAN MUSIC
AND AMERICAN EXPERIENCES

Ives never gave the Second Orchestral Set a programmatic title, but like the First it has a common theme. The last movement may be Ives's most perfect depiction of the way shared singing can bring people together, affect our emotions, and express how we feel. The other two movements, about the feelings embodied in the songs of Stephen Foster, in the hymn tunes of his contemporaries, and in the spirit of singing at a camp meeting, capture the same idea. He might have called the whole set *The Power of Song*—or, picking up a phrase from the title of the finale, *The Voice of the People*.[27]

In his two orchestral sets, Ives celebrated places he knew, commemorated historical events in three of America's most important wars, and employed the classical genre of the symphonic poem to depict how the people of the United States, and especially his region of the Northeast, used music to worship, to march, to come together, to stir feelings, and to have fun. Like the *Holidays Symphony*, both sets bring together all four of his musical traditions. The orchestral sets are among the most important works of his maturity and among the most personal and deeply felt he ever composed, alongside the *Holidays Symphony*, the Third Symphony, and the violin sonatas. In all of these works, Ives placed American music and American experiences at the center, creating new variations on America.

At around the same time, he was also working on music that celebrated some of the most important writers the United States had produced, music that started in orchestral guise and ended up in the piano sonata that in 1921 brought him his first public notice since *The Celestial Country* and, almost two decades later, made his reputation.

· *10* ·

American Literature

$\mathscr{B}$eyond pieces that captured remembered events, during the 1910s Ives also worked on a series of tone poems on American and English literary figures. He collected four of these, in versions for piano solo, in his Piano Sonata No. 2: *Concord, Mass., 1840–1860*, depicting writers who lived in Concord, Massachusetts, in the decades before the Civil War. The first movement contrasts the rambling but powerful essays and speeches of Ralph Waldo Emerson (1803–1882), leader of the Transcendentalist movement, with Emerson's more lyrical poetry. The second movement, a kind of scherzo, evokes episodes from the comic and fantastic tales of Nathaniel Hawthorne (1804–1864). The third movement paints the home life of the Alcott family, including Louisa May Alcott (1832–1888) and her father Bronson Alcott (1799–1888), through a picture of domestic music-making that combines Beethoven—the Transcendentalists' favorite composer—with American hymns and popular songs. The finale is a meditation on Transcendentalist writer Henry David Thoreau (1817–1862) and his memoir *Walden* (1854) on his experiences living alone on the shore of Walden Pond. One theme, which Ives called the "human-faith-melody," unites all four movements.

A health crisis in 1918 drove Ives into partial retirement from insurance and a concentrated effort to get his best music out to the public. His first step was self-publishing the *Concord Sonata*, along with a book that explained his goals for it. The sonata drew scathing reviews, but a few writers and musicians began to promote his music, and the 1920s saw the first public performances of his works since 1902. The 1939 New York premiere of the *Concord Sonata* inspired a review hailing the piece as "exceptionally great music … , the greatest music composed by an American." At sixty-four, Ives finally gained widespread recognition as a composer, and the *Concord Sonata* has remained a pivotal piece for him ever since.

PIANO SONATA NO. 2: *CONCORD, MASS., 1840–1860*

Ives was a professional organist, but left only one major work for organ, the youthful *Variations on "America."* He was an excellent pianist, capable of playing enormously difficult music with expressivity and verve, as is evident from private studio recordings he made between 1933 and 1943, in his late fifties and sixties. He wrote a large amount of piano music: three sonatas, at least eighteen studies (etudes), six marches, and more than a dozen other pieces for piano solo or duet. The sonatas, the studies, and most of the other works are recorded, and all are worth a listen. Yet there is only one Ives work for piano that is widely known and played: Piano Sonata No. 2: *Concord, Mass., 1840–1860*, known as the *Concord Sonata.*[1]

Ives wrote in *Memos* that the idea for the sonata "came originally from working on some overtures representing literary men," referring in a letter to "a series of overtures on 'Men of Literature' [that] either were not completed or ended up in something else." As subjects he lists English poets Robert Browning and Matthew Arnold, American poets Walt Whitman and John Greenleaf Whittier, poet and essayist Ralph Waldo Emerson, and preacher and abolitionist Henry Ward Beecher. Elsewhere he mentions an "Alcott overture" on teacher and reformer Bronson Alcott and his daughter, novelist Louisa May Alcott; pieces based on Nathaniel Hawthorne stories for piano, "for two pianos, or two pianos and four players," or in the form of a piano concerto; and an idea for a piece called "Walden Sounds," drawing on Henry David Thoreau's *Walden.* This is an eclectic mix of writers, partly reflecting the tastes of his Yale literature professor William Lyon Phelps, who taught and wrote about all but Beecher and the Alcotts, and probably also reflecting his current reading in the company of Harmony, who had renewed his interest in literature. Of these projected pieces, he completed only the *Robert Browning Overture* and parts of the *Emerson Overture* for piano and orchestra. Material for the Browning, Whitman, and Arnold overtures ended up in songs setting their poetry.[2]

At some point—apparently on vacation in the Adirondacks in September 1911, when he wrote "Idea of Concord Sonata" in a diary—Ives realized that Emerson, the Alcotts, Hawthorne, and Thoreau all lived in Concord in the mid-nineteenth century and that grouping them together would make an effective piece. He had thought of different instrumentation for each one, but the piano was central to his conception of the Emerson and Hawthorne music and to the story he wanted to tell about the Alcott family, and so the piece became a piano sonata. He worked on it through most of the 1910s, commenting later that "the Sonata was decided and sensed to a great deal by the ear and mind (to say nothing of the left side of the breast) before much went down on paper"; he dated it 1911–1915, though the extant sketches appear to be from about 1914–1919.[3]

In October 1918, Ives suffered a collapse that his family described as a heart attack. As Stephen Budiansky has recently demonstrated, the health crisis was instead triggered by diabetes, first diagnosed when sugar was found in Ives's urine that August. At that time, before the discovery of insulin, diabetes was a virtual death sentence, with a median life expectancy of about five to ten years. The only way to slow it down was to drastically reduce one's food intake, lowering calories and especially carbohydrates—essentially starving oneself to extend life. Ives stayed home from work for most of the next year, and during the 1920s he lost about a third of his weight, becoming in the process weak, frail, anxious, and tired. Things improved when he was put on insulin in 1930, and he lived until 1954, but he never regained the robust athleticism and seemingly tireless energy he had as a young man and maintained until middle age.[4]

Ives turned forty-four in October 1918, with essentially nothing to show for his three decades of composing. As Samuel Johnson famously remarked, "when a man knows he is to be hanged in a fortnight, it concentrates his mind wonderfully." Faced with his own mortality, with perhaps only a few years to live, Ives focused on getting his music out to the public. He chose the *Concord Sonata* as the first vehicle; he had tried repeatedly to interest conductors in his orchestral music, with no success, but for the sonata he had only to interest one performer at a time. That fall and the next year, primarily during an extended vacation with Harmony from January through March 1919 in Asheville, North Carolina, he finalized the sonata, copied it out in ink, and wrote a group of essays to introduce the sonata and explain his intentions for it. In reshaping the sonata for publication, he simplified some passages to make them clearer and less difficult to play, hoping to avoid some of the negative reactions he had encountered when playing his music for professional musicians. The sonata was engraved and printed by G. Schirmer, at Ives's expense. He had meant the essays to be bound with the sonata, but they grew too long to make that practical, so he arranged for them to be published separately by the Knickerbocker Press, again at his own expense, under the title *Essays Before a Sonata*. Both were ready by January 1921, and Ives sent out hundreds of copies to composers, pianists, newspapers, music journals, critics, music schools, and anyone else he could think of who might be interested.[5]

Essays Before a Sonata

Essays Before a Sonata has loomed large in discussions of Ives ever since its publication. There are six essays: a Prologue; an essay for each movement

(Emerson, Hawthorne, The Alcotts, and Thoreau); and an Epilogue. They are wide-ranging and impressionistic, deeply personal rather than scholarly, ruminating on ideas that seem directly relevant to the sonata alongside many that do not. As he wrote in a brief preface, taken together the sonata and book of essays are "an attempt to present (one person's) impression of the spirit of transcendentalism that is associated in the minds of many with Concord, Mass., of over a half century ago."[6]

Ives begins the Prologue by raising questions that challenge the whole idea of a sonata about literature:

> How far is anyone justified, be he an authority or a layman, in expressing or trying to express in music (in sounds, if you like), the value of anything, material, moral, intellectual, or spiritual, which is usually expressed in terms other than music? . . . Does the success of program music depend more upon the program than upon the music? If it does, what is the use of the music? If it does not, what is the use of the program?

He concludes that ultimately all music is program music, in the sense that it is "the translation of an artistic intuition into musical sounds," and that music is capable of expressing things that cannot be expressed in words.[7]

In the Epilogue, Ives focuses on what he calls the "substance" of a musical work, its content or spirit, and the "manner" or means of expression:

> Substance in a human-art-quality suggests the body of a conviction which has its birth in the spiritual consciousness, whose youth is nourished in the moral consciousness, and whose maturity as a result of all this growth is then represented in a mental image. This is appreciated by the intuition, and somehow translated into expression by "manner."

He believes "that substance can be expressed in music, and that it is the only valuable thing in it." In his view, the purpose of music is to embody substance, something of moral and spiritual value, using manner to convey that substance. He rejects music that emphasizes virtuosity or entertainment—or pleasing the audience with familiar sounds, or any other less important goal—over saying anything of value, because such music puts manner over substance. He criticizes the music of Wagner, Debussy, and Richard Strauss for lacking substance, primarily because of the subject matter they chose to depict (although he never criticizes their manner, from which he learned so much). He praises Bach, Beethoven, Brahms, and Franck for writing music of enduring substance that is "always modern" despite changes of style or taste in later generations.[8]

The essays on individual movements convey Ives's impressions of each writer. He presents Emerson, the leading American Transcendentalist, as "a great poet and prophet . . . an invader of the unknown—America's deepest explorer of the spiritual immensities," who believed in "the strength and beauty of innate goodness in man, in Nature, and God—the greatest and most inspiring theme of Concord Transcendental philosophy." In Emerson's essays, "so close a relation exists between his content and expression, his substance and manner, that if he were more definite in the latter he would lose power in the former."[9]

Hawthorne was not a Transcendentalist but a writer of realist novels and fantastic stories. Ives calls him a great artist who was "more interested in psychology than in transcendental philosophy," who "is likely to have more to say about the life around him . . . than a poet of philosophy is," and whose "art was true and typically American," reflecting the people and scenes around him.[10]

The Alcotts essay briefly describes Bronson Alcott as "an exuberant, irrepressible visionary" and his daughter Louisa May Alcott as a writer who "supported the family, and at the same time enriched the lives of a large part of young America, starting off many little minds with wholesome thoughts and many little hearts with wholesome emotions." But Ives centers the essay on the "commonplace beauty" and "spiritual sturdiness" of the house in Concord where they lived.[11]

Ives's Thoreau is the contemplative author of *Walden*, focused on the sights and sounds of nature. He praises Thoreau as "a great musician, not because he played the flute but because he did not have to go to Boston to hear 'the Symphony.' The rhythm of his prose, were there nothing else, would determine his value as a composer. He was divinely conscious of the enthusiasm of Nature, the emotion of her rhythms, and the harmony of her solitude." "Thoreau looked to Nature for his greatest inspirations. In her, he found an analogy to the fundamental of Transcendentalism. The 'innate goodness' of Nature is or can be a moral influence."[12]

The *Essays* can be useful for understanding Ives's intentions, and in what follows we will see that there are comments in the essays on each movement that suggest images in the music. Yet despite the title *Essays Before a Sonata*, Ives wrote them *after* writing the sonata, no doubt shaping the programs he offers to match the music rather than the reverse. And as Kyle Gann usefully cautions, "no specific passages are cited, and we will find ourselves speculating to correlate the hints with the musical events."[13] The interpretations offered here are meant in part to help you grow familiar with the piece and in part to stimulate your own thinking about what it might mean.

Two Editions

After printing and distributing the sonata, Ives continued to tinker with it, penciling revisions into several of the printed copies, and mining the first two movements for material he turned into other pieces. In the 1930s and 1940s he prepared a second edition, professionally published in 1947, in which he restored some of the difficulties and dissonances he had edited out for the first edition and incorporated newer revisions.[14] Almost all performances today are based on the second edition, which represents Ives's final wishes for the piece after almost four decades of living with it.

But some players draw on both or add their own variants, in the spirit of nineteenth-century pianist-composers like Chopin and Liszt, who often altered their own music in performance and sometimes issued more than one version of a piece. Ives explicitly authorized such choices and changes. He considered the written score "a platform for the player to make his own speeches on." In the mid-1930s, when John Kirkpatrick was preparing to premiere the complete sonata, he wrote to Ives about the alternate versions of the Emerson music, and Ives replied, "Do whatever seems natural or best to *you*, though not necessarily the same way each time. The music, in its playing as well as in its substance, should have some of Emerson's freedom in action and thought. . . . It is said that Emerson seldom gave any of his lectures in exactly the same way, and that the published essays were not kept to literally."[15] Ives was not authorizing a kind of indeterminacy or open choice as in music of John Cage or other avant-garde composers of the 1950s and 1960s, which he had not imagined (although they would see Ives as a forebear). Rather, his view of the music as a vehicle for the performer, who must be allowed leeway to play it as inspired on each occasion, reflects a performing tradition that goes back to the nineteenth and eighteenth centuries and beyond.[16]

The Alcotts and the Cyclic Theme

The place to start in understanding the *Concord Sonata* as music is with *The Alcotts*, the third but most accessible movement, and with its theme, the theme that unites the entire sonata.[17] All four of Ives's numbered symphonies are cyclic, bound together by themes that appear in most or all movements, as are several other multimovement works including the First String Quartet and two of the violin sonatas. When Ives pulled together the *Holidays Symphony* and the two orchestral sets from symphonic poems that had begun independently, he did not try to link them together through common themes. But for the *Concord Sonata* he returned to his earlier practice, introducing the theme of *The Alcotts* into all three of the other movements. *The Alcotts* is in cumulative form, culminating in the most complete statement of its theme after a process of building it up from fragments. The whole sonata is a kind of expanded cumulative form, whose first two movements include partial statements of the cyclic theme, which is finally assembled in the third movement, then recalled at the end of the fourth. Each movement has its own themes as well, and the cyclic theme is only one thread in a complex tapestry. But it is the unifying thread, making it a good place to begin.

Ives's other movements in cumulative form typically use an existing tune as a main theme, making it possible for those who know the tune to follow its course through the movement. *The Alcotts* is unique in that its theme, which Ives called the "human-faith-melody," is in part newly composed and in part woven from four existing melodies. One way to learn the theme is simply to listen to a recording of *The Alcotts* two or three times in a row, until the theme that comes at the end is fixed in your memory like an earworm, and you can hear the fragments and variants that precede the final complete statement of the theme. There are many excellent recordings; Ives recorded it himself in 1943 (the only movement from the sonata that he recorded complete), and you can find his version on a CD titled *Ives Plays Ives* or on YouTube or Spotify.[18] If listening to the whole movement is too much or too confusing, start playing the recording about a minute or so from the end of the movement, where the theme appears in its complete form, majestically presented at full volume and accompanied in full chordal harmony. The theme is tonal and in a major key, and it sounds quite different from the constantly moving, harmonically unstable music that immediately precedes it. After the theme is over, a very quiet echo of its opening notes appears before the final chord.

The theme begins with a striking four-note motive, rising two whole steps and leaping down a fifth, in the rhythm short-short-short-long. The first half continues downward by step and skip, then works its way back up the scale to end with the same four notes with which it began, in a new order: rising fifth, falling third, rising step.

The second half of the theme begins with another striking motive, in the same short-short-short-long rhythm: three repeated notes and a falling third, the famous opening motto of Beethoven's Fifth Symphony. The second half continues with what sounds like a variation of the Beethoven motto, featuring the repeated notes followed by a half step up and down before the falling third. Then comes a second variation that skips up from the repeated notes and takes two steps back down before the falling third.

The two halves of the theme are linked by the falling third that appears at the end of the first half and pervades the second half, and by the short-short-short-long rhythm that begins both halves. Yet the first half is more lyrical, flowing up and down, while the second half is more declamatory, focused on the repeating notes and descending third.

Listen again to the theme as it appears in the last minute of *The Alcotts*. As you familiarize yourself with the theme, focus on hearing the shape of each half, including the similarities and differences between them.

The first half is apparently original, while the second half is full of al-lusions to other music. The Beethoven Fifth Symphony motto is the most obvious. Its first "variation" and the texture of pounding repeated chords are both taken from the very opening of Beethoven's Piano Sonata in B-flat Major, Op. 106, known as the *Hammerklavier Sonata*. More subtly, the Fifth Symphony motto shares its contour of repeated notes and a falling third with the opening phrases of two hymn tunes from the 1830s: *Missionary Chant* ("Ye Christian heralds, go, proclaim"), which we encountered in Ives's Second Symphony, and *Martyn* by Simeon B. Marsh, often sung with the words of Charles Wesley's hymn "Jesus, lover of my soul." Indeed, the "variations" of the Beethoven motto in Ives's theme hint at the contour of these two hymns: like them, the first "variation" adds a rising step after the falling third, and the second "variation" shares the melodic contour (though not the rhythm) of the second phrase of *Martyn*.[19]

If you can, listen to *Missionary Chant* and *Martyn* at the Charles Ives Society website (charlesives.org/borrowed-tunes/hymns) and to the opening five to ten seconds of Beethoven's Fifth Symphony and *Hammerklavier So-nata*. After each one, listen again to the theme of *The Alcotts* so you can hear the similarities. Both of these hymn tunes emerge explicitly in the sonata, *Missionary Chant* in *The Alcotts* and *Martyn* in *Hawthorne*. Moreover, the interplay between Beethoven and hymnody is central to the form and mean-ing of *The Alcotts*.

Fundamental to *The Alcotts* is the contrast of musical styles, both familiar and invented ones, akin to the contrasts we have heard in other Ives pieces starting with the song *Memories* in chapter 1. The movement opens with the first phrase of *Missionary Chant*, played softly and in the simple chordal style of hymns, but with the fourth note in the melody altered to form the da-da-da-DUM of the Fifth Symphony; here we have the Beethoven motto played as if it were a hymn. About two minutes later, at a climactic moment not quite halfway through the movement, the third phrase of *Missionary Chant* (which begins with the same four notes as the Fifth Symphony motto) appears with huge pounding chords like those in the *Hammerklavier Sonata*; here the hymn is played as if it were Beethoven. Over the course of the movement, we hear portions of the main theme in hymn-like or Beethoven-like styles, but also in three modernist styles: polytonality, with the accompaniment in a different key than the theme; non-tonal two-part counterpoint, with the theme played over a running line that seems fixed on no key; and a layered texture with the theme over an accompaniment based on the whole-tone scale, reminiscent of Claude Debussy's whole-tone-saturated piano prelude *Voiles*. In the middle is a contrasting section, with three familiar styles of tonal music: a sentimental parlor song in the idiom of Stephen Foster with a touch of Scotch melody;

a march; and a minstrel show song. The gulf between these traditional nineteenth-century tonal styles and the modernist styles around them is huge. After this interlude, the cumulative form resumes, with more modernist counterpoint and increasing hints of the theme's opening motive, culminating in the main theme presented with massive pounding chords like those at the beginning of the *Hammerklavier Sonata*. By starting with hymn style and ending in Beethoven style, by presenting the hymn in Beethoven style and the Beethoven motto in hymn style, and by blending Beethoven motives with phrases from hymn tunes in the main theme, Ives integrates Beethoven and hymnody and uses both to embrace the popular styles in the middle section, whose simple and traditional quality is emphasized by the modern sounds around them, like a frame around a picture.[20]

What does this juxtaposition of styles have to do with the Alcott family and their home in Concord? Ives explains in *Essays Before a Sonata*:

> The Alcott house . . . seems to stand as a kind of homely but beautiful witness of Concord's common virtue—it seems to bear a consciousness that its past is *living*. . . . Here is the home of the "Marches" [the fictional family in Louisa May Alcott's *Little Women* (1868–1869), based on her own family]—all pervaded with the trials and happiness of the family, and telling, in a simple way, the story of "the richness of not having." Within the house, on every side, lie remembrances of what imagination can do for the better amusement of fortunate children who have to do for themselves—much-needed lessons in these days of automatic, ready-made, easy entertainment which deaden rather than stimulate the creative faculty. And there sits the little old spinet piano . . . on which Beth [one of the sisters in *Little Women*] played the old Scotch airs, and played at the *Fifth Symphony*.
> . . . All around you, under the Concord sky, there still floats the influence of that human-faith-melody—transcendent and sentimental enough for the enthusiast or the cynic, respectively—reflecting an innate hope, a common interest in common things and common men—a tune the Concord bards are ever playing while they pound away at the immensities with a Beethoven-like sublimity. . . .
> . . . We won't try to reconcile the music sketch of the Alcotts with much besides the memory of that home under the elms—the Scotch songs and the family hymns that were sung at the end of each day—though there may be an attempt to catch something of that common sentiment (which we have tried to suggest above)—a strength of hope that never gives way to despair—a conviction in the power of the common soul which, when all is said and done, may be as typical as any theme of Concord and its Transcendentalists.[21]

In Ives's account, *The Alcotts* is about a house and the family that lived there. It is about the commonplace—"common virtue," "a common sentiment," "a common interest in common things and common men"—that rises to the level of the transcendent, a *"living"* past that offers "much-needed lessons" in the present. It is a celebration of domestic life, embodied in music-making around the piano. The middle section captures the Scotch songs and other parlor music, from Stephen Foster to marches to minstrel songs, that may seem trivial and sentimental but are part of a greater good. The outer sections feature hymns and Beethoven's Fifth Symphony, not as sung in church or performed at a concert but as played at home on the piano. Hymns and Beethoven are merged in the main theme, the "human-faith-melody," raising Beethoven to the level of the religious and hymns to the transcendent plane of "pounding away at the immensities with a Beethoven-like sublimity," represented in the pounding chords at the final statement of the theme. At the center of it all is a young woman playing the piano, the domestic instrument *par excellence* in the nineteenth century, the instrument legions of girls and women practiced every day as a social accomplishment that could serve to attract a spouse or to entertain family and friends in the evenings. In this sonata about "Men of Literature," this movement is ultimately about women playing the piano and singing hymns with "a strength of hope" as great as anything Beethoven ever expressed, "a conviction in the power of the common soul." This is the substance of this movement, conveyed through the particular styles and juxtapositions—the manner—that Ives deploys. That this movement's main theme links together all four movements of the sonata sends a powerful message that "the power of the common soul" is inherent in both sexes and in all people from every walk of life.

Time to listen to the movement, hear these styles, and experience its substance.

You start the recording and listen to Ives in his late sixties play *The Alcotts*. The 1943 recording is scratchy—it was private, made for his own use, and was never released to the public until 1974, in an LP collection marking the centennial of his birth—but it is exciting to hear the composer himself play.[22]

The movement begins softly, with a hymn, the first phrase of *Missionary Chant*, played twice with subtle variations. If you were not listening closely, you might miss the change to the melody in the opening statement, altered to sound the notes of Beethoven's Fifth Symphony motto, more gentle and plain than you have ever heard it.

As the second statement ends, Ives strums a chord from another key in the accompaniment and repeats it in a rhythm like a slow heartbeat, creating a sense of two keys and two meters at once—polytonality and polyrhythm.

Above it, the main theme enters, its first half truncated, the second half almost complete, its accents shifting against the repeating rhythm in the accompaniment. The main theme begins again, now faster and louder. This time the first half of the theme is presented complete over a running bass line, creating two-part modernist counterpoint. The second half begins with the Fifth Symphony motto, played for the first time loud and in Beethoven's style, followed more quietly by a variant of the next phrase, played in hymn style and sounding like *Missionary Chant*. Ives varies and develops the theme's second half, both the Fifth Symphony motto and the phrase adapted from *Missionary Chant*, mixing them up, changing keys, and growing more intense with dissonant modern harmonies. At a climax, what sounds like the Beethoven motto peals forth in pounding chords, but as it continues you realize that this is the third phrase of *Missionary Chant*, the one that begins like the Fifth Symphony motto ("To distant climes the tidings bear"). By now the sounds of hymns and of Beethoven are thoroughly blended.

The main theme now appears complete for the first time, but not harmonized in *Hammerklavier*-style pounding chords as it will be at the end. The first half is accompanied by tonal chords with chromatic touches, in a style somewhere between hymns and the *Hammerklavier*, closer to a Romantic song. Much more quietly, the second half appears over a repeating figure that uses notes from a whole-tone scale, giving the tune a tentative, incomplete feeling. Here Ives plays with a light, fleet touch, then pauses on a chord that seems to need resolution.

And now for something completely different. What follows is tonal music, in a series of styles from the mid-nineteenth century. The pentatonic melody and lilting rhythms over a simple accompaniment of bass notes and arpeggios remind you of Stephen Foster's sentimental parlor songs, and as the melody descends from a peak you catch what sounds like a bit of the Scotch song *Loch Lomond* (the end of the phrase "But me and my true love will never meet again"). Then comes just a bit of a march: the opening motive of the famous Wedding March from Wagner's opera *Lohengrin*, known far and wide as "Here comes the bride," which Ives had played as an organist.[23] Next is another style of popular song, a bit faster and more bouncy (Ives based this on an obscure minstrel song from the 1840s, A. F. Winnemore's *Stop That Knocking at My Door*). These three vignettes are like a sampler of mid-nineteenth-century music, presenting a picture of playing the piano in the Alcott home, an oasis of domestic calm.

This sampler of piano music repeats, then the pace picks up, and the rising scales of the minstrel song turn into modernist counterpoint. As the music grows more animated, you hear the opening motive of the main theme repeating, starting at different times on different pitches and overlapping itself. The pace, the sound, and the energy build until the apotheosis, when the whole theme emerges at last in all its glory, in powerful chords, "transcendent and sentimental" at once, expressing "a conviction in the power of the common soul." Its last notes grow softer, high in the piano, and a brief recollection of its opening notes leads to the warm major chord that ends the movement.

Perhaps more than any other movement by Ives, *The Alcotts* links the everyday to the mystical, the commonplace to the transcendent. For that reason too, growing familiar with it is a good way to prepare for hearing the other movements of the *Concord Sonata*, which soar into other realms but never lose their connection to the themes of *The Alcotts*—both the musical theme and the programmatic ones.

Emerson

Ives wrote in *Memos* that the *Emerson Overture* "grew into more of a piano concerto, opening with several cadenzas, and gradually becoming more and more unified [over the course of the piece]. The Emerson movement [in the sonata] is a partial reduction for piano from the sketch of this concerto." Ives adds that the concerto "was originally in three movements," although he goes on to list four: the opening movement with cadenzas, a slow movement, a scherzo, and "the last movement," identifying places in the published piano sonata movement that correspond to each of these.[24]

Knowing the origins of *Emerson* as a piano concerto can help us make sense of it. A concerto is a work for a soloist and orchestra, in which the orchestra accompanies and alternates with the soloist, providing a frame and a foil, while the soloist commands our attention and demonstrates impressive skills as a player, including virtuosity, expressivity, emotional power, and creativity. The most intense moments for the soloist are typically the cadenzas, in which the orchestra falls silent and the soloist takes off in rhapsodic flights of fancy. Ives's piano sonata movement of course lacks an orchestra, but the piano textures span the same wide range as a soloist in a concerto, from loud, virtuosic display to soft, relatively simple moments of deep expression. The movement's concerto roots even explain a curious detail. Some performances include a viola playing a brief, meandering line near the end of the movement. This is a misunderstanding of Ives's notation, which indicates that the line, played by the violas in the orchestral version of the Emerson music, may be performed (or omitted) at the discretion of the pianist—but not by a viola!

Several unusual features of *Emerson* reflect aspects of its earlier incarnation as a concerto. These include the movement's extraordinary beginning. Like the first movement of a traditional symphony, such as Ives's First Symphony, the first movement of a sonata or concerto normally starts by presenting the themes, which will be developed and recapitulated later on. *Emerson* begins instead with a kind of rhapsodic fantasy without meter or key, in which fragments of the movement's themes are varied and combined in counterpoint, before the themes have been properly introduced to us in their complete, "original" form. It sounds improvised, or at least like an improvisation—indeed, like a cadenza in a concerto. In the eighteenth and early nineteenth centuries, cadenzas were usually improvised, but nineteenth-century Romantic composers often wrote them out, weaving themes from the movement together with new, highly virtuosic material. *Emerson* opens with exactly this kind of cadenza. Ives adapted it from the concerto's "opening with several cadenzas" by seamlessly blending passages played by the orchestra with the piano's cadenzas and omitting portions of the cadenzas that strayed too far from the thematic material.[25] The second—or fifth or tenth—time you hear the movement, these themes in the opening pages will become easier to hear, and the improvisatory, cadenza-like nature of the passage will become more apparent.

Linking *Emerson* to the Romantic concerto tradition also explains other features. Ives did not invent the idea of a concerto that begins with one or more cadenzas; Beethoven's Piano Concerto No. 5 in E-flat Major (1809), known as the *Emperor Concerto*, opens with a series of cadenzas for the soloist punctuated by the orchestra, and so do Franz Liszt's Piano Concerto No. 1 in E-flat Major (1849, revised 1853 and 1856) and Brahms's Piano Concerto No. 2 in B-flat Major (1881). Most concertos have just three movements, with a slow movement in the middle and no scherzo, but Liszt's First Piano Concerto and Brahms's Second, like Ives's Emerson concerto, have both a slow movement and a scherzo between the two outer movements.

Knowing that Ives merged four movements into one helps to clarify the form of *Emerson*. Once again Liszt offers a precedent: his Piano Sonata in B Minor (1853) is in one movement that combines sonata form with the usual three movements of a piano sonata (sonata form, slow movement, and fast finale). Ives creates a similar compound form in *Emerson*, placing material drawn from the four movements of the Emerson concerto in a frame adapted from sonata form (exposition with first and second themes, development, recapitulation of both themes, and coda).

- The first section, based in part on the opening movement of the concerto, serves as the first theme and transition. The main ideas comprise elements of the "human-faith-melody," including the Beethoven Fifth Symphony motto; a motive unique to this movement that may be identified with Emerson himself; and a theme Ives linked to "the idea of tolerance," embodied by its presentation in parallel whole-tone clusters (that is, in three conflicting keys that coexist and move together despite their dissonance).

- The second theme, a lyrical passage marked "Slowly and quietly," Ives identifies as taken from the concerto's slow second movement.
- A developmental section follows. Then comes a longer lyrical episode, a series of variations on a brief idea, which Ives said "was about the same" as the scherzo of the concerto. After this episode, development resumes, mixing the themes and introducing a brief fugue on a new theme.
- The development culminates in the brief return of two prominent ideas from the first theme area, the opening of the "human-faith melody" and the Emerson motive, and an abbreviated recapitulation of the second theme.
- A short transition leads into a kind of coda, drawn from the last movement of the concerto, which continues to develop the themes and ends with an elegiac interplay of the Emerson motive and the second half of the "human-faith-melody" over a descending bass line.[26]

As is often the case for Ives, several of the thematic ideas are related to each other. The "human-faith-melody" opens with a pentatonic motive, rising two whole steps and falling a fifth. The opening of the scherzo theme reverses the first three notes, falling two whole steps, then a minor third, and adds another whole step down. The Emerson motive follows a similar contour but moves in uneven rhythms and rearranges two notes, falling a whole step, repeating a note, falling a fourth, then skipping up a minor third. The second theme is mostly pentatonic as well and shares some melodic elements with the "human-faith-melody."[27] The small number of motives, the close relationships between them, and the sense of continually developing a few ideas give *Emerson* a sense of coherence, despite the frequent changes in texture and sound.

Ives implies that the style of the music reflects the style of Emerson's writings. He writes in *Essays Before a Sonata* that

> Emerson wrote by sentences or phrases rather than by logical sequence. His underlying plan of work seems based on the large unity of a series of particular aspects of a subject rather than on the continuity of its expression. As thoughts surge to his mind, he fills the heavens with them, crowds them in, if necessary, but seldom arranges them along the ground first. . . .

An apparent confusion, if lived with long enough, may become orderly. . . . What is unified form to the author or composer may of necessity be form-less to his audience. . . . Initial coherence may be dullness tomorrow, prob-ably because formal or outward unity depends so much on repetition. . . .

. . . If Emerson's manner is not always beautiful in accordance with accepted standards, why not accept a few other standards? . . . Jadassohn [author of the harmony textbook Ives used as a teenager and in college], if Emerson were literally a composer, could no more analyze his harmony than a Guide-to-Boston could.[28]

The experience of listening to the Emerson movement and trying to dis-entangle the ideas crowded into the opening cadenza, then hearing each idea worked out in turn and gradually understanding how they are all related, is like the experience of reading Emerson's essays. To convey Emerson's thought and language in music, to capture something of his substance, requires a new manner of expression, full of apparent discontinuities and chords undreamed of in regular music. Ives wrote in one printed copy of the sonata that "the whole [Emerson] movement has more to do (and more than I intended) with the struggles of his soul than [with] that peace of mind which he commands even in his struggles—though the music tries to end with that feeling."[29] Or perhaps, as Kyle Gann suggests, in this description of Emerson's prose writing Ives "is using a vision of Emerson . . . to justify his own composing tenden-cies. . . . Ives is telling us, in his roundabout way, that his music is a reflection or depiction not of outward reality but of consciousness itself."[30]

But Emerson was a poet as well as a speaker and essayist. Ives writes in a note to the score that the lyrical episode in the middle of the movement, based on the scherzo of the concerto, "may reflect some of Emerson's poetry rather than the prose," no doubt because its short phrases and regularly re-peating rhythms parallel the regular line lengths and recurring patterns of accented and unaccented syllables that are characteristic of poetic verse. He adds, "also some of the other passages may lean more towards the poetry than the prose." That he means the second theme is clear from the 1920 edition, where he marks the second theme, the lyrical episode in the middle, and the reprise of the second theme as "verse" and the other sections "prose."[31]

You have come to hear Jeremy Denk play an unusual program, made up of just two piano sonatas, both renowned for their difficulty: Beethoven's *Ham-merklavier Sonata* and Ives's *Concord Sonata*. You are curious about both. You find your seat, perfectly positioned so you can see the piano's keyboard and watch him play.

He comes on to applause and bows to the audience. But before sitting down, he makes a brief announcement: rather than begin with the Beethoven, as indicated on the program, he will play the Ives first.[32] Two thoughts cross your mind. He may have decided to start with the more difficult piece, while he is fresh—but if that were the reason, he probably would have set up the program that way. No, you decide, to announce the program and then switch the order just as he is about to start is a sly way to prevent those who have come for the Beethoven from leaving in the middle of the concert, as some might do to avoid hearing modern music. He sits at the piano bench, composes himself, leans backward with an expression of inspired resolve, and then curls forward to begin.

The first movement starts slowly and majestically, with a gesture like an expanding wedge. Over a descending bass line, you hear the opening motive of the "human-faith-melody," rising by whole step then falling a fifth. Suddenly faster, the music rushes forward in complex counterpoint, and the Beethoven Fifth Symphony motto emerges from the texture. Slower again, the opening motive of the "human-faith-melody" repeats in the bass, under another motive in the highest voice that is harmonized by dissonant chords moving in rhythm with it; this is the Emerson motive, a brief pentatonic tune in uneven rhythm that one could use to dramatically declaim the phrase "Hear!! the herald speaks." The Fifth Symphony motto pounds out in the bass, followed by a softer passage with brief hints of the second theme in the bass and the fugue theme above it (hints you may catch only on the fifth or tenth hearing). The Beethoven motto returns in the bass, only this time it continues with the next phrase from the second half of the "human-faith-melody," with a variant of the Emerson motive above it. Although you can hear these tunes, the meter is irregular, the key is never clear, and the harmony is quite dissonant, sounding more atonal than tonal. The music builds to a new climax, then quiets, developing fragments of the "human-faith-melody" and leading to a gentle statement of the Emerson motive, unharmonized, over a descending bass. The constant changes of tune, texture, rhythm, and tempo, along with the incredible difficulty of playing this music, identify this opening passage as a heroic cadenza in the mold of Beethoven or Liszt.

The music grows faster and louder again, and you hear a variant of the first half of the "human-faith-melody" over its second half in the bass (just the first and last phrases). After a climactic statement of the Emerson motive over rolling chords in the left hand, you hear, high in the piano, the Tolerance theme, a gradually rising, hymn-like tune played in whole-tone clusters, which Denk gently arpeggiates to bring it out from the surrounding texture. The Tolerance theme and Emerson motive alternate and weave in counterpoint with other ideas. Then the music gradually quiets in a transition that begins to drop hints of the second theme. The texture thins, and the harmony grows less dissonant, almost tonal.

The second theme is calm and gentle. A lyrical melody in regular phrases sounds like the most traditional music heard so far. It is in a steady triple meter (for the most part) and is tonal but for the accompanying chords and bass line, which bring in colors from other keys and hint at the fugue theme to come later.

Echoes of the Emerson motive lead into a development section that draws again on both halves of the "human-faith-melody" along with the second theme. After short loud chords and a brief silence seem to signal the end of the exposition, the development begins with a recollection of the movement's expanding opening gesture, the descending bass line now modified to recall the second theme. The music quickly builds to a climax and a varied statement of the second half of the "human-faith-melody," featuring the Beethoven motto in pounding chords and magically changing the last few notes of the theme into the Emerson motive. The development continues, gradually growing more rhapsodic until the pianist swiftly rolls a chord up and down three times, his left hand bouncing rapidly over his other hand from low notes to a high note and back.

Now the development is interrupted by a new lyrical episode representing Emerson's poetry, drawn from the scherzo of the Emerson concerto. Over a repeating arpeggiated chord in the pianist's left hand, a rich and resonant C major embellished with notes from a whole-tone scale, a melody unfolds in short segments, the first almost stepwise, the rest increasingly angular, with large leaps. The phrase repeats, varied, with notes in the melody displaced up or down as the pianist's right hand jumps around on the keyboard. The recurring rhythm and phrasing makes this section sound very different from what preceded it, evoking the regular patterns of poetry as opposed to the irregular rhythms of prose. Another variation brings a faster accompaniment figure, rolling up and down like a swelling sea, as the melody alternates between a single line and a series of chords. A third variation increases the pace of the rolling accompaniment still further, and the melody is now all played in chords, each overlapping with the next as the pianist holds down the damper pedal, creating a marvelously resonant sound like the ringing of church bells (Ives notes in the score that these "melodychords . . . are but to suggest some of the outdoor sounds over the Concord Hills").[33] The music closes on C major, then suddenly quiets and moves to a distant harmonic realm and new material; everything is different except for the texture of a wide-ranging melody over a quickly moving accompaniment. But this turns out to be just a palate cleanser. The phrase that began the lyrical episode returns to bring it to a close, repeating the end of the phrase for emphasis and settling again on C major.

After this lyrical interlude, the development quietly resumes, mixing new material with varied fragments of the themes. You hear the Fifth Symphony motto, very softly, then the music swells to highlight the opening motive of the "human-faith-melody." An angular idea enters, counterpointed by the opening motive of the second theme. The angular theme is then imitated as in a fugue, both right side up and upside down. This fugue theme was anticipated in the opening cadenza and in the accompaniment to the second theme. As the music slows and quiets again, the second theme grows more prominent.

There is a brief pause, then a loud, rhapsodic passage interrupts, leading to an abbreviated recapitulation: the opening motive of the "human-faith-melody" and the Emerson motive to represent the first theme area, and a shortened reprise of the second theme, once again slow and tranquil. The fugue theme sneaks back in, and the cadenza-like texture that opened the movement returns, mixing the Emerson motive with elements of the "human-faith-melody" in a coda that sounds at first like a new development section. A series of climaxes leads to a thundering restatement of an idea from early in the development: the variant of the second half of the "human-faith-melody" that repeats the Fifth Symphony motto in pounding chords and transforms the theme's last notes into the Emerson motive. This time, however, the music gradually grows less intense, slowed and calmed by a recurring idea in the bass that descends by half steps. The Emerson motive is stated loudly one last time, together with the second theme's opening motive. Then as the bass marches slowly downward, the Emerson motive gradually disintegrates, leaving the second half of the "human-faith-melody," which grows softer and fades into silence. The Fifth Symphony motive, which at the beginning of the movement sounded like Beethoven at his most assertive, reaches a kind of transcendence in this passage, heard in hushed echoes, fully absorbed in the spirit of Emerson's vision.

The movement has traveled from the height of complexity at the beginning, a dizzying mélange of themes and other material, through a process of clarification, as each theme gets its moment of prominence in turn, to a culmination where everything becomes simple in the best sense: clear, direct, elemental, deeply felt, achieving what Ives called "that peace of mind [Emerson] commands" after depicting "the struggles of his soul." The experience has been rich, invigorating, inspiring—and at times a bit hard to understand, like Emerson himself. You realize that this is music that calls for repeated hearings, just as Emerson's essays become more meaningful when read more than once.

Now you are ready for something different. And that is what you get.

Hawthorne

The second movement is the scherzo of this four-movement sonata—not a light dance movement, like the scherzo in Ives's First Symphony, but light-hearted and playful, not intended to plumb the philosophical or emotional depths of the other movements. In *Essays Before a Sonata* Ives calls this movement "an 'extended fragment' trying to suggest some of [Hawthorne's] wilder, fantastical adventures into the half-childlike, half-fairylike phantasmal realms." He mentions a number of Hawthorne's short stories, including *Feathertop* and *The Celestial Rail-Road* from *Mosses from an Old Manse*, *The Seven Vagabonds* from *Twice-Told Tales*, and *Circe's Palace* from *Tanglewood Tales*, but does not link any of these to specific passages in the music. By naming several stories that differ greatly in subject and tone, Ives seems to be suggesting that we should expect the movement to be equally diverse, passing from one episode to the next without weaving them together into an overarching form or narrative. In other words, it is like a collection of short stories, rather than a novel. He hints that what is important in the music is "not something that happens, but the way something happens." The only thing he mentions that is explicitly represented in the music is not something from a Hawthorne tale: "the old hymn-tune that haunts the church and sings only to those in the churchyard to protect them from secular noises, as when the circus parade comes down Main Street."[34]

Hawthorne starts with a whirr of sound. The pianist's hands are all over the keyboard, moving faster than seems humanly possible, creating delicate, constantly changing textures. Fragments of melody fly by, including the opening motive of the "human-faith-melody."

After about a minute, the pace suddenly slows, and the texture thins for a quiet melody over thick chords. Then something extraordinary happens. From inside the piano, with his right hand, the pianist picks up a board, about fifteen inches long and two or three inches wide and with a handle attached. He uses it to gently press on the black keys toward his right on the keyboard, creating a high, soft cluster of notes, then moves the block to sound clusters that move lower, then higher, then back and forth. Meanwhile with his left hand he plays chords on the white keys, strumming them like an autoharp or guitar and moving up and down to create a kind of chord-melody. The effect is magical, ethereal, like the "half-fairylike phantasmal realms" Ives mentions in *Essays Before a Sonata*.[35]

The focus shifts to the low range of the piano, the mood grows somber, the pianist puts the board away, and the music gradually speeds up and grows louder and more intense. All of a sudden it becomes very fast and light again as the pianist bounces off the keyboard, playing rapid passagework in the left hand and chords in the right, the opposite of what you expect. The texture thins to a melody in one hand and accompaniment in the other, the two hands trading roles every few seconds. The figuration is constantly changing, and it is fun to watch the pianist play what must be very difficult music.

Every now and then you hear a snippet from the "human-faith-melody." Varied bits of the first half of the melody, beginning with the opening motive and gradually growing longer, appear in the bass under repeating patterns in the right hand, then in the upper reaches of the piano over cascading figures in the left hand. The music swells, and phrases from the second half of the "human-faith-melody," the Beethoven Fifth Symphony motto and the following phrase, sound out in chords over a continually rolling arpeggio in the bass.

A loud swirl of sound creates a dissonant blur as the pianist holds down the damper pedal to sustain the sound. While the piano pulses with resonance, you see the pianist place his fingers on the keyboard, too quietly for you to hear. Then he releases the pedal, the dissonant blur disappears, and you hear a major chord. You recognize the effect as a sonic exuviation. You have heard such an effect more than half a dozen times in Ives's orchestral music, in *Central Park in the Dark*, the *Holidays Symphony*, and *Three Places in New England*, and here it is on the piano. As always, it suggests that the quiet music has been there all along, unheard, covered up by the louder sounds.

Very softly, the pianist repeats the chord and continues with what sounds like a hymn—indeed, like the beginning of *Martyn* ("Jesus, lover of my soul"), one of the hymns blended with Beethoven in the "human-faith-melody." It is interrupted by another loud swirl of sound. A second sonic exuviation reveals the hymn again, which begins like *Martyn* but alters the tune and harmony as it continues.

The hymn seems almost complete when it is interrupted again by loud, fast music that leads into what sounds like a march. Soon you recognize it as the march theme from *Putnam's Camp*. This whole passage, with the hymn surrounded by noisy music that crystallizes into a march, must be what Ives was referring to when he wrote of "the old hymn-tune that haunts the church and sings only to those in the churchyard to protect them from secular noises, as when the circus parade comes down Main Street." The march sounds like it is about to repeat the theme, but then you hear Ives's patented effect of drumming on the piano, sounding the pattern of *Street Beat*, and the march seems to fade into the distance.[36]

A new episode begins with an energetic passage that echoes a tune and texture you heard in the opening section. The music starts to sound something like ragtime, with syncopated figures in the melody over mostly even rhythms in the accompaniment. It builds to a climax, growing faster and more furious. The pianist holds down the damper pedal and begins to play clusters of notes with his fists, first in his right hand and then in both hands, pounding over the whole expanse of the piano, then releases the pedal as he hits the keys with his right fist one last time. You wonder whether attacking the keyboard with fists or playing the keys with a board is the most surprising and extraordinary thing you have ever seen at a concert—surely it is one or the other.

Silence.

What follows is completely different. Softly, the pianist plays a high note and a low note together, then plays high, delicate filigrees that arch down and back. They lead to the first phrase of *Martyn* high in the piano, punctuated with soft dissonant chords and more filigrees.

The quiet hymn tune is interrupted before its last note by a new, more lively section. An arching line in the bass rises and falls repeatedly, moving steadily with occasional dotted rhythms. It is counterpointed by a quicker upper line that mostly moves in the opposite direction. Soon the hands change roles: the melody with dotted rhythms moves to the right hand, often sounding two or three notes moving in parallel, over a rolling accompaniment in the left hand. The rhythms and contour of the melody start to sound familiar, and soon it turns into part of *Columbia, the Gem of the Ocean*. A climax, a pause, more bits from *Columbia*, the Fifth Symphony motto in the bass under running scales, and then the pianist takes off again at amazing speed (Ives marks in the score, "From here on, as fast as possible"). You hear bits of the "human-faith-melody" and of *Columbia, the Gem of the Ocean*. Suddenly everything stops for an echo of *Martyn*. With a loud and very fast upward gesture, hand leaping over hand, the pianist cuts off the hymn, leaves his hands suspended in midair, and slowly lowers them, bringing *Hawthorne* to a close.

It was, as Ives hinted in *Essays Before a Sonata*, a series of episodes of highly contrasting character, like a collection of short stories. The only overarching form you could detect was an alternation between extraordinarily fast sections and slower, quieter ones. But throughout you kept hearing hints of the "human-faith-melody" and of *Martyn*, one of the hymns on which that melody is based. The fantastic virtuosity, lightness of touch, episodic structure, and constant changes of character make it a fascinating foil for the denser, deeper music of *Emerson*, while the presence of the "human-faith-melody" links the two.

The Alcotts (Again)

After a brief silence, the pianist quietly begins the next movement. Having heard *The Alcotts* before, you know what to expect: a cumulative form that juxtaposes and then intertwines hymnody and Beethoven, culminating in the "human-faith-melody" in which they merge. As you listen this time, in the context of the previous two movements, you hear it both as a point of arrival, when the "human-faith-melody" finally appears in its complete form, and as a moment of relaxation, when Emerson's striving after the immensities and Hawthorne's flights of fancy come back down to earth and rest in the pleasant embrace of home and hearth. After much modernist and dissonant music, *The Alcotts* is mostly tonal, at times explicitly old-fashioned, with just enough modern spice to keep it from sounding completely out of place. It is a relief, and a release, like coming home.

Thoreau

The sonata is shaping up like a traditional four-movement work: a serious first movement, with a nod to sonata form; a scherzo, of a novel and episodic sort; a slow movement, with enough of a contrasting middle section to remind you of the ternary structures of the slow movements in Ives's first three symphonies and First String Quartet. What follows, however, is not a bright, fast movement in the manner of a Haydn finale, nor a fast, weighty movement like the finales of Ives's First Symphony, Second Symphony, or First Quartet. Rather, it is a quiet meditation, in the spirit of Thoreau's *Walden*, a memoir of two years living a simple life in a small cabin he had built himself by Walden Pond near Concord.

In *Essays Before a Sonata*, Ives outlines a kind of program for this movement, a series of images of Thoreau at Walden Pond and his thoughts over the course of a single day. It is long and rambling, with many passages quoted or paraphrased from *Walden*. What follows are excerpts that seem most relevant to the music.

> And if there shall be a program for our music, let it follow his thought on an autumn day of Indian summer at Walden—a shadow of a thought at first, colored by the mist and haze over the pond. . . . But this is momentary—the beauty of the day moves him to a certain restlessness—to aspirations more specific—an eagerness for outward action—but through it all he is conscious that it is not in keeping with the mood for this "Day." As the mists rise, there comes a clearer thought, more traditional than the first—a meditation more calm. As he stands on the side of the pleasant hill of pines and hickories in front of his cabin, he is still disturbed by restlessness and goes down the white-pebbled and sandy eastern shore. But it seems not to lead him where the thought suggests—he climbs the path

along the "bolder northern" and "western shore, with deep bays indented," and now along the railroad track, "where the Aeolian harp plays." But his eagerness throws him into the lithe, springy stride of the specie hunter—the naturalist—he is still aware of a restlessness—with these faster steps his rhythm is of shorter span—it is still not the "tempo" of Nature— . . . and he knows now that he must let Nature flow through *him* and slowly—he releases his more personal desires to her broader rhythm, conscious that this blends more and more with the harmony of her solitude; it tells him that his search for freedom on that day, at least, lies in his submission to her, for Nature is as relentless as she is benignant. He remains in this mood, and, while outwardly still, he seems to move with the slow, almost monotonous swaying beat of this autumnal day. . . . At times, the more personal strivings for the ideal freedom—the former more active speculations—come over him, as if he would trace a certain intensity even in his submission. "He grew in those seasons like corn in the night, and they were better than any works of the hands. They were not time subtracted from his life but so much over and above the usual allowance. . . ." "The evening train has gone by, and all the restless world with it. . . ." His meditations are interrupted only by the faint sound of the Concord bell— . . . "a melody as it were, imported into the wilderness. . . . At a distance over the woods the sound acquires a certain vibratory hum, as if the pine needles in the horizon were the strings of a harp which it swept . . . a vibration of the universal lyre. . . ." It is darker—the poet's flute is heard out over the pond and Walden hears the swan song of that "Day"—and faintly echoes. . . . Is it a transcendental tune of Concord? . . . Before ending his day he looks out over the clear, crystalline water of the pond and catches a glimpse of the "shadow-thought" he saw in the morning's mist and haze.[37]

How can we hear these images in the music?

The movement begins very quietly, with a gentle upward sweep across the keyboard like a breath of wind and a slow chromatic motive like a ripple on the water—"a shadow of a thought . . . , colored by the mist and haze over the pond." The effect repeats with a new motive, then again with another, each motive repeating and returning like waves rippling across the pond. A rising, faster, slightly louder gesture, then another, then another, suggests "a certain restlessness . . . an eagerness for outward action." Each rising gesture is answered by a descending one that slows again, and the upward sweep and rippling motives return, restoring "the mood for this 'Day.'"

After a pause, a new idea is heard, sounding stable and tonal in contrast to the chromatic music of the pond and mist. This is "a clearer thought, more traditional than the first—a meditation more calm," that comes after the mists begin to dissipate, clearing his mind as well as the landscape. The thought is clear but brief, followed by a softer echo. But "he is still disturbed by restlessness," depicted by another rising passage, almost in the syncopated style of ragtime, that grows louder and faster before it slows and calms. The alternation of calm meditation and rising restlessness repeats twice more, each time growing louder than before, until it reaches a climax in an emphatic repeating gesture that suggests "eagerness" and a "lithe, springy stride" of "faster steps" whose "rhythm is of shorter span."

The moment does not last. To attain "the 'tempo' of Nature," Thoreau "knows now that he must let Nature flow through *him* and . . . releases his more personal desires to her broader rhythm." That broad rhythm, a "slow, almost monotonous swaying beat," is embodied in a slow, relentlessly repeating figure in the bass, a rising third followed by a rising fifth. Above it, in a different key, comes a new melody that begins with a descent by step and skip, rises to a peak, and descends again. Its opening gesture is the phrase from *Massa's in de Cold Ground* to the words "Down in de cornfield," which you have heard in several Ives pieces already. Although in *The "St. Gaudens" in Boston Common* this tune evoked mourning, here it suggests Thoreau's submission to Nature, the release of his own "personal desires," and the resulting spiritual growth: "He grew in those seasons like corn in the night"—in cornfields in high summer, you can see each morning that the corn is taller than the day before.

Into this meditative moment enter reminiscences of the rippling motives from the movement's opening section. At first these ideas—the "shadow of a thought"—play out over the "monotonous swaying beat" of the repeating figure in the bass, but that figure briefly stops, as his "more personal strivings . . . come over him, as if he would trace a certain intensity even in his submission." The repeating bass figure briefly returns, then stops again, as "his meditations are interrupted . . . by the faint sound of the Concord bell," represented by soft dissonant chords that resemble the clang of distant bells, the left hand arching over the right to strike a high afterbeat like an echo or a "vibration of the universal lyre."

After the bells, you hear what might be a hint of the "human-faith-melody." The music gradually grows louder and faster, developing into a free fantasy that evokes at times the ripple motives and rising passages from the first section, at other times the new idea (the "meditation more calm") from the second section, suggesting that Thoreau's thoughts are ranging, but not with the restless urgency heard before. Two somewhat mechanical passages may depict the passing of "the evening train": one where a dissonant chord in the bass keeps pounding away (Ives marks it "evenly and perversely") as the music above it grows faster and louder, and another where both hands play chords in the same plodding rhythm, starting suddenly loud and far apart and gradually coming together as they slow, quiet, and lose steam.[38] After the latter passage, the "monotonous swaying beat" returns deep in the bass, joined by the melody that begins with "Down in de cornfield." Once again the "broader rhythm" of Nature stops, and fragments of melody from the opening section reappear.

The music builds again, and then you hear it: the "human-faith-melody" that was anticipated in the first two movements, was knit together in the third, and now is recollected as "a transcendental tune of Concord," a "swan song of that 'Day'" by Walden Pond. Remarkably, it is played by a flute offstage, over motives in the piano from the opening section with its images of ripples on the water. This is a literal depiction of the phrase in Ives's program that "the poet's flute is heard out over the pond." (In the score, Ives offers two alternatives: a version with flute, and one where the "human-faith-melody" is played by the piano, with the rest of the texture simplified to fit two hands.) The board and the fists in *Hawthorne* were extraordinary, but to have the sound of a flute float into a piano sonata is even more surprising. You hear the first half of the theme and the beginning of the second half, the Beethoven motto more gentle and placid than ever. The flute wanders off in a new direction and repeats part of the theme's first half in a new key, over rising figures in the piano that recall the restlessness of the opening section. Then the calm, "slow, almost monotonous swaying beat" of Nature returns in the piano, and the "human-faith-melody" sounds out again in the flute, almost complete, but missing its last several notes as the flute fades to nothing.

The "monotonous swaying beat" continues in the piano, and the melody with "Down in de cornfield" returns once more. At the end we hear again sounds from the beginning of the movement, the gentle upward sweep across the keyboard and the slow chromatic motive, "a glimpse of the 'shadow-thought' he saw in the morning's mist and haze," with one last recollection of the "monotonous swaying" motive in the bass and the repeating notes of the Fifth Symphony motto—but not the descending third—in the upper reaches of the piano. What sounded like Beethoven in the opening cadenza of *Emerson* sounds here like Ives: the gentlest echo of that "transcendental tune of Concord," the human-faith-melody.

Minutes later, when Jeremy Denk starts to play the *Hammerklavier Sonata*, you notice something curious, and historically impossible: Ives's sonata that draws on Beethoven is so much in your ears that it sounds like Beethoven borrowed his opening theme from Ives.

Ultimately, the *Concord Sonata* is modern music that reflects an essentially Romantic impulse. Like Mendelssohn's overture *A Midsummer Night's Dream*, Liszt's *Dante Sonata* and *Faust Symphony*, Richard Strauss's *Don Juan* and *Don Quixote*, and countless other nineteenth-century instrumental works, it was inspired by literature. It embraces a wide spectrum of Romantic keyboard styles, from improvisatory fantasies to simple, songlike moments, from intense chromaticism to tonal clarity, from serious statements to light-hearted play. The modern idioms appear where they are needed for rhetorical effect, creating an extreme version of the contrasts between complex and clear textures and between dissonance and consonance that have long been native to piano music and are part of a palette of expressive musical gestures that go back as far as the Renaissance. The *Concord Sonata* challenges you as a listener, but at heart it can be understood in the same way as the piano music of Beethoven, Schumann, or Liszt. It grows on you, this music.

THE IMPACT OF THE *CONCORD SONATA*

When Ives sent out the *Concord Sonata* and *Essays Before a Sonata* to hundreds of newspapers, journals, critics, pianists, and other musicians, most reacted to the modern idiom rather than the Romantic impulse. With few exceptions, Ives did not know the recipients, and they knew nothing about him. A few wrote back, some thanking him while expressing no opinion, some scathing, some encouraging.[39]

Reviewers were not kind. In *Musical America*, A. Walter Kramer called the sonata "without doubt the most startling conglommeration of meaningless notes that we have ever seen engraved on white paper." The *Musical Courier* review is mocking throughout, saying about the book of essays, "There is no music in it," and about the sonata, "Some would insist that there is no music in that, either." Edwin J. Stringham in the *Rocky Mountain News* called the sonata "terribly difficult to perform and, I think, not worth the trouble involved to master it," comparing it to "a boiler-shop or the sounds emanating from a conservatory of music when in full blast." Writing for the English journal *Music and Letters*, Ernest Walker sarcastically commented that

> a reviewer of modernist piano music has necessarily hardened himself to a great deal and is not easily taken aback: but "Concord, Mass." may be safely recommended as a tonic to anyone bored with the reactionary conservatism of European extremists. . . . And every now and then (the oases, if they can be so called, amount to about 2 per cent. of the whole) we come across passages of the plainest common chords that sound exactly like a

beginner's first attempts at harmony exercises. Mr. Ives' style is sadly familiar here: so, indeed, in quite another way, is the style of the 98 per cent., at any rate in households where the baby or the cat has access to the piano.

All four of these writers quoted Ives's dedication in *Essays Before a Sonata*, a witty and self-deprecating attempt to deflect criticism that may have only heightened it: "These prefatory essays were written by the composer for those who can't stand his music—and the music for those who can't stand his essays; to those who can't stand either, the whole is respectfully dedicated." Walker said this "shows that he possesses a sense of humour," but Kramer wrote, "That is why we say the sonata is dedicated to us. *We can't stand either.*"[40]

The most sympathetic review was by Henry Bellamann, a music educator and writer later famous for the novel *King's Row* (1940). Bellamann received the sonata in early 1921 and wrote Ives to thank him, adding,

> I have just recently had time to go over it several times and I want to tell you how remarkable a piece of work it is. Miss [Lenore] Purcell, who is my assistant and who plays a great many modern works for the various lectures I give [to music clubs] . . . , is very delighted with the sonata and we purpose making it the subject of an evening's lecture recital in our series for next year. . . .
>
> An extraordinary work. One feels very happy to know that a creation of such calibre on an American subject may be done in America.

Ives replied with his customary self-deprecation:

> I appreciate your kindness in writing and thank you warmly for your interest. Your proposal to include the Concord Sonata in your lecture-recital programs shows more courage than most musicians care to show. But I am afraid it (at least the first two movements) will arouse little enthusiasm with most audiences (except perhaps in the form of refined abuse or expressive silence).[41]

Bellamann's review, published in the October 1921 issue of the New Orleans journal *The Double Dealer*, offers praise with some qualifications:

> The music is broad and stately, the rhythmic arches are very wide. No fixed tonality, no rhythmic unity. It sways as freely as a tree top in the wind. . . .
> . . . Mr. Ives' sonata is a piece of work sincerely done, and if a failure, a rather splendid one.
> Certainly it must be considered in a class by itself. Conceived independently of any instrumental idiom, it must be regarded as an essay of lofty thought and feeling expressed in musical notation. One arises from a reading of it with much, much more of satisfaction than dissatisfaction.

> Its loftiness of purpose is evident; its moments of achievement elevating
> and greatly beautiful.

Ives was touched by the review and wrote to thank Bellamann. The two developed a friendship, and Bellamann became one of Ives's most avid advocates for the next dozen years.[42]

There were several partial performances of the sonata in the 1920s. Purcell performed excerpts in lecture-recitals with Bellamann in 1921–1922, and Clifton Furness played *The Alcotts* in a lecture-recital on August 3, 1921. Several individual movements were premiered or repeated in 1928: *Emerson* by Katherine Heyman on a Paris radio broadcast on March 5 and by Arthur Hardcastle in a San Francisco concert on September 19; *The Alcotts* by Oscar Ziegler in New York on May 1 and in Salzburg, Austria, on July 31; and *Thoreau* by Clifton Furness on December 12 in Hartford, Connecticut. Keith Corelli toured with *Emerson* in spring 1929.[43]

None of these, however, had the impact of John Kirkpatrick's performances of the entire sonata in 1938–1939. He encountered the sonata in 1927 through Katherine Heyman in Paris, wrote Ives for copies of the sonata and *Essays*, and gradually learned all four movements, starting with *The Alcotts*. By 1935 he was performing *Emerson*, including at a concert at Town Hall in New York on January 28, 1936, at which Harmony and Edith Ives were present. He played the whole sonata in a private concert in Stamford, Connecticut, on June 21, 1938, then gave the public premiere, playing from memory, at Cos Cob, Connecticut, on November 28. Paul Rosenfeld reviewed it enthusiastically for *Modern Music*, calling it "possibly the most intense and sensitive musical experience achieved by an American":

> The structure is Beethoven-like in breadth of conception and cyclic, oftentimes in the grand style . . . ; . . . every note during entire pages is rhapsodically alive, tremulously expressive, fraught with special poetic emphasis and meaning. . . .
> It thrilled, it touched, again and again, the entire work; releasing something in the depths, restoring enchantment to them and to things.[44]

Kirkpatrick repeated the sonata in New York at Town Hall on January 20, 1939, as shown on the concert program in Figure 10.1. Ives was apparently too ill to attend, but his niece Sarane and other family and friends were there. The audience was small but applauded both the *Concord Sonata* and the pianist so enthusiastically that he had to play seven encores. The sonata was rapturously reviewed in the *New York Herald Tribune* by Lawrence Gilman. He had written Ives asking for a score; Harmony sent the sonata and *Essays Before a Sonata*, and Gilman studied them in preparation for the

JOHN

KIRKPATRICK

Piano Recital

TOWN HALL
113 West 43rd Street

FRIDAY EVENING AT 8:30

JANUARY 20th

Sonata in C major, Op. 53   BEETHOVEN

    I.   allegro con brio
   II. Introduzione, adagio molto
        Rondo, allegretto moderato—prestissimo

Concord, Mass., 1840-60   CHARLES E. IVES

SECOND PIANOFORTE SONATA (1911-15)
("an attempt to present one person's impression of the spirit of transcendentalism that
is associated in the minds of many with Concord, Mass., of over a half century ago")

   I. Emerson   ("a composite picture or impression")

  II. Hawthorne (an "extended fragment" reflecting "some of his wilder, fantastical
                     adventures into the half-childlike, half-fairylike phantasmal realms")

  III. The Alcotts ("a sketch")

  IV. Thoreau ("an autumn day of Indian summer at Walden")

FIRST PERFORMANCE

STEINWAY PIANO

Tickets: Box seats $2.75, Orchestra $2.20, $1.65, $1.10, Balcony $.83
Tax included   At Box Office

Management RICHARD COPLEY, Steinway Bldg., 113 West 57th St., New York, N. Y.

Figure 10.1.   Program from John Kirkpatrick's New York premiere of the *Concord Sonata* in Town Hall, January 20, 1939.

MSS 56, The John Kirkpatrick Papers in the Music Library of Yale University, Box 46, Folder 488, January 30, 1939.

concert. His review praises Ives without reserve, calling him "one of the pioneers of modern music, a great adventurer in the spiritual world, a poet, a visionary, a sage, and a seer." Gilman quotes from the *Essays* to characterize each movement, then sums up:

> This sonata is exceptionally great music—it is, indeed, the greatest music composed by an American, and the most deeply and essentially American in impulse and implication. It is wide-ranging and capacious. It has passion, tenderness, humor, simplicity, homeliness. It has imaginative and spiritual vastness. It has wisdom and beauty and profundity, and a sense of the encompassing terror and splendor of human life and human destiny—a sense of those mysteries that are both human and divine.[45]

This review, more than any other single event during Ives's lifetime, made his reputation as a composer of greatness. The national newsmagazine *Time* quoted Gilman's review and echoed his praise, introducing Ives to a national audience and declaring that despite the scarcity of performances of Ives's works,

> little by little the few music-lovers who did hear them began to realize that Ives was neither a trickster nor a crackpot, but a writer of real, live music. Today Ives is regarded even by conservative critics as one of the most individual and authentically American of all U. S. composers.

Nothing could be further from the mocking reviews of eighteen years earlier.

At Gilman's suggestion, Kirkpatrick repeated the sonata for a packed house in Town Hall on February 24 in the first all-Ives concert ever. Olin Downes's review of this concert for the *New York Times* was more measured, saying of the sonata that "its structural form will be clearer with later hearings" and reserving final judgment, but praised it as "a creation spun out of a man's home memories and consciousness—not a fabric of tone to fit a model outside of himself. An American composer thus dares be himself. . . . The stuff of a fearless man and artist is in it."[46]

Not everyone was enthusiastic, however. After the first New York performance, Irving Kolodin wrote in the *New York Sun* that

> simply a page of this music is enough to impress the listener with Ives's musicality, the fervor of his desire to write music, the amazing perception which enabled him to anticipate, by a score of years, some of the most recent developments in writing here and abroad. Yet none of these things, as isolated phenomena, was equivalent to music. It was the reaction of this listener that Ives's single, most serious deficiency was a lack of discipline, an inability to distinguish between the gold and the dross that issued from his imagination.

Oscar Thompson reviewed the February concert for the same paper and wrote that the sonata

> is essentially a work of associations. . . . An earnest effort last night to hear this sonata purely as music left with this reviewer substantial doubts as to whether the work possesses the basic stuff to make a strong and intelligible appeal direct to the ear, without which the most ingenious of program music is unable to maintain itself.

In *Modern Music*, the composer Elliott Carter, who had been a friend of Ives since he was a teenager in the 1920s and had heard Ives play excerpts from the sonata, said he was "sadly disappointed" at hearing the whole work, which he called "formally weak," "full of the paraphernalia of the overdressy sonata school, cyclical themes, contrapuntal development sections that lead nowhere, constant harmonic movement which does not clarify the form, and dramatic rather than rhythmical effects." He disparaged the "quotation of well-known American tunes with little comment, possibly charming but certainly trivial." Yet he asserted that "while his music is more often original than good, the good is really very personal and beautiful." Carter concluded, "it is not until we have had a much greater opportunity to examine and hear his music, that Ives' position as a composer can be determined. The present canonization is a little premature."[47]

The disagreements continued throughout Ives's lifetime and beyond, but the *Concord Sonata* has remained one of his best-known works. It has been recorded dozens of times, beginning with Kirkpatrick's 1948 performance on Columbia Records, and has been played by hundreds of pianists worldwide. Considered virtually unperformable when first published in 1921, it is now played by students in colleges and conservatories and is regarded as difficult but hardly inaccessible.

One can sympathize with the negative reviewers; most had heard little or none of his other music, and the *Concord Sonata* is a difficult piece to digest on first hearing. But their complaints that Ives lacked discipline in writing the sonata, or that it is "formally weak" or does not have "the basic stuff to make a strong and intelligible appeal direct to the ear" purely as music, can best be answered by getting to know it through repeated listenings and considering it alongside his earlier major works. The composer of Ives's first three symphonies—none of which had been heard yet in 1939—did not lack discipline or craft or control of form or the ability to create pieces that work purely as music without a program to sustain them. Carter's objections to "cyclical themes" and "contrapuntal development sections" are matters of taste, reflecting his neoclassical orientation versus Ives's essential Romanticism. And he was dead wrong about Ives's use of borrowed melodies; from the

First String Quartet and Second Symphony through the orchestral sets and *Concord Sonata*, we have seen Ives's masterful reworking of borrowed material, which allows him to achieve effects that cannot be accomplished in any other way, such as the interplay of Beethoven with hymnody to convey subtle and profound meanings in *The Alcotts*. For all its individuality, the *Concord Sonata* is quintessentially a creation of the same composer as *Memories*, *Variations on "America*," the first three symphonies, the violin sonatas, the *Holidays Symphony*, and *Three Places in New England*, a composer who weaves together the musical traditions present in his American environment in ever new and fascinating variations.

• *11* •

Transcendent Journeys

$\mathscr{F}$rom *Central Park in the Dark* to *Three Places in New England* and the *Concord Sonata*, many of Ives's pieces are about places and the people in them. As Larry Starr has pointed out, several others are about journeys, from the stroll through the hills in *Walking* to the march off to war in *The "St. Gaudens" in Boston Common*.[1] Two are about journeys that culminate in an experience of transcendence, one in a real terrestrial space, the other in an imagined spiritual realm. In the Second String Quartet, Ives depicts four men who converse, argue, and then walk up a mountain to commune with the divine, culminating in "Nearer, my God, to Thee." In his Fourth Symphony, Ives drew on movements from the Second Quartet and three other works to create a mystical experience, posing a question about the pursuit of meaning in the first movement, giving views of the too lazy or too convention-bound religious life in the middle movements, and in the finale achieving an apotheosis that again reaches "Nearer, my God, to Thee." In both pieces, Ives used all the resources he had developed over his career, from innovative sounds and techniques of his experimental music to genres and procedures of the classical tradition, from hymn tunes to patriotic songs, from cumulative form to collage, from tonality to atonality and everything in between, to convey the journey from the human to a transcendent plane.

STRING QUARTET NO. 2

Ives assembled his orchestral sets, *Holidays Symphony*, and *Concord Sonata* from single-movement tone poems he had begun separately. His Second String Quartet, composed around 1911–1914, is different: it is apparently his only completed programmatic work that he imagined from the start as a multimovement piece. It depicts four men—embodied by the four players and their four instruments—who have a conversation in the first movement, get into an argument in the second movement, and then in the finale stop talking and walk up a nearby mountain together to contemplate the heavens. He summarized the string quartet's program in a note on the first page of his pencil sketch: "S.Q. for 4 men—who converse, discuss, argue (in re 'Politick'), fight, shake hands, shut up—then walk up the mountain side to view the firmament!"[2]

Ives was inspired to write the piece as a protest against what he saw as the timidity of string quartet performers and the complacency of audiences for chamber music. The metaphor of a string quartet as a conversation between the players goes back to the time of Haydn, when it was primarily a genre for home music-making, a way for friends to pass the time together, akin to playing cards or a parlor game. Stating a musical idea in one instrument, then passing it around to others, each offering a new variation or contrasting it with new ideas, is typical of quartets by Haydn, Mozart, Beethoven, and later composers, evoking the exchange of ideas in a conversation and the conviviality that can engender. But if the ideas are trite or banal, or have been heard many times before, what is the point of having a conversation?

As Ives recalled in *Memos*, around 1911

> it used to come over me—especially after coming from some of those nice Kneisel Quartet concerts—that music had been, and still was, too much of an emasculated art. Too much of what was easy and usual to play and to hear was called beautiful, etc.—the same old even-vibration, Sybaritic apron-strings, keeping music too much tied to the old ladies. The string quartet music got more and more weak, trite, and effeminate. After one of those Kneisel Quartet concerts in the old Mendelssohn Hall [in New York], I started a string quartet score, half mad, half in fun, and half to try out, practise, and have some fun with making those men fiddlers get up and do something like men.

He wrote that the piece "is one of the best things I have, but the old ladies (male and female) don't like it anywhere at all. It makes them mad."[3]

Ives's language here requires some unpacking. He had been attending Kneisel Quartet concerts since college and was growing tired of their repertoire.[4] "Nice" is not a term of praise in Ives's vocabulary; he means by it something (or someone) that is deliberately inoffensive, and therefore lacking in the character or wit it takes to say something meaningful. Music that is "easy and usual to play and to hear" should not be praised as "beautiful," nor held up as a model to follow. That is lazy thinking, typical of those accustomed to luxury and pleasure ("Sybaritic," after the luxurious ancient city of Sybaris). Better music, like life itself, offers a challenge, a kind of mental and musical exercise for both players and listeners. Music that does not make us work is "emasculated," "weak," "effeminate," "too much tied to the old ladies" (a term equally applicable to either sex)—unable to do its job of telling us something new and taking us to a place we have never been.

Ives's use of gendered language in passages like this has led some writers to castigate him as anti-woman. But such a view is contradicted by his devotion to and collaborations with his wife Harmony; his respectful treatment of the women he worked with; his support for the right of women to vote, one of the great causes of his time; and his positive portrayal of women in his music, from *The Alcotts* to the Goddess of Liberty in *Putnam's Camp* and in several songs. As Judith Tick has argued, in attacking as "emasculated" and "effeminate" the music promoted by the classical music establishment, Ives was inverting and redirecting then-current ideas about music and gender. It was widely believed that only men were capable of composing in classical genres and forms, while women were regarded as able to write only short pieces like songs and piano music. The male-dominated music of orchestras and professional string quartets was praised as "masculine" and "cerebral" and considered superior to the "feminine" music of the home, of popular entertainment, or of the church. Ives flipped this formula, praising hymns and popular music as strong, reflecting the strength of the everyday women and men who performed them, and castigating what was formulaic and routine in classical music—"the same old even-vibration"—as emasculated, rather than virile as other writers had claimed. If "old ladies" was a term of derision suitable for both sexes, that was because Ives believed that both men and women were capable of working hard as performers and listeners and meeting every challenge music can pose, if they chose to do so.[5] It was in the spirit of critiquing the status quo in the concert hall that Ives sought to "have some fun with making those men fiddlers get up and do something like men."

Looking beyond the gendered language and the attack on the musical establishment, the Second Quartet embodies a transcendent journey for the men portrayed in it. They start and end as friends yet experience something important together and are transformed by the experience. The discussion in the first movement is civil, sometimes marked by agreement, even though it touches on "politick" in ways that invoke the Civil War. But the arguments in the second movement start shrill and get worse, rising to mockery, out-shouting each other, and heated exchanges that threaten to restage the war right then and there. The only possible resolution—a lesson for our own times, and every time—is to go back to what they have in common: here, for these four, a quiet and ultimately spiritual walk together, side by side, blessed at the end by a shared experience that seems revelatory.

Ives seems to have modeled his picture of four men on those he knew. In notes he added in the margins of the sketch, reprinted in the 2016 critical edition of the piece but not in the first published score from 1954, Ives refers in the first movement to his Poverty Flat apartment mate Keyes Winter and to his Yale fraternity, DKE. In the middle movement, Ives casts the second violinist as a virtuoso with conservative tastes, like the ones who hated his violin sonatas when they played through them; in marginal notes, Ives calls him "Rollo," after the main character in a nineteenth-century series of didactic books for children, who became for Ives, in John Kirkpatrick's words, "a symbol of the literal mind unable to imagine anything beyond what he'd been taught." And in the finale, the walk up the mountain reflects Ives's many vacations in the Adirondack Mountains and rugged hikes with the Twichells.⁶

First Movement: *Discussions*

The first movement, *Discussions* (or *Conversations and Discussions*), starts quietly. All four instruments begin together on a sustained chord that would be consonant if not for the note in the viola. The viola is the first to speak, rising through new notes and stopping on one that is dissonant against all the other instruments. The first violin moves in response, arching down and leaping up to a note that is dissonant with the cello, who moves in turn, echoing part of the violin's line then continuing on. It is easy to hear this as a conversation, each speaking in turn and sparking a response. The viola speaks again briefly, then the second violin, who repeats himself and develops his thought. The others chime in, overlapping each other. All of this is atonal, with no sense of a pitch center despite the many sustained tones. Then suddenly everyone converges on the same regular rhythm, moving together on a few chords that sound tonal—a point of agreement.

The moment quickly passes, and they arrive back on the opening chord. This time, the second violin speaks first, and the others soon join in. Suddenly—sudden change seems to be the norm here—everyone is again playing in the same rhythm, but now the rhythm is irregular and most chords are dissonant until without warning they converge on a single pitch and resolve to a major chord as if in tonal music. For just a moment the music sounds traditional, as the first violin plays a melody over a bass line in the cello and the two inner instruments murmur between them, but the lines quickly diverge and the music reverts to atonality. We are not even two minutes into the movement, and it is growing harder to follow the conversation. This is not music that is "easy and usual to play and to hear," but it is endlessly new and full of intriguing gestures and sonorities.

As the movement continues, there are moments where one instrument parallels or echoes another, or all four come together in a dissonant crunch or what sounds like a tonal chord progression, or everyone pauses to take a breath. But mostly each instrumental line is independent of the others, and the overall texture is constantly changing, like the flow of a good conversation. After a slower, more lyrical moment, suddenly—that word again—the first violin plays the first few notes of *Columbia, the Gem of the Ocean* over dissonant, rapidly flowing lines in the other instruments. It is answered by the beginning of *Dixie* in the viola, part of *Marching Through Georgia* in the second violin (with a bit of *Turkey in the Straw* in the viola), and the opening notes of *Hail! Columbia* in the first violin and cello. We are not to assume that the four men have suddenly burst into song; instead, these familiar fragments of melody tell us that the conversation has turned to politics, as an appeal to national pride is interrupted by a southerner (*Dixie*), who is countered by a northerner (*Marching Through Georgia*), until both are shouted down by the other two players invoking *Hail! Columbia* and its salute to national unity from the era when George Washington and John Adams were president. The moment is over quickly, and the texture returns to the interplay between free counterpoint and moments of similar rhythm or parallel motion.

After awhile, the music grows louder and faster again. (Ives wrote in his sketch at this moment, "Keyes takes exception 'on that point'—So do the others [and] each has his say DKE.") A brief pause, and everyone joins in a rich C major ("But on this—they all say Eyah! Everybody can see that!"). After the phrase quietly resolves, three loud and dissonant chords interrupt. Now the music moves more slowly and softly, in a texture reminiscent of passages earlier in the movement. At the end, we hear once again the opening chord and the first few notes in the viola and violin, as if we have cycled back to the beginning of the conversation and there is no more to say ("enough discussion for us!").[7]

Second Movement: *Arguments*

The second movement, *Arguments*, sounds angry from the start. It opens with each instrument in turn playing wicked dissonances. The lower instruments settle into repeating figures ("Saying the same thing over & over & louder & louder—ain't arguing," comments Ives in the sketch) while the violins spin out ideas above them. Tired of the cacophony, the second violin bursts into a solo cadenza in lyrical Romantic style (marked in the score "Andante Emasculata: Alla Rubato ELMAN!," referring to violin virtuoso Mischa Elman and the Romantic practice of freely bending the rhythm, known as *rubato*). The others cut him off with loud dissonant chords (marked "Allegro con fisto," made-up Italian for "fast with a fist"; on the sketch, Ives wrote by the second violin part, "Cut it out! Rollo!"). After a back-and-forth, the viola plays a melody with all twelve chromatic notes in it, imitated by all the others in a complex atonal canon. A hint of *Columbia, the Gem of the Ocean* is tucked into the counterpoint. The second violin is the last to enter and the first to drop out (Ives writes "Prof. M [violinist Franz Milcke] stops, 'Too hard to play—so it just can't be good music'—Rollo"), then starts to keep time by playing on every beat ("Beat time Rollo"). He comes back in when everyone starts playing scales in the key of C, the simplest key ("all in key of C. You can do that 'nice' & pretty"). But then everyone gets mad, shouting in turn ("all mad!").[8]

The tempo slows and all four play together in dissonant counterpoint, out of which emerges a dialogue of familiar tunes: *Hail! Columbia* in the first violin; the theme from the third movement of Tchaikovsky's *Pathétique Symphony* (the model for Ives's First Symphony finale) in the cello, echoed by the violins in parallel thirds; a theme from the first movement of Brahms's Second Symphony in the first violin; *Columbia, the Gem of the Ocean* in parallel fourths in the viola and cello; the "Ode to Joy" theme from Beethoven's Ninth Symphony finale in the second violin; the opening notes of the verse and then of the chorus from *Marching Through Georgia* in the first violin. The debate here is not about the Civil War or domestic politics but seems to concern the relative merits of European and American music or of symphonies versus popular songs. Over rich harmonies in the other instruments, we hear "Down in de cornfield" from *Massa's in de Cold Ground* in the first violin, followed by more shouts, more C major scales, what sounds like tuning up, and two fast dissonant chords (marked "Allegro con fistiswatto") to end the movement.

Third Movement: *The Call of the Mountains*

The finale, *The Call of the Mountains*, is almost as long as the other two movements put together, and it has an entirely different spirit. It begins softly, with rich, dissonant chords. After the references to familiar music we just heard, which reminded us of human conversation, this rich quiet feels like an awed silence, as if we have come outdoors to see a landscape full of beauties and with no one in it but us. A hint of *Nettleton* ("Come, Thou Fount of ev'ry blessing") in the violins lends a religious cast. Wisps of melody appear among the sonorous chords. The pace picks up, as if we have begun walking, then moves a bit faster still. At times it sounds like the violins are in step with each other, moving more quickly, while the lower instruments walk on with slower tread.

All at once the texture changes: the cello marches down and up by whole steps at a steady pace, while the viola, in long notes and double stops, plays Lowell Mason's *Bethany*, the most famous tune for Sarah Adams's hymn "Nearer, my God, to Thee":

Nearer, my God, to Thee, nearer to Thee!
E'en tho' it be a cross that raiseth me.
Still all my song shall be, nearer, my God, to Thee,
Nearer, my God, to Thee, nearer to Thee!

The whole steps in the cello echo and reinforce the two descending whole steps that begin the hymn's first, second, and fourth phrases. Above them the violins quietly perform arabesques, like leaves fluttering on the trees or the glitter of fireflies or the buzz of tree frogs and insects as we walk through the woods toward the mountaintop. Halfway through the hymn tune, the viola weaves in a motive from *Westminster Chimes*, the time-keeping melody named for the chimes in the Clock Tower (Big Ben) at London's Westminster Palace, a tune Ives had grown fond of while listening to the steeple chimes at Bloomfield's First Presbyterian Church. As the viola resumes the second half of the hymn tune, the cello changes from whole steps to half steps. Bits of *Westminster Chimes* mix again with the hymn. As is typical with Ives, the chime tune and the hymn tune are melodically related, so blending one into the other makes a lovely pun—which in this case is also deeply meaningful. In the context of a "walk up the mountain side to view the firmament," the hymn expresses the exaltation of being nearer to the divine, and the chime tune conveys the sense of height and space Ives must have identified with hearing the bells from a steeple or clock tower pealing over a landscape.

Loud scurrying in all four instruments cuts off this transcendent vision, and the music returns to the slow, quiet richness of the opening of the movement. Again the music builds, the players sometimes moving together, sometimes separately as the walk continues. Echoes and variants of *Westminster Chimes* and *Bethany* can be heard now and then, as if the very landscape is sparkling with height and space and signs of God. Suddenly and unexpectedly, all four instruments join in a brief, passionate, angular melody, a moment of communion, the only time in the whole quartet they all play the same line at once.

Moments later, the music rushes forward to reveal a vision of the divine, the end of their transcendent journey. The cello plays a repeated whole tone scale descending from D to D in the lowest part of its range, while above in the stratosphere the first violin sounds out in long notes the third phrase of *Bethany*—"Still all my song shall be, nearer, my God, to Thee"—overlapping with *Westminster Chimes*, both in a glorious D major. In between them, the other instruments play repeating figures that embellish and reinforce D major, a key long associated with triumph and rejoicing, as in the *Hallelujah Chorus* from Handel's *Messiah* and the finale of Beethoven's Ninth Symphony. In a piece that has been almost unrelentingly atonal, this is a moment of revelation, a deep experience of the divine in the heavens and in the natural world around the four men, and of communion among the companions who have shared the same remarkable experience. The music gradually grows quieter, the violins float down into a more human level, and with bits of *Bethany* in the inner instruments, the quartet calms to a haunting close on a chord that is both major and minor, embracing the full range of human experience.

"A Musical Revelation"

The Second String Quartet was premiered by a student quartet from the Juilliard School on May 11, 1946, in the same concert at Columbia University in New York where *The Unanswered Question* and *Central Park in the Dark* were first performed. Its first professional performances came later that year by the Walden String Quartet, at the Yaddo Music Festival on September 15 and at Town Hall in New York on October 7. Lou Harrison, who had conducted the premiere of the Third Symphony that April and had proofread and corrected the parts for the quartet before its premiere, reviewed the Yaddo Festival in the *New York Herald Tribune*, and he described the quartet in glowing terms:

> This work is, for this reporter, the finest piece of American chamber music yet. It is difficult going for a while but one becomes increasingly aware of the vast mastery in Ives's composing means, and in the final movement, in which the men, who have been demonstrated as discussing and then arguing things in the two preceding movements, walk up to the hills and "gaze into the firmament," a musical revelation occurs. It is hard to convey in words what every one present felt at this moment. Music of this kind happens only every fifty years or a century, so rich in faith and so full of the sense of completion.[9]

Throughout the quartet, Ives uses sounds and textures like those he had developed over decades of writing experimental pieces. But it is far less consistent than those pieces, and it cannot be reduced to a small number of specific procedures, as can works like *From the Steeples and the Mountains* or *Scherzo: All the Way Around and Back*. Rather, it flows from moment to moment, developing ideas and following threads like conversations between people with interesting thoughts and strong opinions, impossible to predict but seemingly right in retrospect. It is radically different from the First String Quartet, but it feels equally at home in the tradition of the string quartet, and its fundamental metaphor of a conversation between friends reaches right back to the origins of the genre.

SYMPHONY NO. 4

While the Second String Quartet was conceived from the start as a whole, Ives's Symphony No. 4 is a prime example of his fondness for recycling existing works into new ones. Every movement is based on a movement we have already encountered in another piece. The first movement incorporates the setting of *Watchman* ("Watchman, tell us of the night") from the middle of the First Violin Sonata finale, which Ives also recast as a song. The second movement is an orchestral version of Ives's tone poem for piano, *The Celestial Railroad*, which itself was adapted from portions of the *Hawthorne* movement of the *Concord Sonata*. The third movement is the original first movement of the First String Quartet, the fugue on *Missionary Hymn* ("From Greenland's icy mountains"), with a few added instruments and passages. The finale is mostly new but ends with the transcendent closing passage of the Second String Quartet finale, revised and rescored for chorus and orchestra.

The remarkable thing is that somehow all this music, drawn from three decades of Ives's career, fits together in a coherent statement that makes sense. The secret lies in Ives's program for the symphony as a whole. When the second movement was published in Henry Cowell's *New Music* in January 1929, it included the following program note from Ives for the entire symphony:

> This symphony, the fourth, consists of four movements—a "prelude," a second movement "in comedy vein," the third, a "fugue," and a finale, etc.
>
> The aesthetic program of the work is that of the searching questions of What? and Why? which the spirit of man asks of life. This is particularly the sense of the prelude. The three succeeding movements are the diverse answers in which existence replies.
>
> The second movement is not a scherzo in an accepted sense of the word, but rather a comedy—in which an exciting, easy and worldly progress through life is contrasted with the trials of the Pilgrims in their journey through the swamps and rough country. The occasional slow episodes—Pilgrims' hymns—are constantly crowded out and overwhelmed by the former. The dream, or fantasy, ends with an interruption of reality—the Fourth of July in Concord—brass bands, drum corps, etc.
>
> The Fugue is an expression of the reaction of life into formalism and ritualism.
>
> The last movement is an apotheosis of the preceding content, in terms that have something to do with the reality of existence and its religious experience.[10]

A longer version of the note, included in the program for the partial premiere of the Fourth Symphony two years earlier, observes that the first movement reflects the soul asking "questions of the ultimate meaning of existence," explains that Nathaniel Hawthorne's short story *The Celestial Rail-Road* "may be considered as a sort of incidental program" for the second movement, and refers to the finale as having "transcendental spiritual content."[11]

In brief, the four movements fit together as stages in a spiritual journey. The first movement poses questions about the search for meaning, hope, joy, and fulfillment. The second offers a false answer, a trip to Heaven in comfort and ease that ends up at a different destination, as in Hawthorne's fable. The third embodies another false path, the routines of organized religion, representing "formalism" through a fugue in C major and the "ritualism" of church services through a theme drawn from a hymn tune with a missionary text. The finale then charts a true course, gradually drawing closer to the divine through a cumulative form on *Bethany*, so that the inner pilgrimage exemplified in the whole symphony culminates in coming "nearer, my God, to Thee."

Ives dated his first work on the symphony to 1910, and sketches exist from about 1912 to 1918, but the piece as we know it seems to have come together between 1921 and 1925. During that time, Ives reworked about half of the *Hawthorne* movement into *The Celestial Railroad*, reordering passages and adding new material to create a piano piece that closely follows the scenes and events in Hawthorne's story. We know he cannot have begun that work before 1921, since some passages are clipped out of a published copy of the *Concord Sonata* (printed in January 1921) and pasted on the pages of music paper on which *The Celestial Railroad* is written, making the latter in part a literal cut-and-paste job. Then, on the score of *The Celestial Railroad*, Ives added other musical lines in pencil, augmenting the piece beyond what a pianist could play, as he sketched in material for an orchestral version of the music that became the second movement of the Fourth Symphony. In the same years of 1921–1925, Ives worked on the other movements of the symphony and brought all four into near-final form. It seems likely that he came up with the program around the same time, incorporating the journey in Hawthorne's story into a larger inner journey toward transcendence.[12]

The Fourth Symphony not only represents a journey, it also is in many ways the culmination of Ives's musical journey, combining in one work most of the procedures and approaches that had become characteristic of his compositions. Most of the experimental techniques Ives had explored, from polytonality to dissonant clusters, appear in this symphony. All the movements but the third feature multiple simultaneous streams of music, often in different keys, meters, or tempos, reaching in the second movement a level of complexity far surpassing any of Ives's experimental works or indeed any piece yet composed. All four movements incorporate borrowed melodies, including about thirty in the second movement, more than in any other movement Ives ever wrote.

The symphony is suffused with hymn tune material on almost every page, and the second movement draws on popular songs, patriotic songs, and band music as well. In the first, second, and fourth movements, Ives uses collage, not to suggest memories, as in *Washington's Birthday* and *The Fourth of July*, but to convey a sense of a stream of consciousness, as in a dream or mystical experience. At the same time, the piece fits neatly into the symphonic tradition, with serious first and last movements, a second movement that serves as a scherzo, a slow third movement that most differs from the others and provides a point of respite, and cyclic connections between the movements, sharing common themes as in Ives's First, Second, and Third Symphonies. The Fourth Symphony offers an adventure that reaches to the heavens, but its roots lie deep in the music Ives had been hearing and composing over his half century on the planet.

As you wait for the symphony to begin, you notice the performers arranged on stage: a large orchestra, with a piano in front for a soloist, two pianos and a celesta tucked further back, and lots of percussion instruments; a chorus of women and men on risers behind the orchestra; and at the back of the stage, behind and above the chorus, a handful of violins and a harp. The chorus and the spatial separation of instruments reminds you of the voices in *Thanksgiving and Forefathers' Day* and of the offstage chorus and instruments in *From Hanover Square North*. But you have learned by now that even someone who has heard dozens of Ives pieces cannot predict what the next one will sound like or what might happen. You sit waiting for the conductor's first wave of the baton, open to anything. That openness, and your openmindedness, will come in handy for the next half hour, as four very different movements come your way, all of which feature constrasts of style and texture within them as well as between them.

First Movement: *Prelude*

The low strings and a solo piano start the journey with a dynamic unison melody, answered by high strings and a distorted trumpet fanfare. These loud gestures cut off, and you hear the distant group of violins and harp quietly playing sweet dissonant chords and melodic motives from *Bethany*, like a celestial vision of being "Nearer, my God, to Thee." Beneath them, back on Earth, the low strings and piano briefly resume their melody. The contrast of sounds loud and soft, close and far, creates a sense of vast space—not a real space as in *From Hanover Square North*, but an imagined space as if you were seeing an apparition of Heaven from afar.

As the distant violins and harp continue, and the piano and plucked string basses softly play circling, irregular patterns, into this space comes a solo violin (or cello) playing the first phrase of *In the Sweet By-and-By*. While the melody occupies the middle space between the deep basses and the high and far-off violins, like a human realm between Earth and the heavens, the unsung text—"There's a land that is fairer than day"—offers an image of the Promised Land. The melody turns to repeating a few tightly circling notes, and some other instruments enter, including the celesta with snippets of *Bethany*. The many simultaneous layers of music are rhythmically independent from each other, reinforcing the sense of multiple beings moving through a great visionary space.

Then the chorus comes in, singing in unison Lowell Mason's hymn *Watchman* with words by John Bowring, joined by a trumpet and accompanied by the piano and strings:

> Watchman, tell us of the night,
> What its signs of promise are.
> Trav'ler, o'er yon mountain's height,
> See that glory-beaming star!

The star in this Christmas hymn is the one heralding Jesus's birth, a sign of promise. As you listen, the vision of the star seems to be embodied in the distant violins and harp with their music from *Bethany*, and in the high, shimmering celesta mixing motives from *Bethany* with *Westminster Chimes*. Quietly in the background you hear the percussion playing *Street Beat*, like a great but distant procession, and a flute weaving together melodically related motives from several other hymns (*Proprior Deo*, *Something for Thee*, *Bethany*, and *Crusader's Hymn*), as if one thought leads to another, too quickly to follow but all leading in the same direction, toward contemplation and prayer.

Then Ives alters both the tune and the text of the hymn *Watchman*. Bowring's original poem continues the dialogue, the traveler asking questions and the watchman answering with affirmation:

> Watchman, does its beauteous ray
> Aught of joy or hope foretell?
> Trav'ler, yes; it brings the day,
> Promised day of Israel.

Ives makes the exchange more dramatic and open-ended. He shortens the traveler's question: "Watchman, aught of joy or hope?" Everyone pauses, breathless, waiting for the answer. "Trav'ler, Yes!" comes the reply from the chorus, accompanied by piano and a few solo strings. The full texture returns for the last two lines of the hymn, then all the other instruments stop again as the chorus and accompaniment add a final question: "Dost thou see its beauteous ray?" They hush, and the distant violins and harp playing bits of "Nearer, my God, to Thee" are heard again; clearly these represent the star. The chorus reenters, repeating their question and exhorting the traveler to *see* the star and its beautiful ray of light. With a touch of *Bethany* in the piano, orchestral strings, and distant instruments, the first movement comes to a close. It has posed "the searching questions of What? and Why? which the spirit of man asks of life" by converting a hymn of affirmation into a question that asks us to see the "signs of promise" and "see that glory-beaming star!" and by suggesting that what we are seeking is to draw nearer to God.

Second Movement: *Comedy*

You know from reading the program booklet for the concert that the second movement closely parallels the events in Hawthorne's 1843 story *The Celestial Rail-Road*, a relationship that was first described in detail by Thomas M. Brodhead. According to Brodhead, "The Hawthorne story is itself a comic trope on John Bunyan's *The Pilgrim's Progress*," the great seventeenth-century allegory that traces the laborious journey of a pilgrim from his home in the City of Destruction, representing the sins of this world, to deliverance in Heaven, the Celestial City. In his story, Hawthorne satirizes what he saw as charlatans who offer a false religion—one that asks of its adherents no effort, no work, no commitment, and no self-sacrifice— through the metaphor of a train that supposedly can take people along the pilgrim's path to Heaven without the exertion of actually walking there on foot. Brodhead summarizes the plot:

> Like Bunyan's book, Hawthorne's tale begins with a nameless narrator who falls asleep and starts to dream. The narrator finds himself at a [railroad] depot in the City of Destruction, where he is befriended by a Mr. Smooth-it-away who escorts him aboard a waiting train. Once inside, the narrator learns that the locomotive speeds its passengers to the Celestial City in nineteenth-century comfort. The train then departs with its whistle blowing, passes through scenery known to readers of *The Pilgrim's Progress* (even stopping at the town of Vanity Fair [where vendors sell goods to suit worldly tastes]), and finally comes to rest in Beulah Land [from which Heaven is visible]. All the passengers leave the train and board a ferry that they are told will carry them across the River Jordan to the Celestial City. Once in the water, the narrator sees Mr. Smooth-it-away back on shore reverting to his true demonic form. The narrator realizes that all has been

a hoax and leaps into the river to escape. The impact wakes the narrator and brings the story to a close.[13]

You wonder how you will be able to follow this complicated plot as the movement unfolds, how Ives will suggest the sound and motion of the train and depict the places it passes through, and how he will contrast the passengers with the pilgrims.

The movement begins as if in a dream, as suggested by Hawthorne's story. Ever so softly, the piano, clarinets, bells, percussion, and strings each present independent layers of music, creating once again the sense of a vast imagined space like in the first movement. Amidst this the string basses twice play an urgent gesture that rises and falls; only because you are following Brodhead's summary of the plot do you realize that this is a distorted phrase from the gospel hymn *Beulah Land*, a reference to the train's destination. After a brief outburst by the full orchestra, the strings quietly play a kind of chorale, based on a phrase from the hymn tune *Martyn*, with occasional interjections by the piano and other instruments. The strings sound out of tune; they are playing chords with quarter tones, notes that fall between the notes that can be played on a piano, making a sound that perfectly captures the gray, ugly, troubling atmosphere of the City of Destruction.

The flute and violins play part of William G. Toner's gospel hymn *God Be With You* ("God be with you till we meet again"), as the passengers and friends say their goodbyes. The train ride begins with an unmistakable imitation of a steam train starting to move and gaining momentum, using dissonant clusters of notes in low strings and pianos. The whistle blows as the train reaches full speed. You hear a boisterous noise including bits of the Civil War tunes *Tramp, Tramp, Tramp* ("In the prison cell I sit") and *Marching Through Georgia* in the trombones and the gospel hymn *Throw Out the Life-Line* ("Throw out the Life-Line! Someone is drifting away") in the low strings. Perhaps this depicts the passengers singing songs and hymns to pass the time as they travel, although the reference to prison in the words of *Tramp, Tramp, Tramp* and the inclusion of *Throw Out the Life-Line*, a song about having to rescue a lost soul, strongly hint that the passengers themselves may need to be saved from damnation.

In an instant the noise of the train vanishes, and you hear soft, slow hymns in the strings, phrases from *In the Sweet By-and-By* and *Nettleton*. This must be one of the "slow episodes—Pilgrims' hymns" Ives mentions in his program. Suddenly the train noises return, then almost as quickly fade away to reveal the pilgrims' hymns still going on. The effect is cinematic, as if we have changed perspective, trudging along with the pilgrims and watching the train roar by. The passage brings to life the contrast Ives describes in his program note, between "the trials of the Pilgrims in their journey through the swamp" and the "exciting, easy, and worldly progress through life" enjoyed by the passengers on the train.

The train approaches again and, with another change of perspective, we are back on board and leave the pilgrims behind. The texture becomes incredibly complex, with layers of music piled on top of each other, some in different meters, in a carefully calculated chaos. Fragments of tunes fly by too quickly to grasp, as in a dream. You catch a few, most of them hard to hear amid all the confusion: the trombones play the Civil War tunes again, then *In the Sweet By-and-By*; the piano plays a distorted version of *Camptown Races* as other tunes swirl around; the brass play a snippet of *Hail! Columbia*; the strings, winds, and brass play bits of *In the Sweet By-and-By* and *Nettleton*; the trumpets play distorted variants of *Columbia, the Gem of the Ocean*; high bells play *Beulah Land*; and cellos and trombones play part of *Columbia, the Gem of the Ocean*. It is like the stream of consciousness in a dream, one thing after another, some images more memorable than others. The hymn tunes all point toward Heaven, the secular tunes toward worldly concerns, and the many layers of repeating figures suggest the noises of the train itself. There is so much going on at once that you cannot possibly catch everything—and that is part of the point. It is a dream, and in dreams, despite a moment-to-moment logic, more flits by than can be grasped and remembered. Although you cannot pay attention to everything that is happening in this music, if there were less of it, it would not so wonderfully represent a dream.

The music slows, quiets, and thins out. This must be the stop at Vanity Fair. The piano plays a free fantasy. A few instruments repeat figures in the background. Among them a single viola quietly spins out a reminiscence of *In the Sweet By-and-By*, reminding us of the journey's ultimate destination and of the pilgrims we passed by. Then the piano starts to play in a kind of ragtime style with trumpet and percussion, while the flutes float above with *In the Sweet By-and-By*, a contrast of the worldly goods available at Vanity Fair with the spiritual hymns of the pilgrims.

The train starts up again, with the piano playing music you remember from *Hawthorne* (including part of the human-faith-melody), augmented by added layers in other instruments. Once again the texture builds as one idea after another piles on, most prominently *Throw Out the Life-Line* in various instruments and *Beulah Land* in the trombones. Suddenly everything stops, and a sonic exuviation reveals a quiet hymn in the piano, adapted from *Martyn* ("Jesus, lover of my soul . . . / O receive my soul at last")—a vision of the pilgrims outside the train window. The train comes roaring back, then cuts off in a second sonic exuviation.

This time, the quiet hymn in the piano is joined by an almost complete statement of *Beulah Land* by a solo violin. We must have arrived at Beulah Land, the end of the journey by train, with a view of the pilgrims entering the Celestial City across the River Jordan. For those who know them, the melody of the gospel hymn evokes the words by Edgar P. Stites, which paint the scene:

I've reached the land of corn and wine,
And all its riches freely mine
Here shines undimmed one blissful day,
For all my night has passed away.

Refrain
O Beulah Land, sweet Beulah Land,
As on thy highest mount I stand
I look away across the sea,
Where mansions are prepared for me,
And view the shining glory-shore,
My Heav'n, my home forevermore!

It is a vision of hope. Yet in the background plays another piano, tuned in quarter tones and moving in undulating patterns. The rippling music suggests the movement of the water, but, as at the beginning of the movement, the quarter tones hint that something is not right, sounding out of tune and sickly.

The whole orchestra suddenly erupts in a huge noise, the biggest shock yet, almost blowing you out of your seat. This must be the moment the narrator realizes he has been tricked by a demon and is on his way to hell. Rising and falling waves of dissonance suggest his struggle to flee and his leap into the water, shocking him awake. Here Ives's program adds to Hawthorne's story: "The dream, or fantasy, ends with an interruption of reality—the Fourth of July in Concord—brass bands, drum corps, etc." You hear the march theme from *Putnam's Camp*, surrounded and followed by a collage of other music that might be heard on that holiday, from patriotic tunes like *Marching Through Georgia* and *Yankee Doodle* to fiddle tunes like *Turkey in the Straw* and popular songs like *Camptown Races*.

"Reality" is just as confusing as the dream. The effect of this movement, with its many simultaneous layers and frequent changes of texture and style, is overwhelming. Everything Ives learned from his experimental music, his experience writing symphonies, and his familiarity with hymn tunes and with popular music, is blended together here in a vast fantasy, the most complex piece of music that anyone had composed by the 1920s. But the lesson is clear: no one is going to get to Heaven by taking a train. It is a journey that must be made step by step. If the search for the meaning of life means seeking to be nearer to God, as implied by the first movement, the path described in the second movement is not the way to get there.

You are both exhilarated and exhausted. What could possibly come next?

Third Movement: *Fugue*

Having heard two movements in Ives's most expansive idiom, with multiple simultaneous streams of music, you expect the next movement to be in the same vein. What you hear instead is the cellos playing a tune in good old C major, imitated by violas, horn, and violins in turn. It is a fugue, in a traditional tonal style; indeed, it is the fugue on *Missionary Hymn* ("From Greenland's icy mountains") from the first movement of his First String Quartet, described in chapter 4, adapted from a fugue Ives composed in college.

As you listen, you realize that in almost any other context, this movement would sound like normal music, but after the first two movements of the symphony it is shockingly different, surprising, even strange and disorienting. It really *feels* like a "reaction . . . into formalism and ritualism," as Ives put it in the program. A fugue is both a traditional form and an academic ritual, a rite of passage for composers and students learning counterpoint. A hymn is likewise a form that goes back centuries and a part of church ritual. The way Ives presents the melody—phrase by phrase, the first phrase in a fugue, the second in a fugue with a countermelody, the third as a melodic climax marked by a return to the home key, and the last as a slow chorale—recalls the traditional ways that Bach and many other composers set chorale tunes in their organ works, cantatas, and other service music. This hymn in particular is focused on the forms and rituals of the church itself, urging the faithful to build up the church through missionary work—quite a different focus from the hymns in the first two movements that center on salvation in Heaven, nearness to God, and a direct, personal experience of the divine. The orchestration is much less colorful than the earlier movements: mostly strings with occasional melodies for a solo wind or brass instrument, like a score by Bach or Handel. After the soul-searching, dramatic, and musically adventurous movements that precede it, this movement, however beautiful, feels like a loss of nerve.

As you listen further, you begin to notice changes from the version of this fugue that you remember from the First String Quartet, changes that reinforce the meaning this movement conveys in the context of this symphony. In some passages, the string basses playing descending lines add unexpected pulsations, making the music sound a bit unsettled. The allusion to church services is deepened when for a brief moment the orchestra cuts off and you hear the sound of an organ, the quintessential church instrument, softly echoing what the orchestra just played. Minutes later, the organ comes back at the climactic presentation of the third phrase of *Missionary Hymn* and plays alongside the orchestra from there to the end.

Soon you notice another insertion Ives added to the fugue, a gradual piling up of dissonance that sounds completely different in style and brings the music to a dead stop; it serves as a reminder of the dissonant world of the first two movements, disturbing the comfort you have fallen into while listening to the beautiful melodies and smooth counterpoint. The jolt reminds you of the shock you felt at the beginning of this movement when the juxtaposition of traditional and modernist styles went in the other direction. The music restarts, smooths out the harmonies, and returns to the original course of the movement, but the sense of disturbance lingers.

Near the end of the movement, Ives adds two hymn tunes, the chorus of *Welcome Voice* in the clarinet and part of *Antioch* (better known as *Joy to the World*) in the trombone, and he changes the very end so that it sounds like an Amen. All of these are comforting and familiar sounds that reinforce the church-like atmosphere. Yet the questions raised by the first movement are still unresolved. If sitting in a church service were enough to answer "the searching questions of What? and Why? which the spirit of man asks of life," churches would all be full, and no one would still be asking the questions.

Fourth Movement: *Finale*

The finale gives the impression that it has been going on long before you were aware of it, like a procession approaching from a distance. Almost inaudibly, a small group of percussionists—on snare drum, Indian drum, bass drum, cymbals, and gong—begins to play, combining *Street Beat* and other repeating patterns in a quiet march they will keep up during the whole movement. Next to enter, soft and very low in their range, are the string basses, with the third phrase of *Bethany* ("Still all my song shall be, nearer, my God, to Thee"). Then comes a reminiscence of the opening of the symphony's first movement, quieter now, with the strings, piano, and brass alternating with the distant violins and harp playing part of *Bethany*. For a song about being near to God, it sounds very far away, very soft and in low and high ranges few human voices can reach. The strings, piano, and brass repeat and develop their gestures, swelling in intensity, then stop.

Very quietly, a few violins begin to play a hymn-like melody, combining motives from *Dorrnance* (which you earlier heard in *The Housatonic at Stockbridge*), *Missionary Chant* (heard in *The Alcotts*), and *Bethany*, punning on melodic similarities between the hymn tunes. The texture gradually grows denser and louder as more instruments enter. Out of the fog of sound, another melody begins to emerge that weaves together the third phrase of *Bethany*, a bit of *Westminster Chimes*, and the second half of *Missionary Chant*. A sudden hush, and you hear birdcalls in the flutes and piccolo (the song of the thrush, according to Ives's note in a sketch). Then the melody woven from segments of *Bethany*, *Westminster Chimes*, and *Missionary Chant* returns in the violins.

The music becomes suddenly louder, and, over descending scales in the basses, the horns and trumpets play almost all of *Missionary Chant*, punning near the beginning on its resemblance to *Dorrnance* and at the end eliding with part of *Azmon* (theme of the Third Symphony's first movement). Meanwhile other instruments add layers of melody, from repeating figures to bits of *Bethany* and *Westminster Chimes*. The music grows louder still, and trumpets and violas sound out the melody woven from *Bethany*, *Westminster Chimes*, and *Missionary Chant* while fragments of these and other melodies flow around them.

By now you have realized that this movement is as full of simultaneous layers as the second movement, but there is no plot to follow—or to hang onto. There is a logical sequence of events, but it is entirely musical, the spinning out of melodic threads drawn from hymn tunes, with *Bethany* a nearly constant presence even when it is not the most prominent melody. There is not a popular or patriotic song in sight, or in hearing.

Suddenly the loud music cuts off in a sonic exuviation, and you hear again the soft march in the percussion, the distant instruments, and the birdcalls in flutes and piccolo. Quietly, over a repeated descending whole-tone scale in the bass, you hear many layers of hymn tune melodies, *Bethany* most prominent, melded or overlapping with *Missionary Chant* or *Westminster Chimes*, with parts of *Martyn* and several others as well.

Finally, the chorus—which has been sitting in silence since the end of the first movement—rises and sings, on a wordless "Ah," the complete second half of *Bethany* over the descending whole tone scales, with the melody woven from *Bethany*, *Westminster Chimes*, and *Missionary Chant* as its main countermelody. The entire movement has been a cumulative form with the second half of *Bethany* as its theme. This culminating passage you recognize from the end of the Second String Quartet, and you hear the same repeating figures elaborating D major. This is not tonality as an easy cop-out, as the C major fugue in the third movement would have been, but a gloriously expanded major key that in retrospect was the goal all along, resolving all the tensions between tonal and atonal elements in the entire symphony.

The solution to the questions posed in the first movement is not an easy trip to Heaven on a false promise of effortless salvation, nor the ease of sitting in church waiting for form and ritual to do it all for you, but the gradual journey over the course of the finale to come "nearer, my God, to Thee." *Bethany* is anticipated in the first movement; absent from the second and third, revealing them as false answers and misdirected paths; in sight yet still far away at the beginning of the fourth movement, deep in the basses and high in the distant violins and harp; and finally reached at this moment, embodied in human voices, an achievement as sweet as it is hard won. The transcendent moment lingers as voices and instruments slowly fade to silence. The last to be heard is the group of percussion instruments, continuing their march into the distance, perhaps forever.

Performance and Publication: A Hard Won Apotheosis

The first and second movements of the Fourth Symphony were performed soon after Ives completed them, the first of his orchestral works to be played in public. They appeared on a concert at Town Hall in New York on January 29, 1927, sponsored by Pro Musica, an organization led by E. Robert Schmitz that was committed to presenting new music, especially by French and American composers. British conductor Eugene Goossens, who had developed a reputation for learning new and complex music quickly, directed members of the New York Philharmonic in the performance, with Schmitz playing the solo piano. According to Henry Cowell, Goossens's first reaction at seeing Ives's symphony was that it was impossible to conduct, but then "he wound a towel about his head, drank gallons of coffee, sat up nights, learned the score, and found a way to conduct it successfully in public." Ives and Harmony came to the rehearsals, listening from backstage in the green room (where soloists wait before coming on stage) because he was too nervous to meet the players or sit in the hall, and Goossens came to Ives to consult about performance details. Ives did work up his nerve and attended the concert.[14]

Reviews were mixed. The *Musical Courier* called it a "dreadful symphony" and said Ives "lacked both talent and technic to accomplish his aims." On the other hand, W. J. Henderson wrote in the *New York Sun* that "at first hearing it seems to possess strong individuality," and Olga Samaroff in the *New York Evening Post* mentioned its "freshness of musical utterance." Robert A. Simon in *The New Yorker* called it "rather too peculiar" and said it had a "quality of madness," but added, "we should like to hear more of Mr. Ives' output. He seems to be thumbing his nose most of the time, but, after all, it is his own nose."[15] Writing in the *New York Herald Tribune*, Lawrence Gilman hailed Ives's "sureness of touch" in deploying modernist techniques and said, "This music is as indubitably American in impulse and spiritual texture as the prose of [eighteenth-century theologian] Jonathan Edwards; and, like the writing of that true artist and true mystic, it has at times an irresistable veracity and strength, and uncorrupted sincerity." Most positive of all was Olin Downes in the *New York Times*, who wrote, "There is something in this music: real vitality, real naivete and a superb self respect. . . . There is 'kick' in the piece, regardless of the composer's philosophic or moral purpose, his scheme of rhythms, and all the rest. It is genuine, if it is not a masterpiece, and that is the important thing."[16]

The second movement appeared two years later in the January 1929 issue of Henry Cowell's *New Music*, a quarterly that printed scores of what Cowell called "ultramodern" music. The published version was the most meticulously notated orchestral score Ives ever produced, no doubt because he had heard the piece in rehearsal and performance by a group of professionals and had the opportunity to make adjustments. He included indications for how close to or distant from the audience each group of players should be, to create the sense of space he wanted.

There were no further performances of the second movement for almost forty years. The third movement was premiered on May 10, 1933, by the New Chamber Orchestra conducted by Bernard Herrmann, in a concert at the auditorium of the New School for Social Research in New York, where Cowell was teaching. Herrmann repeated the first and third movements at Town Hall on February 25, 1934, and the third movement was performed separately a few more times, including by the Columbia Symphony Orchestra on the CBS radio program *Everybody's Music*, broadcast nationwide on September 27, 1936.

Finally, on April 26, 1965, the entire symphony was played for the first time, by Leopold Stokowski conducting the American Symphony Orchestra at Carnegie Hall, with assistant conductors David Katz and José Serebrier leading portions of the ensemble in passages with more than one simultaneous meter or tempo. Critics called it a masterpiece, and *Newsweek* declared that "Ives' pre-eminence among American composers is now beyond question." Columbia Records issued a recording, and a manuscript facsimile of the symphony was published that same year.[17]

Almost a half century later, after more than thirty years' work by a team of editors, a critical edition of the symphony was issued in 2011, paired with a performing version that resolved problems of notation and coordination that orchestras had faced in the existing score and parts.[18] Both were computer-engraved by Thomas M. Brodhead, who modified existing software to make it possible to present the music as Ives intended it, with all the multiple layers, conflicting meters, and special notations. Because of these new scores and performing parts, in recent years the Fourth Symphony, once considered too difficult to perform, has been played in concert more frequently than ever before. For fans of Ives's music, that accomplishment is an apotheosis as hard won and dear to the heart as that reflected in the symphony itself.

Collecting Songs and Late Works

$\mathcal{T}$he journeys to transcendence in the Second String Quartet and the Fourth Symphony represent Ives at his most grand. Yet from his 1918 health crisis until the Fourth Symphony premiere in 1927, he also produced over sixty smaller works that in their own way show his breadth as a composer.

In his campaign to get his music before the public, Ives followed up his self-publication of the *Concord Sonata* with a collection of *114 Songs*, printed and distributed in 1922. About a fifth of the songs were newly composed, and another fifth were new as songs but based in some way on earlier pieces. The rest span his entire career. Together these songs represent the whole sweep of Ives's output, from Romantic art songs and popular-style love songs to comic songs, personal statements, and modernist settings of great poets. Like the sonata, the book of songs brought mocking reviews but also found several sympathetic musicians.

A few late works followed the publication of the songbook. The remarkable diversity of Ives's music is still evident in four works from the years 1923 to 1924: a post-impressionist song, *Yellow Leaves*; a satirical song, *The One Way*; the experimental *Three Quarter-Tone Pieces*; and *Psalm 90*, a masterpiece of choral music.

SONGS OLD AND NEW FOR *114 SONGS*

Although popular songs were usually published individually as sheet music, there was a tradition of printing art songs in groups; Brahms, for example, typically published his in groups of four to fifteen. By the late 1910s, Ives had been writing songs for over thirty years, more than 120 of them. He had gathered some into small collections since 1898, at first in his own ink copies, then professional ones, and then lithographed copies around 1917–1919. When he began to focus on getting his musical legacy into print and performance, it must have seemed natural to assemble an anthology of songs representing all stages of his career, and sometime in 1920 he set to work in earnest.[1]

Once the project began, it stimulated a new wave of creativity. Between 1919 and 1921, he composed about forty-five new songs, including twenty-two that were entirely new, five that reused material from his previous compositions, five he rescored from choral works, and thirteen he adapted for voice and piano from pieces for chamber orchestra or other groups of instruments. He also gave some of his German songs from the 1890s new English texts, revised at least a handful of other songs, and included about twenty other songs he had adapted or retexted before 1919. As H. Wiley Hitchcock has suggested, Ives probably included so many arrangements so that "he could display as many of his earlier types of music as possible to a public that, up to then, had experienced almost none."[2] Although he did not include every song he had ever written, the collection ballooned until there were 114 of them, far larger than the typical publication by a composer of art songs—but then, it was meant to represent everything he had done as a song composer.

He assembled his songbook for the most part with the most recent songs near the beginning, to represent his current approach and no doubt to place what he considered his best songs near the front of the book, where readers were most likely to see them. On the first page of each song, he put the song's title and the name of the poet whose words he was setting; at the back of the book, he wrote in a note that "when no author is indicated the words are by Harmony Twichell Ives or her husband."[3] He also provided in parentheses the year he wrote the song (or arranged it for voice and piano), to make clear to the reader that these songs were indeed produced over more than three decades and, no doubt, to suggest an explanation for why they differed so greatly in their musical language and style. Songs in the first third of the book are dated 1921 or 1920, and from there to the end the collection is arranged mostly in reverse chronological order by Ives's dates: about fifteen songs from the 1910s, about three dozen from his first decade in New York, about seventeen from his college years, two or three from Danbury, and a few recent songs mixed in, out of order. The last song is the oldest in the collection: *Slow March*, which Ives wrote in the summer of 1887 or 1888 to words by his Uncle Lyman Brewster. His mother found it in the cellar in May 1921, while he was putting together the songbook, and he touched it up and included it.[4]

Song Groups

One reason the book is not strictly in reverse chronological order is that Ives made several groupings of songs related by subject or type and placed together in the collection. A group of "5 Street Songs and Pieces" spans from the recently composed *Down East* (1919, see chapter 1) to a song in popular style from college days. It includes two songs adapted from band music he had written in the 1890s, among them *The Circus Band* (see chapter 1), arranged sometime between 1899 and 1921. Another group features "8 Sentimental Ballads," most composed during college, but including his 1906 courting song *The World's Highway* to words by Harmony, another song from his early New York years, and *A Song—for Anything*.

Ives gave this last song its satirical title when assembling *114 Songs* because the tune proved so flexible that he had used it for three different texts: a sacred text sung at a church service in Danbury around 1892; a farewell to Yale in 1898; and a love song at some point in between. None of these was comic, but the effect of giving all three texts as verses of one song (in the order romantic, collegiate, and religious) made the song into a commentary on songwriting and a critique of melodies so lacking in individuality that they could be married to words with such disparate meanings. The gently pulsing accompaniment underlies a tune that would be lovely, even beautiful and moving, if left alone with just one set of words; but with three, sung one after the other, it becomes ridiculous. Ives added a footnote that begins with this observation: "*NOTE:*—The song above is a common illustration (and not the only one in this book) of how inferior music is inclined to follow inferior words and 'vice-versa.'" (To reinforce the point, he wrote a new song in 1920, *On the Counter*, that satirizes songs of the day that were still using old styles from the 1890s, and in it he echoes the melody of his own *A Song—for Anything* from that decade. *On the Counter* appears earlier in *114 Songs*, with the self-deprecating footnote, "*NOTE:* Though there is little danger of it, it is hoped that this song will not be taken seriously, or sung, at least, in public.")[5]

Other groups by subject or type are more concentrated chronologically. There are four German songs from his college days and early years in New York, including *Ich grolle nicht* and *Feldeinsamkeit* (see chapter 3). Four songs in French represent his interest in expanding his palette of art song styles in the years just after college. There are two arias from *The Celestial Country*, with the organ and instrumental parts transcribed for piano. Three songs from 1920 set texts on months of the year, all translated by Dante Gabriel Rossetti from sonnets by fourteenth-century Italian poet Folgore da San Geminiano.

The "4 Songs Based on Hymntune Themes" are all adapted from instrumental movements in cumulative form. Three of them, taken from violin sonatas, include only the final complete statement of the hymn tune and a few measures of the preceding material: *Watchman!* (1913) from the middle section of the First Violin Sonata finale, based on *Watchman* ("Watchman, tell us of the night"); *At the River* (1916) from the Fourth Violin Sonata finale, based on *The Beautiful River* ("Shall we gather at the river"); and *His Exaltation* (1913) from the first movement of the Second Violin Sonata, based on *Autumn* (sung in the song to the second stanza of Robert Robinson's hymn text "Mighty God, while angels bless Thee"). Since there is little or no development of the hymn melody, these songs are not in cumulative form themselves. But the fourth song in this group, *The Camp-Meeting* (1912), is a real cumulative form based on the Third Symphony finale, combining portions of its first and third sections that develop *Woodworth* ("Just as I am") with the entire final section that presents the hymn complete.

Of the song groupings, perhaps the most significant is the set "3 Songs of the War," all composed during the first months after the United States entered World War I on April 6, 1917. The text for *In Flanders Fields* was the most widely read poem about the war, written in May 1915 by John McCrae, a Canadian doctor who had worked for Mutual Life in Montreal before the war and was serving in the Canadian Expeditionary Force in Belgium. Because of the Mutual Life connection, Julian Myrick suggested Ives set the poem and arranged for the song to be professionally performed at an insurance luncheon in April 1917. Ives's setting is somber, dissonant, and filled with patriotic and military quotations. By contrast, *He Is There!* is like a musical recruiting poster. Ives's text relates the story of a young man who has sailed for Europe to fight for the righteous cause of liberty, as his grandfather fought in the Civil War. With its patchwork of phrases from patriotic songs, this song may sound humorous or even satirical to us today, but Ives was completely in earnest. The gem of the war songs, again with words by Ives, is *Tom Sails Away*, which captures the ambivalent emotions of a sibling whose younger brother has just left to fight in the war.[6]

An Early Song and an Adaptation

You are back in the recital hall for another voice recital. This time the singer is an alto, and she has chosen to end her concert with a set of Ives songs selected from *114 Songs*. Unlike Ives, she will present them in chronological order, ending with four of the most recent.

First up is *Slow March*, the oldest song in the collection. You see in your program booklet that Ives wrote it for the funeral of the family pet, and to set the tone he quotes the "Dead March" from Handel's oratorio *Saul*, which was played at Civil War funerals and remained the most common funeral piece until gradually replaced by the funeral march from Chopin's Piano Sonata in B-flat Minor.[7] The song begins with a piano prelude, featuring slowly pulsing chords, low in the piano, that blossom into quicker motions as the bass continues a steady pulse. This must be the "Dead March." After it sinks to a close, the singer enters, describing the burial at sunset, the loyal pet, the solemn family march through the garden. Over stately chords, the vocal melody unfolds in four phrases, all featuring the same rhythmic figure that subtly echoes the march. The last phrase in the voice is the same as the first, linking the image of the garden to the sunset and the grave, and the piano adds a postlude that repeats the beginning of the march. As you play over the song in your mind, you realize that, other than the piano prelude and postlude borrowed from Handel, there is nothing in the song to identify it as a march or as funeral music. The vocal line gently rises and falls, moving almost entirely by step with an occasional skip, in a smooth curve equally well suited to a hymn or a love song. Its elegance shows a gift for melody, but Ives's sensitivity to differences between styles and the associations they carry was clearly not yet developed when he was twelve or thirteen.

Next is *The Camp-Meeting*. The program booklet tells you Ives adapted this song from his Third Symphony finale, which was based on the hymn "Just as I am" (*Woodworth*). Having heard the symphony, you wonder how he will rework the finale in the song. It starts with a long prelude in the piano. You recognize phrases from the countermelody, taken from the middle of the finale's first section, and then the very opening of the movement, with its fragments and variants of the hymn tune. The singer enters with a melody you remember: the distorted paraphrase of the hymn tune that began the third section of the finale. She is singing words by Ives that speak of a song coming from a distance over the summer fields, a song of prayer and praise. As the melody winds upward to a peak, then gradually subsides, the words tell of exulting in God and yielding to his love. When she starts to sing the hymn, over the countermelody and accompaniment in the piano, you realize that this is the song heard from afar: "Just as I am, without one plea, / But that Thy blood was shed for me, / And that Thou bidd'st me come to Thee, / O Lamb of God. . . ." The sense of the hymn text, summoning us to the divine, merges with the words Ives added before it, suggesting that we—you, the singer, everyone in the audience—have come over the fields to hear the singing at the camp meeting. Ives has condensed and reordered the material, but every note of the song is from the symphony movement, leading from fragments and paraphrases to the complete statement of the theme with its countermelody, in the same way hearing the song has led us over the meadows. Transferring this music from symphony to song helps us to hear the ideas develop, as the words guide us from distant hints to the hymn itself. And in the song, the long wait to hear the final notes of the melody is made even more meaningful, as the voice also waits to give us the final words: "I come! I come!" As wonderful as the Third Symphony finale is in its orchestral garb, this song offers a brilliant fusion of words and music and of the journeys they evoke.

Songs of the War

Next are the three songs Ives wrote in 1917 about World War I, which the United States joined that spring. *In Flanders Fields* begins with tolling low notes in the piano and continues with dramatic, dissonant music. Throughout, the song blends original material with a patchwork of military and patriotic references, including *Columbia, the Gem of the Ocean*, *The Battle Cry of Freedom*, and the drum pattern *Street Beat*, later joined by *America* (the same tune as the British national anthem, *God Save the King*) and the bugle call *Reveille*. The poem speaks solemnly in the voice of the dead Allied soldiers who have fallen and are buried in Flanders. When they call for new volunteers to take up the cause ("To you from failing hands we throw / The torch"), the voice quotes the phrase "Aux armes, citoyens" (To arms, citizens) from the French national anthem *La Marseillaise* over *America* in the piano. The overlapping of these two tunes is a musical symbol for the torch being passed from the dead French, British, and Canadian soldiers to the Americans who were just entering the war.

If *In Flanders Fields* pictures war in somber tones, *He Is There!* waves the flag and celebrates the cause of freedom. In an upbeat march tempo and bright tonal style, it tells the story of a boy who fifteen years earlier marched in the Decoration Day parade next to his grandfather, a German immigrant who came to the United States after the failed 1848 revolutions in Germany and fought for the Union in the Civil War. Now the boy is grown up, and it is his turn to finish the job, fighting for liberty and democracy in Europe. The words are Ives's, and you find it remarkable that in 1917—at a time when German Americans were suspected of sympathy for the enemy, German-language newspapers were being closed down, and German immigrant musicians were being fired from their jobs—he framed the war as a fight not against Germans as people but on behalf of everyone in the world against the "medieval stuff" embodied by the warlords of Europe. The music for the three verses borrows from the march theme in *Putnam's Camp* and from the Civil War songs *Marching Through Georgia* and *Tenting on the Old Campground*. The chorus adds *Columbia, the Gem of the Ocean*; *Tramp, Tramp, Tramp*; and *The Battle Cry of Freedom*. An optional flute or violin countermelody to the chorus is made almost entirely of patriotic tune fragments: *Dixie*; *Marching Through Georgia*; *Maryland, My Maryland* (the same tune as *O Tannenbaum*); *La Marseillaise*; *The Battle Cry of Freedom*; and *The Star Spangled Banner*. Like the text, the prominence of Union songs among these borrowed tunes links the new war to the idealism of the Civil War, and *Dixie* reminds you that young men from both South and North were going off to fight in Europe, side by side.

Tom Sails Away creates an entirely different mood, with neither the stern call to duty of *In Flanders Fields* nor the idealistic rallying cry of *He Is There!* The song opens with soft, fleet arpeggios in the piano, akin to the figures Ives used in *Thoreau* to conjure up the mists on Walden Pond. Here they evoke the mistiness of memory. A lilting melody in the piano is echoed by the voice; this is the opening of *The Old Oaken Bucket*, a sentimental song from the 1820s that begins with the line "How dear to this heart are the scenes of my childhood." The singer quotes the music to the first half of this phrase—"dear to this heart are the scenes"—while singing words adapted from the second half—"scenes from my childhood are with me." She does not tell us how she feels about these visions of the past, but she does not have to: the music fills in the words she does not say. It is a beautiful way to suggest how we often leave unspoken our deepest feelings. Speaking in present tense, as if she really were back in the days of her childhood, she shares a vivid memory: a sunset in spring, the garden behind her house, her mother walking toward her carrying her younger brother Tom, a view of town, a breeze, factory whistles, a train in the valley, her father coming home from work, and running to greet him. The figuration in both voice and piano changes for every phrase in the text, as if each image is distinct and clear in her mind. The music fades, and she returns to present reality: this day Tom, now a young man, has sailed away to war. The piano sounds the beginning of *Columbia, the Gem of the Ocean*, and the singer joins in patriotic affirmation, sounding proud of Tom's choice to serve his country and the cause of freedom. But soon she falls into dull recitation, as if unable to sustain the feeling. The piano continues its tune, fading into a kind of wistful stasis, as the singer tells us where Tom is bound: "over there." She sings the notes of George M. Cohan's powerful recruiting song *Over There* (1917), which stirred so many Americans to volunteer, yet she sings the phrase so slowly and quietly that the effect becomes entirely different: not stirring, but laden with sorrow at parting and with fear for what will happen to Tom. The song ends as it began, cloaked with the soft, haunting mists of childhood memories.

Songs of 1921

You check your program again and see that four songs from 1921 will end the concert: *Two Little Flowers*, on a poem by Harmony and Charles Ives about their daughter Edith and her best friend Susanna Minturn; *The Greatest Man*, to a poem by Anne Collins that speaks in the voice of a boy who admires his father; *The White Gulls*, on a translation by Maurice Morris of a Russian poem that compares seagulls to restless souls; and *Evening*, setting seven lines from John Milton's epic *Paradise Lost* that depict evening in Eden. The selection of texts illustrates the range of Ives's tastes: Milton was a classic English poet he had studied with Phelps at Yale, and he found the Collins and Morris poems in the New York newspaper *The Evening Sun*.

Two Little Flowers begins with a short piano introduction, repeating a pattern of seven widely spaced notes, arching up and back down. As the pattern continues in the piano, the voice enters with a melody that sounds like a sentimental song of the late nineteenth century, with lyrics about two flowers that appear in the back yard on sunny days. The accompaniment is static, motoric, entirely unsentimental, and out of sync with the melody. The harmony too seems disengaged from the voice, remaining stuck on a single sonority for long stretches. As the singer describes in turn the beauty of marigolds, roses, violets, orchids, and wildflowers, the harmony changes at the beginning of each phrase, but the rhythmic pattern continues on its own independent path. Then suddenly, after the voice rises to a peak, the harmony and rhythm begin to move in coordination with the melody, and the singer declares that the fairest and rarest flowers are the two girls in the back yard: Edith and her friend Susanna. What would have been merely sentimental in an ordinary musical setting becomes deeply moving when the obsessive rhythmic pattern and nonfunctional chords give way to the ordinary motions of phrase and harmony, a musical reassurance that captures both the very ordinariness of the domestic scene and how precious it is to the Iveses.

The Greatest Man is much more sprightly. Over light chords in the piano, the singer declaims in a boy's drawl in lilting rhythm. His teacher asked the class to write about a great man, and he thought of his pa, who is no hero but can ride horses, swim, fish, hunt, and take care of a sick kid, all of which seems great to the boy. The music is mostly tonal with sweet chromatic touches, each image in the text prompting a new figure or texture in the accompaniment. The melody wanders too much and repeats too little to be a real folk song, but it has a folk-like quality that matches the boy's down-home way of speaking. You think you may hear familiar bits of melody—is that a phrase from *On the Banks of the Wabash*? is that *I've Been Working on the Railroad*?—but they fit in so perfectly with the rest that it hardly matters, the vernacular style of the music matching the vernacular text like a twin.[8]

After these two cheerful, essentially tonal songs, *The White Gulls* sounds completely different. Its opening is soft but bleak: a dissonant chord in the pianist's right hand over a descending scale in the bass, repeated three times. The singer enters, describing white seagulls flying back and forth over gray waters, calling and crying. The melody wanders up and down in seemingly aimless curves, evoking the flight of the birds, as the piano cycles through a series of dissonant chords. The piano settles on a soft, arpeggiated chord and repeats it while the voice sings a slow, hymn-like melody to the words "The white gulls sink to rest / On the tide's slow-heaving breast." After a quiet interlude, both voice and piano grow louder, faster, and more restless, describing "souls of men" that fly as aimlessly as the gulls over cold waters, calling and crying. Then the soft arpeggiated chord and the hymn-like phrase return for the words "Souls of men that sink to rest / On an all-receiving breast." The parallels in the music reinforce those in the text, creating a powerful metaphor. On the last word, the piano resolves its dissonant arpeggiated chord to the clear major chord that would be its natural resolution in tonal music, confirming the sense of coming to rest. As you hum the hymn-like phrase in your mind, it reminds you of the middle part of *Shining Shore*—or maybe *Dorrnance* or *Bethany* or *Nettleton*. It certainly sounds like a hymn, but which hymn is not important; it is not the words of a particular hymn that it calls to mind, but the general style of slow hymns like these that offer comfort, solace, and trust in the divine.[9]

Evening begins with a gentle rocking in the piano, like a lullaby. The harmony is mildly dissonant yet calm, needing no resolution. The voice enters with a description of evening, set to a descending melody that evokes the setting sun. The melody's rhythm and falling contour remind you of *Bethany* ("Nearer, my God, to Thee"), and you wonder if you think of the hymn tune only because you have heard it so often in Ives's music. As dimming twilight shades the scene, the vocal melody now rises, and chords shift to suggest new colors, growing denser and more dissonant. Silence comes, depicted by a new, more consonant swaying figure and a brighter melody in the voice, which again reminds you of *Bethany*. The peaceful swaying continues while the melody and harmony subtly change to reflect the animals settling down to sleep. Yet the nightingale stays awake, singing her song, imitated by both piano and voice over a repeated descending figure in the bass that—once again—sounds like the first few notes of *Bethany*. As the singer echoes the nightingale's song, the opening rocking figure returns in the piano. Then the piano turns back to the chirping of the nightingale over the repeated descending figure in the bass, while the singer adds her final words—"Silence is pleased"—set to a melody identical to the first four notes of *Bethany*. The gesture is too brief and too primal to be sure that Ives intended a reference, though the idea of nearness to God is appropriate to the scene, and the second verse of the hymn mentions sunset, darkness, rest, and dreams. Reference or not, thinking of the hymn tune makes you aware of how often in this short song you have heard descending steps, an image at the outset for the coming of evening and at the end for the embrace of silence, binding the whole song into one unified thought.[10]

The meaning of the three war songs relies a great deal on the tunes Ives weaves into them and the words and associations they carry. But these four songs from 1921 seem to represent a new approach for him: more laconic and economical with material, often with no borrowing or only subtle allusions. These suggest a late style, in the sense that Ives, like Beethoven, seems to have entered his last style period around the age of forty-five.

All four of these songs—like so much of Ives's music—neatly combine elements of tonal music with modern sounds and procedures. While other composers of his generation tended either to write tonal music or to use an entirely new musical language, Ives used whatever resources seemed most expressive and appropriate to the occasion. As he once wrote,

> Why tonality as such should be thrown out for good, I can't see. Why it should always be present, I can't see. It depends, it seems to me, a good deal—as clothes depend on the thermometer—on what one is trying to do, and on the state of mind, the time of day or other accidents of life.[11]

Reception

When he was finished assembling and proofreading *114 Songs* in the summer of 1922, Ives had 1,500 copies printed—twice as many as the *Concord Sonata*—and sent them out to the same mix of musicians, music schools, libraries, periodicals, and critics.[12] A decade later, he wrote in *Memos* that he had planned to begin the songbook with *Evening*, an attractive miniature that would have intrigued singers and pianists and encouraged them to keep exploring the collection. But in what may be his most self-defeating act of his entire career, the complaints he had received about his music, perhaps especially the recent mocking reviews of the *Concord Sonata*, "made me feel just mean enough to give all the 'old girls' another ride." So he placed as number 1 the song *Majority*, whose first page bristles with massive clusters of notes to be played on the piano with the forearm, knowing that "it would keep them from turning any more pages and finding something 'just too awful for words, Lily!'" He acknowledged that this was "another instance of how opinions, remarks, etc., which to the recipient seem either stupid or unfair, will cause one to do something that his better judgment knows it's not quite best perhaps to do."[13]

Critical reception for *114 Songs* was mixed. *The Musical Courier* treated it as a joke. John Philip Sousa, the famous band conductor and composer of marches and operettas, thanked Ives for sending it but noted that "some of the songs are most startling to a man educated by the harmonic methods of our forefathers." Many musicians, however, were intrigued. One old friend from Yale, fellow music student and organist W. Woods Chandler, wrote Ives that "the one thing that impressed me most, in looking over the songs, was to trace the development from College Days, down to the World War, then through that period and so on to the present. Looking at it in this way, one could better understand the why and wherefore of present day development."[14]

Over time, the songbook found singers. George Madden performed two of the songs from the 1890s in a recital at Town Hall on November 28, then sang *The Greatest Man* and *The White Gulls*, among the most appealing and expressive of the recent songs, in another Town Hall concert on February 28, 1924. Mary Holley had already premiered *The White Gulls* and two earlier songs in Danbury on June 8, 1922, even before the book was printed. Other songs appeared on programs in New Orleans in 1924 and at Carnegie Chamber Music Hall in New York in 1929, and from 1932 on came a steady run of performances across the United States and in Europe, along with a few recordings. Interest was spurred especially by the performance of seven songs, including *Evening*, by Hubert Linscott with Aaron Copland at the piano, at the Yaddo Festival in Saratoga Springs, New York, on May 1, 1932. These seven songs were published as a group later that year, in the first commercial publication of Ives's songs, with *Evening* placed first—finally. Numerous other collections followed, some including songs Ives had omitted from *114 Songs* or composed later.[15] By the mid-to-late 1930s, Ives's songs had taken on a life of their own, and they have been more widely sung and heard in every decade since.

THE MUSIC OF 1923–1924

After completing *114 Songs*, Ives turned his attention primarily to getting his major chamber and orchestral works in shape, revising and polishing the First and Second Violin Sonatas, *Holidays Symphony*, Second Orchestral Set, and Fourth Symphony, as well as working on a Third Orchestral Set and an ambitious *Universe Symphony* that he was unable to complete beyond a few sketches and fragments. He also found he had a few more songs in him, writing seven between 1922 and 1926, along with a scattering of new pieces for other media. Comparing four works he wrote in 1923–1924 shows that in his late forties, near the end of his composing career, the music that came out of him was as diverse as ever.

Henry Bellamann became friends with Ives after his review of the *Concord Sonata*, and Bellamann and his wife visited the Iveses at their West Redding home for several days in August 1922 and in New York on other occasions; Ives inscribed one copy of *Essays Before a Sonata* to Bellamann on

January 1, 1924 (the same copy six-year-old Edith had inscribed in pencil on the back flyleaf, "Edith Ives to Susanna Minturn / May 1920"—which presumably Ives did not notice when he presented it to Bellamann).[16] Their personal connection prompted Ives to set two of Bellamann's poems in 1923. Bellamann wrote poetry that is perhaps best described as imagist: free verse, with no rhyme or meter, featuring clear images, lean language, little connective tissue, and feelings that are implied rather than stated. His poem *Yellow Leaves* paints a picture of fall leaves, bright yellow against their brown twigs, like flames from church candles or gold coins seen through water pooled under a fountain. Ives's music for it is equally lean, with brief phrases of melody standing out against repeating figures that change from phrase to phrase, and a bit of rapid movement to suggest the images of the flames and of the moving water. The song is not atonal—there are too many repeated pitches and traditional sounds for that—but there is no key, rather a sense of suspended harmony, floating from image to image.

By contrast, *The One Way*, a satirical song about songwriting that Ives composed in 1923 to his own words, is as tonal as it gets. There is not a note or harmony in it that could not have been written by a composer of operettas or popular songs, and that is the point. The text is about songs that sound just like songs everyone has heard before, with the same kinds of rhymes, rhythms, chord progressions, and ideas, put out by songwriters who are making money by playing "the same old game." Everything is a cliché: the melody is full of familiar gestures; simple harmonies turn to more intense chromatic chords, change keys, and return home; rhythms start plain and grow more march-like, with a RUM-tid-dle-y-*Tum*-tum drum figure, and build to a climax. Ives wrote that he was inspired by a concert in New York's Aeolian Hall at which "a young [man] with a dumb look sang some songs by F[rank La Fo]rge and Oley Speaks!" A particular model—"target" might be a better word—is Speaks's biggest hit, *On the Road to Mandalay* (1907), an earnest if pompous song in a conservative idiom.[17] There is no overt borrowing, just unmistakable echoes of the style, form, and manner. Listen to *On the Road to Mandalay* followed by *The One Way* and the parallels will be hard to miss.

From the conventional tonality of *The One Way* to the strange sounds of the *Three Quarter-Tone Pieces* for two pianos, composed in 1923–1924 and premiered in 1925, is quite a leap. There are eighty-eight keys on a piano, each tuned to a note exactly a semitone (half step) away from the notes just above and below it. Yet this piece explores quarter tones—intervals half the size of a semitone—by using two pianos, with every string in Piano II tuned a quarter tone lower than the corresponding string in Piano I. This is a fully worked-out composition in three movements lasting about twelve minutes in performance, but in spirit it is a return to Ives's experimental pieces of two and three decades earlier, trying something out to see what possibilities there are. Ives explores a variety of effects: chords that use notes from both pianos and so include intervals that cannot be played on a normal piano; melodies with quarter tones, played by alternating between pianos; gestures played on one piano, then the other, so one hears the idea repeat a quarter tone higher or lower; and alternating chords between the pianos, creating an effect like quarter-tone melodies in several voices at once. The fast middle movement borrows material from Ives himself (three songs and two *Ragtime Dances*) and from *The Battle Cry of Freedom*, and the third movement varies *America* ("My country, 'tis of thee") as a quarter-tone melody, building to a climactic statement in counterpoint with a phrase from *La Marseillaise*; for anyone familiar with those pieces it is fascinating to hear them recast in quarter tones, like viewing them in a funhouse mirror. A decade after the *Three Quarter-Tone Pieces* were composed and performed, Ives wrote in *Memos* that "as far as I was concerned, these pieces were not presented as definitely completed works of art (or attempts at works of art). They were simply studies within the limited means we had with which to study quarter tones." Indeed, they served as studies for his Fourth Symphony, one of his most ambitious works of art; soon after writing the *Three Quarter-Tone Pieces*, he used some of the same quarter-tone effects in the symphony's second movement.[18]

The masterpiece among Ives's works of 1923–1924 is *Psalm 90* for choir, organ, and bells, setting the King James version of the psalm. John Kirkpatrick reported that "Mrs. Ives recalled his saying that it was the only one of his works that he was satisfied with."[19] In it Ives draws on the experiments of his earlier psalm settings but, as in his mature orchestral music, goes beyond merely demonstrating the possibilities of new resources and uses them for their rhetorical effect. Like all psalms, this one comprises a series of verses, each containing an idea, often made more pointed by contrast between the two halves of the verse. This psalm juxtaposes God as eternal with humankind's mortality, prays for forgiveness from sin, and closes with a vision of rejoicing in God's mercy and beauty and in doing God's work. Ives's setting unfolds over a repeated low C in the organ pedals, a representation of God's eternal presence that continues throughout the entire piece.

In a slow prelude before the choir sings, Ives presents the basic materials he will use during the work, and in the score he gives each chord or gesture a label. These are in some ways like the leitmotives in a Wagner opera, motives that are each associated with a particular person, thing, or concept. The sketches show that this prelude was among the last things Ives wrote for *Psalm 90*, revealing that he worked out these associations while setting the text, rather than in advance:

- "The Eternities": a C major chord with an added D (C-G-D-E-E).
- "Creation": a chord of stacked fifths (C-G-D-A-E) containing the notes of the previous sonority, showing the close relationship between the concepts.
- "God's wrath against sin": a chord of stacked thirds, very dissonant.
- "Prayer and Humility": a descending fourth in the melody, over parallel mostly whole-tone chords in the middle range of the organ.
- "Rejoicing in Beauty and Work": bells, playing three brief melodies over a low C.

———〜———

As you listen, you hear the first three chords on the organ, loud and full, each leading right into the next. Then, much softer, you hear the misty whole-tone chords of "Prayer and Humility," which are then joined by bells for "Rejoicing in Beauty and Work."

The choir begins by addressing the Lord as "our dwelling place from one generation to another," singing a unison melody over the first sonority, then over the second, and then turns to dissonant chords of stacked thirds—evolving swiftly from "The Eternities" through "Creation" to sin. In chords of fifths and fourths they chant of the creation and acknowledge "thou art God." Man turns to destruction—again the stacked thirds—and the Lord (set as a tenor solo) summons them to return.

The contrast of God's eternal being with humans' brief lifespan—"a thousand years in thy sight are but as yesterday when it is past"—is noted with the "Prayer and Humility" leitmotive. There follows a series of bitter images for humanity's condition, each set to a different musical idea. God carries people away like a flood, depicted by an expanding wedge and the dissonant stacks of thirds; they are like grass that grows in the morning and is cut down in the evening, with brief canons between voices giving way to a sentimental melody (based on a hymn tune that was adapted from Louis Moreau Gottschalk's *The Last Hope*). We are consumed by God's anger, again with stacked thirds; our secret sins, set to a soft chromatic descending melody, contrast with the light of God's countenance in strong rising chords made of thirds and fourths. Our days pass away, as an expanding wedge builds to a huge whole-tone cluster, each chord coming thicker and faster, then contracts in an exact retrograde. We may live eighty years, set to gradually thickening chords of fifths and fourths that link our lives to "Creation," but we live in labor and suffering, depicted by soft chromatic descending lines. God's anger—the stacked thirds again—is more powerful than we can know.

"So"—the psalmist entreats—"teach us to number our days, that we may apply our hearts unto wisdom." Here Ives draws on a trick he had used before: the mysterious series of rising minor chords that begins the development in the first movement of his First Symphony (described in chapter 3). The secret to the trick is that the chords themselves are moving down a whole-tone scale, but Ives rearranges the notes of each chord so that every voice is singing a rising line. The result is a musical paradox, a mystery—like the mysteries and paradoxes of faith that lead to wisdom. The voices rise for the first half of the psalm verse, then descend through the same chords in reverse order in the second half, returning to where they started, having raised their voices to God and brought their lessons home to earth. Then, over the chords that signify "Prayer and Humility," which also gently rise and fall, a solo soprano begs the Lord to return and to forgive his servants.

Now the culmination. As the choir asks for mercy, for gladness in re-sponse to affliction and evil, for work to do as servants of the Lord, and for the beauty of the Lord to be upon us, the bells come in with the leitmotive "Rejoicing in Beauty and Work," repeating their fragments of melody like the sparkling of the starry firmament or of sunbeams through clouds. The ending is calm and fulfilling, like the apotheosis at the end of the Fourth Symphony, and seems to go on forever, moving gently through beautiful sonorities. This is not beauty as "something that lets the ears lie back in an easy chair," a concep-tion Ives mocked in *Essays Before a Sonata*, but beauty that is hard won and well earned.[20] One phrase of the psalm—"and establish thou the work of our hands upon us"—comes into relief when the choir sings it in old-fashioned tonal harmony like Ives used in his church anthems of two to three decades earlier. For years, his church music was literally "the work of his hands." To hear him evoke it so directly near the end of his last piece of sacred music, more than two decades after he retired from his career as a church musician, is profoundly moving. At the very end comes an Amen, like a benediction on Ives's whole composing career.

The new songs and other pieces of the early 1920s show that Ives was continu-ing to evolve as a composer. Having developed sophisticated ways to blend his four traditions, to rework borrowed melodies, and to convey meanings through novel chords, textures, and procedures, in these late pieces we see him writ-ing music that is just as diverse and well crafted yet often more concentrated, more succinct. Putting his thoughts into dozens of songs rather than into new orchestral works or sonatas, his music was becoming more lyric, less epic.

But his life as a composer was about to change, one more time.

Epilogue

$\mathcal{A}$fter years of renting, in 1926 the Iveses bought a house in New York at 164 East 74th Street, a few blocks east of Central Park, where they would spend the winter months for the rest of their lives. It was a four-story townhouse with Ives's music room on the top floor. According to Harmony, soon after they moved in, her husband "came downstairs one day with tears in his eyes, and said he couldn't seem to compose any more—nothing went well, nothing sounded right." He was fifty-two. Exhausted from hard work, diabetes, and a starvation diet, he had run out of energy, and perhaps out of new ideas. As Harmony would write to Nicolas Slonimsky a decade later, Ives had "worked tremendously hard in his quarry all those years & exhausted the vein I suppose."[1]

This time he did not "quit music" as he had in 1902. He made sketches toward a new choral work, *Johnny Poe* (ca. 1927–1928), wrote a setting for the African American spiritual *Give Me Jesus* (titled *In the Mornin'*, 1929), and wrote new words for *He Is There!* to suit it for World War II (as *They Are There!*, 1942). He continued to revise his major works, including adding revisions to printed copies of the *Concord Sonata* and *114 Songs*, completing and scoring the Second Orchestral Set, supervising the publication of the Fourth Symphony second movement, getting the *Holidays Symphony* in shape, reworking *Three Places in New England* for chamber orchestra, revising *Central Park in the Dark* and *The Unanswered Question*, preparing the second edition of the *Concord Sonata*, and changing the ending of the Second Symphony.

Most important, he kept up his campaign to promote his music and continued to find allies and advocates to help. Ives's first biographers, Henry Cowell and his wife Sidney Robertson Cowell, called this stage "the career of Ives's music," as his compositions left home and began to circulate like baby birds flying out of the nest. Earlier chapters have recounted the premieres and publication of individual works, but a quick summary will make clear how crucial was the role played by Ives's supporters. As Cowell and Cowell wrote,

"Composers are born, but a career is always made. Even the greatest music has always had to establish itself through the interest and effort of many people who are able to forward it.... Fame never arrives untouched by human hands." The relationships were mutually beneficial: early on, Ives typically paid the expenses for performances and publications of his own music, but also gave crucial financial support to the broader activities of groups that were working to put the music of modern American composers before the public.[2]

Ives met pianist and entrepreneur E. Robert Schmitz in 1923, and soon he was helping to fund the organization Schmitz had founded in 1920 as the Franco-American Musical Society and later renamed Pro Musica, which had chapters across the country and overseas. It was probably Schmitz who stimulated Ives to compose the *Three Quarter-tone Pieces*, which premiered on a concert sponsored by Schmitz's group in February 1925. Pro Musica also sponsored the premiere of the first two movements of the Fourth Symphony in January 1927 and the New York premiere of *The Celestial Railroad* in November 1928.

Henry Cowell, founder of the California-based New Music Society, wrote Ives in 1927 inviting him to subscribe to his new project, a quarterly publication containing new music by American modern composers, to become a member of the advisory board, and to submit some of his own music. Ives responded enthusiastically, subscribed to *New Music* from its first issue, and eventually became its largest funder. Cowell went on to print many of Ives's works in the journal, including the second movement of the Fourth Symphony in 1929, *The Fourth of July* in 1932, two collections of songs in 1933 and 1935, *Washington's Birthday* in 1937, and the Third Violin Sonata in 1951. *New Music* also issued recordings, including several of Ives's works. Cowell was a tireless promoter of Ives's music, including it on New Music Society concerts and writing laudatory articles about Ives from 1928 on, and in 1949–1951 Cowell helped to prepare the Second Symphony for performance and saw it into print. Through Cowell, Ives met Nicolas Slonimsky, who conducted the premieres and other performances of *Three Places in New England* and *Washington's Birthday* in 1931 and *The Fourth of July* in 1932, on concerts in the United States, Cuba, and Europe that Ives underwrote.

As interest in Ives's music grew, musicians increasingly approached him. Lou Harrison was a teenaged college student in Cowell's San Francisco orbit when he wrote Ives a fan letter in 1936. Ives began to send him printed and photostated scores, and a decade later Harrison prepared the Third Symphony and Second String Quartet for performance and conducted the premiere of the symphony, awarded the Pulitzer Prize in 1947. Lehman Engel launched Ives's choral music into the public eye with performances of *Psalm 67* in 1937 and a recording of it two years later. John Kirkpatrick's performances of the *Concord Sonata* in the late 1930s and 1940s brought Ives more attention than ever, and his recording became the best-selling classical album for months after it was issued in 1948. Internationally famous violinist Joseph Szigeti performed and recorded the Fourth Violin Sonata in 1942, and violinist Sol Babitz and composer Ingolf Dahl played the public premiere of the Third Violin Sonata (the last of the four to be premiered) in 1942, recorded it, and edited it for publication. In 1948 the popular organist E. Power Biggs asked Ives for organ music and in response received the fifty-six-year-old *Variations on America*, which he prepared for publication, played often, and helped to make into one of Ives's most widely known pieces.[3] The Boston Symphony played *Three Places in New England* in 1948, the piece's first performance in almost sixteen years and the first performance of any Ives work by a major American orchestra. The 1951 premiere and radio broadcast of the Second Symphony by the New York Philharmonic conducted by Leonard Bernstein brought Ives new fans.

By the time of his death on May 19, 1954, the momentum had become self-sustaining. Ives's stature continued to rise, as new performers and listeners took up his music every year, and he became an inspiration for and influence on younger generations of composers, from Bernard Herrmann and John Cage to Frank Zappa and John Adams. Today he is part of the canon, played by almost every orchestra or band and taught in every music school, culminating a remarkable career.

EXTRAORDINARY YET TRADITIONAL, AMERICAN YET UNIVERSAL

In some ways, Ives was an ordinary composer. He studied music as a child, working his way up to master teachers of organ and composition. He became a virtuoso performer on organ and piano. He had a successful career as a church musician while composing both for church and for other venues, as countless others have done. He wrote hundreds of pieces in a wide variety of genres, from songs to symphonies.

In other ways, he was extraordinary. He made his living outside music, as a businessman, and was remarkably successful and influential in his field. Most of his music was performed and published long after it was written, and musicians and the public got to know his major works in roughly reverse chronological order. After years of obscurity, he published his own music in his mid-forties, subsidized performances of it in his fifties, finally gained a national reputation as a composer in his mid-sixties, and at his death at seventy-nine was hailed as one of his country's great composers.

His music is extraordinary as well. Taken as a whole, it has an unprecedented diversity, encompassing four different traditions, and spanning from pieces that follow the conventions of their type to pieces that mix, rethink, upend, or replace those conventions to create music unlike anything heard before. Because of that diversity, there is something to appeal to everyone in his music, as well as pieces that may not suit your tastes.

One secret of his success has been his ability to attract different audiences for different reasons, or different aspects of his music. Stephen Budiansky notes that as Ives's music became known from the 1920s through the 1940s, "everyone saw in his music what they wanted to: the mystics saw mysticism, the radicals radicalism, the modernists modernism, the nativists nativism." David Paul makes a similar point in his book on how Ives and his music have been regarded during the last hundred years by critics, composers, musicians, cultural historians, musicologists, and others, who all see him differently because of their own points of view.[4] Few composers attract fans for such a wide range of reasons.

What often astonishes listeners most as they get to know Ives's music is how varied in style it can be, not only from piece to piece but within a single movement. No other composer from his era or before has the range of styles he exhibits, even in the six songs we began with in chapter 1. Over and over, in *Memories*, *Down East*, *Psalm 67*, *Central Park in the Dark*, the Second Symphony, *Holidays Symphony*, *The Alcotts*, the Fourth Symphony, and countless other pieces, we have seen how Ives uses contrasts of style to delineate the piece's form and to convey meanings through the associations carried by the musical styles he invokes. It may be even more surprising to realize that employing style contrasts in this way is not unusual in the least but is part of the classical tradition, used by opera composers to set off one character or scene from another, and by composers of sonatas and symphonies to distinguish themes from each other and from transitions or codas. If you think about it, the same use of contrasting styles is what makes film music work, giving a different atmosphere to a love scene, a battle scene, a chase, a Mexican street scene, or a Hindu temple. It even shows up in popular music, as in the wildly disparate styles in the songs on the Beatles' album *Sgt. Pepper's Lonely Hearts Club Band*. What is different about Ives is that the contrasts of style can seem more extreme, perhaps because we know the styles so well (as in *Memories*) or because he places a familiar style side by side with a style he made up, something you have never encountered before (as in *Washington's Birthday* or *Psalm 90*). Getting to know Ives, and hearing such obvious contrasts in *his* music, can help us be more attentive to the ways other musicians use the same device.

Likewise, Ives's use of fictional music—music that acts the part of other music, played by different musicians from a faraway place or time, and invites us to imagine ourselves there, listening to that music—is not new. Characters in operas often sing drinking songs, lullabies, or serenades to other people on stage, and we listen in as if we were there. In the finale to the first act of his opera *Don Giovanni*, Mozart gets three dances going at once, played by three different bands, and it is as if we are at the party, too, rather than sitting in our seats in the opera house—just as the Second Violin Sonata and *Washington's Birthday* can make us imagine we are at a barn dance. Ives's use of borrowed melodies is also not new; that has been part of music since the Middle Ages, and major composers like Bach and Beethoven use borrowed material in almost as many different ways as Ives does. Breaking rules to make music more expressive, as Ives often does, goes back to sixteenth-century madrigals and seventeenth-century operas.[5] In these ways, too, getting to know Ives's music can make us more attentive to what other composers are doing. Like Ives, they often had to do something out of the ordinary to get their listeners' attention, but recognizing what is new or unusual in music that has long been recognized as a classic can take an act of imagination; knowing Ives can help us hear such music with new ears.

Ives's music is as American as that of Stephen Foster, John Philip Sousa, Bessie Smith, Duke Ellington, Elvis Presley, or Prince, but more deliberately and purposefully so, because he was working in the imported tradition of European classical music. By integrating American popular music and church music with the genres, forms, and methods of the classical tradition, Ives sought to represent America on the world stage—and especially his region of the Northeast, New England and New York, whose music and culture he knew as a native. In his First String Quartet and Second Symphony, he imported American material into the two most prestigious genres of instrumental music, adjusting the American melodies through paraphrase so they would work as themes in the characteristic classical forms of fugue, sonata form, and ternary form. In his Third Symphony and violin sonatas, he raised American hymn melodies to a new level of seriousness by making them his themes with little or no alteration, adopting the methods of classical music but changing the forms. In his *Holidays Symphony* and orchestral sets, he moved beyond celebrating the music of America to depict its holidays, its history, its places, and especially the way Americans use music to dance, commemorate, remember, have fun, aspire, march, dream, worship, and join together in song. In the *Concord Sonata*, he celebrated American literature, and in his Second String Quartet and Fourth Symphony he imagined Americans engaging in discussions, arguments, journeys, and trials and experiencing moments of transcendence, all represented in part through music that is familiar to them.

These pieces speak from Ives's own experience as a human being familiar with a wide range of music from Bach to ragtime, who sought to integrate it all and show how all of it can be reconciled in one person's life. In *Essays Before a Sonata*, he wrote that by capturing the spirit of music one has known deeply, through personal experience and the lives of those around him, one "may find there a local color that will do all the world good. . . . If local color, national color, any color, is a true pigment of the universal color, it is a divine quality, it is a part of substance in art—not of manner."[6] That he aspired to express and embrace the universal is clear in works like *The Unanswered Question*, his unfinished *Universe Symphony*, and late pieces such as *Evening*, *Yellow Leaves*, and *Psalm 90*, which have nothing particularly American about them. But Ives also believed that the truest expression is deeply personal, and his most personal—and perhaps ultimately most universal—music springs from blending all the aspects of his musical personality.

WHY DOES IVES MATTER?

In the end, why does Ives's music matter? In part, because it lifts a mirror so we can see ourselves in ways that we may instantly recognize—yes, that reminds me of when I was a child—and in ways we would never have imagined—yes, that chaos, that gradual coming to clarity, that lack of resolution at the end, that unanswered question, that vision of the beyond, I never heard anything like it before, but it resonates with my own experience.

The concert hall is an odd place, where we gather together in community to have an individual encounter with music, where we stay silent so that we can listen intently to noise. Listening to recordings alone is even more strange; music has always been a social glue, something everyone in the room participates in as performer or dancer or worshiper or listener, but recordings allow us to hear music with no one else around.

Whether in concert or through recordings, Ives's music pulls us in by simultaneously being music we hear and being *about how we hear music*—how it sounds and how we encounter it as part of our daily life: outdoors, indoors, at "the opera house," at a parade, on a walk, at home, at an organ recital, at a football game, sitting in Central Park, in a religious service, at a camp meeting, in our memories, at a dance, at a memorial service, on the Fourth of July, in the military, in our dreams, from across a river, on an elevated train platform, around the family piano, wafting over a pond, from a distance, close by, clearly heard, barely noticed. Every bit of Ives's music comes with some of that "social glue" attached, inviting us to be a part of a community that knows and uses the kinds of music and sounds he evokes. As he weaves his many variations on America, even if we are listening all alone, the people connected with this music are all around us.

Notes

ABBREVIATIONS

Budiansky   Budiansky, Stephen. *Mad Music: Charles Ives, the Nostalgic Rebel.* Lebanon, NH: ForeEdge, 2014.

Correspondence   Ives, Charles. *Selected Correspondence of Charles Ives.* Ed. Tom C. Owens. Berkeley: University of California Press, 2007.

Essays   Ives, Charles. *Essays Before a Sonata, The Majority, and Other Writings.* Ed. Howard Boatwright. New York: W. W. Norton, 1970.

Feder   Feder, Stuart. *Charles Ives, "My Father's Song": A Psychoanalytic Biography.* New Haven: Yale University Press, 1992.

Grove   Burkholder, J. Peter. "Ives, Charles (Edward)." In *The New Grove Dictionary of Music and Musicians,* 2nd ed., ed. Stanley Sadie, and *Grove Dictionary of American Music,* 2nd ed., ed. Charles Hiroshi Garrett. Work-list with James B. Sinclair and Gayle Sherwood Magee. At Grove Music Online via http://oxford musiconline.com.

Ives World   Burkholder, J. Peter, ed. *Charles Ives and His World.* Princeton: Princeton University Press, 1996.

Magee   Magee, Gayle Sherwood. *Charles Ives Reconsidered.* Urbana: University of Illinois Press, 2008.

Memos   Ives, Charles. *Memos.* Ed. and with appendices by John Kirkpatrick. New York: W. W. Norton, 1972.

Perlis   Perlis, Vivian. *Charles Ives Remembered: An Oral History.* New Haven: Yale University Press, 1974.

Rossiter   Rossiter, Frank R. *Charles Ives and His America.* New York: Liveright, 1975.

Sinclair   Sinclair, James B. *A Descriptive Catalogue of the Music of Charles Ives.* New Haven: Yale University Press, 1999.

Swafford   Swafford, Jan. *Charles Ives: A Life with Music.* New York: W. W. Norton, 1996.

INTRODUCTION

1. Gayle Sherwood, "The Choral Works of Charles Ives: Chronology, Style, Reception" (PhD dissertation, Yale University, 1995); "Questions and Veracities: Reassessing the Chronology of Ives's Choral Works," *Musical Quarterly* 78 (Fall 1994): 429–47; and "Redating Ives's Choral Sources," in *Ives Studies,* ed. Philip Lambert (Cambridge: Cambridge University Press, 1997), 77-101. She also established dates for pieces discussed in J. Peter Burkholder, *All Made of Tunes: Charles Ives and the Uses of Musical Borrowing* (New Haven: Yale University Press, 1995). For Sinclair and *Grove,* and for sources cited in the next paragraph, see above under "Abbreviations."

2. Unless otherwise cited, these appear in my *All Made of Tunes* or in my chapter "The Symphonic Works of Charles Ives," in *The Symphonic Repertoire, Volume 5: The Symphony in the Americas,* ed. Brian Hart (Bloomington: Indiana University Press, 2021).

CHAPTER 1: A MOST UNUSUAL CAREER— AND A RECITAL OF SONGS

1. The idea for this chapter was inspired by a voice recital by my former student Reuben Walker that began with *Dichterliebe* followed by Ives's *General William Booth Enters into Heaven.* Thanks to Reuben for the inspiration.

2. Nicholas Vachel Lindsay, *General William Booth Enters into Heaven and Other Poems* (New York: Mitchell Kennerly, 1913). Ives set only the excerpts from the poem he found in a review of this book, "A Poet of Promise," *The Independent,* January 12, 1914, 72.

3. *Essays,* 97.

4. Rossiter, 180–83; Swafford, 325.

5. Reprinted in *Ives World,* 309. See also Swafford, 325–28.

6. *Memos,* 127.

7. See J. Peter Burkholder, *Charles Ives: The Ideas Behind the Music* (New Haven: Yale University Press, 1985), 85–86. The term was introduced by Peter J. Rabinowitz, "Fictional Music: Toward a Theory of Listening," *Bucknell Review* 26, no. 1 (1981): 193–208.

8. On this aspect of Ives's music, see Larry Starr, *A Union of Diversities: Style in the Music of Charles Ives* (New York: Schirmer Books, 1992); and J. Peter Burkholder, "Stylistic Heterogeneity and Topics in the Music of Charles Ives," *Journal of Musicological Research* 31, nos. 2–3 (2012): 166–99, which discusses *Memories* on pp. 177–81.

9. For a discussion of *Walking* as a journey through contrasting styles, see Starr, *A Union of Diversities,* 35–43.

10. The description here draws on J. Peter Burkholder, "Ives and the Four Musical Traditions," in *Ives World,* 3–34. For different views, see Starr, *A Union of Diversities,* 93–103; Swafford, 268–69; and Magee, 106–14.

CHAPTER 2: AN AMERICAN MUSICAL CHILDHOOD

1. Rossiter, 3–8; Feder, 1–18 and 85; Swafford, 3–6, 27–30, and 60–61; Budiansky, 17–31.

2. *Memos*, 245; Rossiter, 8–10; Feder, 12–22; Swafford, 6–11; Budiansky, 24–25; Burkholder, *Charles Ives: The Ideas Behind the Music*, 33–36.

3. *Memos*, 245–46; Rossiter, 10–11; Feder, 19–30, 47–48, 54–58, and 85; Swafford, 11–18; Budiansky, 25–26 and 38–39.

4. *Memos*, 247–48; Rossiter, 20–22; Feder, 59–76, 81–84, and 108; Swafford, 38–43 and 49; Budiansky, 42.

5. *Memos*, 247–48; *Correspondence*, 7–12; Rossiter, 21; Feder, 87–88, 91, 96, 108–9, and 118–21; Swafford, 44–47 and 55–59; Budiansky, 42–46.

6. Feder, 79–81 and 88–93; Swafford, 43–44 and 48–49; Budiansky, 31–37.

7. Burkholder, "Ives and the Four Musical Traditions," in *Ives World*, 3–34.

8. Rossiter, 12; Feder, 31–43 and 99–100; Swafford, 19–26; Budiansky, 39–40.

9. *Memos*, 246–47; Rossiter, 12–13, 16–21, and 37–39; Feder, 51–59, 66–67, 76–79, 85–87, and 105–6; Swafford, 32–38, 40–42, and 61; Magee, 8–13 and 16–18; Budiansky, 34–35 and 40–42.

10. Feder, 95; Swafford, 52. Magee, 19–21, errs in asserting that there is a repetition of the first half after the trio, which causes her to see the march as more old-fashioned than it is.

11. Reprinted in *Ives World*, 274–75.

12. *Ives World*, 275.

13. Sinclair, 95–96; Rossiter, 44; Swafford, 53.

14. Rossiter, 28 and 39–40; Paul D. Weber, "Charles Ives and Nineteenth Century American Church Music" (MMA Thesis, Yale University, 1979), 31; Feder, 100–101, 105, and 127; Swafford, 49 and 95–98; Magee, 13–15; *Correspondence*, 27–29, quoting p. 28.

15. Rossiter, 28–29; Weber, "Charles Ives and Nineteenth Century American Church Music," 51–91; William Osborne, "Charles Ives the Organist," *The American Organist* 24, no. 7 (July 1990): 58–64; Feder, 104–5 and 107–8; Swafford, 48–51; Magee, 20–22; Budiansky, 44–45; J. Peter Burkholder, "The Organist in Ives," *Journal of the American Musicological Society* 55 (Summer 2002): 255–310.

16. *Memos*, 69 and 132–33.

17. Weber, "Charles Ives and Nineteenth Century American Church Music," 9–11 and 19–20.

18. Rossiter, 11–12; Feder, 29, 48–51, 91–93, and 97; Swafford, 17–18; Magee, 11–12 and 17; Burkholder, *All Made of Tunes*, 12–20.

19. Swafford, 66–69; Magee, 34.

20. Rossiter, 29; Weber, "Charles Ives and Nineteenth Century American Church Music," 56–62; Osborne, "Charles Ives the Organist," 58–59.

21. Rossiter, 29–32; Weber, "Charles Ives and Nineteenth Century American Church Music," 67–69 and 74–75; Osborne, "Charles Ives the Organist," 59; Swafford, 57; Magee, 22–27.

22. Sinclair, 247–48; Rossiter, 45–47; Osborne, "Charles Ives the Organist," 59; Feder, 113–15; Swafford, 62–64; Budiansky, 54–56. The following description draws on Weber, "Charles Ives and Nineteenth Century American Church Music," 77–81.

23. Osborne, "Charles Ives the Organist," 61; Burkholder, "The Organist in Ives," 265–70; Magee, 34; Budiansky, 61.

24. Burkholder, *All Made of Tunes*, 22 and 432n25; Sinclair, 247–48.

25. Burkholder, "The Organist in Ives," 285–86.

26. See David Nicholls, *American Experimental Music, 1890–1940* (Cambridge: Cambridge University Press, 1990).

27. *Memos*, 47.

28. J. Peter Burkholder, "The Critique of Tonality in the Early Experimental Music of Charles Ives," *Music Theory Spectrum* 12 (Fall 1990): 203–23; Swafford, 89–92.

29. *Memos*, 42–43.

30. Charles Ives, "Some 'Quarter-tone' Impressions," in *Essays*, 110–11; *Memos*, 115; Rossiter, 13–15; Burkholder, *Charles Ives: The Ideas Behind the Music*, 43–57; Feder, 88–90 and 93–94; Swafford, 44 and 94–95; Budiansky, 46–49.

31. *Correspondence*, 12–29; Rossiter, 22, 47–48, and 84; Weber, "Charles Ives and Nineteenth Century American Church Music," 31–32; Burkholder, *Charles Ives: The Ideas Behind the Music*, 76–78; Feder, 120–22 and 124–28; Swafford, 72–73 and 76–80; Magee, 27; Budiansky, 57–58 and 61.

32. Rossiter, 21–22; Feder, 122–23; Swafford, 73.

33. Swafford, 73–76; Magee, 29–30.

34. *Memos*, 281; Weber, "Charles Ives and Nineteenth Century American Church Music," 86; Feder, 123; Swafford, 73–74; Magee, 7–8 and 28–34.

35. Burkholder, *Charles Ives: The Ideas Behind the Music*, 61–65; Magee, 33–37.

36. Burkholder, "The Organist in Ives."

CHAPTER 3: APPRENTICESHIP

1. For an overview, see J. Peter Burkholder, "Ives and Yale: The Enduring Influence of a College Experience," *College Music Symposium* 39 (1999): 27–42.

2. Rossiter, 50; Feder, 103, 106, 120–21, and 128; Budiansky, 61–62.

3. Ives's transcript is in *Memos*, 180–83. On the old-fashioned curriculum, see Rossiter, 68–69, and Feder, 133.

4. Quoted in Burkholder, *Charles Ives: The Ideas Behind the Music*, 74. For more on Phelps, see ibid., 72–76.

5. *Memos*, 83.

6. Rossiter, 70.

7. Rossiter, 65 and 68–78; Feder, 151–61; Swafford, 104–7, 116–19, 129–30, and 132–34; Budiansky, 63–71 and 87–88.

8. Rossiter, 64–65; Budiansky, 71–73.

9. Reprinted in Perlis, 22–23.

10. Sinclair, 134–35, 194, and 549–50.

11. *Correspondence*, 23.

12. *Memos*, 182–83; Magee, 41–43.

13. *Memos*, 48.

14. Magee, 47–48.

15. *Memos*, 49.

16. On the Beethoven arrangement, see Burkholder, *All Made of Tunes*, 46–49.

17. Quoted in Sinclair, 113–14.

18. *Memos*, 49.

19. *Memos*, 47.

20. Ives himself changed the way he described Parker's influence, and writers followed suit; these changes are traced briefly in Burkholder, "Ives and Yale," 35–38.

21. *Memos*, 49.

22. Burkholder, *Charles Ives: The Ideas Behind the Music*, 61–62.

23. Burkholder, *Charles Ives: The Ideas Behind the Music*, 62–66.

24. *Memos*, 183; Burkholder, *All Made of Tunes*, 27; Bryan R. Simms, "The German Apprenticeship of Charles Ives," *American Music* 29 (Summer 2011): 139–67.

25. Charles E. Ives, *114 Songs* (Redding, CT: C. E. Ives, 1922; reprinted New York: Peer International, Associated Music Publishers, and Theodore Presser, 1975), 192. Reprinted with altered punctuation in *Memos*, 184.

26. *Memos*, 183–84.

27. Thomas Willis, quoted in Burkholder, *All Made of Tunes*, 89.

28. *Memos*, 29, 51, and 87; Sinclair, 3–5; Burkholder, *All Made of Tunes*, 89 and 441n2.

29. Burkholder, "The Organist in Ives," 273–76 (cited in chapter 2).

30. Magee, 90–93.

31. *Memos*, 51 and 86–87. The editor's italic brackets, used to mark material Ives inserted into the text, are omitted here.

32. Budiansky, 61. On Griggs, see *Memos*, 253–58; Burkholder, *Charles Ives: The Ideas Behind the Music*, 68–72; and Feder, 143–46.

33. *Memos*, 237; *Correspondence*, 19–20, 26–27, 30, and 33; Osborne, "Charles Ives the Organist," 59–60 (cited in chapter 2); Swafford, 121; Magee, 34–35.

34. Perlis, 21.

35. On the anthems for Center Church, see Gayle Sherwood, "Redating Ives's Choral Sources," in Lambert, *Ives Studies*, 87–89 and 97–98, and "'Buds the Infant Mind': Charles Ives's *The Celestial Country* and American Protestant Choral Traditions," *19th-Century Music* 23 (Fall 1999): 170–86.

CHAPTER 4: WEAVING THE THREADS

1. Osborne, "Charles Ives the Organist," 60 (cited in chapter 2); "Our Historic Sanctuary," Bloomfield Presbyterian Church on the Green, http://bpcog.org/our-historic-sanctuary (accessed July 18, 2019); Sinclair, 248.

2. Osborne, "Charles Ives the Organist," 60–61 and 62.

3. *Memos*, 269; Amelia Van Wyck, quoted in Perlis, 10.

4. Perlis, 34; a differently edited version is in *Memos*, 269. For an alternate account, see Budiansky, 101–2.

5. On Poverty Flat, see *Memos*, 262–67; Swafford, 143 and 149–51; Magee, 67–68, who points out that "Poverty Flat" was "a popular nickname for the bachelor apartment of the early [twentieth] century"; and Budiansky, 90, who suggests a link to Poverty Flats, Colorado. Of the three buildings, only 34 Gramercy Park, built in 1883, still exists; 317 West 58th Street was later demolished to erect a skyscraper covering half the block, and the current building at 65 Central Park West was erected in the 1920s, long after Ives moved out.

6. *Memos*, 265; *Correspondence*, 34. "Hence the pyramids" was used in Ives's Yale crowd as a jesting non sequitur. It came from a bawdy song or monologue that has several variants. The closest to Ives's orbit I have found is from *Immortalia: An Anthology of American Ballads, Sailor's Songs, Cowboy Songs, College Songs, Parodies, Limericks, and other Humorous Verses and Doggerel* (Philadelphia: Privately printed, 1927), 154, which cites the hippopotamus, "Who has a square ass-hole and eats mud. Every time he shits he shits bricks, Hence the pyramids and Stanford University." See Budiansky, 71.

7. *Memos*, 61.

8. Sinclair, 106; *Memos*, 266.

9. *Memos*, 55.

10. Quoted in *Memos*, 264. Ives wrote two settings of the poem, the first revised and the second composed around 1901.

11. Quoted in *Memos*, 267. For the nickname, see *Memos*, 262.

12. *Memos*, 56–57; Burkholder, *All Made of Tunes*, 277 and 344; Swafford, 149–50 and 151–52; Magee, 56–58. On the offensive practice of blackface minstrelsy, see the section on "A Synthesis of Traditions" in chapter 6.

13. Sinclair, 657.

14. Burkholder, *All Made of Tunes*, 34–35.

15. Sherwood, "'Buds the Infant Mind,'" 175–83 (cited in chapter 3); Magee, 61–64.

16. Sinclair, 139–40.

17. Burkholder, *All Made of Tunes*, 436–37, note 16.

18. Sinclair, 264–76; *Memos*, 47, 115, 148, 153–54, and 178–79; Sherwood, "Redating Ives's Choral Sources," in Lambert, *Ives Studies*, 88–90 and 97–98. In an early list of his works, Ives listed "About 10 Psalms—100th, 24th, 90th—*23rd Psalm* (Center Church and Newark Presbyterian, Bloomfield Presbyterian) 1897–98—(*90th Psalm* 1923–24)." Sinclair applies the date 1897–98 to *Psalm 100* and *Psalm 24*, but Ives probably meant both that date and the performances in church to apply only to *Psalm 23*; this setting of one of the most popular texts in the entire Bible does not survive, and most likely was in Romantic style like Ives's setting of *Psalm 42 (As Pants the Hart)* from ca. 1892.

19. *Memos*, 178.

20. The following discussion is based on my analyses in Burkholder, "The Critique of Tonality," 209–15 (cited in chapter 2), and "Stylistic Heterogeneity and Topics in the Music of Charles Ives," 183–86 (cited in chapter 1).

21. Sinclair, 280–83.

22. *Memos*, 43; Burkholder, "The Critique of Tonality," 215–19; Burkholder, "Ives and Yale," 40–41 (cited in chapter 3).

23. Sinclair, 131; Burkholder, *All Made of Tunes*, 342–43 and 484n4.

24. *Memos*, 40.

25. *Memos*, 40; Sinclair, 130–32.

26. Sinclair, 264–76; Rossiter, 270–71.

27. Sinclair, 139–40.

28. *Memos*, 262–64 and 327–28; Sinclair, 256; Rossiter, 146–47; Burkholder, *Charles Ives: The Ideas Behind the Music*, 78–81; Feder, 171–75; Magee, 61–66.

29. Horatio Parker, introduction to *Music and Public Entertainment* (Boston: Hall and Locke, 1911; reprint ed., New York: AMS Press, 1980), xvi.

30. Reviews reprinted in *Ives World*, 275–77.

31. "A Danbury Composer," *Danbury Evening News*, April 26, 1902; quoted in Budiansky, 98.

32. *Memos*, 148; Burkholder, *Charles Ives: The Ideas behind the Music*, 84.

33. *Memos*, 57.

CHAPTER 5: SEEKING AND FINDING

1. Michael Broyles, "Charles Ives and the American Democratic Tradition," in *Ives World*, 135–37.

2. Broyles, "Charles Ives and the American Democratic Tradition," 137–39; Feder, 183–86, 187, and 198–99; Budiansky, 118–25; Gayle Sherwood, "Charles Ives and 'Our National Malady,'" *Journal of the American Musicological Society* 54 (Fall 2001): 555–84; Magee, 74–82.

3. Broyles, "Charles Ives and the American Democratic Tradition," 139–41; *Memos*, 270; Perlis, 36 and 46–47; Rossiter, 111–13; Feder, 199; Swafford, 194–98; Magee, 68–70 and 78–79; Budiansky, 125–27, 147–48, and 153.

4. Perlis, 35–36.

5. Rossiter, 113; Feder, 258; Swafford, 197, 205, 216, 267, and 344; Budiansky, 126–27, 153–54, 158, and 229. Inflation-adjusted equivalents from the US Inflation Calculator at https://www.usinflationcalculator.com.

6. Perlis, 36 and 65; Rossiter, 115–16, quoting p. 116; Swafford, 203–5; Budiansky, 156. Portions of the revised version of *The Amount to Carry* are reprinted in *Essays*, 232–40, and are quoted or summarized in Swafford, 203–4. *Broadway* is in *Memos*, 229–35.

7. See Perlis, 56–58, for a program of study and George Hofmann's reminiscences about teaching the classes. See also Rossiter, 117; Swafford, 201–6; and Budiansky, 154.

8. *Essays*, 238–39. See also Swafford, 206–12, on Ives's insurance ideals.

9. Broyles, "Charles Ives and the American Democratic Tradition," 141–42.

10. Advertisement in *The Eastern Underwriter*, September 19, 1930, p. 18; reprinted in Perlis, 41.

11. *Memos*, 120, 259–60, and 274; Burkholder, *Ideas*, 95 and 140n1.

12. *Memos*, 274–76, quoting from "The Nurse's Gain" on p. 275; Perlis, 37. On nursing, see also Magee, 71–73 and 79–80, and Budiansky, 135–36.

13. *Memos*, 277; Burkholder, *Charles Ives: The Ideas behind the Music*, 141n8; *Ives World*, 204–10; *Correspondence*, 35–43; Feder, 203–6; Swafford, 169, 176, and 182–87; Budiansky, 128–30 and 136–38.

14. *Memos*, 260; Henry Cowell and Sidney Cowell, *Charles Ives and His Music*, rev. ed. (London: Oxford University Press, 1969), 46; Burkholder, *Charles Ives: The Ideas Behind the Music*, 95 and 140n2; Swafford, 188 and 191–92; Budiansky, 140–41.

15. *Correspondence*, 42.

16. *Memos*, 277; Burkholder, *Charles Ives: The Ideas Behind the Music*, 97 and 141n8; *Correspondence*, 37–38 and 48–50; Feder, 204–5; Swafford, 183–84.

17. Rossiter, 173; Burkholder, *Charles Ives: The Ideas Behind the Music*, 100 and 95; Perlis, 38; *Memos*, 277.

18. *Memos*, 114.

19. Perlis, 95; Burkholder, *Charles Ives: The Ideas Behind the Music*, 96.

20. See Burkholder, *Charles Ives: The Ideas Behind the Music*, 96–102, summarized in the following paragraphs. Feder, 213–14, suggests that Harmony was echoing back Ives's own ideas to him, but to judge from the surviving letters they appear in her letters first. See also Magee, 82–83.

21. *Ives World*, 204.

22. Quoted in Burkholder, *Charles Ives: The Ideas Behind the Music*, 96, and Feder, 213–14. See also Swafford, 188–90.

23. *Correspondence*, 38 and 95–96, quoting p. 38; Burkholder, *Charles Ives: The Ideas Behind the Music*, 98.

24. See *Memos*, 318–24; her letter is quoted on p. 324.

25. Burkholder, *Charles Ives: The Ideas Behind the Music*, 100; transcribed differently in Rossiter, 173.

26. Magee, 67 and 73–74.

27. *Memos*, 277; Swafford, 183.

28. Other famous palindromes include these: "Madam, I'm Adam." "Red rum, sir, is murder." "Do nine men interpret? Nine men, I nod." "Straw? No, too stupid a fad. I put soot on warts." "Doc, note: I dissent. A fast never prevents a fatness. I diet on cod."

29. *Memos*, 61–62.

30. *Memos*, 125.

31. Sinclair, 102. For a full analysis of this piece, see J. Peter Burkholder, "The Evolution of Charles Ives's Music: Aesthetics, Quotation, Technique" (PhD dissertation, University of Chicago, 1983), 494–520.

32. "Note," in Charles E. Ives, *Central Park in the Dark* (Hillsdale, NY: Boelke-Bomart, 1973), 31.

33. Burkholder, "The Organist in Ives," 273–76 (cited in chapter 2).

34. Burkholder, "The Organist in Ives," 282–85.

35. *Memos*, 50.

36. Nicolas Slonimsky, *Music Since 1900*, 5th ed. (New York: Schirmer Books, 1994), 1171; Burkholder, "The Organist in Ives," 276–82.

37. *Memos*, 159; Sinclair, 129. Ives wrote on the manuscript his address at the Charles Raymond agency, good only through December 1906, but using addresses to date his manuscripts has proven unreliable; sometimes the date was entered before the music, and sometimes it was entered much later.

38. Sinclair, 103 and 129; *Ives World*, 340–41.

39. *Ives World*, 342.

40. *Essays*, 81–82; John Jeffrey Gibbens, "Debussy's Impact on Ives: An Assessment" (DMA dissertation, University of Illinois at Urbana-Champaign, 1985); David Michael Hertz, *Angels of Reality: Emersonian Unfoldings in Wright, Stevens, and Ives* (Carbondale and Edwardsville: Southern Illinois University Press, 1993), 93–113; and David Michael Hertz, "Ives's Concord Sonata and the Texture of Music," in *Ives World*, 75–117.

41. Sinclair, 103 and 129.

42. Sinclair, 103–4, 160, and 177.

43. *Memos*, 277.

CHAPTER 6: SYNTHESIZING AMERICAN AND EUROPEAN MUSIC

1. *Memos*, 51–52 and 155; Sinclair, 8–9.

2. Dates in *Grove*, modifying her preliminary dates in Burkholder, *All Made of Tunes*, 103 and 443n20.

3. Burkholder, *All Made of Tunes*, 105–7, 111–13, 116–19, 120–24, 126–27, 128–29, and notes 26, 28, 32–35, 40, 42–46, 49, 54, 56, and 66 on pp. 444–48; Burkholder, "Symphonic Works of Charles Ives."

4. *Memos*, 87; Sinclair, 8–10; *Correspondence*, 54–55 and 294–96.

5. Sinclair, 8; Cowell and Cowell, *Charles Ives and His Music*, 135; Swafford, 427–29; *Correspondence*, 355; Perlis, 98.

6. See Walter Frisch, *Brahms and the Principle of Developing Variation* (Berkeley: University of California Press, 1984).

7. Ives had played a transcription of the prelude to *Tristan und Isolde* on the organ; see Weber, "Charles Ives and Nineteenth Century American Church Music," 41 (cited in chapter 2).

8. *Memos*, 155.

9. Perlis, 98. This contradicts the story in Cowell and Cowell, *Charles Ives and His Music*, 136, that he listened "on the maid's little radio in the kitchen" and did "an awkward little jig of pleasure and vindication."

10. *Correspondence*, 357.

11. Quoted in *Ives World*, 358. On the revisions to the ending, see Sinclair, 10, and Magee, 175–80.

12. *Correspondence*, 356.

13. Quoted in *Ives World*, 352, 354, and 355.

14. For Brahms, see *Memos*, 95.

15. *Memos*, 237.

16. Rossiter, 38–39; Feder, 76; Swafford, 17 and 41; Magee, 13; Budiansky, 41 and 71–72.

17. See Burkholder, *Charles Ives: The Ideas Behind the Music*, 34–36, 40, and 99; *Memos*, 53 and 250–52; *Essays*, 79; and Perlis, 59.

18. *Correspondence*, 294–95.

19. Antonín Dvořák, "Music in America," *Harper's* 90 (February 1895), partly reprinted in *Composers on Music: Eight Centuries of Writings*, edited by Josiah Fisk (Boston: Northeastern University Press, 1997), 163; Joseph Horowitz, *Moral Fire: Musical Portraits from America's Fin de Siècle* (Berkeley: University of California Press, 2012), 36, 91, 187, 200, and 235.

20. Magee, 88.

CHAPTER 7: A NEW FORM

1. *Memos*, 87n8; Swafford, 193; Sinclair, 669; Feder, 215.

2. *Memos*, 278 and 329; Feder, 215–17; Swafford 213–14; Magee, 94–96; Budiansky, 148.

3. *Memos*, 278.

4. Sinclair, 722–23; *Memos*, 279; Rossiter, 88; Swafford, 216–17.

5. *Memos*, 279; Perlis, 48–49; Rossiter, 88; Feder, 220–22; Swafford, 273–76, quoting p. 275; Magee, 120–24; Budiansky, 164–66; *Correspondence*, 74–75 and 290–92, quoting pp. 75 and 290. Edith's letter is a joy to read.

6. Perlis, 116.

7. See also the vivid descriptions of Ives's working methods by Swafford, 154, and Budiansky, 145–46.

8. Sinclair, 12–14; *Memos*, 55, 150, and 160; Burkholder, *All Made of Tune*, 143, 151, 238, 450n5, 451n8, and 466n41; Burkholder, "Symphonic Works of Charles Ives." Ives changed the date from 1911 to 1904 in his later work-lists, but there is no corroboration for the earlier date. Mark Zobel, *The Third Symphony of Charles Ives*, CMS Sourcebooks in Music 6 (Hillsdale, NY: Pendragon Press, 2009), offers background and an interpretation of the work.

9. See *Memos*, 55, and Sinclair, 14. Omitted in the 1947 and 1964 published scores, the shadow parts were included as a performance option in the 1990 critical edition. See Charles Ives, *Symphony No. 3: "The Camp Meeting,"* edited by Kenneth Singleton (New York: Associated Music Publishers, 1990).

10. On cumulative form, see Burkholder, *All Made of Tunes*, 137–266.

11. Arnold Schoenberg, "Folkloristic Symphonies," in *Style and Idea: Selected Writings of Arnold Schoenberg*, edited by Leonard Stein with translations by Leo Black (London: Faber & Faber, 1975), 164.

12. *Memos*, 69.

13. Burkholder, "The Organist in Ives," 302–5 (cited in chapter 2).

14. Burkholder, "The Organist in Ives," 301–2.

15. These dates follow those in *Grove*, based on Gayle Sherwood Magee's revisions of her preliminary dates in Burkholder, *All Made of Tunes*, 154, 163, 170, 174, 177–78, 181, 193, 200, 201, 206, 234, 236–37, 315, 452n17, 454n28, 454n31, 455n39, 456n45, 458n65, 460n81, 460n83–84, and 465–66n37–39. See Ives's dates in *Memos*, 67–72, 150–51, 156, 160, 161–62, 163, and 165, and Sinclair, 145, 147–49, 150–51, 153–54, and 156–58.

16. See for instance the reviews by Anthony Tommasini, "Review: Jeremy Denk and Stefan Jackiw's Lessons in Ives's Nostalgic Sonatas," *New York Times* (November 22, 2015), and by Andrew L. Pincus, "When It Comes to Charles Ives, Play It Slugarocko," *The Berkshire Eagle* (July 26, 2019), at https://www.berkshireeagle.com/stories/when-it-comes-to-charles-ives-play-it-slugarocko,580518.

17. *Memos*, 72.

18. Burkholder, *All Made of Tunes*, 455n39.

19. *Memos*, 69.

20. *Memos*, 69.

21. *Memos*, 69.

22. *Memos*, 68.

23. *Memos*, 70.

24. *Memos*, 123.

25. *Memos*, 118.

26. *Memos*, 69–70 and 118; Sinclair, 148, 151, 154, and 157; reviews in *Ives World*, 291–92 and 337.

27. *Memos*, 121; *Correspondence*, 54–56.

28. *Ives World*, 338–39.

29. Sinclair, 13–14; Feder, 347–48; Swafford, 421–22.

CHAPTER 8: AMERICAN HOLIDAYS

1. *Memos*, 95.

2. Quoted at greater length in chapter 5 above and in Burkholder, *Charles Ives: The Ideas behind the Music*, 96, and Feder, 213–14. See also Swafford, 188–90.

3. See Magee, 126.

4. *Memos*, 96.

5. *Memos*, 94.

6. Swafford, 229.

7. *Memos*, 95.

8. *Memos*, 97–99, 150, and 160; Sinclair, 22–23; Burkholder, *All Made of Tunes*, 497–98n42.

9. *Memos*, 98.

10. Quoted, in slightly different versions, in *Memos*, 96–97n1, and in Charles E. Ives, *Washington's Birthday*, ed. James B. Sinclair (New York: Associated Music Publishers, 1991), 31. Ives's quotation from Whittier reverses the first two lines; see Burkholder, "Symphonic Works of Charles Ives."

11. *Memos*, 97–98.

12. On collage, see Burkholder, *All Made of Tunes*, 369–71 and 376–85.

13. *Memos*, 96.

14. *Memos*, 97.

15. *Essays*, 3.

16. Burkholder, "The Organist in Ives," 285–89 (cited in chapter 2).

17. Sinclair, 24–26; Burkholder, *All Made of Tunes*, 486n14.

18. *Memos*, 102–3.

19. *Memos*, 103; Burkholder, "The Organist in Ives," 269–71.

20. Budiansky, 27.

21. Charles E. Ives, *Decoration Day*, ed. James B. Sinclair (New York: Peer International, 1989), 33.

22. *Memos*, 102; Stuart Feder, "Decoration Day: A Boyhood Memory of Charles Ives," *Musical Quarterly* 66 (April 1980): 234–61; Feder, 237–43; and Swafford, 251–53.

23. *Memos*, 104, 150, and 160; Sinclair, 26–28; Burkholder, *All Made of Tunes*, 495n21.

24. Perlis, 38. This probably happened when the Ives & Myrick offices moved from 38 Nassau Street to 46 Cedar Street in late April 1923, or possibly later moves in 1926 or 1930; the previous move in 1914 is too early. See Sinclair, 723, for the addresses.

25. Sinclair, 27; Rossiter, 230–32.

26. *Memos*, 104. Ives's probable source is the end of chapter 28 of *Huckleberry Finn* (1884), but according to William Safire, Twain was quoting a saying that originated in Britain and was apparently first published in *Punch* in 1846. See William Safire, "On Language: You Pays Yer Money," *The New York Times Magazine* (February 28, 1988), 16.

27. *Memos*, 104n1.

28. Translated in Rossiter, 230–31.

29. *Memos*, 38–39.

30. Sinclair, 245–46 and 30–31; *Memos*, 95; Burkholder, *All Made of Tunes*, 456n50.

31. See Rossiter, 101–2 and 107, and the title of Budiansky's *Mad Music: Charles Ives, The Nostalgic Rebel*, among others.

CHAPTER 9: AMERICAN HISTORIES

1. Denise Von Glahn, "From Country to City in the Music of Charles Ives," in *The Sounds of Place: Music and the American Cultural Landscape* (Boston: Northeastern University Press, 2003), 66–67, quoting p. 66.

2. Sinclair, 41; Perlis, 147–51; Rossiter, 223–25; Feder, 321and 325; Swafford, 377–79 and 380–81; Budiansky, 208–11.

3. Perlis, 150–51.

4. *Ives World*, 228–29.

5. Sinclair, 41; Perlis, 150; Swafford, 381–83.

6. Rossiter, 225–26; *Ives World*, 299.

7. Translated in *Ives World*, 301–2.

8. Translated in *Ives World*, 303–4.

9. Sinclair, 40–41; Rossiter, 237, 254, and 298–99.

10. Sinclair, 39–40; Burkholder, *All Made of Tunes*, 481n33; Burkholder, *Charles Ives: The Ideas Behind the Music*, 34–36 and 99–100; Feder, 231–37; Swafford, 218–19; Denise Von Glahn Cooney, "New Sources for *The 'St. Gaudens' in Boston Common (Colonel Robert Gould Shaw and his Colored Regiment)*," *The Musical Quarterly* 81 (Spring 1997): 13–50; *Correspondence*, 295. Magee, 125–26, links the movement to World War I as well as the anniversary of the Civil War.

11. See Von Glahn Cooney, "New Sources," 28–42.

12. Charles E. Ives, *Three Places in New England: An Orchestral Set* (Boston: C. C. Birchard, 1935; repr. Bryn Mawr, PA: Mercury Music), 20. See *Memos*, 84–85, for the words to the song.

13. Sinclair, 39–41, 89–90, and 106–7; Burkholder, *All Made of Tunes*, 386–89 and 499n56. Denise Von Glahn Cooney offers an analysis in "A Sense of Place: Charles Ives and 'Putnam's Camp, Redding, Connecticut,'" *American Music* 14 (Fall 1996): 276–312. Magee, 125–26, links the movement to World War I. See also Feder, 244–47, and Swafford, 167–68 and 243–45. Brewster's libretto is in *Memos*, 281–317.

14. Perlis, 16; Rossiter, 15–16 and 100–101; Feder, 59 and 78–79; Swafford, 34–35; Magee, 18.

15. *Memos*, 87.

16. The poem was first published in 1897; see Von Glahn, "From Country to City," 72.

17. *Memos*, 87n8; Sinclair, 40 and 399; Burkholder, *All Made of Tunes*, 482–83n50; Swafford, 193, 242, and 245–47. For analyses, see Starr, *Union of Diversities*, 115–26, and Von Glahn, "From Country to City," 64–92.

18. Robert Underwood Johnson, *Poems*, 2nd ed. (New York: Century, 1908), 105–7; H. Wiley Hitchcock, "Ives as Songwriter and Lyricist," in Charles Ives, *129 Songs*, edited by H. Wiley Hitchcock, Music of the United States of America 12 (Middleton, WI: American Musicological Society and A-R Editions, 2004), lx–lxii.

19. See Burkholder, *All Made of Tunes*, 327–30. Despite Nicolas Slonimsky's claim in Perlis, 152, Ives's melody is not based on the opening of Beethoven's Fifth Symphony.

20. As Von Glahn argues in "From Country to City," 64–92.

21. Sinclair, 44–45; Burkholder, *All Made of Tunes*, 481n31; Charles Hiroshi Garrett, "Charles Ives's *Four Ragtime Dances* and 'True American Music,'" in *Struggling to Define a Nation: American Music and the Twentieth Century* (Berkeley: University of California Press, 2008), 17–47; Burkholder, "Symphonic Works of Charles Ives."

22. *Memos*, 92; Sinclair, 45–46; Burkholder, *All Made of Tunes*, 212–14 and 461n94; Burkholder, "Symphonic Works of Charles Ives."

23. Gayle Sherwood Magee's dates in Burkholder, *All Made of Tunes*, 471n83. See the detailed analysis of this movement in Von Glahn, "From Country to City," 92–109, and shorter accounts in Swafford, 269–71, and Magee, 118–20.

24. *Memos*, 92.

25. Gayle Magee, "'Every Man in New York': Charles Ives and the First World War," in *Over Here, Over There: Transatlantic Conversations on the Music of World War I*,

edited by William Brooks, Christina Bashford, and Gayle Magee (Urbana: University of Illinois Press, 2019), 37–44.

26. *Memos*, 92–93. Italic parentheses used to mark an insertion have been omitted.

27. See Burkholder, "Symphonic Works of Charles Ives."

CHAPTER 10: AMERICAN LITERATURE

1. Two indispensable guides to the *Concord Sonata* are Kyle Gann, *Charles Ives's Concord: Essays After a Sonata* (Urbana: University of Illinois Press, 2017), and Geoffrey Block, *Ives: Concord Sonata* (Cambridge: Cambridge University Press, 1996). For overviews, see Feder, 260–72, and Swafford, 256–66. Magee, 132–37, reads the sonata in relation to the Civil War and World War I. On his skill as a player, see Burkholder, "The Organist in Ives," 264–71 (cited in chapter 2). Ives's recordings are available on the CD *Ives Plays Ives*, cited below.

2. *Memos*, 65, 76–77, 81, 163, and 199; Sinclair, 64–65, 85–89, 92–95, 195, 590, 597–99, 612, and 614; Burkholder, *Charles Ives: The Ideas Behind the Music*, 74–75 and 100. The *Emerson Overture* (or *Emerson Concerto*) was reconstructed in the 1990s by David G. Porter and has been recorded.

3. Sinclair, 193–94; *Essays*, 84n; *Memos*, 79–83, 195, and 202; Burkholder, *All Made of Tunes*, 458n71; Swafford, 256; Block, *Ives: Concord Sonata*, 4 and 20–30; Magee, 132; Gann, *Charles Ives's Concord*, 7–10.

4. Budiansky, 170–76, 193–95, and 213–17, based on Stephen Budiansky, "Ives, Diabetes, and His 'Exhausted Vein' of Composition," *American Music* 31 (Spring 2013): 1–25. See also *Correspondence*, 98–99 and 102–11.

5. Sinclair, 193; Burkholder, *All Made of Tunes*, 458n71; *Memos*, 82; Burkholder, *Charles Ives: The Ideas Behind the Music*, 110–12; Rossiter, 180 and 183; Swafford, 289–90 and 305; Magee, 141 and 146–48; Budiansky, 177–79, 183, and 185–86; Gann, *Charles Ives's Concord*, 10–11. On revisions to *Concord Sonata* prior to printing, see Geoffrey Block, "Remembrances of Dissonances Past: The Two Published Editions of Ives's *Concord Sonata*," in *Ives Studies*, edited by Philip Lambert (Cambridge: Cambridge University Press, 1997), 27–50. For Johnson's comment, see the entry for September 19, 1777, from James Boswell, *Boswell's Life of Johnson*, edited by George B. Hill, rev. ed. L. F. Powell, vol. 3 (Oxford: Clarendon Press, 1934), 167.

6. *Essays*, xxv. On *Essays*, see Swafford, 291–301, and the detailed discussion of the individual essays in Gann, *Charles Ives's Concord*, 27–39, 57–73, 135–36, 210–16, 230–41, and 269–99.

7. *Essays*, 3–8, quoting 3, 4, and 7.

8. *Essays*, 70–102, 75, 77, and 85.

9. *Essays*, 11–36, quoting 11, 34, and 29–30.

10. *Essays*, 39–42.

11. *Essays*, 45–48.

12. *Essays*, 51–69, quoting 51 and 53–54.

13. Gann, *Charles Ives's Concord*, 27.

14. Rossiter, 290–91; Block, "Remembrances of Dissonances Past"; Block, *Ives: Concord Sonata*, 28–29; Swafford, 415–16; Budiansky, 245–47; Gann, *Charles Ives's Concord*, 10, 17, 20–22, 122–34, 139–56, and especially 345–72.

15. *Memos*, 191 and 200–201. See also Gann, *Charles Ives's Concord*, 351 and 368–72, on why the 1947 edition is better and what variants performers might consider.

16. See also Block, "Remembrances of Dissonances Past," 43, and Gann, *Charles Ives's Concord*, 370.

17. Gann, *Charles Ives's Concord*, 40–56, traces the theme's role through every movement and links it to an overall harmonic plan.

18. The CD is *Ives Plays Ives*, CRI CD 810 (New York: Composer Recordings, Inc., 1999; rereleased as New World Records 80642-2, 2006), track 42. The theme appears at 3:58 and ends at 4:42; the movement concludes at 4:54. On YouTube or Spotify, search for "Ives Plays Ives The Alcotts."

19. For these relationships and an analysis of the movement, see Burkholder, *All Made of Tunes*, 195–200 and 356, especially Example 5.22 on p. 198. See also Block, 32–41 and 80–84, for the relationship of this theme to its sources and other motives in the sonata. Some analysts have suggested borrowings in the first half of the theme, but none have been widely accepted.

20. Burkholder, "Stylistic Heterogeneity," especially 168–70 and 189–97 (cited in chapter 1).

21. *Essays*, 47–48.

22. *Charles Ives: The Hundredth Anniversary*, Columbia M4 32504 (New York: Columbia Records/CBS, 1974). Ives's performance of *The Alcotts* is available on the CD *Ives Plays Ives*, cited above.

23. Weber, "Charles Ives and Nineteenth Century American Church Music," 41 (cited in chapter 2).

24. *Memos*, 77.

25. See Gann, *Charles Ives's Concord*, 113–19.

26. See also Block, *Ives: Concord Sonata*, 42–45 and 85. Gann, *Charles Ives's Concord*, offers a somewhat different analysis related to sonata form on pp. 74–110 and a comparison with the *Emerson Concerto* on pp. 111–22. On the Tolerance theme, see *Memos*, 199n3.

27. Burkholder, *All Made of Tunes*, 352–54, especially p. 353.

28. *Essays*, 22–24.

29. Quoted in *Memos*, 199n3.

30. Gann, *Charles Ives's Concord*, 60.

31. Charles Ives, *Piano Sonata No. 2: "Concord, Mass., 1840–1860,"* 2nd ed. (New York: Associated Music Publishers, 1947), 73; Block, *Ives: Concord Sonata*, 69–71 and 85; Gann, *Charles Ives's Concord*, 83.

32. This happened at Denk's recital in Auer Concert Hall in Bloomington, Indiana, on March 27, 2008.

33. Ives, *Piano Sonata No. 2*, 73.

34. *Essays*, 42. See also his description in *Memos*, 187–88, which suggests a series of images for the movement; Block, *Ives: Concord Sonata*, 72–74, 103n20, and 103–4n22;

and Gann, *Charles Ives's Concord*, 135–209, who offers a complete formal outline in relation to such images.

35. Ives wrote in *Memos*, 81, that these high clusters "originally were intended to be played by a second piano off the stage," giving "a kind of sound of distant reverberations that one may hear in the woods under certain conditions."

36. Ives writes in a note, "A Drum Corps gets the best of the Band—for a moment"; Ives, *Piano Sonata No. 2*, 73.

37. *Essays*, 67–69. See Block, *Ives: Concord Sonata*, 75–78, and Gann, *Charles Ives's Concord*, 243–45, for parallels in the music.

38. These passages seem more train-like than the passage, just before the "Concord bell," where Ives marked "a train passes by" in one copy of the sonata; see Gann, *Charles Ives's Concord*, 245. Perhaps there is more than one train.

39. *Correspondence*, 56–59, 67, 69–74, 77–78, and 80–92; Rossiter, 183–85; Swafford, 318–23; Budiansky, 187–93.

40. *Ives World*, 278–80 and 284–88; Rossiter, 186–87; Block, *Ives: Concord Sonata*, 7–9. Emphasis original.

41. *Ives World*, 214–16; *Correspondence*, 83–84; Rossiter, 196–97.

42. *Ives World*, 280–84 and 216–17; Rossiter, 198–200; Block, *Ives: Concord Sonata*, 9–10.

43. Sinclair, 194; *Memos*, 201n17; Gann, *Charles Ives's Concord*, 15–17; *Correspondence*, 89.

44. *Memos*, 198; Sinclair, 194–95; Rossiter, 277–78; Block, *Ives: Concord Sonata*, 11–12; Budiansky, 236–39; Gann, *Charles Ives's Concord*, 18–19; *Ives World*, 313–16.

45. Rossiter, 278–80; Swafford, 411; Block, *Ives: Concord Sonata*, 12–13; Magee, 166–68; *Ives World*, 316–21. By coincidence, Gilman had been acquainted with Harmony in Hartford in the 1890s, and he was surprised to learn that she was married to Ives; see Swafford, 411.

46. Sinclair, 194–95; Rossiter, 280–81; *Ives World*, 323–24 and 326–28.

47. Rossiter, 284–87; Block, *Ives: Concord Sonata*, 13–15; *Ives World*, 321–22 and 330–37.

CHAPTER 11: TRANSCENDENT JOURNEYS

1. Starr, *Union of Diversities*, 33–35.

2. Sinclair, 142–43; Burkholder, *All Made of Tunes*, 348 and 441n60.

3. *Memos*, 73–74.

4. *Correspondence*, 30–31.

5. See Catherine Parsons Smith, "'A Distinguishing Virility': Feminism and Modernism in American Art Music," in *Cecilia Reclaimed: Feminist Perspectives on Gender and Music*, edited by Susan C. Cook and Judy S. Tsou (Urbana: University of Illinois Press, 1994), 90–106; and Judith Tick, "Charles Ives and Gender Ideology," in *Musicology and Difference: Gender and Sexuality in Music Scholarship*, edited by Ruth A. Solie (Berkeley: University of California Press, 1993), 83–106. For Ives's respect for women he worked with, see the interviews in Perlis, 48–50, 62–64, 114–19, 190–92,

and 209–11; for his support for the right of women to vote, see his praise for "suffrage extension" in *Essays*, 34; for his depiction of a strong woman devoted to hymn singing, see his portrait of "Aunt Sarah" in *Essays*, 80–81. Tom C. Owens points out that some of Ives's seemingly gendered language relates to class rather than gender; see *Correspondence*, 125–26.

6. *Memos*, 26–27n1; Mark Tucker, "Of Men and Mountains: Ives in the Adirondacks," in *Ives World*, 161–96; Swafford, 237–41.

7. Charles E. Ives, *String Quartet No. 2*, ed. Malcolm Goldstein (New York: Peer International, 2016), 8–10.

8. Ives, *String Quartet No. 2*, 11–16.

9. *Ives World*, 345; Feder, 346–47. On Harrison's work on the Second Quartet, see *Correspondence*, 306–9.

10. Charles E. Ives, *The Fourth Symphony for Large Orchestra*, in *New Music* 2, no. 2 (January 1929): ii.

11. Reprinted in Charles E. Ives, *Symphony No. 4*, edited by James B. Sinclair, William Brooks, Kenneth Singleton, and Wayne D. Shirley (New York: Associated Music Publishers, 2011), xiii.

12. See Thomas M. Brodhead, "Ives's *Celestial Railroad* and His Fourth Symphony," *American Music* 12 (Winter 1994): 389–424, especially 394–410 and 415–19; Sinclair, 18 and 221; Burkholder, *All Made of Tunes*, 490–91n56 and 500n61; Swafford, 342–45; Magee, 156–57; and Burkholder, "Symphonic Works of Charles Ives." Swafford, 349–64 (with extensive notes on 491–96) offers an accessible analysis.

13. Brodhead, "Ives's *Celestial Railroad*," 389–90. The following analysis draws on Brodhead's discussion of music in relation to this program. See also Gann, *Charles Ives's Concord*, 139–56.

14. Sinclair, 18; *Memos*, 12 and 68; Cowell and Cowell, *Charles Ives and His Music*, 165, drawing on Elliott Carter, "The Case of Mr. Ives," *Modern Music* 16 (1939): 173; Feder, 319; Swafford, 366–68; Magee, 149–50; Budiansky, 203.

15. Rossiter, 208–9; Swafford, 368.

16. *Ives World*, 293–96.

17. Sinclair, 18–19; Rossiter, 248, 304, and 366n52–53; Swafford, 368, 394, and 407; Budiansky, 204–6.

18. Ives, *Symphony No. 4*; Charles E. Ives, *Symphony No. 4*, performance edition, realized and edited by Thomas M. Brodhead (New York: Associated Music Publishers, 2020).

CHAPTER 12: COLLECTING SONGS AND LATE WORKS

1. Sinclair, 657. On *114 Songs*, see Feder, 309–17, who reads it as autobiography, and Swafford, 325–28. H. Wiley Hitchcock offers a typology of the songs in *114 Songs* in "Ives as Songwriter and Lyricist," xvii–lxxi (cited in chapter 9).

2. Hitchcock, "Ives as Songwriter and Lyricist," xlii. Hitchcock's count of new and adapted works from 1919–1921 (pp. xli–xlv and lxvi) differs from mine due to uncertainty about dates.

3. Ives, *114 Songs*, 260 (cited in chapter 3). Hitchcock, "Ives as Songwriter and Lyricist," lii–lv, identifies all the poets, including both Iveses.

4. Sinclair, 496.

5. Ives, *114 Songs*, 206 and 68; Burkholder, *All Made of Tunes*, 278–81.

6. Sinclair, 410–11; Magee, "'Every Man in New York,'" 45–46 (cited in chapter 9). See the different interpretations of the war songs in Burkholder, *All Made of Tunes*, 313–15 and 363–64; Alan Houtchens and Janis P. Stout, "'Scarce Heard Amidst the Guns Below': Intertextuality and Meaning in Charles Ives's War Songs," *Journal of Musicology* 15 (Winter 1997): 66–97; and Magee, 126–31.

7. Sinclair, 496–97; Rossiter, 44; Feder, 39 and 104; Burkholder, *All Made of Tunes*, 16–17; Budiansky, 52–54. Sinclair, Rossiter, and Budiansky say that it was the family dog, Feder that it was "the family cat, Chin-Chin."

8. Burkholder, *All Made of Tunes*, 286–87.

9. Burkholder, *All Made of Tunes*, 291–94; Magee, 144–46.

10. Burkholder, *All Made of Tunes*, 83–84.

11. Charles Ives, "Some 'Quarter-tone' Impressions," in *Essays*, 117.

12. Sinclair, 658; Rossiter, 180–83; Swafford, 325; Budiansky, 183–86. The first printing in August 1922 was of five hundred copies bound in green paper; the second printing of a thousand copies bound in blue buckram came in April 1923.

13. *Memos*, 126–27. One such reaction is in *Correspondence*, 68.

14. *Ives World*, 288–90 and 213; *Correspondence*, 60–69, 75–80, and 91–92, quoting p. 75. See also Rossiter, 185–87, and Swafford, 333–35.

15. See the chronology in Sinclair, 672–79; published song collections on pp. 658–63; and individual songs on pp. 334, 338, 341–43, 346, 348–49, 355–58, 366, 369, 374–75, 381, 387, 390–91, 393–95, 399–401, 405–7, 413, 417–19, 421, 423–25, 430–32, 439, 447–51, 464, 467, 472, 474, 478–80, 486, 490, 494–95, 511, 514–15, 522–23, 527, 530–33, 536–37, and 542–45. For the Madden concerts, see Swafford, 335 and 339, and Magee, 142–46. Charles Ives, *Seven Songs* (New York: Cos Cob Press, 1932; repr. Association Music Publishers, 1957). See also Rossiter, 238–40; *Correspondence*, 64.

16. Cowell and Cowell, *Charles Ives and His Music*, 99–100; Rossiter, 198–200; Swafford, 333. I have this copy of *Essays Before a Sonata*, a unique document.

17. Sinclair, 465; Burkholder, *All Made of Tunes*, 279.

18. *Memos*, 110–11; Burkholder, *All Made of Tunes*, 276 and 473n23. Ives claimed that the third movement was based on a piece for strings composed years earlier, but all the sketches for all three movements date from 1923–1924, and annotations for string scoring are on an ink copy of the completed movement, suggesting that the string version came later. See *Memos*, 163; Sinclair, 236–37 and 594; Burkholder, *All Made of Tunes*, 472–73n22; and *Grove*.

19. "Editor's Notes," in Charles Ives, *Psalm 90*, edited by John Kirkpatrick and Gregg Smith (Bryn Mawr, PA: Merion Music, 1970), 3. Ives dated *Psalm 90* 1923–1924 (*Memos*, 148), and all the sources are from then; Sherwood, "Redating Ives's Choral Sources," 90 and 100, calls *Psalm 90* "entirely new" in 1923–1924. References to working on "part of the 90th [Psalm]" with his father (*Memos*, 47) and to a copy in the choir library at Central Presbyterian Church suggest that an earlier setting may

have existed, but the sketches from 1923 indicate that Ives was composing a new piece, not reconstructing an old one. See Sinclair, 271–72, and Burkholder, *All Made of Tunes*, 493n75. On *Psalm 90*, see also Swafford, 346–47.

20. *Essays*, 97; quoted above in chapter 1.

EPILOGUE

1. *Memos*, 279; *Correspondence*, 128.

2. Cowell and Cowell, *Charles Ives and His Music*, 98. The next three paragraphs draw on ibid., 98–123; Rossiter, 206–311; Feder, 319–21 and 346–50; Swafford, 335–40, 369–73, 377–87, and 395–430; Sinclair, 674–83; Magee, 149–56; and Budiansky, 199–253. See also *Correspondence*, 140–89 and 209–366, and Perlis, 123–226, for primary documents related to his advocates and collaborators.

3. Osborne, "Charles Ives the Organist," 61 (cited in chapter 2).

4. Budiansky, 223; David C. Paul, *Charles Ives in the Mirror: American Histories of an Iconic Composer* (Urbana: University of Illinois Press, 2013).

5. See Rabinowitz, "Fictional Music" (cited in chapter 1); the comparison to Beethoven and others in Burkholder, *All Made of Tunes*, 415–17; and J. Peter Burkholder, "Rule-Breaking as a Rhetorical Sign," in *Festa musicologica: Essays in Honor of George J. Buelow*, edited by Thomas J. Mathiesen and Benito V. Rivera (New York: Pendragon Press, 1995), 369–89.

6. *Essays*, 81.

Selected Reading

IVES'S WRITINGS

Ives, Charles. *Essays Before a Sonata, The Majority, and Other Writings.* Ed. Howard Boatwright. New York: W. W. Norton, 1970.
    Collection of Ives's writings, including the essays written to introduce the *Concord Sonata* and several smaller works.
Ives, Charles. *Memos.* Ed. and with appendices by John Kirkpatrick. New York: W. W. Norton, 1972.
    Ives's informal reminiscences and discussions of dozens of pieces, with numerous helpful appendices by John Kirkpatrick.
Ives, Charles. *Selected Correspondence of Charles Ives.* Ed. Tom C. Owens. Berkeley: University of California Press, 2007.
    Letters to and from Ives, full of interesting insights on Ives, his family, and his friends.

BIOGRAPHIES

Budiansky, Stephen. *Mad Music: Charles Ives, the Nostalgic Rebel.* Lebanon, NH: ForeEdge, 2014.
    A recent biography with new information on Ives's health.
Cowell, Henry, and Sidney Cowell. *Charles Ives and His Music.* Rev. ed. London: Oxford University Press, 1969.
    The first biography of Ives, written by close associates. While more a publicity release than objective biography, it is still valuable for the account of Ives's career and the analyses of his music.
Feder, Stuart. *Charles Ives, "My Father's Song": A Psychoanalytic Biography.* New Haven: Yale University Press, 1992.
    A biography from a psychoanalytic perspective, focusing on Ives's relationship with his father.
Feder, Stuart. *The Life of Charles Ives.* Cambridge and New York: Cambridge University Press, 1999.
    A brief biography.

Horowitz, Joseph. *Moral Fire: Musical Portraits from America's Fin de Siècle*. Berkeley: University of California Press, 2012.

　　Fascinating look at four figures active in the late nineteenth century who believed in music as a force for moral values, including Ives alongside a patron, a music critic, and a feminist writer.

Magee, Gayle Sherwood. *Charles Ives Reconsidered*. Urbana: University of Illinois Press, 2008.

　　A biography based on the revised chronology of Ives's works, full of fresh insights.

Rossiter, Frank R. *Charles Ives and His America*. New York: Liveright, 1975.

　　A thoroughly researched biography, once the standard. Rossiter's focus on psychosexual issues and his argument that Ives wrote dissonant music to assert his masculinity lend it a contentious tone.

Swafford, Jan. *Charles Ives: A Life with Music*. New York: W. W. Norton, 1996.

　　A warm-hearted view of Ives, which quickly became the standard biography.

IVES'S MUSIC AND THOUGHT

Block, Geoffrey. *Ives: Concord Sonata*. Cambridge and New York: Cambridge University Press, 1996.

　　A study of the piece that made Ives's reputation, from a number of perspectives.

Block, Geoffrey, and J. Peter Burkholder, eds. *Charles Ives and the Classical Tradition*. New Haven: Yale University Press, 1996.

　　A collection of essays arguing that Ives's music is rooted in the European tradition and parallels the music of his European contemporaries in significant ways.

Burkholder, J. Peter. *All Made of Tunes: Charles Ives and the Uses of Musical Borrowing*. New Haven: Yale University Press, 1995.

　　A detailed study of Ives's uses of existing music across his career, showing his evolution from traditional uses to extraordinary ones.

Burkholder, J. Peter. *Charles Ives: The Ideas Behind the Music*. New Haven: Yale University Press, 1985.

　　A brief intellectual biography, examining what concerns Ives sought to address in *Essays Before a Sonata*, why those issues were important to him, and who were his important influences.

Burkholder, J. Peter. "The Symphonic Works of Charles Ives." In *The Symphonic Repertoire, Volume 5: The Symphony in the Americas*, ed. Brian Hart (Bloomington: Indiana University Press, 2021).

　　A deep dive into all six works Ives called "symphony" plus the three he called "orchestral sets." Part of a multivolume reference work on the history of the symphony.

Burkholder, J. Peter, ed. *Charles Ives and His World*. Princeton: Princeton University Press, 1996.

　　Essays on Ives, selected correspondence, and early reviews and articles on Ives.

Gann, Kyle. *Charles Ives's Concord: Essays After a Sonata*. Urbana: University of Illinois Press, 2017.

A fascinating study of the *Concord* Sonata and its accompanying *Essays Before a Sonata*, illuminating Ives's ideas, music, and compositional procedures.

Hertz, David Michael. *Angels of Reality: Emersonian Unfoldings in Wright, Stevens, and Ives.* Carbondale and Edwardsville: Southern Illinois University Press, 1993.
An examination of the influence of Emerson and Transcendentalism on Ives, Frank Lloyd Wright, and Wallace Stevens.

Hitchcock, H. Wiley. *Ives: A Survey of the Music.* Brooklyn: Institute for Studies in American Music, 1977.
An excellent brief introduction to Ives's music, organized by genre.

Hitchcock, H. Wiley, and Vivian Perlis, eds. *An Ives Celebration: Papers and Panels of the Charles Ives Centennial Festival-Conference.* Urbana: University of Illinois Press, 1977.
Papers and panels from the 1974 Centennial Conference.

Johnson, Timothy. *Baseball and the Music of Charles Ives: A Proving Ground.* Lanham, Md.: Scarecrow Press, 2004.
What baseball meant to Ives, and how he used it as an inspiration for his music.

Lambert, Philip. *The Music of Charles Ives.* New Haven: Yale University Press, 1997.
Technical discussion of Ives's characteristic musical procedures.

Lambert, Philip, ed. *Ives Studies.* Cambridge and New York: Cambridge University Press, 1997.
A collection of essays on Ives.

McDonald, Matthew. *Breaking Time's Arrow: Experiment and Expression in the Music of Charles Ives.* Bloomington: Indiana University Press, 2014.
Analytical studies of several Ives pieces, seeking to demonstrate how he manipulated time in his music.

Nicholls, David. *American Experimental Music, 1890–1940.* Cambridge: Cambridge University Press, 1990.
A study of experimental music in the United States that begins with a chapter on Ives.

Paul, David C. *Charles Ives in the Mirror: American Histories of an Iconic Composer.* Urbana: University of Illinois Press, 2013.
A history of how Ives's music and career have been regarded and described by his biographers, by historians, and by musicologists, showing a fascinating pattern of change over time.

Perry, Rosalie Sandra. *Charles Ives and the American Mind.* Kent, Ohio: Kent State University Press, 1974.
A study that links Ives to trends in American aesthetics and philosophy, including Transcendentalism, realism, revivalism, the social gospel, and pragmatism.

Solie, Ruth, ed. *Musicology and Difference: Gender and Sexuality in Music Scholarship.* Berkeley: University of California Press, 1993.
Includes an insightful essay on Ives and gender issues by Judith Tick.

Starr, Larry. *A Union of Diversities: Style in the Music of Charles Ives.* New York: Schirmer Books, 1992.
Examines stylistic diversity as an element of form and expression in Ives's music.

Von Glahn, Denise. *The Sounds of Place: Music and the American Cultural Landscape.* Boston: Northeastern University Press, 2003.

Looks at how American composers have evoked places in their music, including a chapter on Ives's *Three Places in New England* and *From Hanover Square North.*

Zobel, Mark. *The Third Symphony of Charles Ives.* Hillsdale, NY: Pendragon Press, 2009.

A study and interpretation of Ives's Third Symphony.

CATALOGUE AND SOURCE BOOKS

Henderson, Clayton. *The Charles Ives Tunebook.* 2nd ed. Bloomington: Indiana University Press, 2008.

A very useful book, gathering together the melodies to (almost) all the music Ives borrowed and indexing the borrowings in each Ives work. Use in tandem with the lists in Burkholder's *All Made of Tunes* and Sinclair's catalogue.

Perlis, Vivian. *Charles Ives Remembered: An Oral History.* New Haven: Yale University Press, 1974; repr., Urbana: University of Illinois Press, 2002.

An outstanding oral history, with transcripts from interviews with family, friends, business associates, and musical collaborators of Ives.

Sinclair, James B. *A Descriptive Catalogue of the Music of Charles Ives.* New Haven: Yale University Press, 1999.

The standard catalogue of Ives's music, with many useful features.

BIBLIOGRAPHIES AND RESEARCH GUIDES

Block, Geoffrey. *Charles Ives: A Bio-Bibliography.* New York: Greenwood Press, 1988.

An excellent annotated bibliography of materials on Ives, still useful though dated. For material after 1987, see Magee's guide.

Burk, James Mack. *A Charles Ives Omnibus.* Ed. Michael J. Budds. Hillsdale, NY: Pendragon Press, 2008.

A compendium of Ivesiana, including reviews, recordings, and Ives's appearances in film, art, literature, and more.

Magee, Gayle Sherwood. *Charles Ives: A Research and Information Guide.* New York: Routledge, 2010.

A bibliographic guide to writings on Ives, updating Block's *Bio-Bibliography.*

Selected Listening

To make it easy to find one or more recorded performances for each piece mentioned in this book, these recordings are grouped by genre and, within each group, presented in alphabetical order by artist. In the last four categories (Orchestral Music, Other Instrumental Music, Songs, and Choral Music), recordings are numbered and preceded by an alphabetical list of pieces, each followed by numbers indicating on which of the following CDs that piece appears. Many of the recordings listed here also include other pieces by Ives that are not mentioned in this book, which you are encouraged to explore as well. Information is given here for these recordings as released on CDs; most are also available via Spotify, YouTube, and other streaming services.

IVES PLAYS IVES

Ives, Charles, piano. *Ives Plays Ives*. CRI CD 810, 1999; New World Records 80642-2, 2006. CD. All the known recordings of Ives performing at the piano. Includes parts of the *Concord Sonata* (all of *The Alcotts* and excerpts from *Emerson* and *Hawthorne*) and the song *They Are There!*

CONCORD SONATA
(PIANO SONATA NO. 2: CONCORD, MASS., 1840–1860)

Aimard, Pierre-Laurent, piano. *Ives: Concord Sonata, Songs*. Warner Classics 2564 60297-2, 2004. CD.

Denk, Jeremy, piano. *Jeremy Denk Plays Ives*. Think Denk Media TDM 2567, 2010. CD.

Hamelin, Marc-André, piano. *Ives: Concord Sonata; Barber: Piano Sonata*. Hyperion CDA 67469, 2004. CD.

Kalish, Gilbert, piano. *Charles Ives: Piano Sonata No. 2, "Concord, Mass., 1840–60"*. Elektra Nonesuch 9 71337-2, 1977. CD.

Mayer, Steven, piano. *Charles Ives: Piano Sonata No. 2 "Concord"; The Celestial Railroad*. Naxos 8.559127, 2006. CD.

VIOLIN SONATAS NOS. 1–4

Dicterow, Glenn, and Israela Margalit, piano. *Songs, Piano Trio, Violin Sonatas Nos. 2 and 4*. EMI Classics 5099923444959, 2008. CD. [Nos. 2 and 4 only.]

Fulkerson, Gregory, violin, and Robert Shannon, piano. *Charles Ives: The Sonatas for Violin and Piano*. Bridge BCD 9024, 1991. CD.

Hahn, Hilary, violin, and Valentina Lisitsa, piano. *Charles Ives: Four Sonatas*. Deutsche Grammophon 477 9435, 2011. CD.

Thompson, Curt, violin, and Rodney Waters, piano. *Charles Ives: Violin Sonatas Nos. 1–4*. Naxos 8.559119, 2004. CD.

STRING QUARTETS NOS. 1 AND 2

Blair String Quartet. *String Quartets*. Naxos 8.559178, 2006. CD.

Emerson String Quartet. *Ives: String Quartets Nos. 1 and 2; Barber: String Quartet*. Deutsche Grammophon 435 864-2, 1992. CD.

Lydian String Quartet. *The String Quartets*. Centaur CRC 2069, 1990. CD.

ORCHESTRAL MUSIC

Central Park in the Dark: 2, 6, 12, 16, 17, 18, 21, 23
Country Band March: 18, 19
Emerson Concerto for Piano and Orchestra: 15
Orchestral Set No. 1: *Three Places in New England*: 1, 10, 12, 19, 20, 21, 24
Orchestral Set No. 2: 5, 10, 13, 24
Overture and March "1776": 18
Ragtime Dances: 19
Robert Browning Overture: 14
A Symphony: New England Holidays (complete): 1, 2, 12, 17, 24
  Washington's Birthday: 18
  Decoration Day: 9
  The Fourth of July: 9
  Thanksgiving and Forefathers' Day: 9
Symphony No. 1 in D Minor: 3, 6, 8, 11, 15
Symphony No. 2: 7, 8, 11, 14, 16
Symphony No. 3: *The Camp Meeting*: 5, 7, 13, 16, 18, 20, 21, 22, 23
Symphony No. 4: 3, 4, 6, 13, 22, 23
The Unanswered Question: 2, 4, 12, 17, 18, 20, 21, 23
Yale–Princeton Football Game: 9, 19

1. Baltimore Symphony Orchestra and Chorus, conducted by David Zinman. *Ives: Three Places in New England; New England Holidays; They Are There!* Argo 444 860-2, 1996. CD.

2. Chicago Symphony Orchestra and Chorus, conducted by Michael Tilson Thomas. *Charles Ives: Holiday Symphony; The Unanswered Question; Central Park in the Dark.* CBS Records Masterworks MK 42381, 1988. CD.
3. Chicago Symphony Orchestra and Chorus, conducted by Michael Tilson Thomas. *Charles Ives: Symphonies Nos. 1 and 4.* Sony Classical SK 44939, 1991. CD.
4. Cleveland Orchestra and Chorus, conducted by Christoph von Dohnányi. *Ives: Symphony No. 4; The Unanswered Question; Varèse: Amériques.* London 443 172-2, 1994. CD.
5. Concertgebouw Orchestra, conducted by Michael Tilson Thomas. *Charles Ives: Symphony No. 3/Orchestral Set No. 2.* CBS Records Masterworks MK 37823, 1985. CD.
6. Dallas Symphony Orchestra, conducted by Andrew Litton. *Ives: Symphonies Nos. 1 and 4; Central Park in the Dark.* Hyperion CDA 67540, 2006. CD.
7. Dallas Symphony Orchestra, conducted by Andrew Litton. *Ives: Symphonies Nos. 2 and 3; General William Booth Enters into Heaven.* Hyperion CDA 67525, 2006. CD.
8. Detroit Symphony Orchestra, conducted by Neeme Järvi. *Ives: Symphony No. 1; Symphony No. 2.* Chandos Classics CHAN 10031, 2002.
9. Malmö Symphony Orchestra and Chamber Chorus, conducted by James Sinclair. *Charles Ives: Decoration Day; Fourth of July; Thanksgiving.* Naxos 8.559370, 2009. CD.
10. Malmö Symphony Orchestra and Chamber Chorus, conducted by James Sinclair. *Charles Ives: The Three Orchestal Sets.* Naxos 8.559353, 2008. CD.
11. Melbourne Symphony Orchestra, conducted by Sir Andrew Davis. *Charles Ives: Symphonies Nos. 1 and 2.* Chandos CHSA 5152, 2015. CD.
12. Melbourne Symphony Orchestra, conducted by Sir Andrew Davis. *Charles Ives: A Symphony "New England Holidays"; Three Places in New England; Central Park in the Dark; The Unanswered Question.* Chandos CHSA 5163, 2016. CD.
13. Melbourne Symphony Orchestra, conducted by Sir Andrew Davis. *Charles Ives: Symphony No. 3: The Camp Meeting; Symphony No. 4; Orchestral Set No. 2.* Chandos CHSA 5174, 2017. CD.
14. Nashville Symphony Orchestra, conducted by Kenneth Schermerhorn. *Charles Ives: Symphony No. 2; Robert Browning Overture.* Naxos 8.559076, 2000. CD.
15. National Symphony Orchestra of Ireland, conducted by James Sinclair; Alan Feinberg, piano. *Charles Ives: Emerson Concerto; Symphony No. 1.* Naxos 8.559175, 2003. CD.
16. New York Philharmonic, conducted by Leonard Bernstein. *Ives: Symphonies No. 2 and 3; Central Park in the Dark.* Sony Classical SMK 47568, 1990. CD.
17. New York Philharmonic, conducted by Leonard Bernstein. *Contemplations.* Sony Classical SMK 60203, 1998. CD.
18. Northern Sinfonia, conducted by James Sinclair. *Charles Ives: Symphony No. 3; Washington's Birthday; Two Contemplations.* Naxos 8.559087, 2003. CD.
19. Orchestra New England, conducted by James Sinclair. *The Orchestral Music of Charles Ives.* Koch International Classics 3-7025-2, 1990. CD.
20. Orpheus Chamber Orchestra. *A Set of Pieces: Music by Charles Ives.* Deutsche Grammophon 439 869-2, 1994. CD.

21. Saint Louis Symphony Orchestra, conducted by Leonard Slatkin. *Ives: Symphony No. 3; The Unanswered Question; Three Places in New England.* RCA Victor Red Seal 09026-61222-2, 1992. CD.
22. San Francisco Symphony, conducted by Michael Tilson Thomas. *Charles Ives: Symphony No. 3: The Camp Meeting; Symphony No. 4.* SFS Media 0076, 2019. CD.
23. Seattle Symphony, conducted by Ludovic Morlot. *Ives: Symphony No. 4; The Unanswered Question; Central Park in the Dark; Symphony No. 3.* Seattle Symphony Media SSM 1009, 2016. CD.
24. Seattle Symphony, conducted by Ludovic Morlot. *Ives: Three Places in New England; Orchestral Set No. 2; New England Holidays.* Seattle Symphony Media SSM 1015, 2017. CD.

OTHER INSTRUMENTAL MUSIC

The Celestial Railroad: 25, 32
From the Steeples and the Mountains: 29, 31
Holiday Quickstep: 27
March "Intercollegiate": 35
Scherzo: All the Way Around and Back: 27, 29
Scherzo for String Quartet: 28
Three Quarter-Tone Pieces: 25, 33
Variations on "America": 26, 30, 34
Variations on "America" (arranged for band): 35

25. Berman, Donald, piano, with Stephen Drury, piano. *The Unknown Ives, Volume 2.* New World Records 80618-2, 2004. CD.
26. Davis, Andrew, organ. *Andrew Davis Plays the Organ at Roy Thompson Hall.* Marquis Classics MAR-109, 2014. CD.
27. Detroit Chamber Winds and Friends, conducted by H. Robert Reynolds. *Remembrance: A Charles Ives Collection.* Koch International Classics 3-7182-2 H1, 1993. CD.
28. Emerson String Quartet. *Ives: String Quartets Nos. 1 and 2; Barber: String Quartet.* Deutsche Grammophon 435 864-2, 1992. CD.
29. Ensemble Modern, conducted by Ingo Metzmacher. *A Portrait of Charles Ives.* EMI Classics CDC 7 54552 2, 1992. CD.
30. John, Keith, organ. *Keith John Plays the Organ of the Kallio Church, Helsinki, Finland.* Priory PRCD 638, 1999.
31. London Gabrieli Brass Ensemble, conducted by Christopher Larkin. *From the Steeples and the Mountains: American Brass Music.* Hyperion CDA 66517, 1991. CD.
32. Mayer, Steven, piano. *Charles Ives: Piano Sonata No. 2 "Concord"; The Celestial Railroad.* Naxos 8.559127, 2004. CD.
33. Quattro Mani (Steven Beck and Susan Grace, pianos). *Lounge Lizards.* Bridge 9486, 2017. CD.
34. Quinn, Iain, organ. *Variations on America.* Chandos CHAN 10489, 2009. CD.

35. United States Marine Band, conducted by Colonel Timothy W. Foley. *Charles Ives: Variations on "America"; Old Home Days; The Alcotts.* Naxos 8.570559, 2003. CD.

SONGS

All (or almost all) of Ives's songs, including songs not listed here: 44, 45
At the River: 37, 38, 39, 40
Autumn: 36
The Cage: 36, 38, 41, 42
The Camp-Meeting: 37
Chanson de Florian: 37
The Circus Band: 37, 38, 40, 42
Down East: 36, 40, 43
Élégie: 37, 39, 41
Evening: 36, 39, 40, 43
Feldeinsamkeit: 37, 41, 43
General William Booth Enters Into Heaven: 41, 43
The Greatest Man: 36, 39, 41, 43
His Exaltation: 37
The Housatonic at Stockbridge: 36, 38, 39, 41, 42, 43
Ich grolle nicht: 37, 41
In Flanders Fields: 40
In the Mornin': 38
Memories: 36, 38, 39, 41, 42
My Native Land (first setting): 40
On the Counter: 36, 39, 40
The Sea of Sleep: 43
Slow March: 36, 39, 40
A Song—for Anything: 41
Spring Song: 36
They Are There!: 37, 40
Tom Sails Away: 36, 41, 43
Two Little Flowers: 36, 39, 40, 43
Walking: 39, 41
Watchman!: 37, 40, 43
Yellow Leaves: 41

36. Alexander, Roberta, soprano, and Tan Crone, piano. *Charles Ives: Songs.* Etcetera ETC 1020, 1984. CD.
37. Alexander, Roberta, soprano, and Tan Crone, piano. *Charles Ives: Songs, Vol. 2.* Etcetera ETC 1068, 1989. CD.
38. DeGaetani, Jan, mezzo-soprano, and Gilbert Kalish, piano. *Charles Ives: Songs.* Nonesuch 9 71325-2, 1976. CD.

39. Feldman, Jill, soprano, and Jeannette Koekkoek, piano. *Charles Ives: Songs.* Olive OM 011, 2007. CD.
40. Finley, Gerald, baritone, and Julius Drake, piano. *Romanzo di Central Park: Songs by Charles Ives.* Hyperion CDA67644, 2008. CD.
41. Finley, Gerald, baritone, and Julius Drake, piano. *A Song—for Anything: Songs by Charles Ives.* Hyperion CDA67516, 2005. CD.
42. Graham, Susan, soprano, and Pierre-Laurent Aimard. *Ives: Concord Sonata, Songs.* Warner Classics 2564 60297-2, 2004. CD.
43. Narucki, Susan, soprano, and Donald Berman, piano. *The Light That Is Felt: Songs of Charles Ives.* New World Records 80680-2, 2008. CD.
44. Ohrenstein, Dora, soprano; Mary Ann Hart, mezzo soprano; Paul Sperry, tenor; and William Sharp, baritone; with Philip Bush, Dennis Helmrich, Irma Vallecillo, and Steven Blier, piano. *The Complete Songs of Charles Ives.* 4 vols. Albany Troy 077, 078, 079, and 080, 1992–94. CD.
45. Various artists. *Charles Ives: Songs.* 6 vols. Naxos 8.559269-8.559274, 2008; whole set 8.506030, 2013. CD.

CHORAL MUSIC

All-Forgiving: 47
The Celestial Country: 46, 47
Crossing the Bar: 46, 47
Easter Carol: 46, 47
I Come to Thee: 47
Psalm 24: 48
Psalm 42 (As Pants the Hart): 48
Psalm 54: 46, 48
Psalm 67: 46, 48
Psalm 90: 46, 48
Psalm 100: 48
Psalm 150: 48
Turn Ye, Turn Ye: 47

46. BBC Singers, conducted by Stephen Cleobury. *Charles Ives: The Celestial Country, Psalm Settings, Easter Carol, Crossing the Bar.* Collins Classics 14792, 1996.
47. The Gregg Smith Singers, conducted by Gregg Smith. *The Young Ives: Early Choral Music of Charles Ives.* Newport Classic NPD 85677, 2006.
48. SWR Vokalensemble Stuttgart, conducted by Marcus Creed. *Charles Ives: Psalms, Complete Recording.* SWR Music/Hänssler Classic CD 93.224, 2007.

Index of Ives's Compositions

Page references for the primary discussion of a piece are in **boldface**. Page references for figures are in *italics*.

General Index

Page references for figures are in *italics*.

About the Author

J. Peter Burkholder is Distinguished Professor Emeritus of Musicology at the Indiana University Jacobs School of Music and past president of the American Musicological Society and the Charles Ives Society. He has been listening to and thinking about Ives's music since he was a teenager. He has written or edited four previous books on Ives and dozens of articles on Ives, modern music, musical borrowing, and meaning in music. He is the primary author of the most widely used music history textbook, and his award-winning writings have been published in eight languages. He lives in Bloomington, Indiana, with his husband Doug and three cats. Like the young Ives, he plays hymns every Sunday, and "Nearer, my God, to Thee" is a favorite.

CPSIA information can be obtained
at www.ICGtesting.com
Printed in the USA
BVHW092150100121
597121BV00003B/4